Shojo Beat

S·A

Special A

Hikari & kei middle school

Volume 1

Story & Art by

Maki Minami

Contents

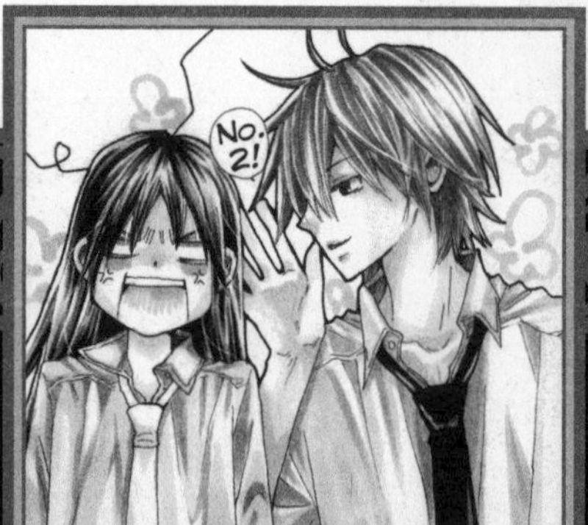

No. 2!

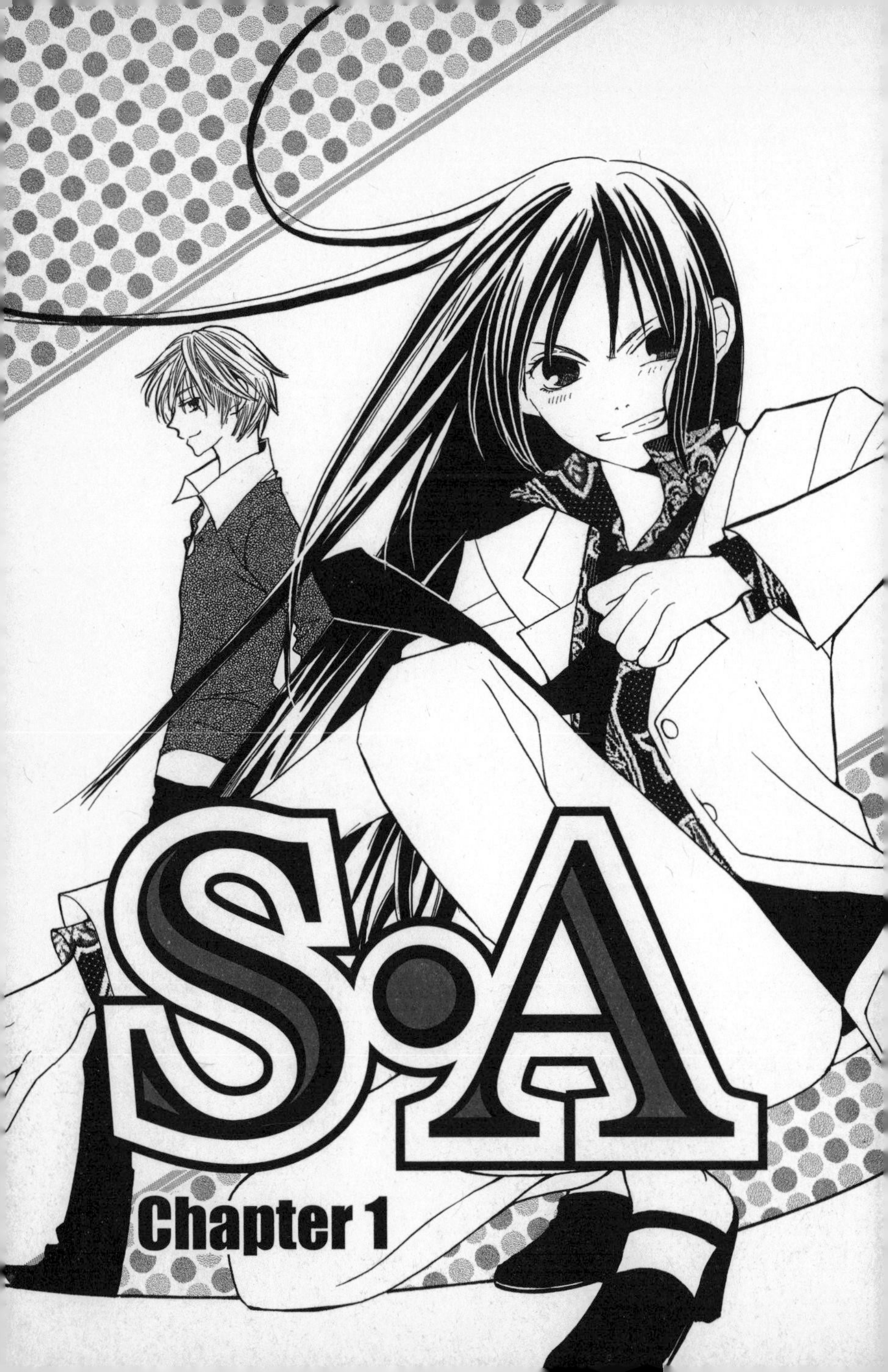
S·A
Chapter 1

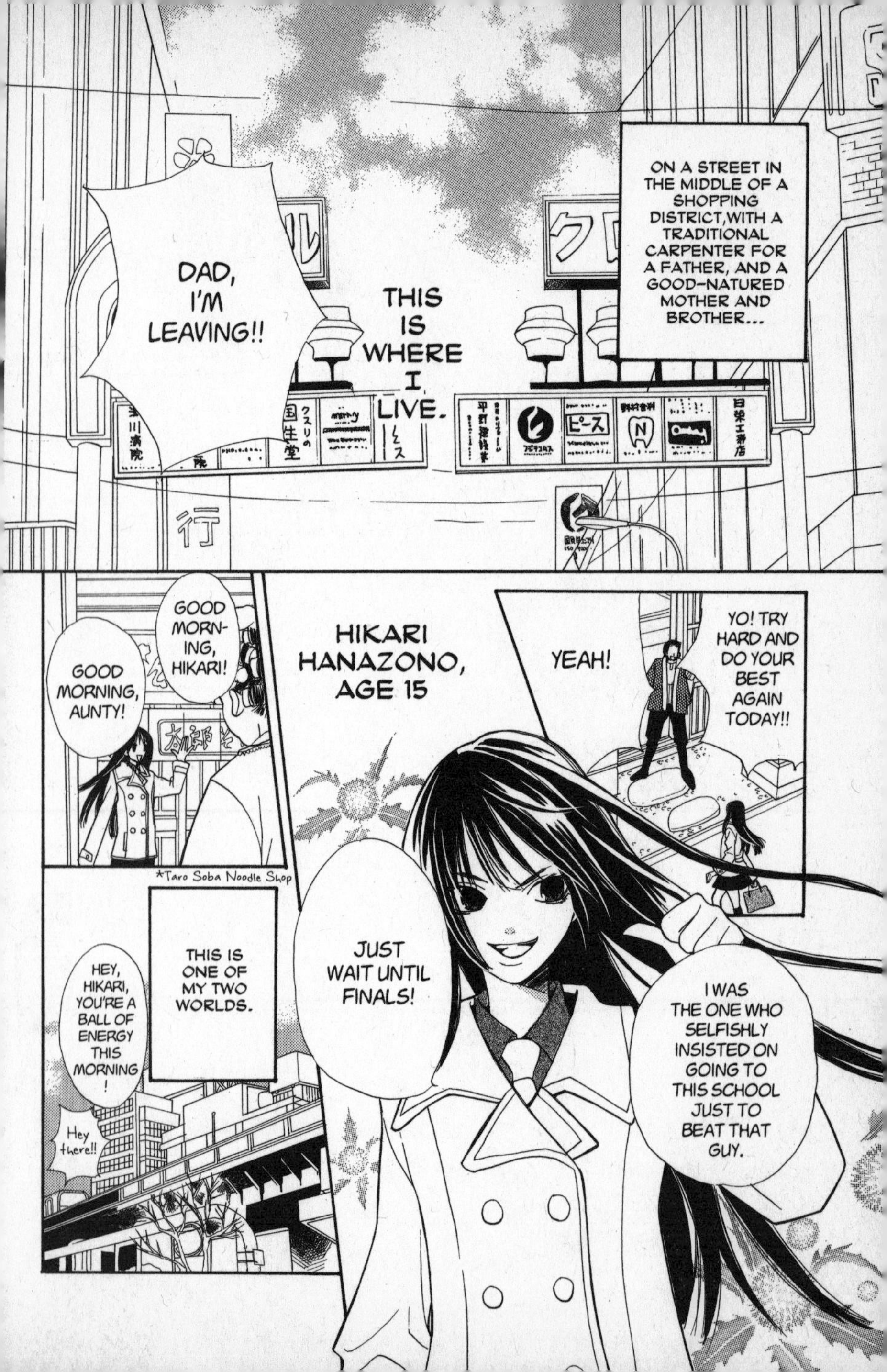
ON A STREET IN THE MIDDLE OF A SHOPPING DISTRICT, WITH A TRADITIONAL CARPENTER FOR A FATHER, AND A GOOD-NATURED MOTHER AND BROTHER...
THIS IS WHERE I LIVE.
DAD, I'M LEAVING!!
YO! TRY HARD AND DO YOUR BEST AGAIN TODAY!!
YEAH!
HIKARI HANAZONO, AGE 15
GOOD MORNING, HIKARI!
GOOD MORNING, AUNTY!
*Taro Soba Noodle Shop
I WAS THE ONE WHO SELFISHLY INSISTED ON GOING TO THIS SCHOOL JUST TO BEAT THAT GUY.
JUST WAIT UNTIL FINALS!
THIS IS ONE OF MY TWO WORLDS.
HEY, HIKARI, YOU'RE A BALL OF ENERGY THIS MORNING!
Hey there!!

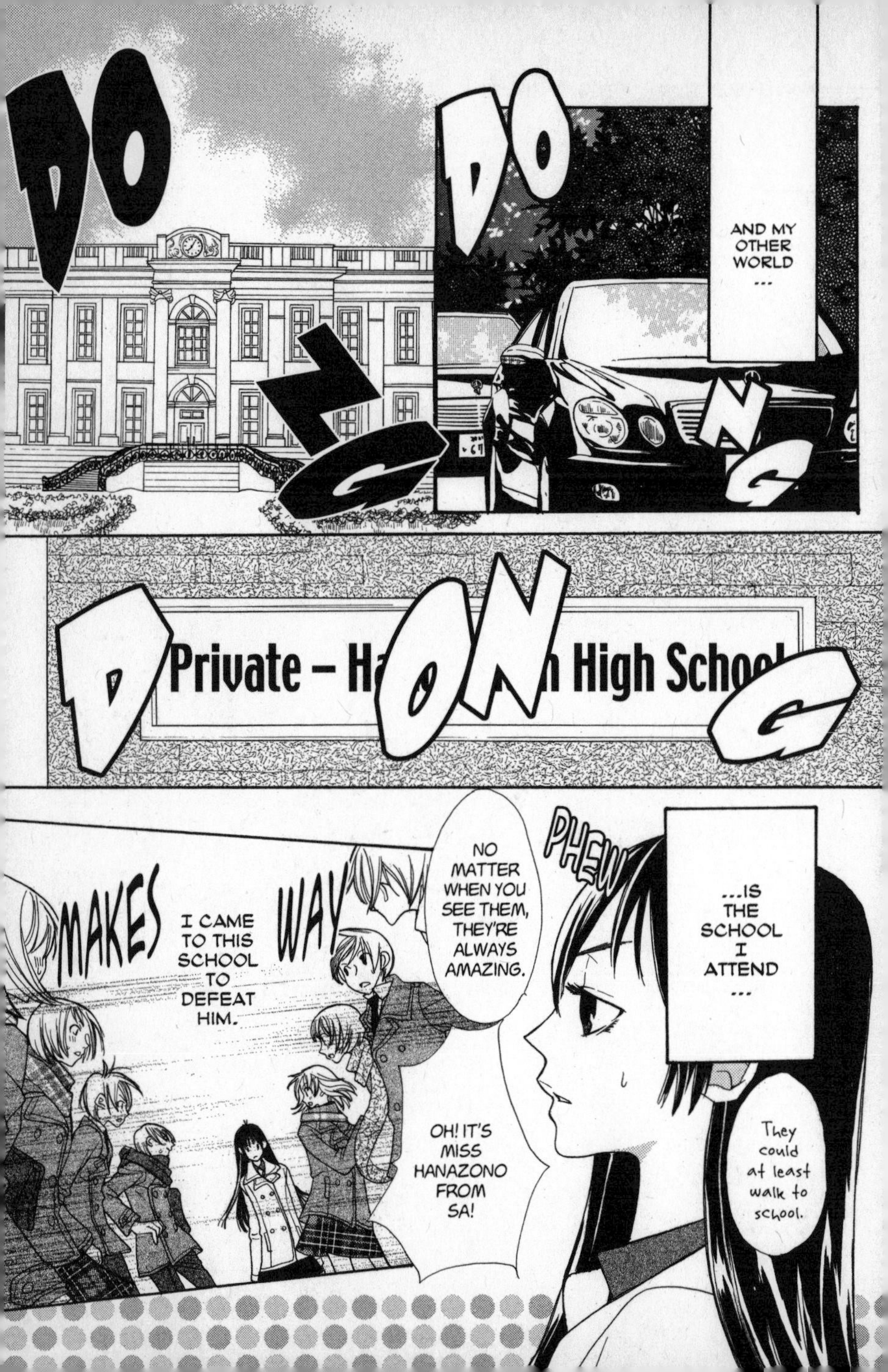
AND MY OTHER WORLD ...
DONG
DONG
Private – Ha h High Schoo
DONG
...IS THE SCHOOL I ATTEND ...
PHEW
They could at least walk to school.
NO MATTER WHEN YOU SEE THEM, THEY'RE ALWAYS AMAZING.
OH! IT'S MISS HANAZONO FROM SA!
MAKES WAY
I CAME TO THIS SCHOOL TO DEFEAT HIM.

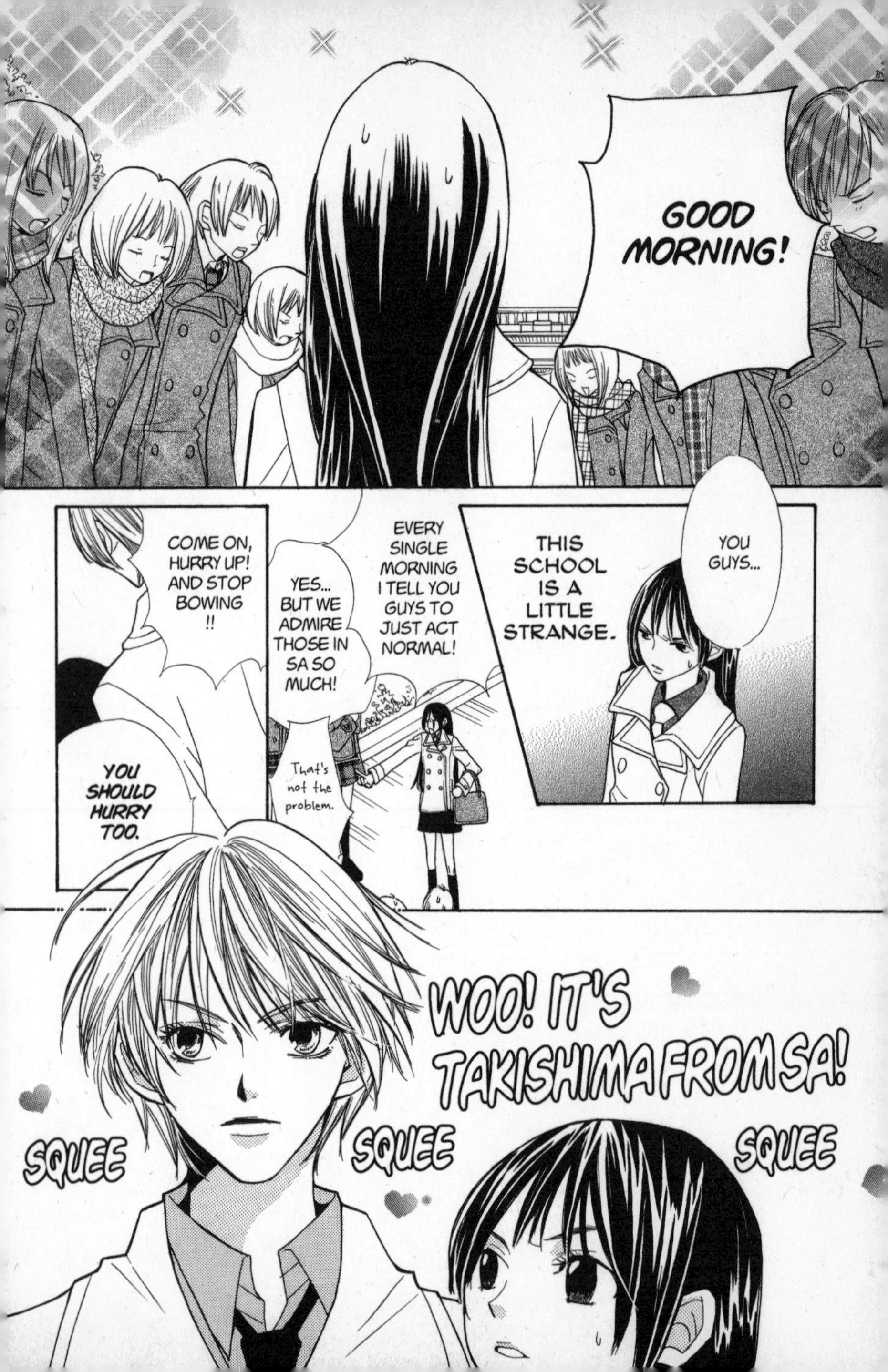
GOOD MORNING!
YOU GUYS...
THIS SCHOOL IS A LITTLE STRANGE.
EVERY SINGLE MORNING I TELL YOU GUYS TO JUST ACT NORMAL!
YES... BUT WE ADMIRE THOSE IN SA SO MUCH!
COME ON, HURRY UP! AND STOP BOWING !!
That's not the problem.
YOU SHOULD HURRY TOO.
WOO! IT'S TAKISHIMA FROM SA!
SQUEE
SQUEE
SQUEE

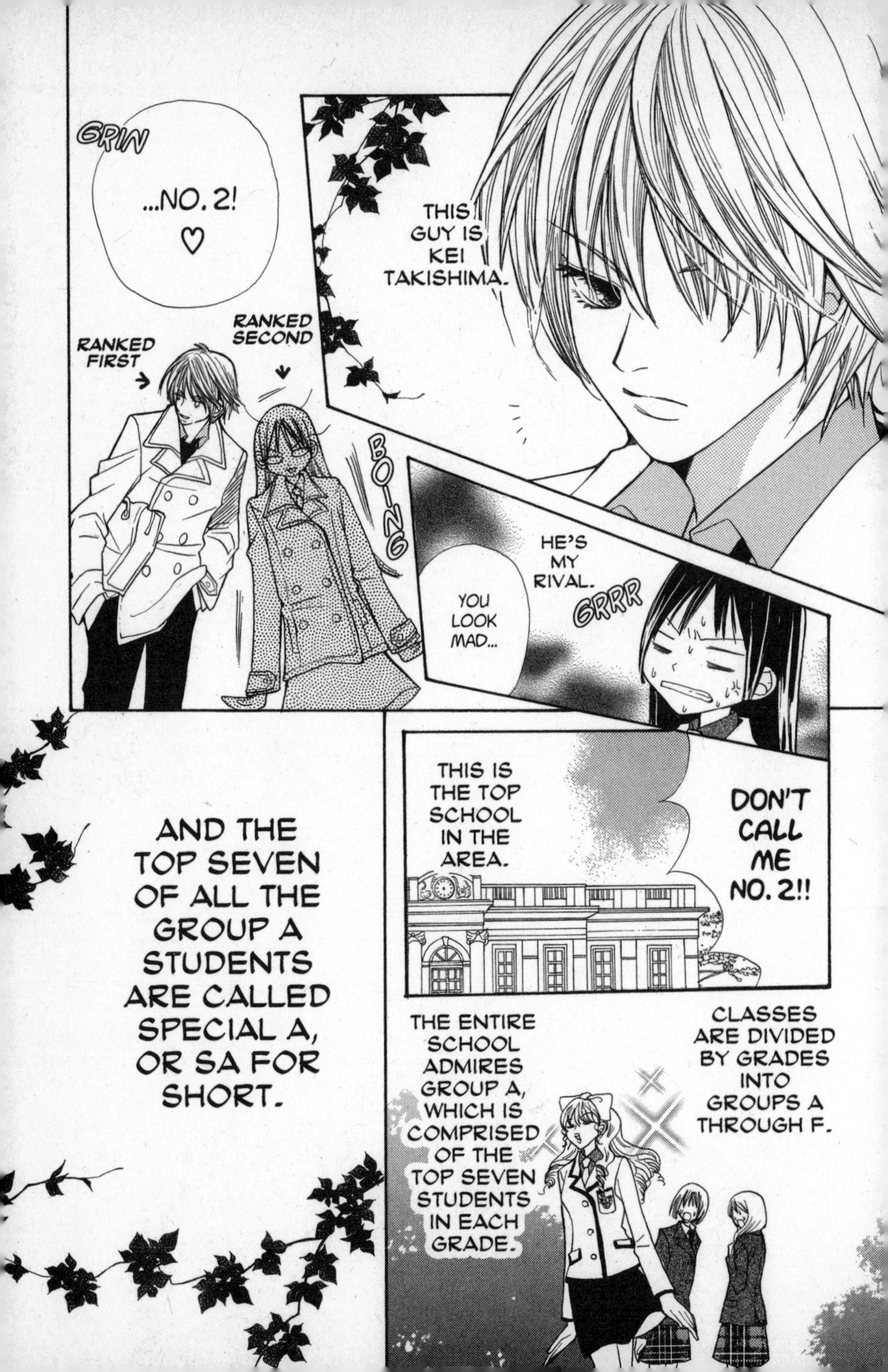
THIS GUY IS KEI TAKISHIMA.
HE'S MY RIVAL.
GRRR
YOU LOOK MAD...
GRIN
...NO. 2! ♡
RANKED SECOND
RANKED FIRST
BOING
THIS IS THE TOP SCHOOL IN THE AREA.
DON'T CALL ME NO. 2!!
CLASSES ARE DIVIDED BY GRADES INTO GROUPS A THROUGH F.
THE ENTIRE SCHOOL ADMIRES GROUP A, WHICH IS COMPRISED OF THE TOP SEVEN STUDENTS IN EACH GRADE.
AND THE TOP SEVEN OF ALL THE GROUP A STUDENTS ARE CALLED SPECIAL A, OR SA FOR SHORT.

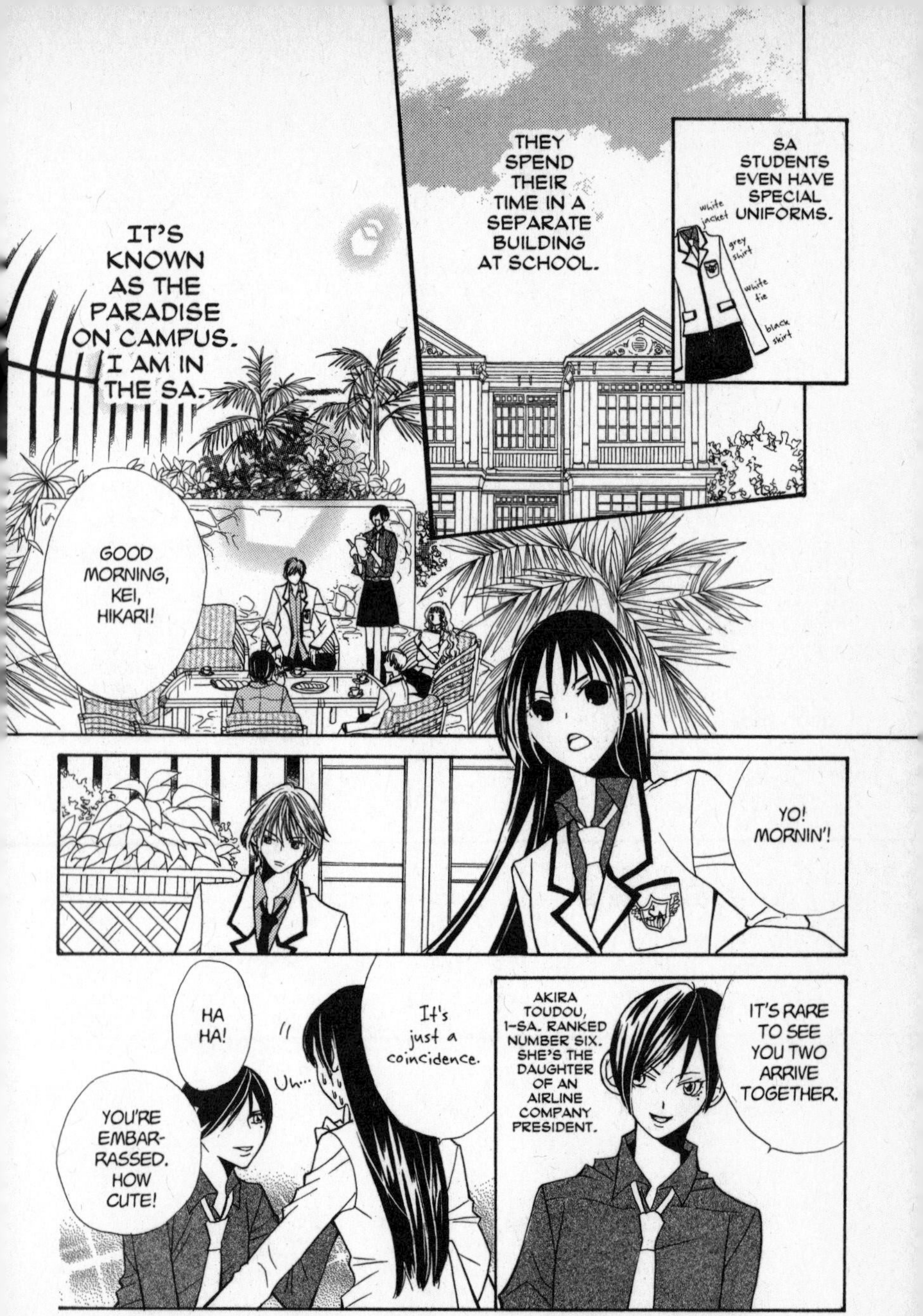
SA STUDENTS EVEN HAVE SPECIAL UNIFORMS.
white jacket
grey shirt
white tie
black skirt
THEY SPEND THEIR TIME IN A SEPARATE BUILDING AT SCHOOL.
IT'S KNOWN AS THE PARADISE ON CAMPUS. I AM IN THE SA.
GOOD MORNING, KEI, HIKARI!
YO! MORNIN'!
IT'S RARE TO SEE YOU TWO ARRIVE TOGETHER.
AKIRA TOUDOU, 1-SA. RANKED NUMBER SIX. SHE'S THE DAUGHTER OF AN AIRLINE COMPANY PRESIDENT.
It's just a coincidence.
Uh...
HA HA!
YOU'RE EMBAR-RASSED. HOW CUTE!

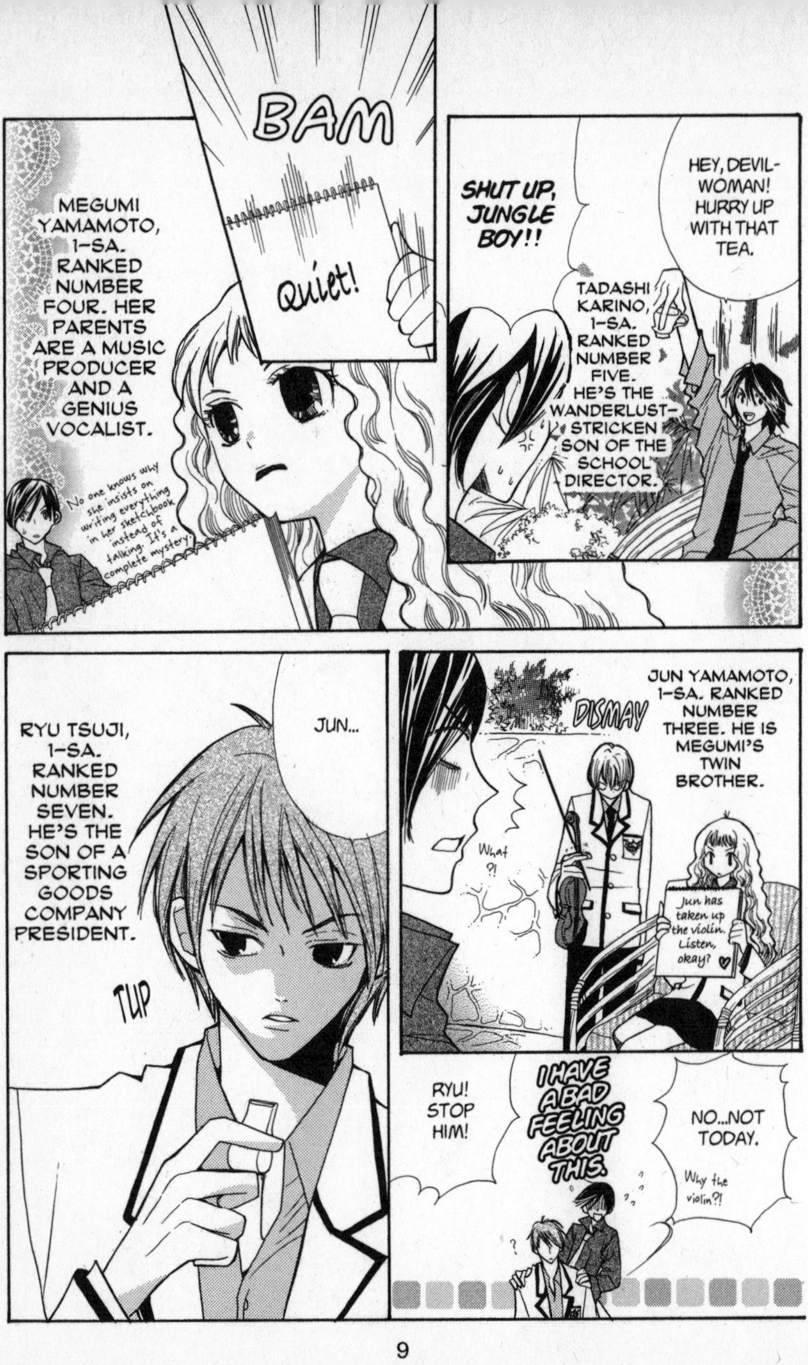
HEY, DEVIL-WOMAN! HURRY UP WITH THAT TEA.
SHUT UP, JUNGLE BOY!!
TADASHI KARINO, 1-SA. RANKED NUMBER FIVE. HE'S THE WANDERLUST-STRICKEN SON OF THE SCHOOL DIRECTOR.
BAM
Quiet!
MEGUMI YAMAMOTO, 1-SA. RANKED NUMBER FOUR. HER PARENTS ARE A MUSIC PRODUCER AND A GENIUS VOCALIST.
No one knows why she insists on writing everything in her sketchbook instead of talking. It's a complete mystery.
JUN YAMAMOTO, 1-SA. RANKED NUMBER THREE. HE IS MEGUMI'S TWIN BROTHER.
DISMAY
What?!
Jun has taken up the violin. Listen, okay? ♥
NO...NOT TODAY.
Why the violin?!
I HAVE A BAD FEELING ABOUT THIS.
RYU! STOP HIM!
JUN...
RYU TSUJI, 1-SA. RANKED NUMBER SEVEN. HE'S THE SON OF A SPORTING GOODS COMPANY PRESIDENT.
TUP

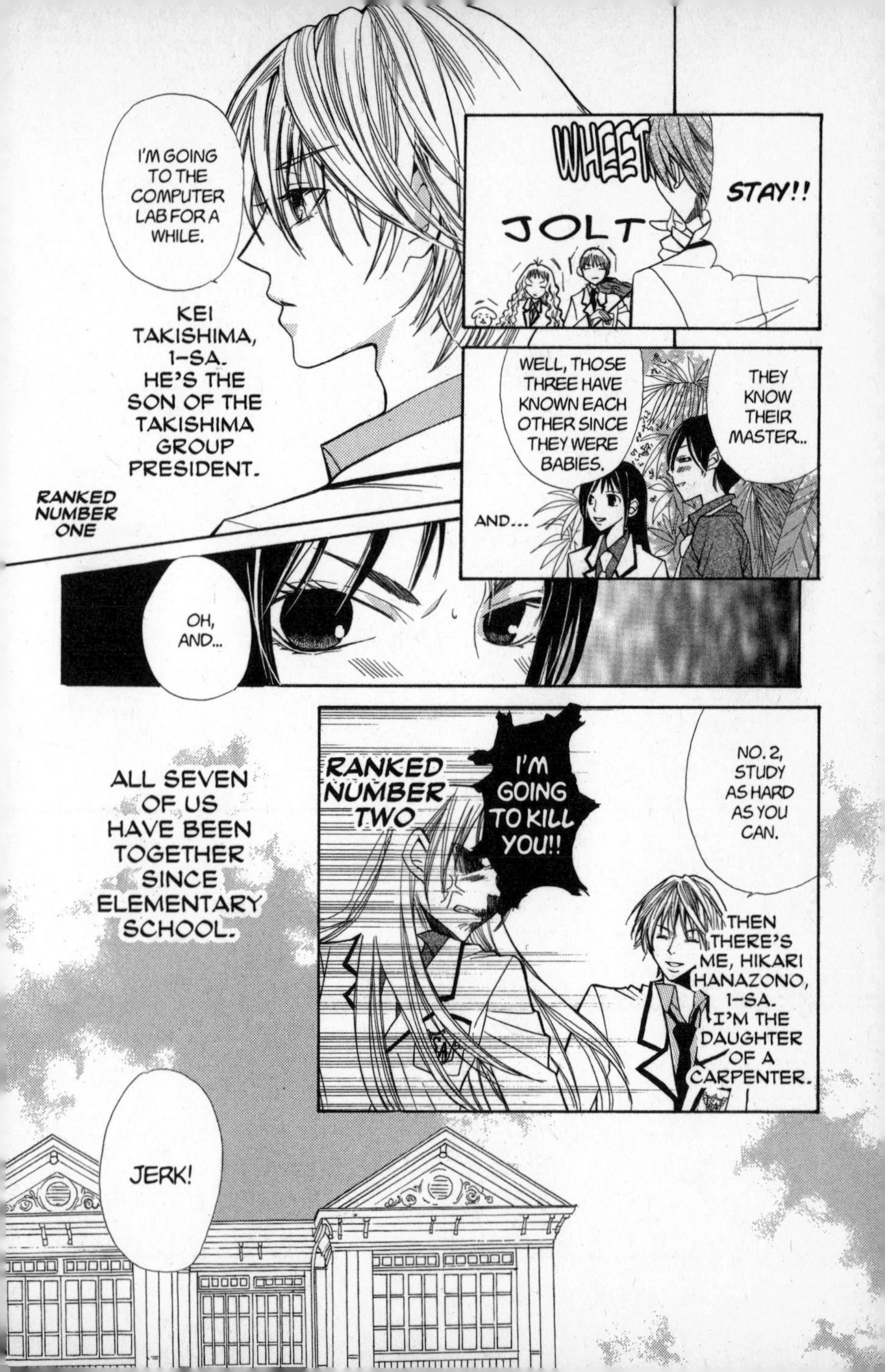
WHEET
STAY!!
JOLT
THEY KNOW THEIR MASTER...
WELL, THOSE THREE HAVE KNOWN EACH OTHER SINCE THEY WERE BABIES.
AND...
I'M GOING TO THE COMPUTER LAB FOR A WHILE.
KEI TAKISHIMA, 1-SA. HE'S THE SON OF THE TAKISHIMA GROUP PRESIDENT.
RANKED NUMBER ONE
OH, AND...
NO. 2, STUDY AS HARD AS YOU CAN.
I'M GOING TO KILL YOU!!
RANKED NUMBER TWO
THEN THERE'S ME, HIKARI HANAZONO, 1-SA. I'M THE DAUGHTER OF A CARPENTER.
ALL SEVEN OF US HAVE BEEN TOGETHER SINCE ELEMENTARY SCHOOL.
JERK!

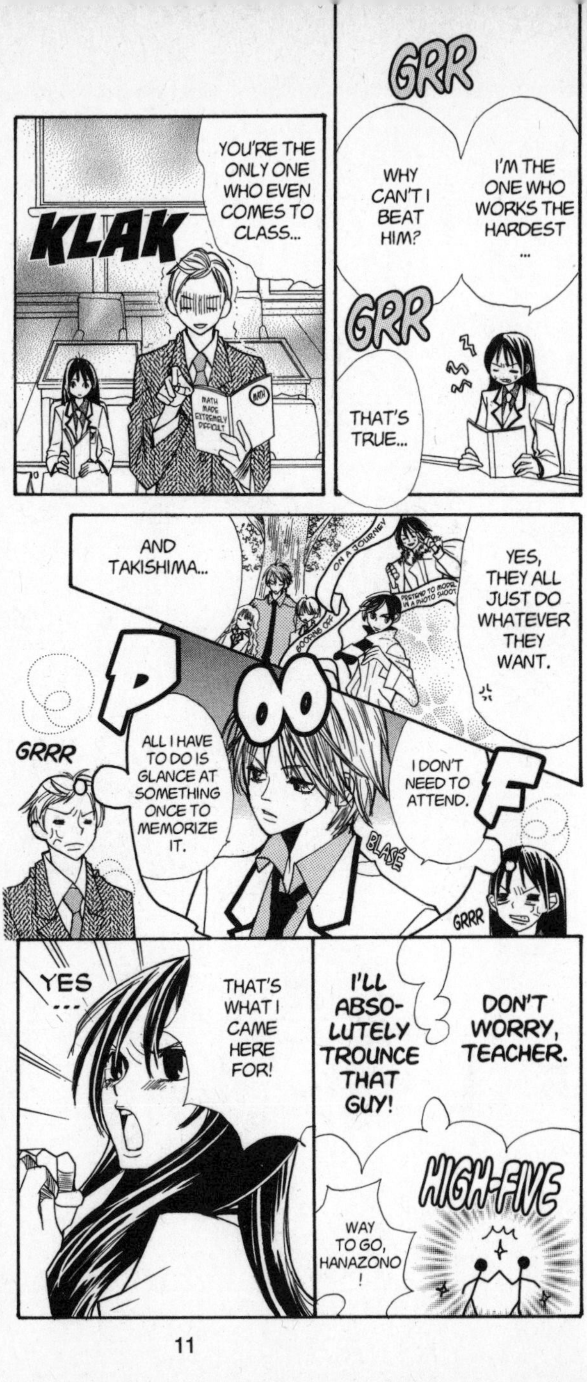
GRR
I'M THE ONE WHO WORKS THE HARDEST ...
WHY CAN'T I BEAT HIM?
GRR
THAT'S TRUE...
YOU'RE THE ONLY ONE WHO EVEN COMES TO CLASS...
KLAK
MATH MADE EXTREMELY DIFFICULT
MATH
YES, THEY ALL JUST DO WHATEVER THEY WANT.
ON A JOURNEY
PRETEND TO MODEL IN A PHOTO SHOOT
GOOFING OFF
AND TAKISHIMA...
POOF
I DON'T NEED TO ATTEND.
BLASÉ
ALL I HAVE TO DO IS GLANCE AT SOMETHING ONCE TO MEMORIZE IT.
GRRR
GRRR
DON'T WORRY, TEACHER.
I'LL ABSOLUTELY TROUNCE THAT GUY!
HIGH-FIVE
WAY TO GO, HANAZONO!
THAT'S WHAT I CAME HERE FOR!
YES ...

1

HELLO! HOW ARE YOU?!

I'M MAKI MINAMI. THIS IS MY FIRST MANGA! I'M VERY, VERY... ***HAPPY!*** I WOULD LIKE TO SAY TO EVERYONE WHO WAS ROOTING FOR ME, TO EVERYONE WHO COLLABORATED WITH ME, AND TO MY EDITOR, THANK YOU ALL SO VERY MUCH! (YELLING OUT LOUD)

THIS IS WHAT HAPPENED WHEN THE EDITOR TOLD ME ABOUT THE MANGA...

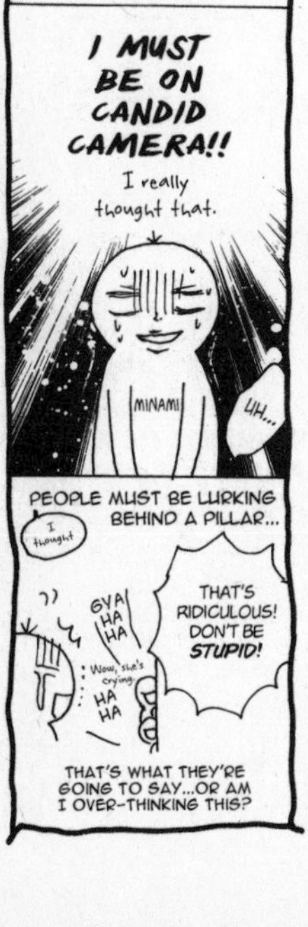
I MUST BE ON CANDID CAMERA!!
I really thought that.
MINAMI
UH...
PEOPLE MUST BE LURKING BEHIND A PILLAR...
I thought
THAT'S RIDICULOUS! DON'T BE STUPID!
GYA HA HA
Wow, she's crying.
HA HA
THAT'S WHAT THEY'RE GOING TO SAY...OR AM I OVER-THINKING THIS?

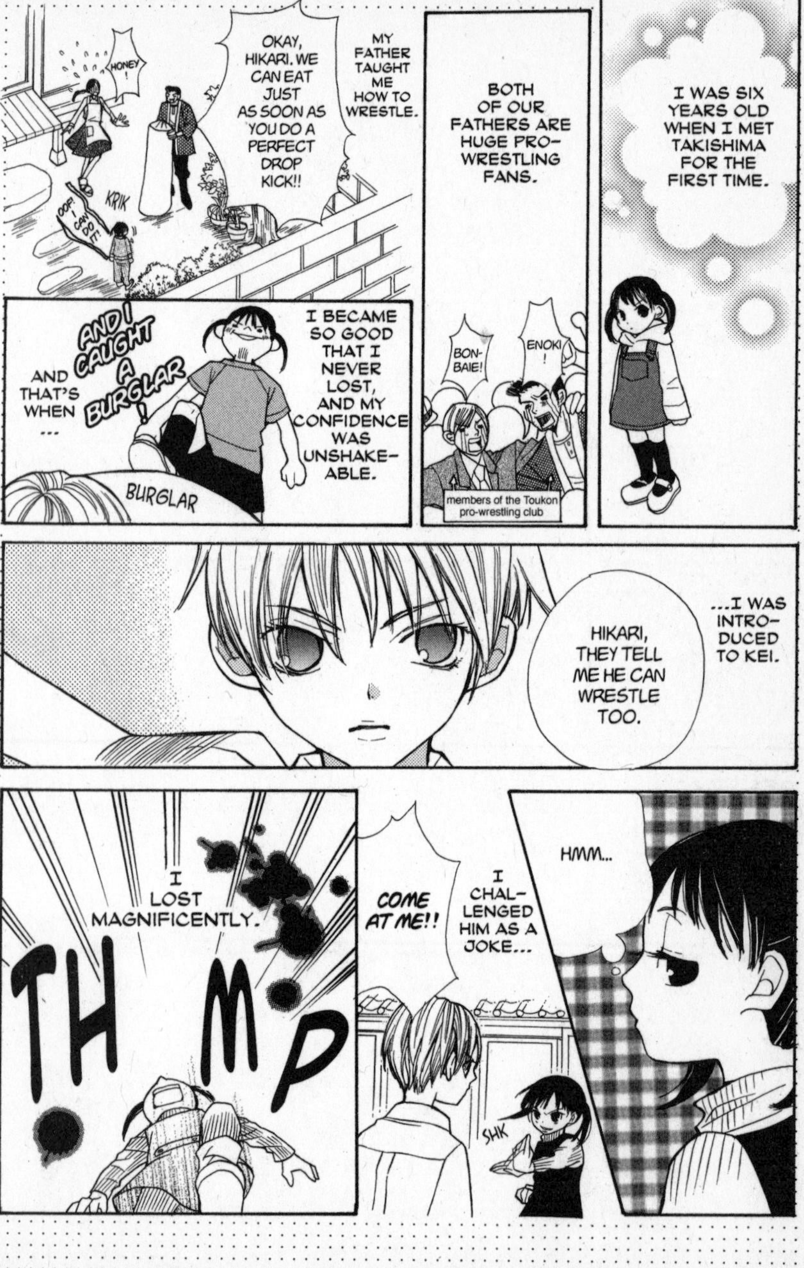
I WAS SIX YEARS OLD WHEN I MET TAKISHIMA FOR THE FIRST TIME.
BOTH OF OUR FATHERS ARE HUGE PRO-WRESTLING FANS.
ENOKI!
BON-BAIE!
members of the Toukon pro-wrestling club
MY FATHER TAUGHT ME HOW TO WRESTLE.
OKAY, HIKARI. WE CAN EAT JUST AS SOON AS YOU DO A PERFECT DROP KICK!!
HONEY!
KRIK
OOF! I CAN DO IT!
I BECAME SO GOOD THAT I NEVER LOST, AND MY CONFIDENCE WAS UNSHAKE-ABLE.
AND I CAUGHT A BURGLAR!
BURGLAR
AND THAT'S WHEN ...
...I WAS INTRODUCED TO KEI.
HIKARI, THEY TELL ME HE CAN WRESTLE TOO.
HMM...
I CHAL-LENGED HIM AS A JOKE...
COME AT ME!!
SHK
I LOST MAGNIFICENTLY.
THMP

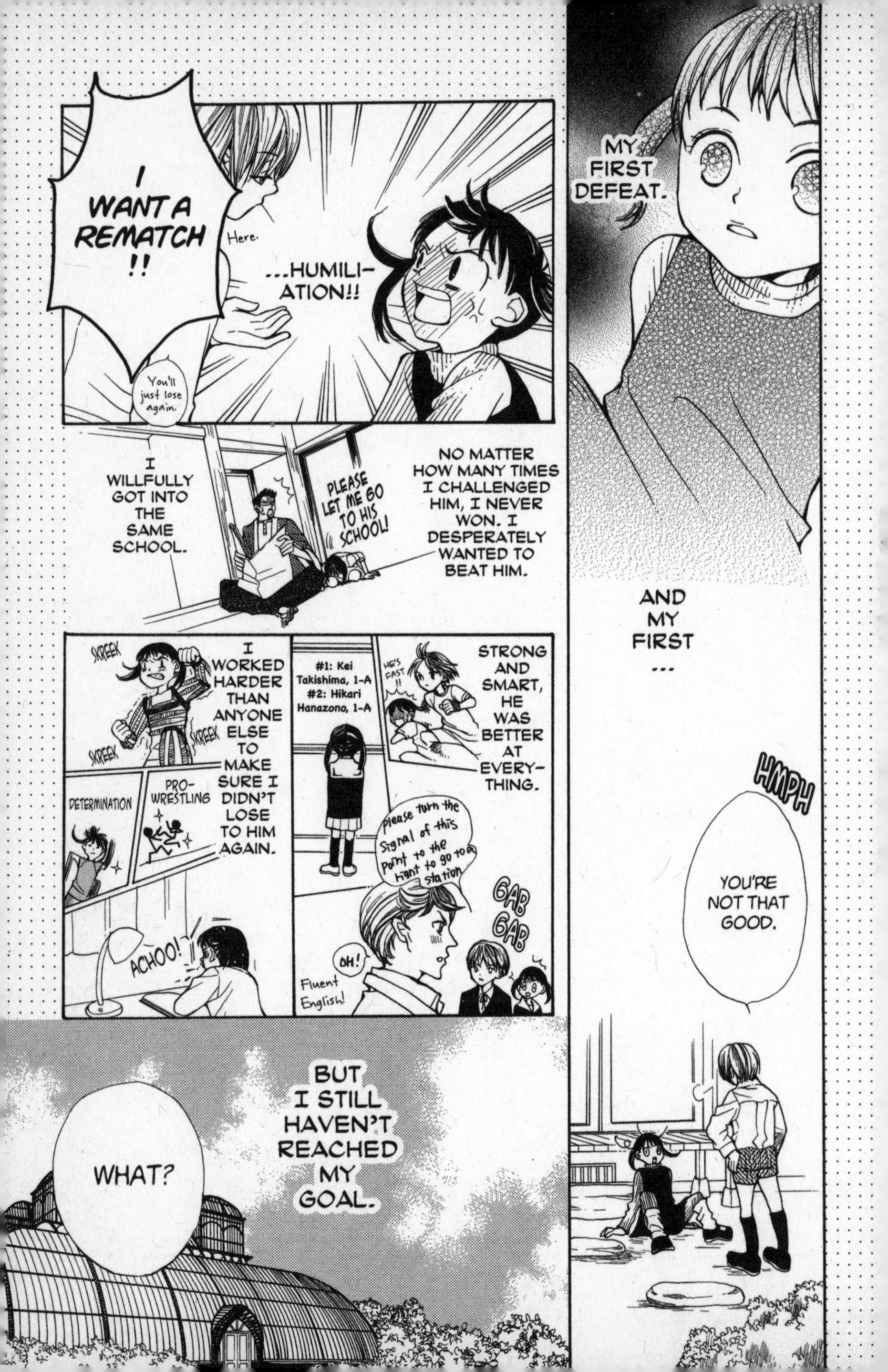
MY FIRST DEFEAT.
AND MY FIRST ...
HMPH
YOU'RE NOT THAT GOOD.
...HUMILI-ATION!!
Here.
I WANT A REMATCH!!
You'll just lose again.
NO MATTER HOW MANY TIMES I CHALLENGED HIM, I NEVER WON. I DESPERATELY WANTED TO BEAT HIM.
PLEASE LET ME GO TO HIS SCHOOL!
I WILLFULLY GOT INTO THE SAME SCHOOL.
STRONG AND SMART, HE WAS BETTER AT EVERY-THING.
HE'S FAST!!
#1: Kei Takishima, 1-A
#2: Hikari Hanazono, 1-A
please turn the Signal of this Point to the right to go to station
GAB GAB
OH!
Fluent English!
I WORKED HARDER THAN ANYONE ELSE TO MAKE SURE I DIDN'T LOSE TO HIM AGAIN.
SKREEK
SKREEK
SKREEK
DETERMINATION
PRO-WRESTLING
ACHOO!
BUT I STILL HAVEN'T REACHED MY GOAL.
WHAT?

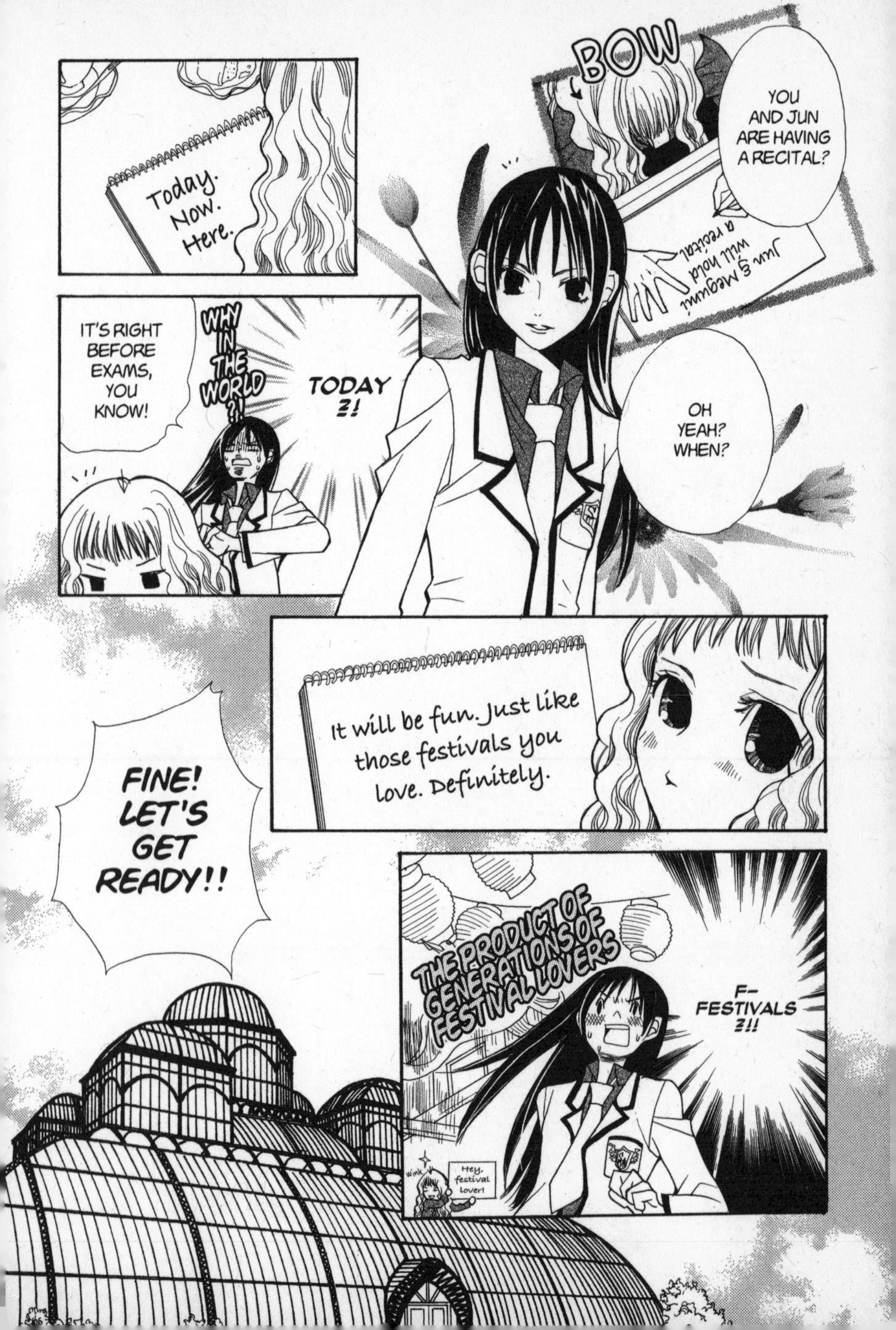
BOW
YOU AND JUN ARE HAVING A RECITAL?
Jun & Megumi will hold a recital
...
OH YEAH? WHEN?
Today. Now. Here.
WHY IN THE WORLD?!
TODAY?!
IT'S RIGHT BEFORE EXAMS, YOU KNOW!
It will be fun. Just like those festivals you love. Definitely.
F-FESTIVALS?!!
THE PRODUCT OF GENERATIONS OF FESTIVAL LOVERS
wink
Hey, festival lover!
FINE! LET'S GET READY!!

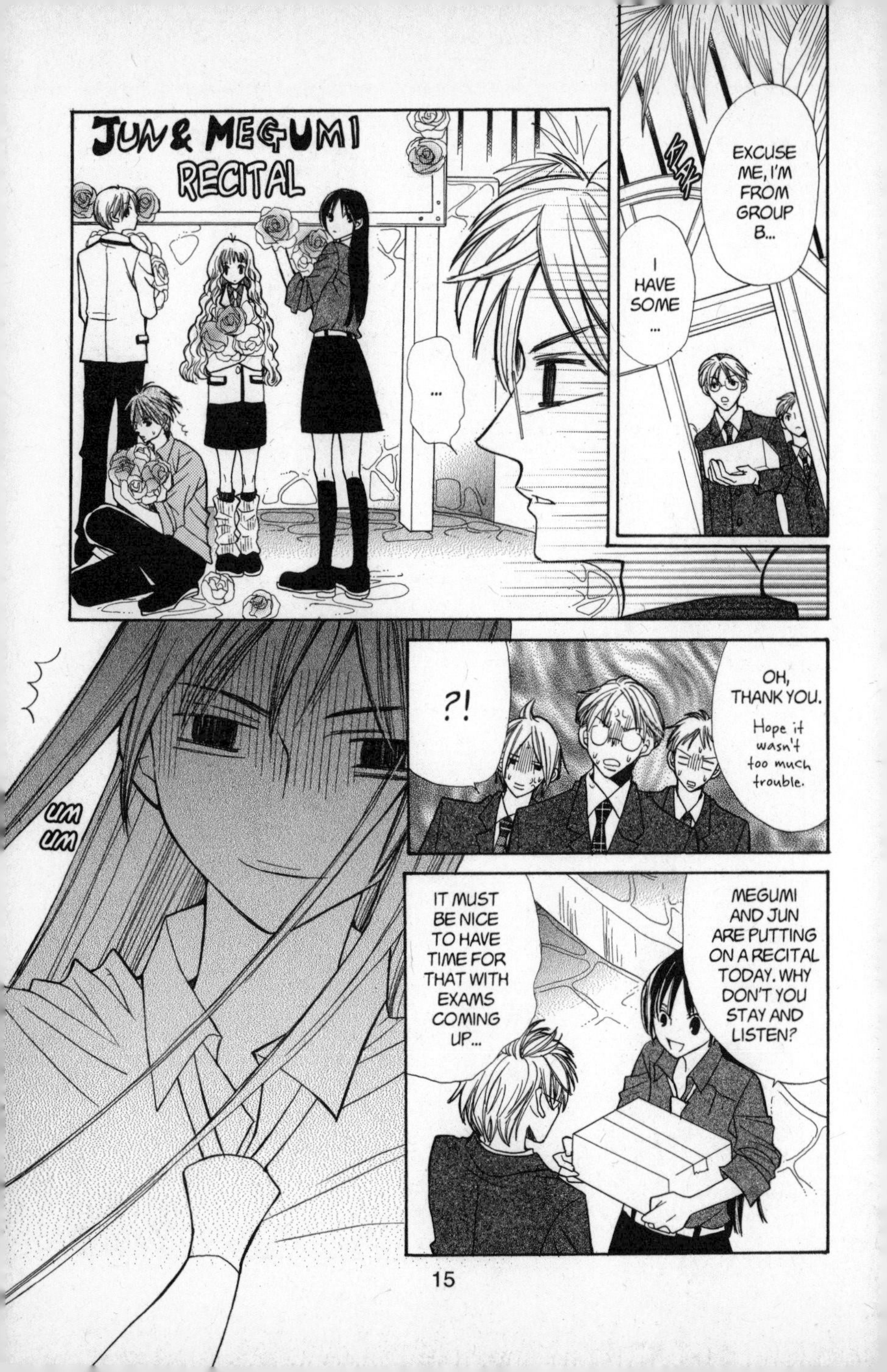
KLAK
EXCUSE ME, I'M FROM GROUP B...
I HAVE SOME ...
...
JUN & MEGUMI RECITAL
OH, THANK YOU.
Hope it wasn't too much trouble.
?!
MEGUMI AND JUN ARE PUTTING ON A RECITAL TODAY. WHY DON'T YOU STAY AND LISTEN?
IT MUST BE NICE TO HAVE TIME FOR THAT WITH EXAMS COMING UP...
UM UM

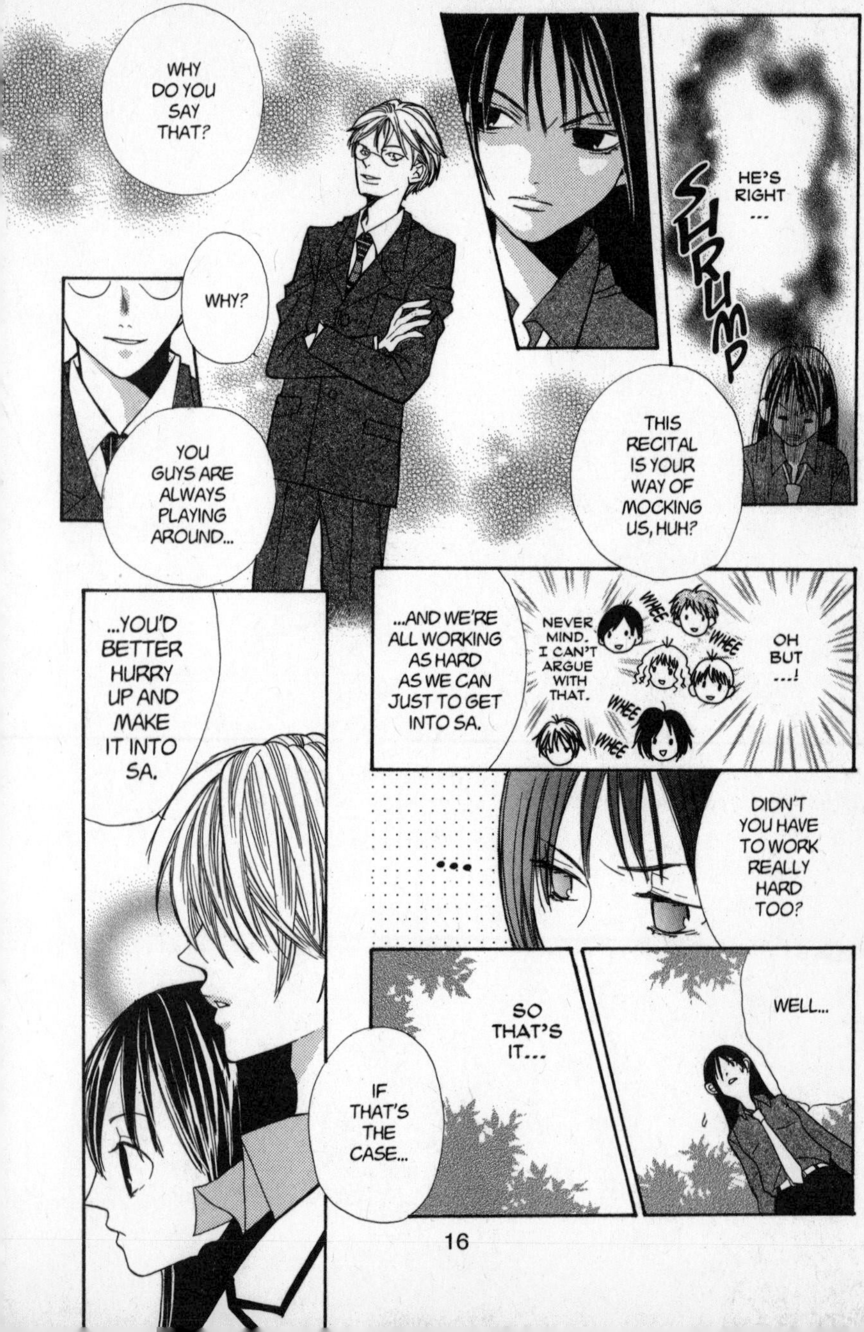
HE'S RIGHT...
SHRUMP
THIS RECITAL IS YOUR WAY OF MOCKING US, HUH?
WHY DO YOU SAY THAT?
WHY?
YOU GUYS ARE ALWAYS PLAYING AROUND...
...AND WE'RE ALL WORKING AS HARD AS WE CAN JUST TO GET INTO SA.
OH BUT...!
WHEE
WHEE
NEVER MIND. I CAN'T ARGUE WITH THAT.
WHEE
WHEE
...
DIDN'T YOU HAVE TO WORK REALLY HARD TOO?
WELL...
SO THAT'S IT...
IF THAT'S THE CASE...
...YOU'D BETTER HURRY UP AND MAKE IT INTO SA.

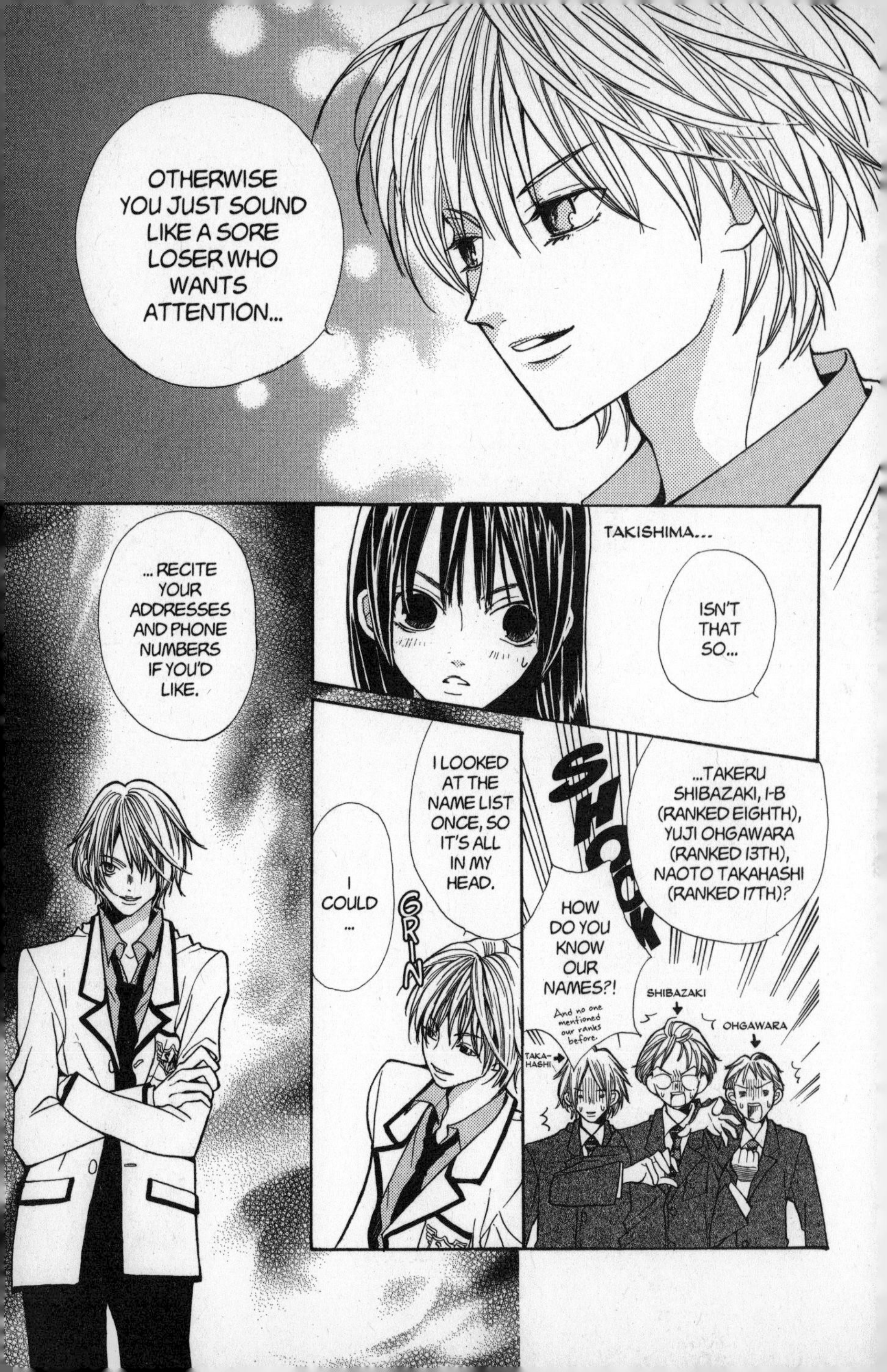
OTHERWISE YOU JUST SOUND LIKE A SORE LOSER WHO WANTS ATTENTION...
TAKISHIMA...
ISN'T THAT SO...
...TAKERU SHIBAZAKI, I-B (RANKED EIGHTH), YUJI OHGAWARA (RANKED 13TH), NAOTO TAKAHASHI (RANKED 17TH)?
SHOCK
HOW DO YOU KNOW OUR NAMES?!
OHGAWARA
SHIBAZAKI
And no one mentioned our ranks before.
TAKA-HASHI
I LOOKED AT THE NAME LIST ONCE, SO IT'S ALL IN MY HEAD.
GRIN
I COULD ...
... RECITE YOUR ADDRESSES AND PHONE NUMBERS IF YOU'D LIKE.

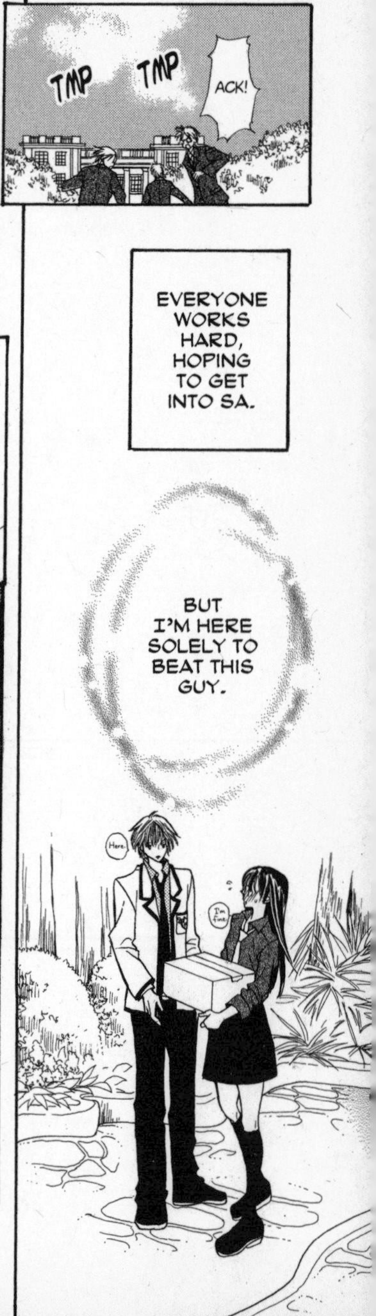
TMP TMP
ACK!
EVERYONE WORKS HARD, HOPING TO GET INTO SA.
BUT I'M HERE SOLELY TO BEAT THIS GUY.
Here.
I'm fine.

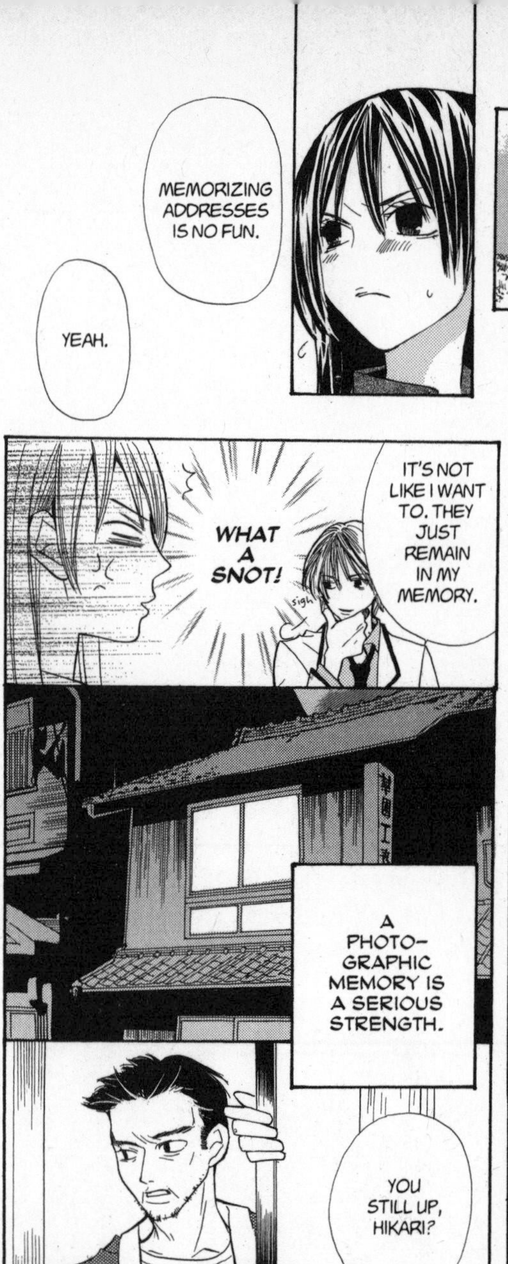
MEMORIZING ADDRESSES IS NO FUN.
YEAH.
IT'S NOT LIKE I WANT TO. THEY JUST REMAIN IN MY MEMORY.
WHAT A SNOT!
sigh
A PHOTOGRAPHIC MEMORY IS A SERIOUS STRENGTH.
YOU STILL UP, HIKARI?

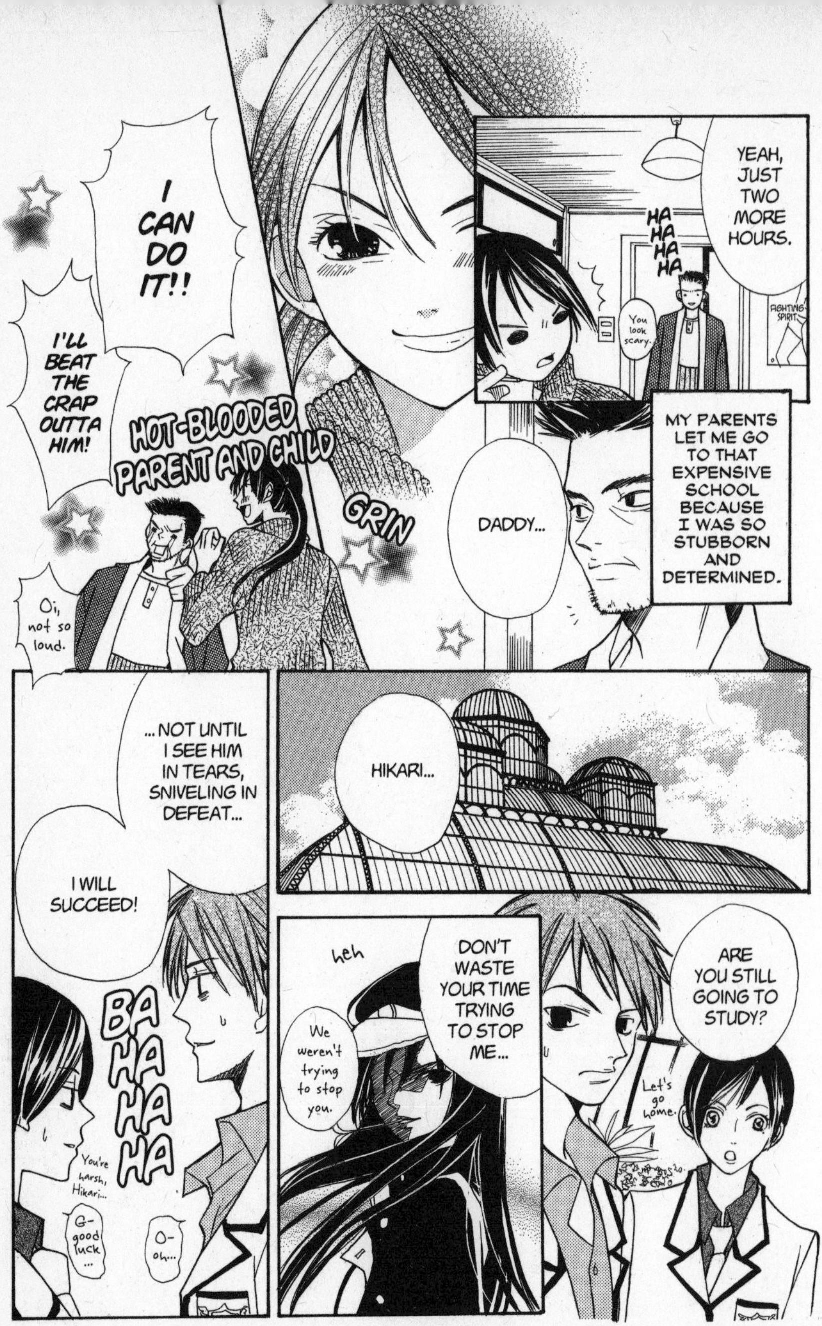
YEAH, JUST TWO MORE HOURS.
HA HA HA HA
You look scary.
FIGHTING SPIRIT
MY PARENTS LET ME GO TO THAT EXPENSIVE SCHOOL BECAUSE I WAS SO STUBBORN AND DETERMINED.
DADDY...
GRIN
I CAN DO IT!!
I'LL BEAT THE CRAP OUTTA HIM!
HOT-BLOODED PARENT AND CHILD
Oi, not so loud.
HIKARI...
ARE YOU STILL GOING TO STUDY?
Let's go home.
DON'T WASTE YOUR TIME TRYING TO STOP ME...
heh
We weren't trying to stop you.
...NOT UNTIL I SEE HIM IN TEARS, SNIVELING IN DEFEAT...
I WILL SUCCEED!
BA HA HA HA HA
You're harsh, Hikari...
O-oh...
G-good luck...

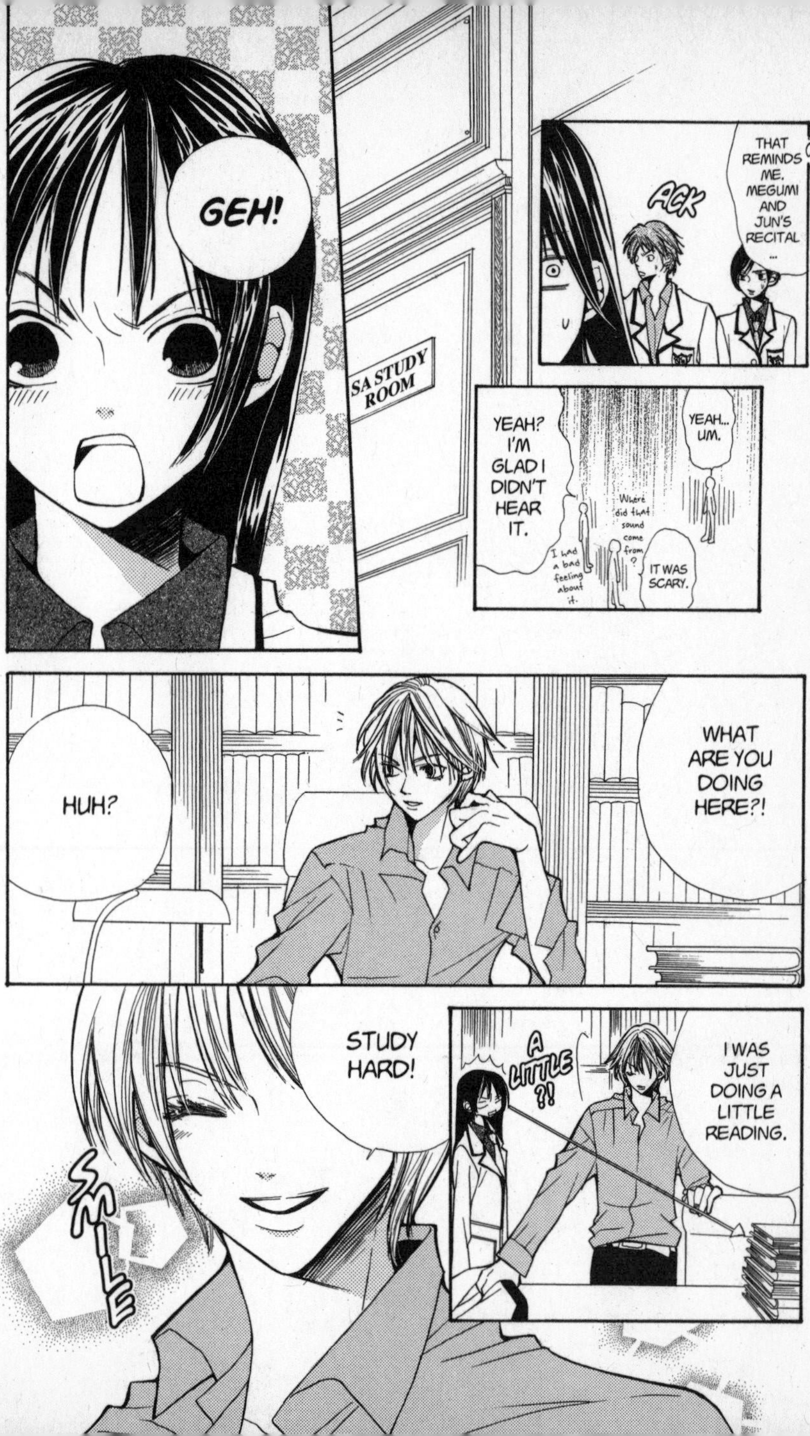
OH!
THAT REMINDS ME. MEGUMI AND JUN'S RECITAL ...
ACK
YEAH... UM.
Where did that sound come from?
IT WAS SCARY.
YEAH? I'M GLAD I DIDN'T HEAR IT.
I had a bad feeling about it.
SA STUDY ROOM
GEH!
WHAT ARE YOU DOING HERE?!
HUH?
I WAS JUST DOING A LITTLE READING.
A LITTLE?!
STUDY HARD!
SMILE

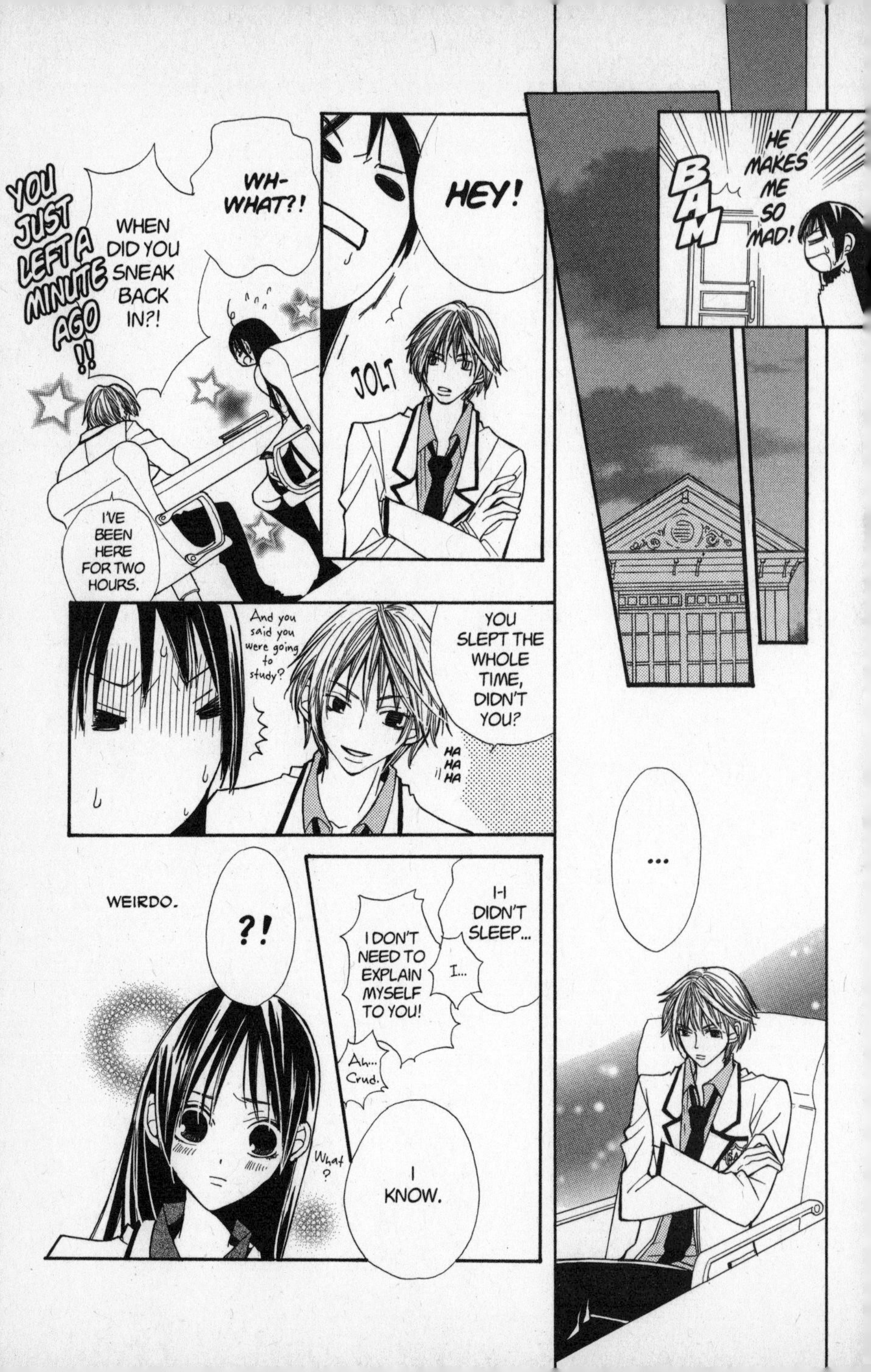
HE MAKES ME SO MAD!
BAM
...
HEY!
JOLT
WH-WHAT?!
WHEN DID YOU SNEAK BACK IN?!
YOU JUST LEFT A MINUTE AGO!!
I'VE BEEN HERE FOR TWO HOURS.
YOU SLEPT THE WHOLE TIME, DIDN'T YOU?
HA HA HA
And you said you were going to study?
I-I DIDN'T SLEEP...
I...
I DON'T NEED TO EXPLAIN MYSELF TO YOU!
Ah... Crud.
I KNOW.
What?
?!
WEIRDO.

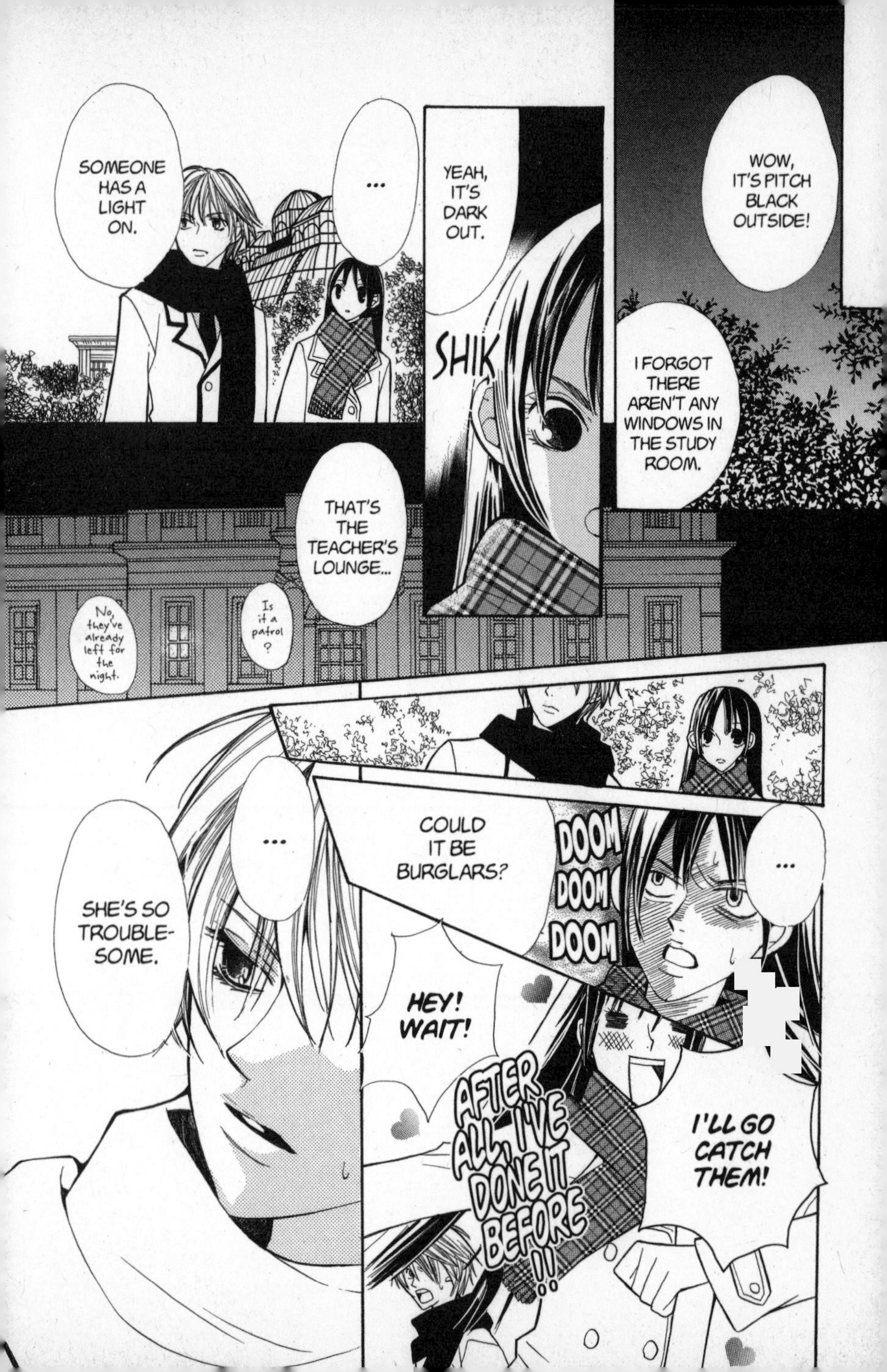
WOW, IT'S PITCH BLACK OUTSIDE!
I FORGOT THERE AREN'T ANY WINDOWS IN THE STUDY ROOM.
YEAH, IT'S DARK OUT.
SHIK
...
SOMEONE HAS A LIGHT ON.
THAT'S THE TEACHER'S LOUNGE...
Is it a patrol?
No, they've already left for the night.
...
COULD IT BE BURGLARS?
DOOM DOOM DOOM
I'LL GO CATCH THEM!
AFTER ALL, I'VE DONE IT BEFORE!!
HEY! WAIT!
...
SHE'S SO TROUBLE-SOME.

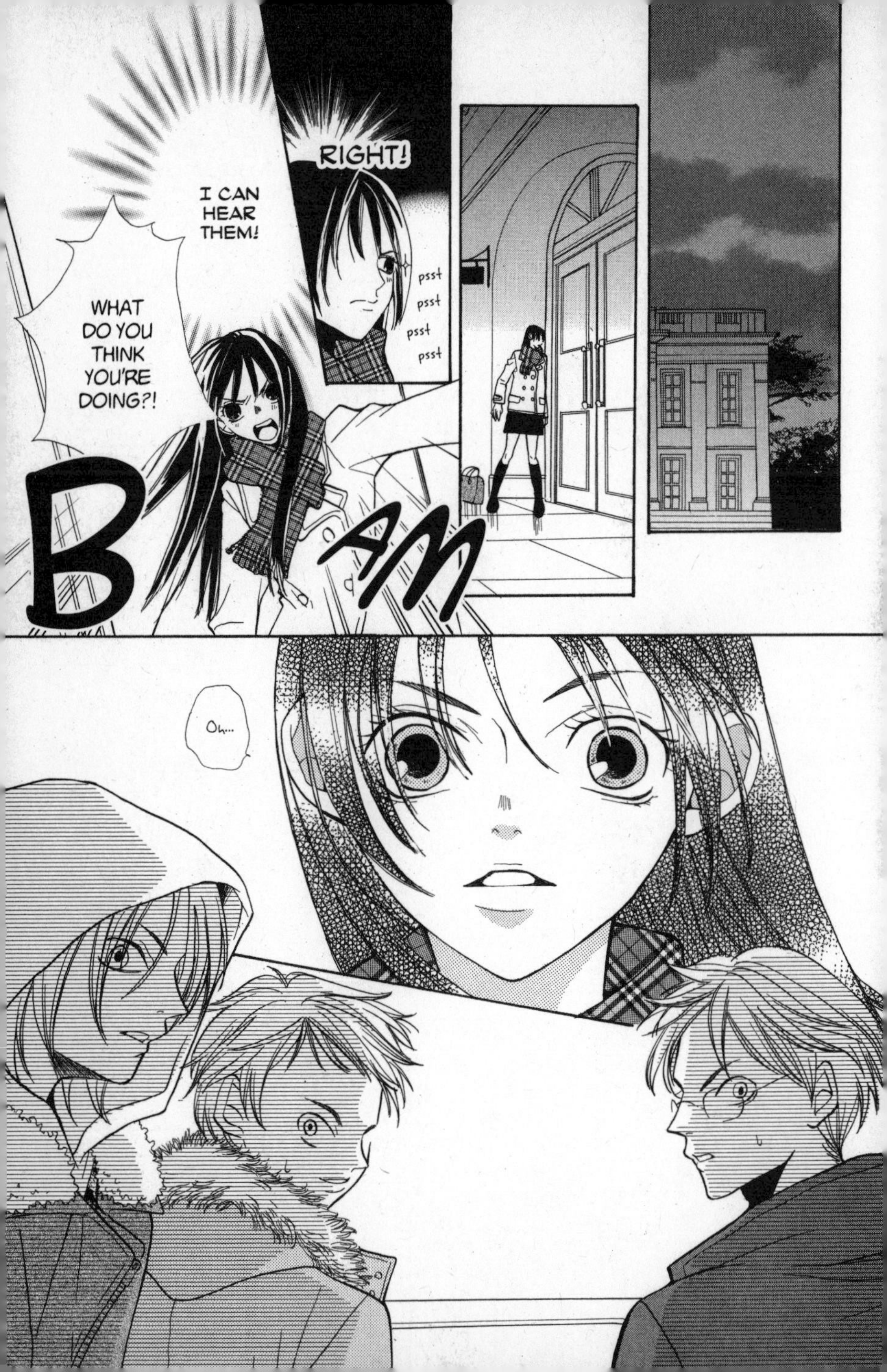
RIGHT!
psst
psst
psst
psst
I CAN HEAR THEM!
WHAT DO YOU THINK YOU'RE DOING?!
BAM
Oh...

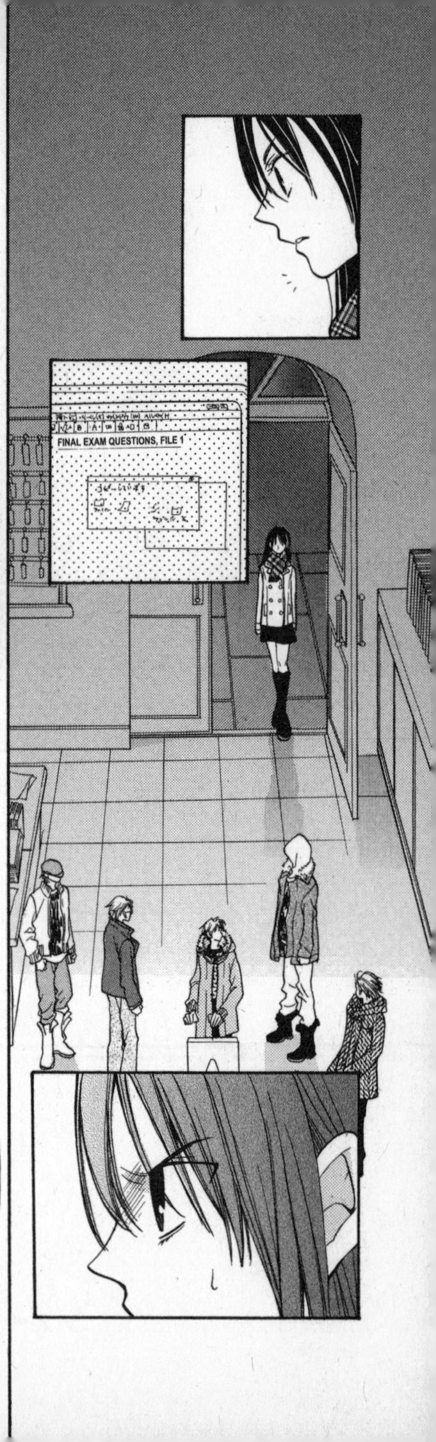
FINAL EXAM QUESTIONS, FILE 1

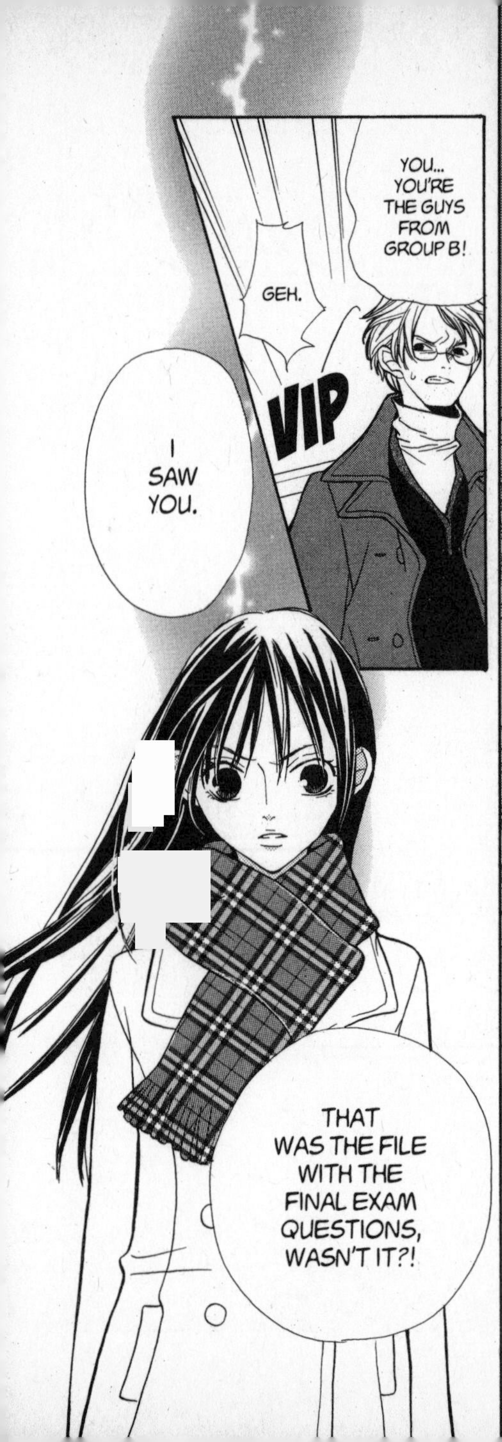
YOU... YOU'RE THE GUYS FROM GROUP B!
GEH.
VIP
I SAW YOU.
THAT WAS THE FILE WITH THE FINAL EXAM QUESTIONS, WASN'T IT?!

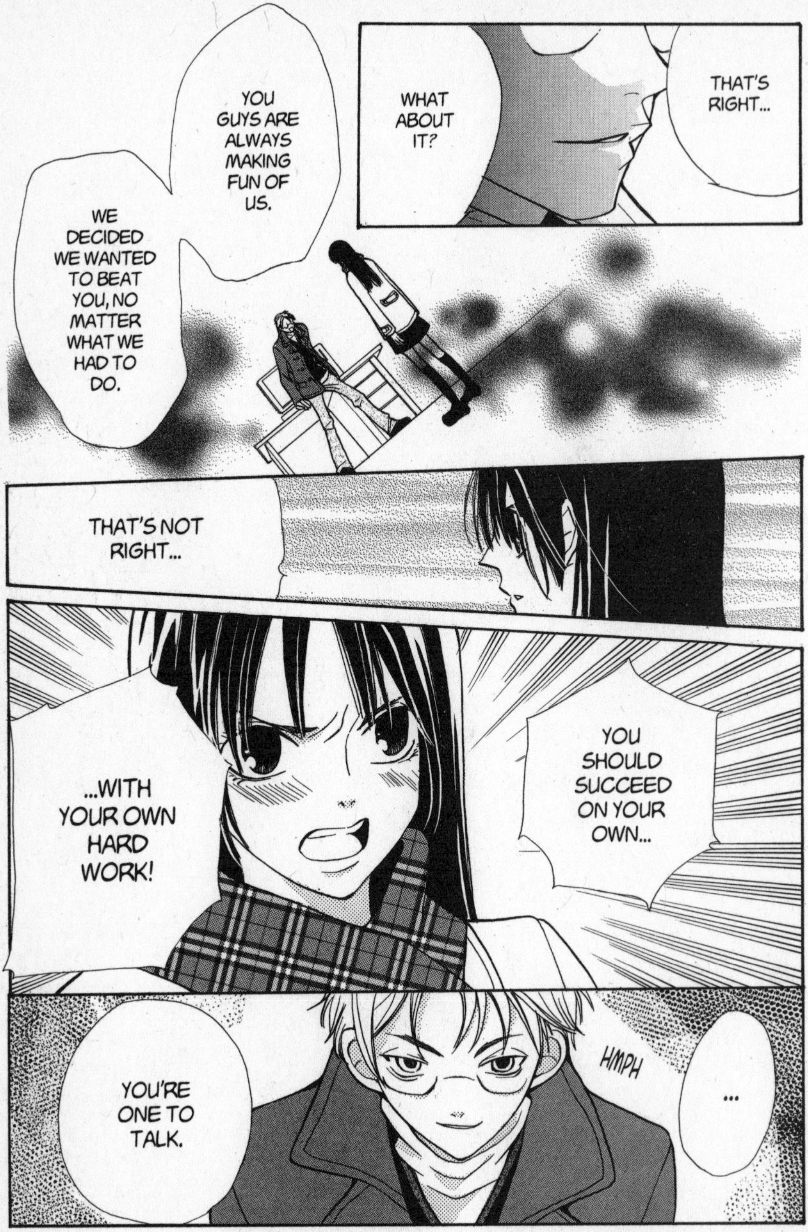
THAT'S RIGHT...
WHAT ABOUT IT?
YOU GUYS ARE ALWAYS MAKING FUN OF US.
WE DECIDED WE WANTED TO BEAT YOU, NO MATTER WHAT WE HAD TO DO.
THAT'S NOT RIGHT...
YOU SHOULD SUCCEED ON YOUR OWN...
...WITH YOUR OWN HARD WORK!
...
HMPH
YOU'RE ONE TO TALK.

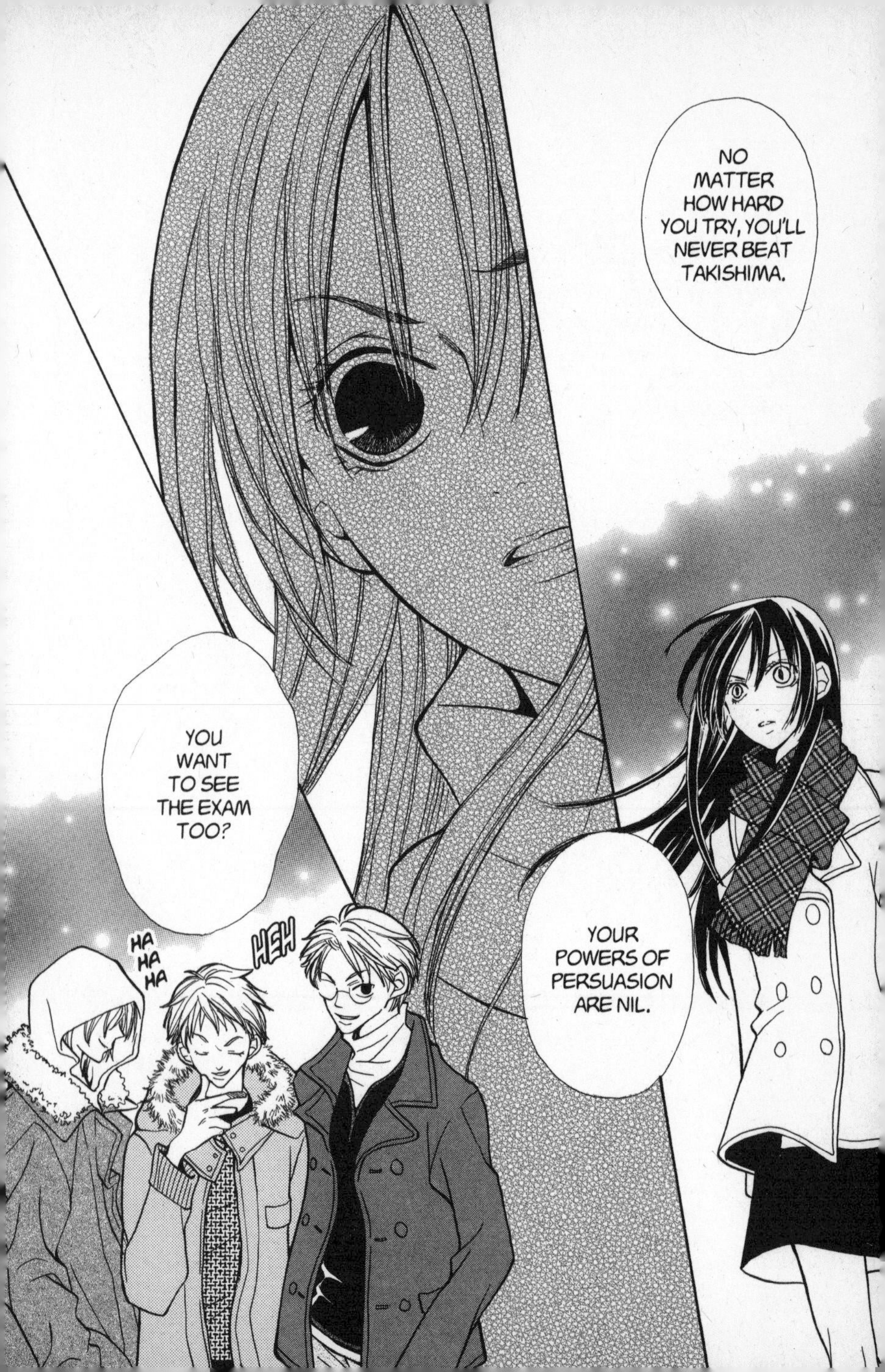
NO MATTER HOW HARD YOU TRY, YOU'LL NEVER BEAT TAKISHIMA.
YOU WANT TO SEE THE EXAM TOO?
HEH
HA HA HA
YOUR POWERS OF PERSUASION ARE NIL.

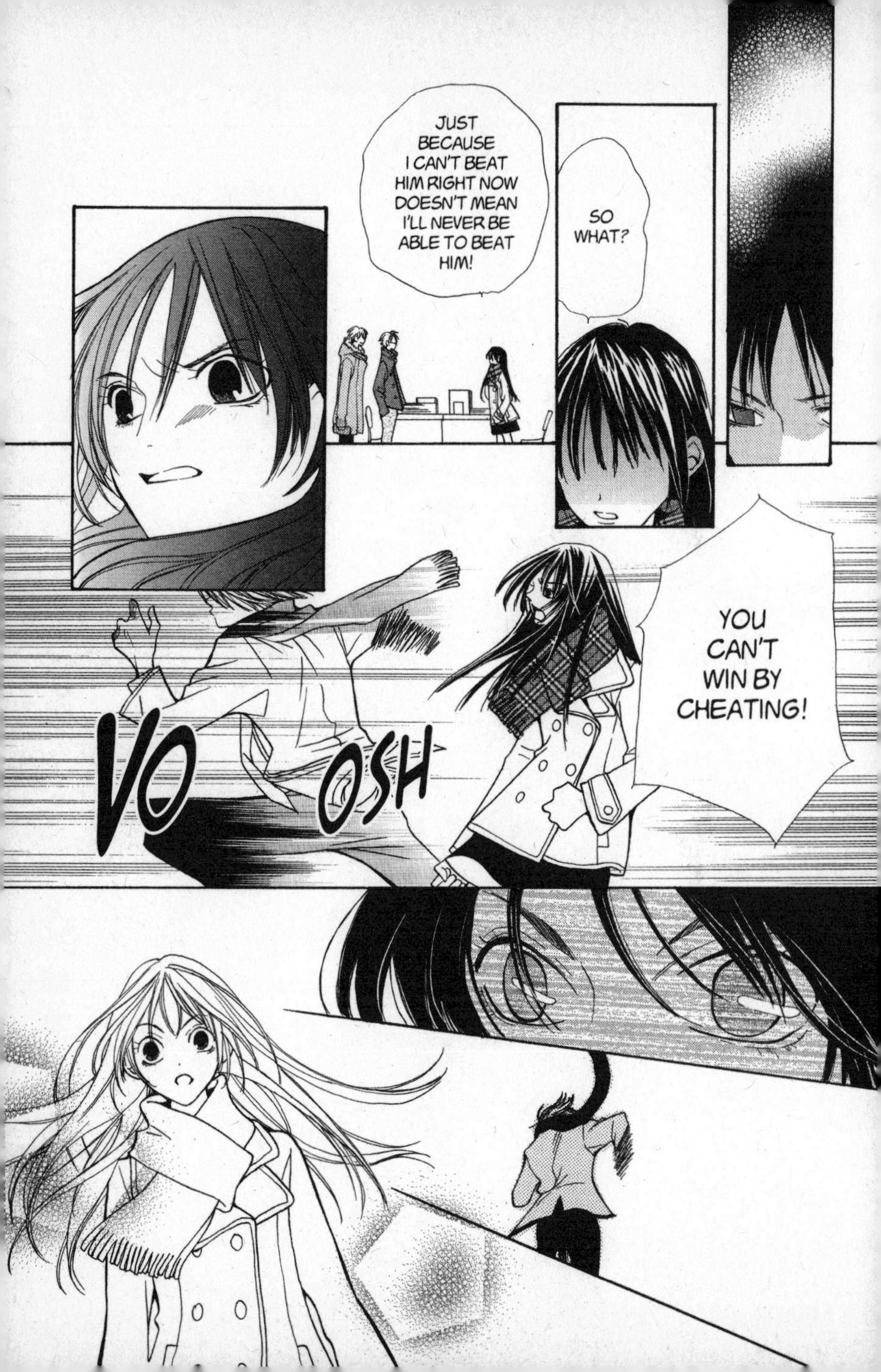
SO WHAT?
JUST BECAUSE I CAN'T BEAT HIM RIGHT NOW DOESN'T MEAN I'LL NEVER BE ABLE TO BEAT HIM!
YOU CAN'T WIN BY CHEATING!
VO OSH

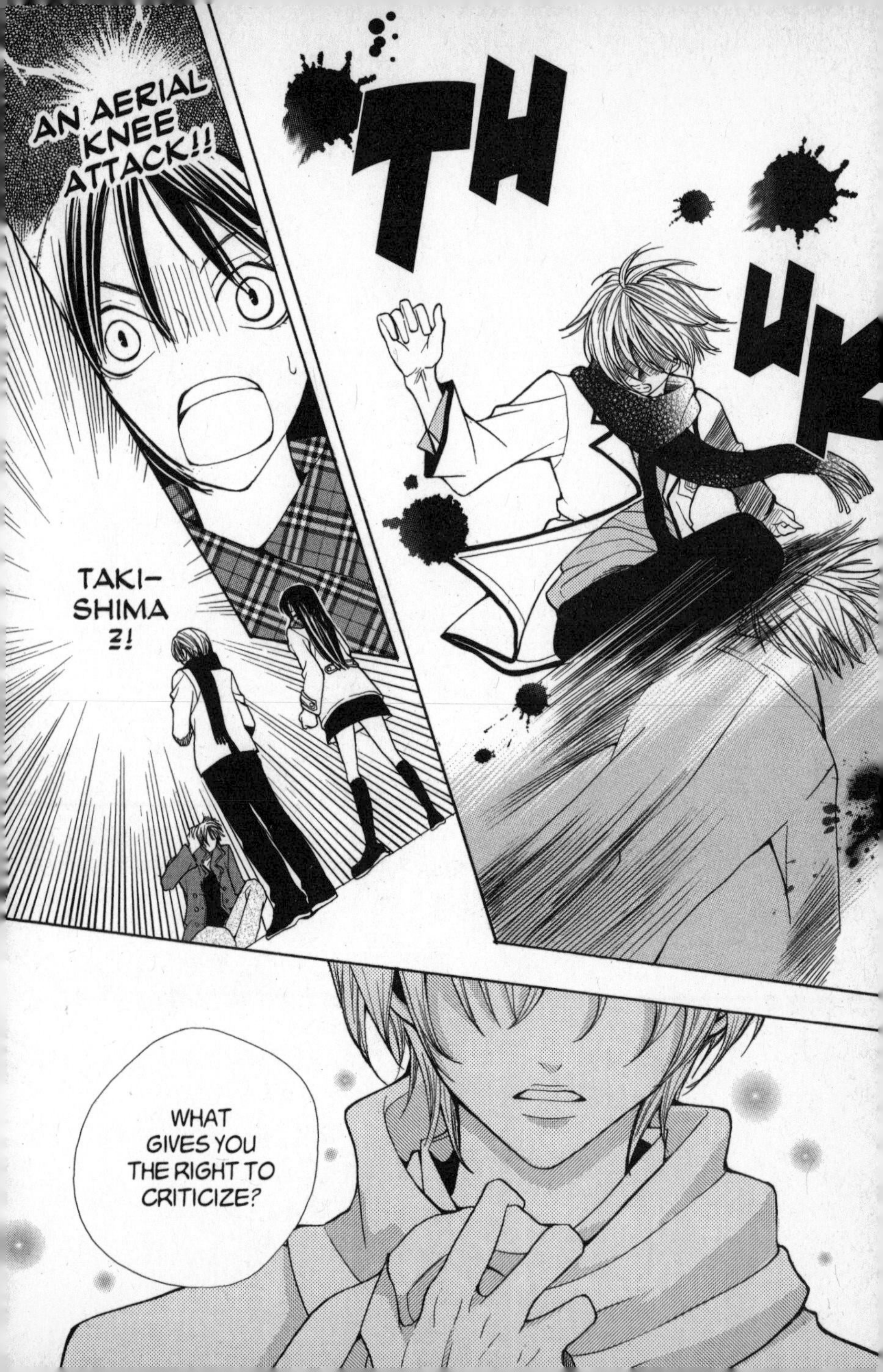
TH
UK
AN AERIAL KNEE ATTACK!!
TAKI-SHIMA?!
WHAT GIVES YOU THE RIGHT TO CRITICIZE?

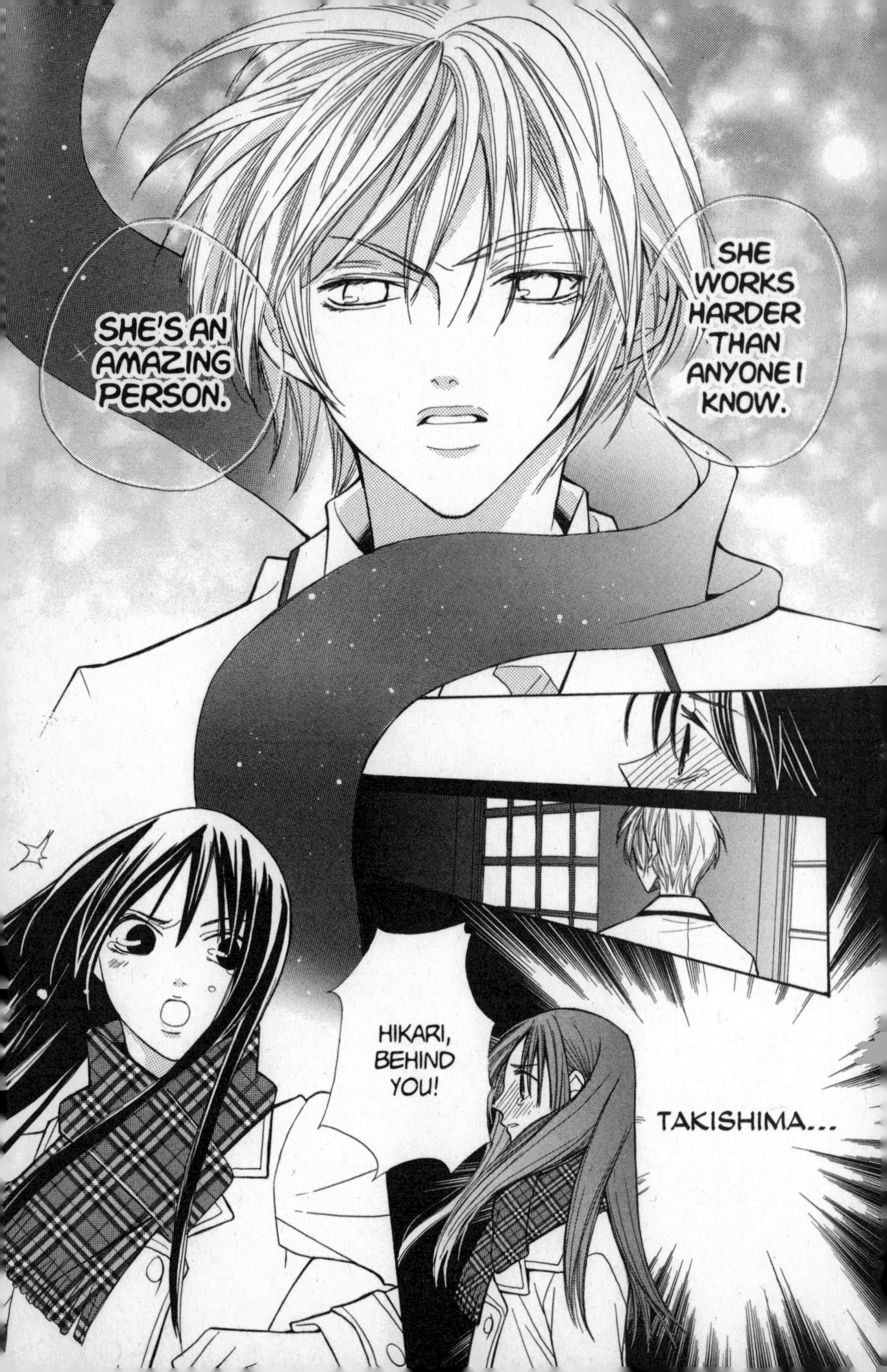
SHE WORKS HARDER THAN ANYONE I KNOW.
SHE'S AN AMAZING PERSON.
TAKISHIMA...
HIKARI, BEHIND YOU!

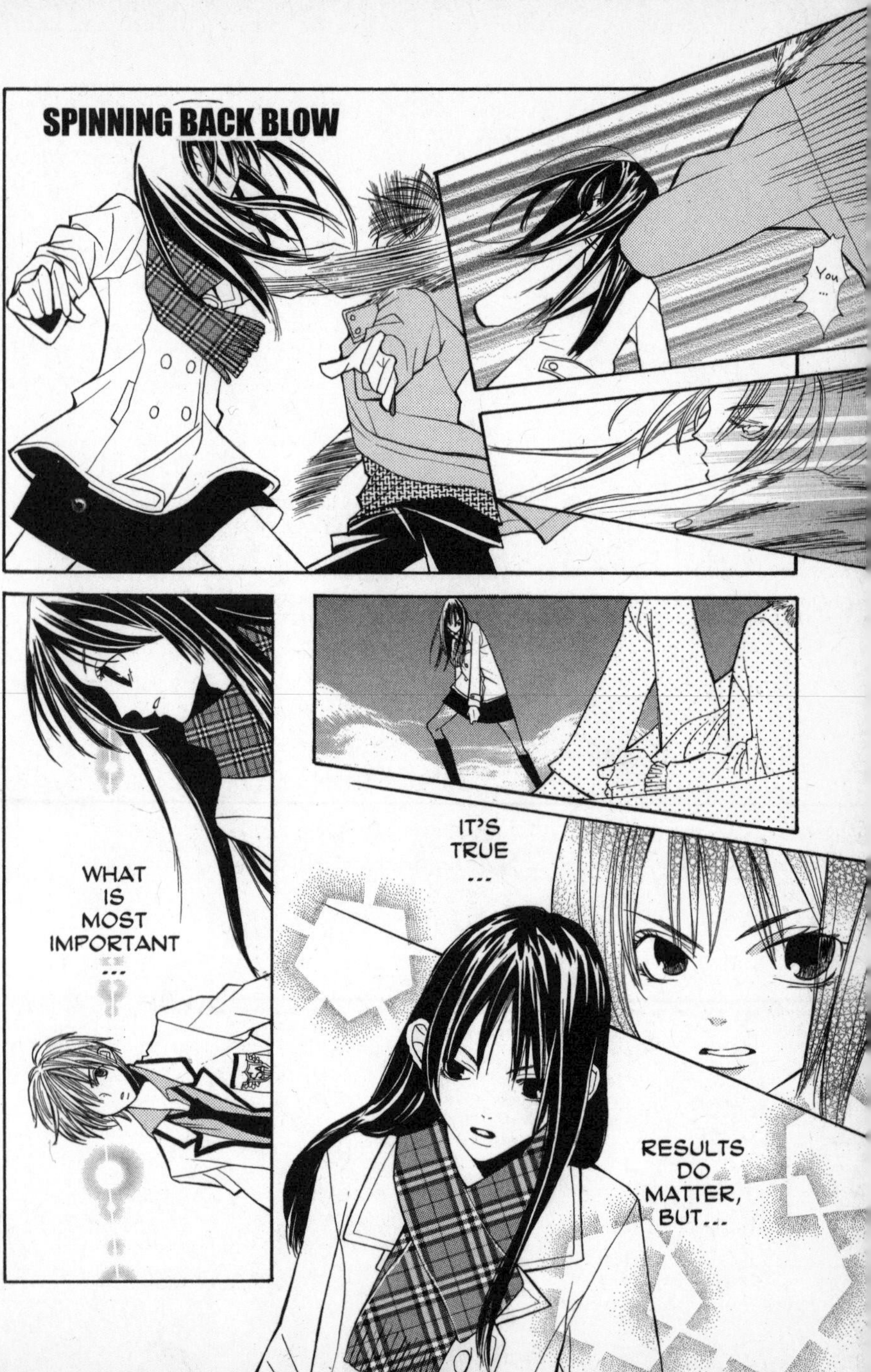
You ...
SPINNING BACK BLOW
IT'S TRUE ...
RESULTS DO MATTER, BUT...
WHAT IS MOST IMPORTANT ...

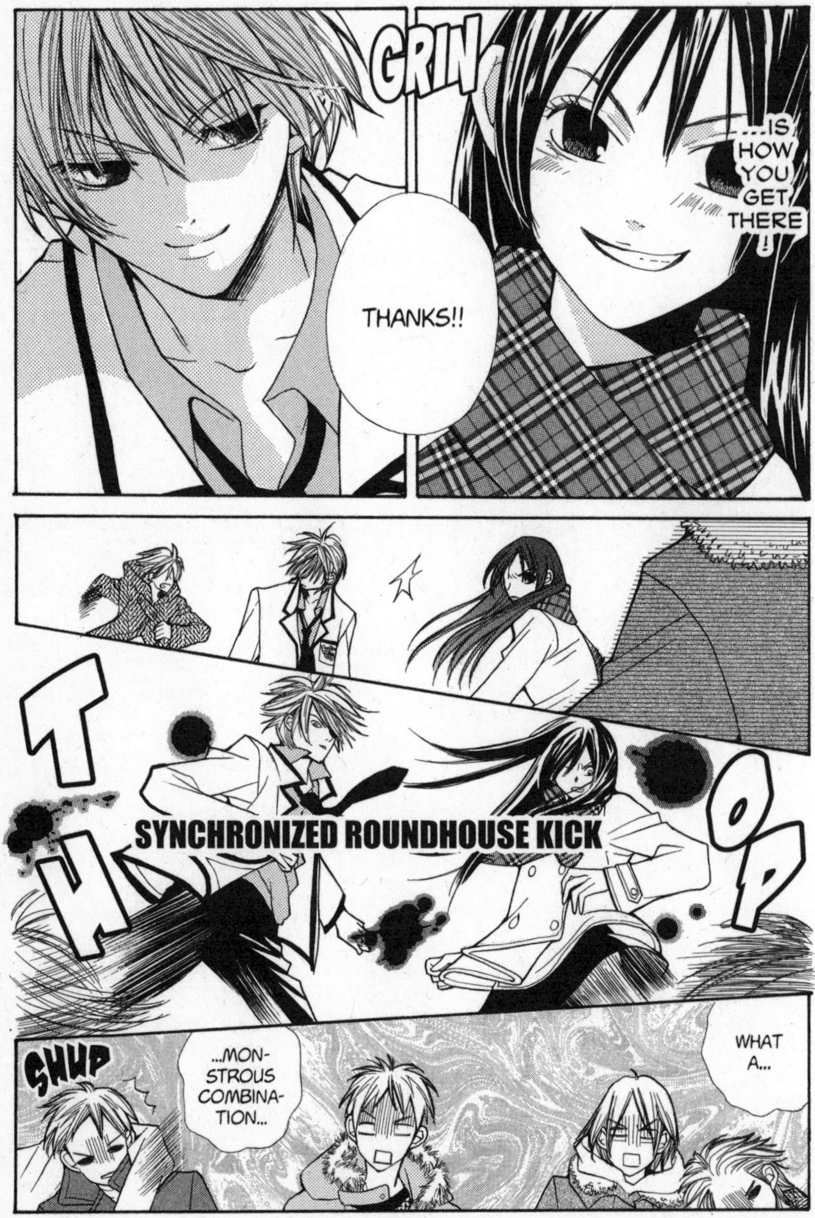
GRIN
...IS HOW YOU GET THERE!
THANKS!!
THOP
SYNCHRONIZED ROUNDHOUSE KICK
WHAT A...
...MON-STROUS COMBINA-TION...
SHUP

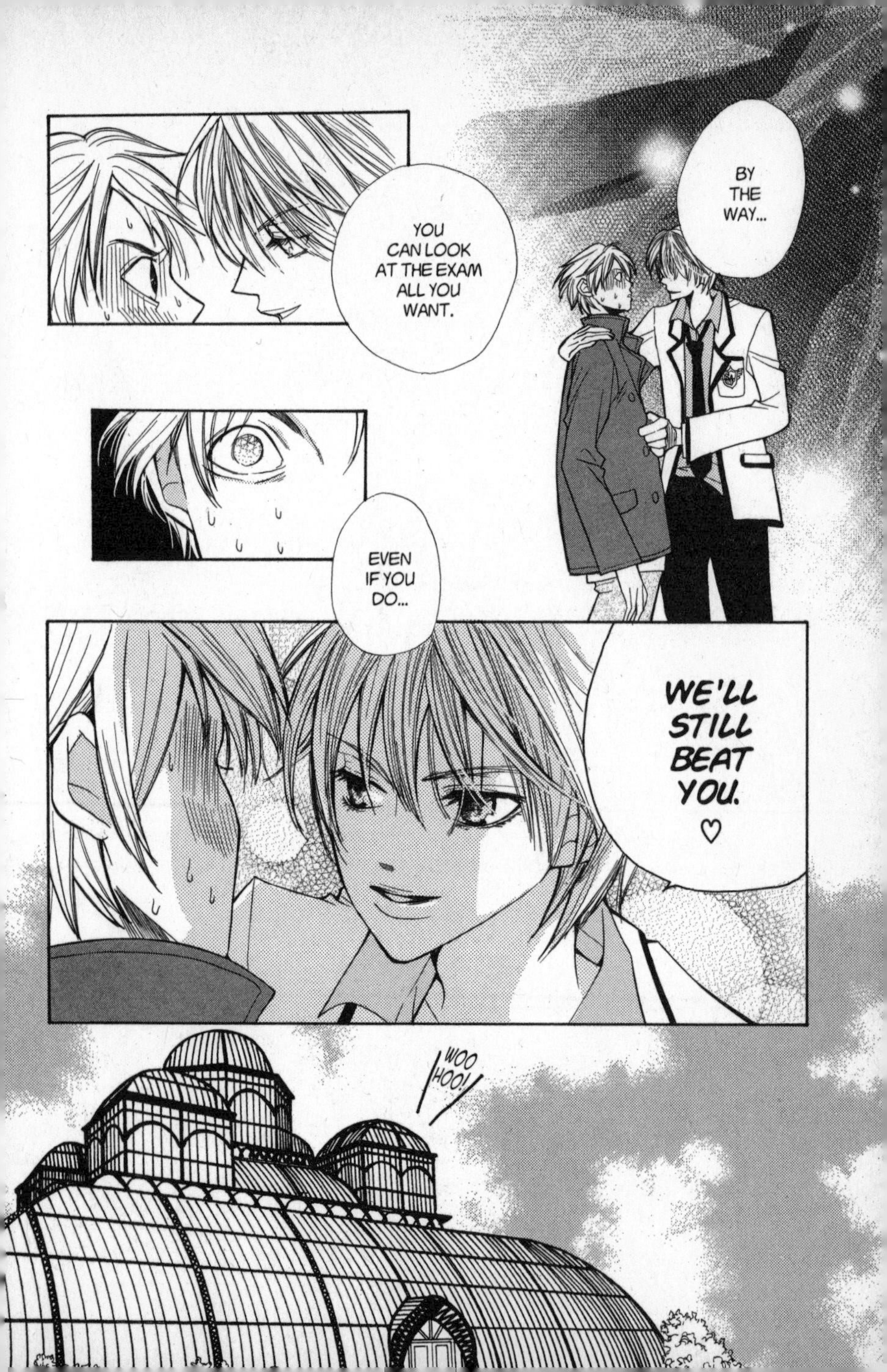
BY THE WAY...
YOU CAN LOOK AT THE EXAM ALL YOU WANT.
EVEN IF YOU DO...
WE'LL STILL BEAT YOU. ♡
WOO HOO!

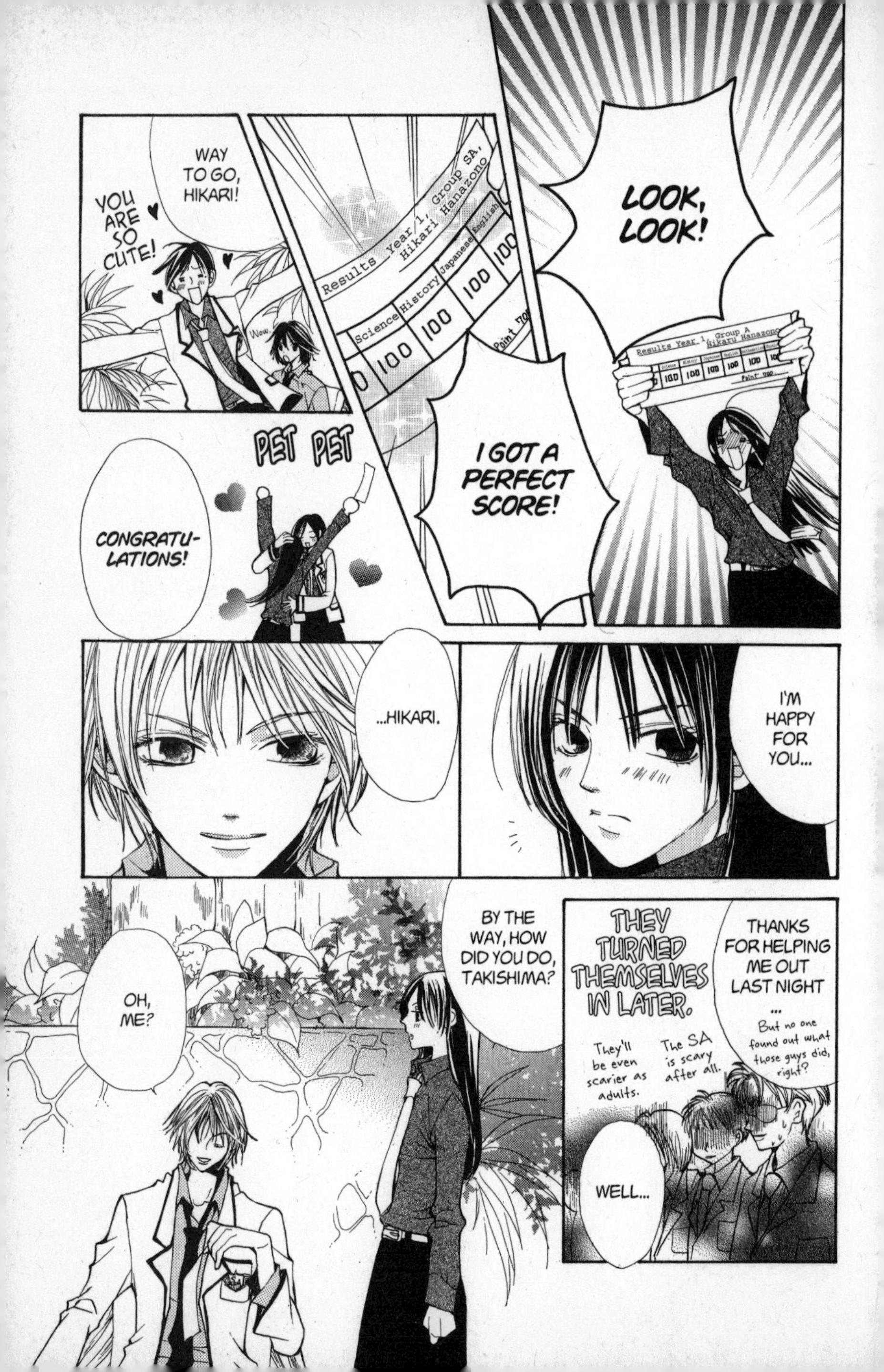
LOOK, LOOK!
I GOT A PERFECT SCORE!
Results Year 1, Group SA, Hikari Hanazono
Science History Japanese English
100 100 100 100
Point 700
WAY TO GO, HIKARI!
YOU ARE SO CUTE!
Wow.
PET PET
CONGRATULATIONS!
I'M HAPPY FOR YOU...
...HIKARI.
THANKS FOR HELPING ME OUT LAST NIGHT ...
But no one found out what those guys did, right?
WELL...
THEY TURNED THEMSELVES IN LATER.
The SA is scary after all.
They'll be even scarier as adults.
BY THE WAY, HOW DID YOU DO, TAKISHIMA?
OH, ME?

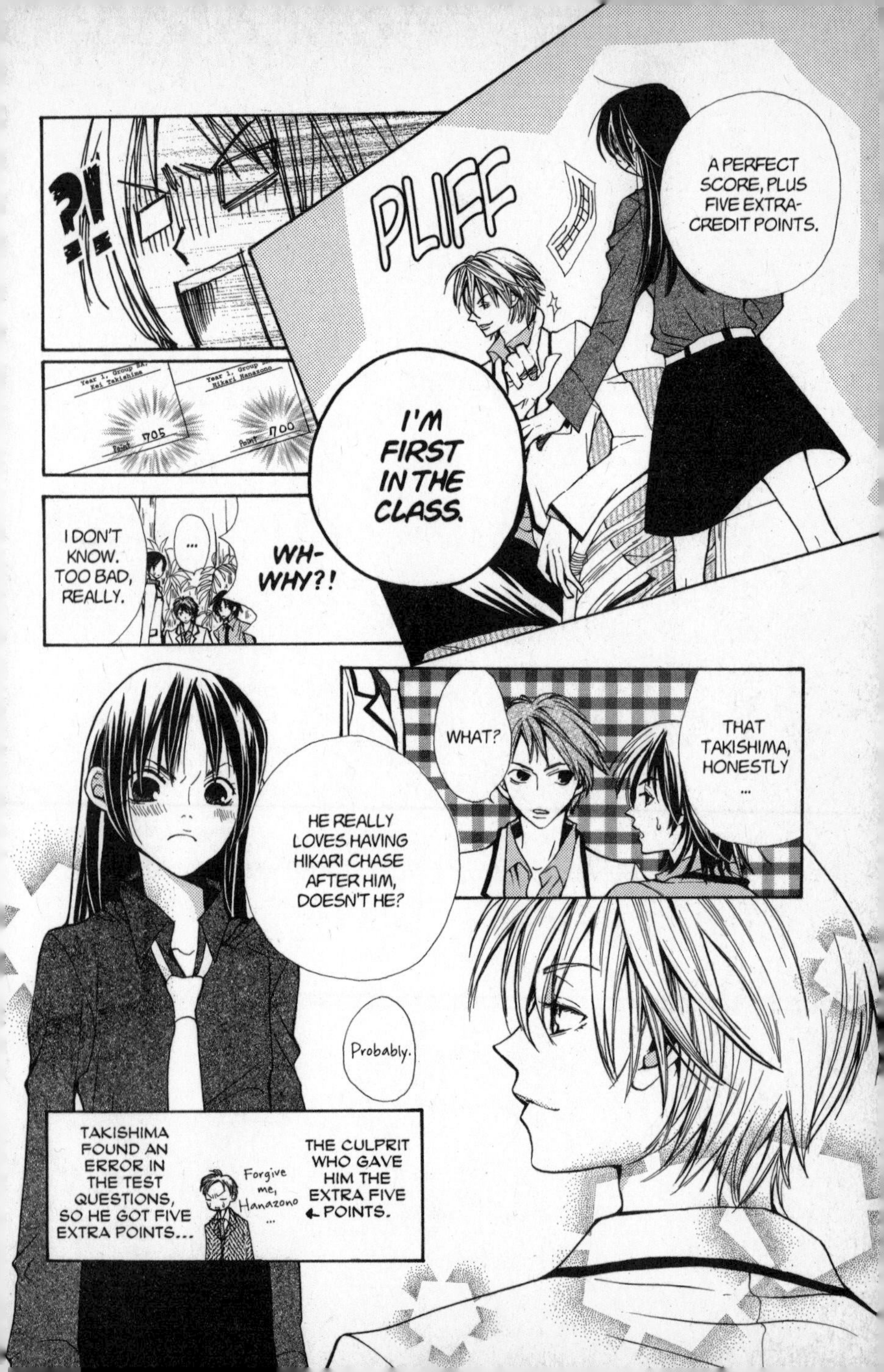
PLIFF
A PERFECT SCORE, PLUS FIVE EXTRA-CREDIT POINTS.
I'M FIRST IN THE CLASS.
?!
Year 1, Group
Hikari Hanazono
Point 1700
Year 1, Group
Kei Takishima
Point 1705
WH-WHY?!
...
I DON'T KNOW. TOO BAD, REALLY.
THAT TAKISHIMA, HONESTLY ...
WHAT?
HE REALLY LOVES HAVING HIKARI CHASE AFTER HIM, DOESN'T HE?
Probably.
TAKISHIMA FOUND AN ERROR IN THE TEST QUESTIONS, SO HE GOT FIVE EXTRA POINTS...
Forgive me, Hanazono ...
THE CULPRIT WHO GAVE HIM THE EXTRA FIVE POINTS.

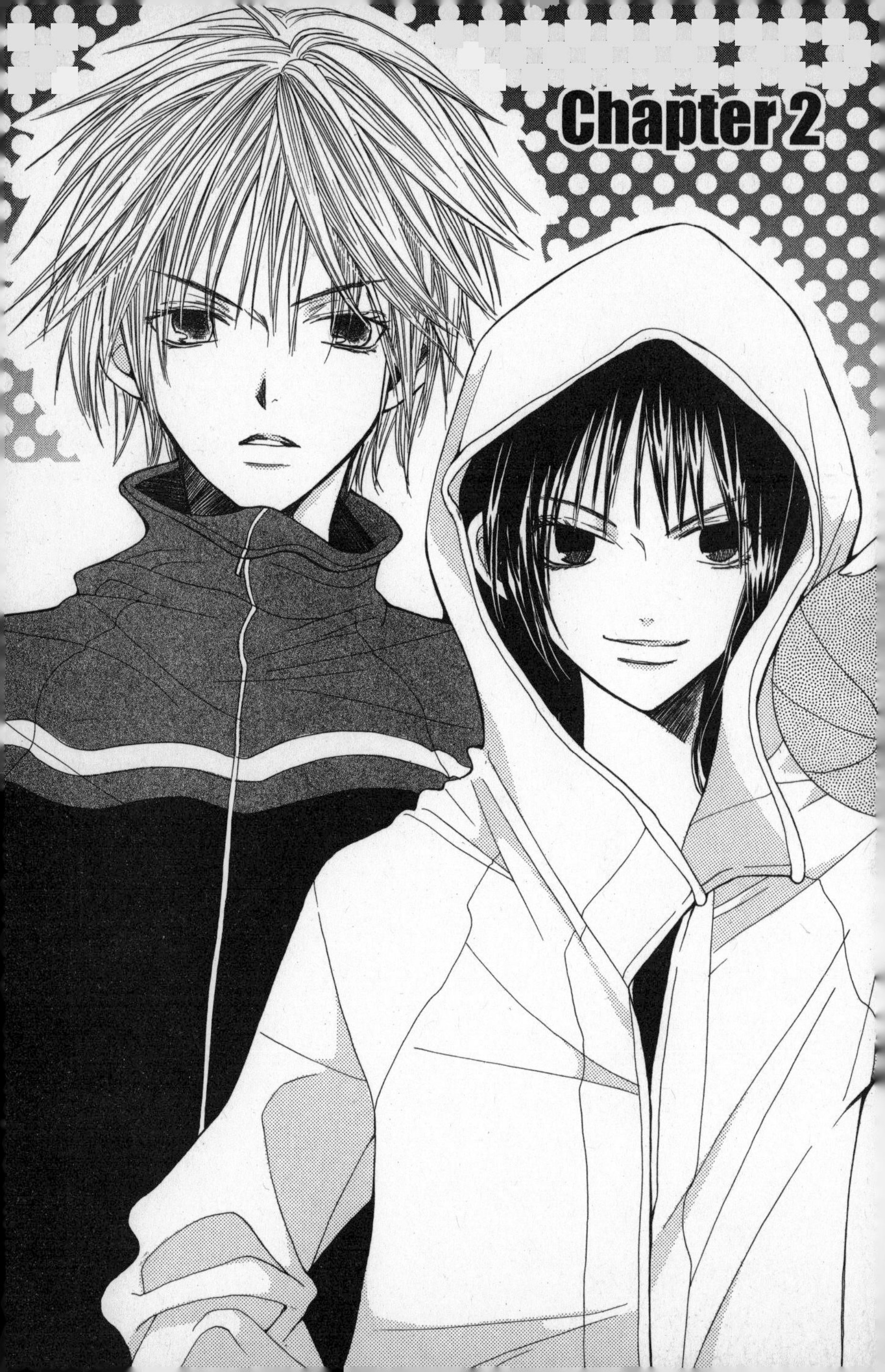
Chapter 2

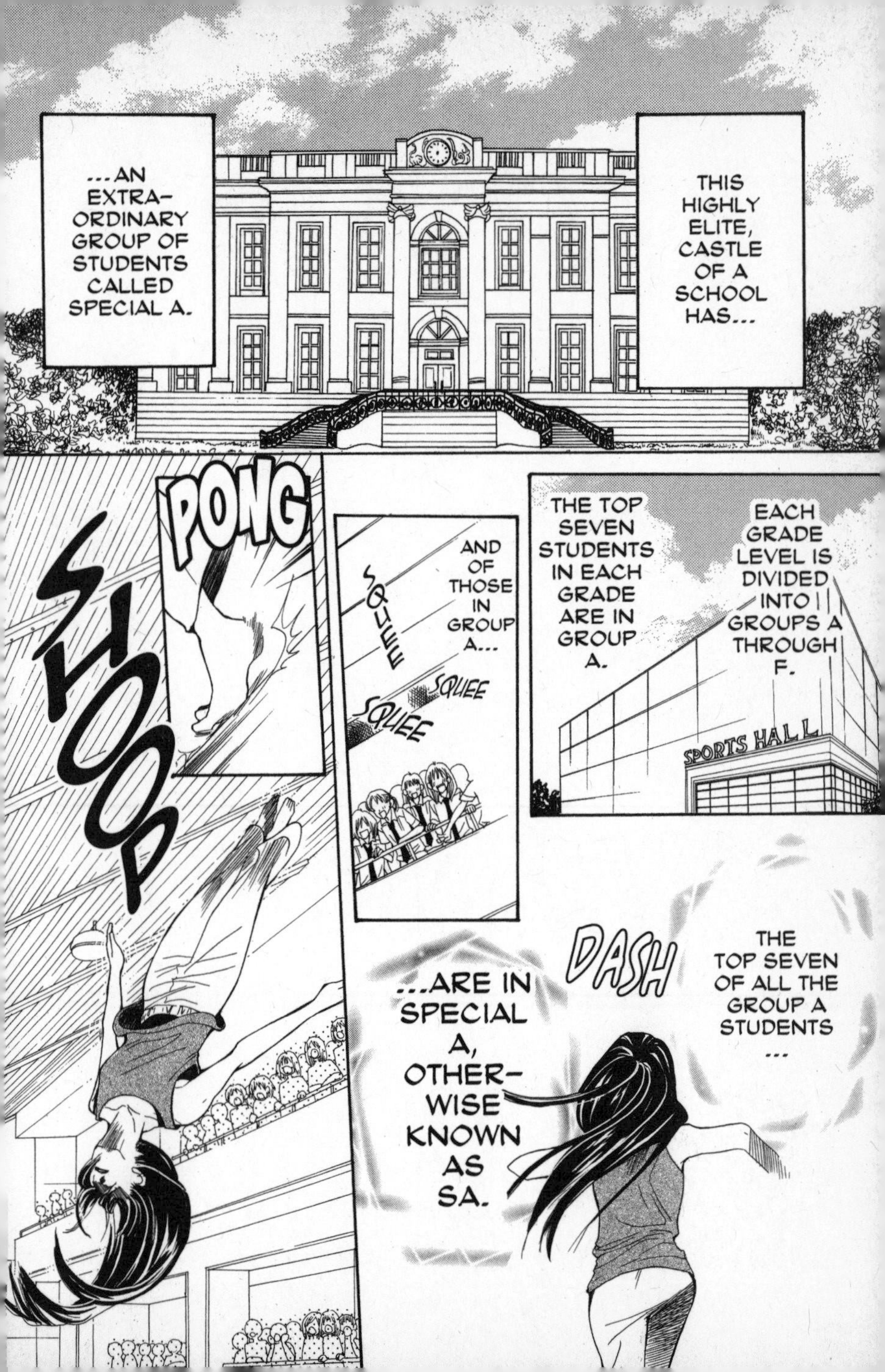
THIS HIGHLY ELITE, CASTLE OF A SCHOOL HAS...
...AN EXTRA-ORDINARY GROUP OF STUDENTS CALLED SPECIAL A.
EACH GRADE LEVEL IS DIVIDED INTO GROUPS A THROUGH F.
THE TOP SEVEN STUDENTS IN EACH GRADE ARE IN GROUP A.
SPORTS HALL
AND OF THOSE IN GROUP A...
SQUEE
SQUEE
SQUEE
THE TOP SEVEN OF ALL THE GROUP A STUDENTS ...
DASH
...ARE IN SPECIAL A, OTHER-WISE KNOWN AS SA.
PONG
SHOOP

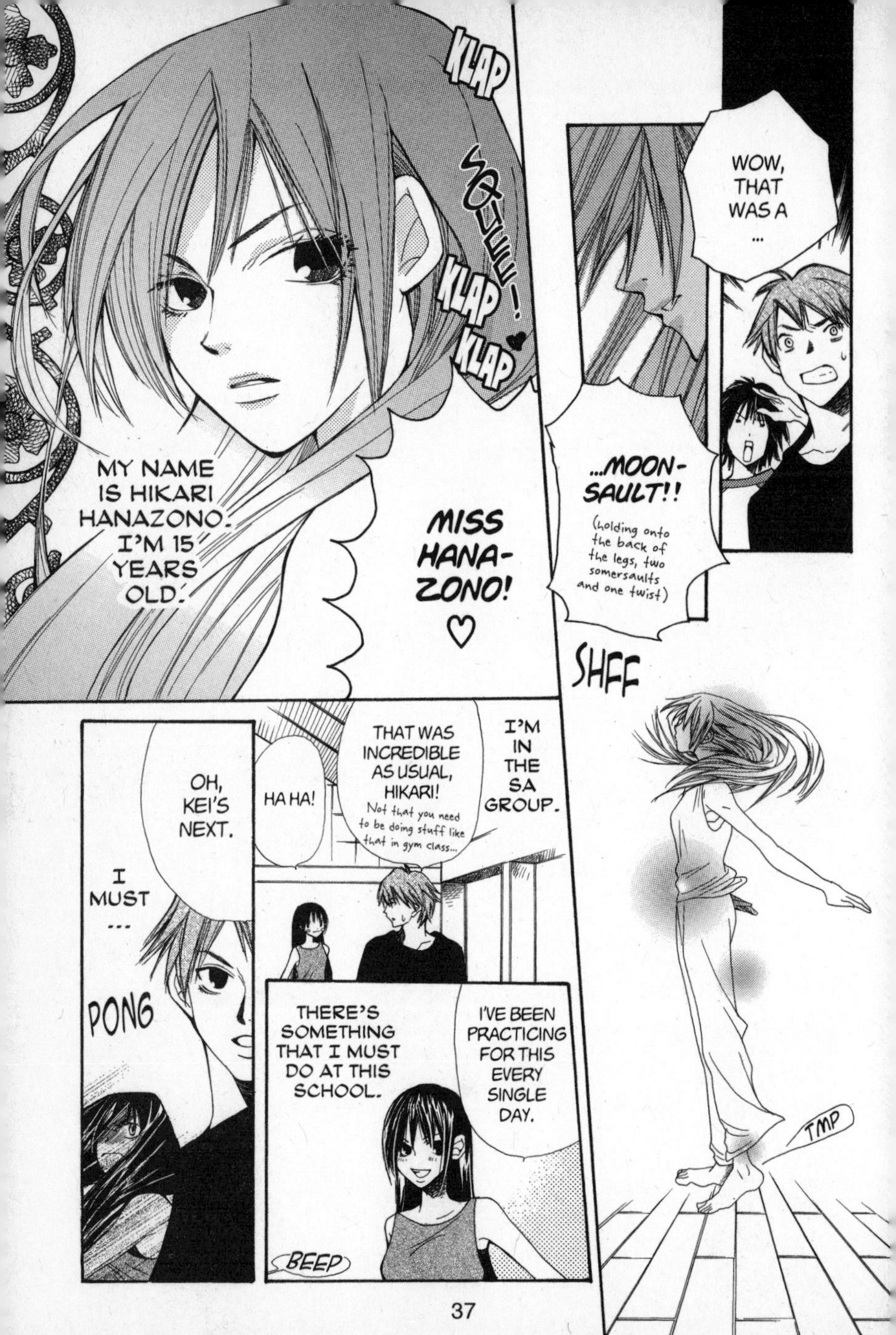
WOW, THAT WAS A ...
...MOON-SAULT!!
(holding onto the back of the legs, two somersaults and one twist)
SHFF
TMP
KLAP
KLAP
KLAP
KLAP
MISS HANA-ZONO! ♡
MY NAME IS HIKARI HANAZONO. I'M 15 YEARS OLD.
I'M IN THE SA GROUP.
THAT WAS INCREDIBLE AS USUAL, HIKARI! Not that you need to be doing stuff like that in gym class...
HA HA!
OH, KEI'S NEXT.
I MUST ...
PONG
I'VE BEEN PRACTICING FOR THIS EVERY SINGLE DAY.
THERE'S SOMETHING THAT I MUST DO AT THIS SCHOOL.
BEEP

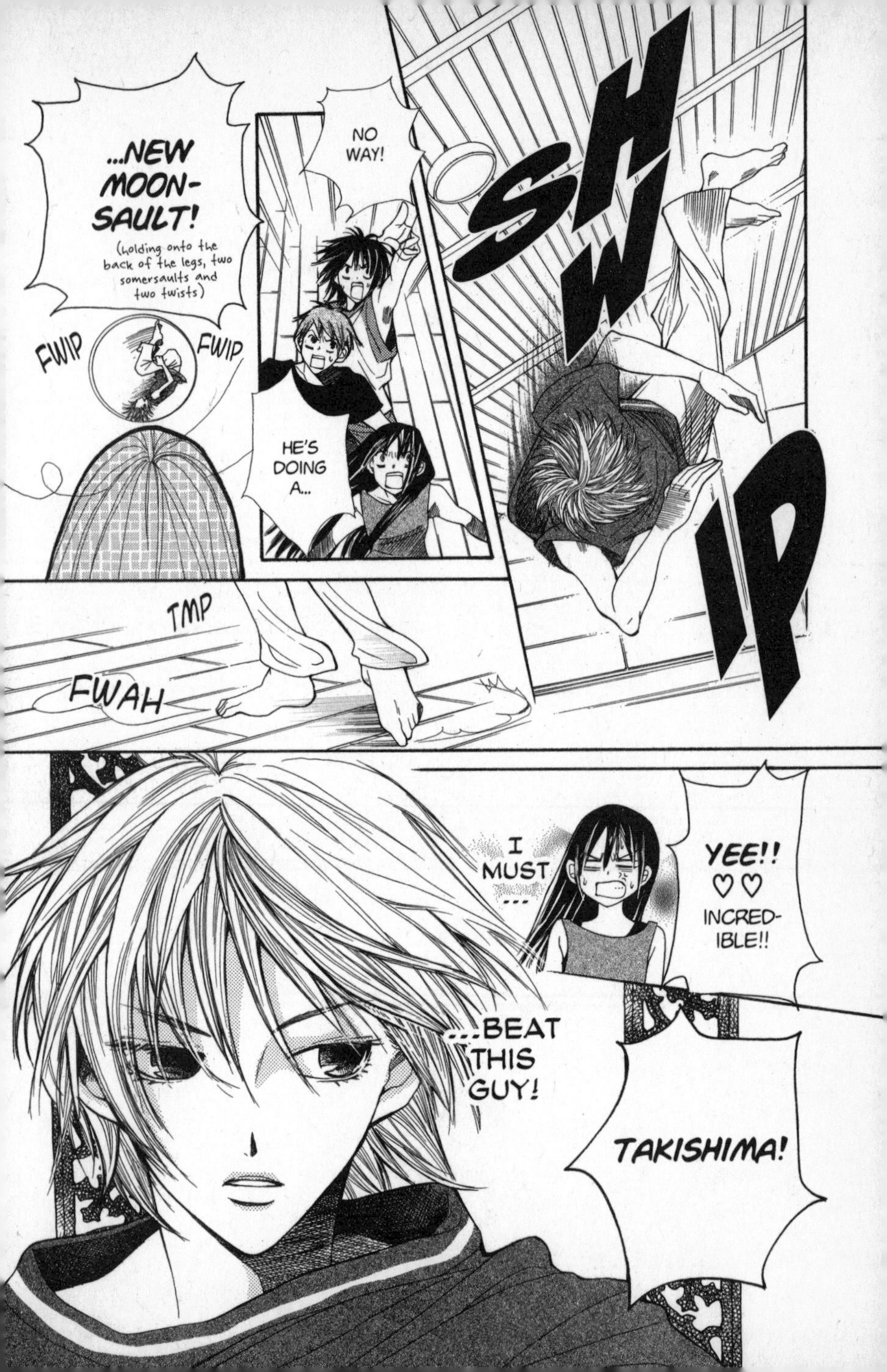
SHWIP
NO WAY!
HE'S DOING A...
...NEW MOONSAULT!
(holding onto the back of the legs, two somersaults and two twists)
FWIP
FWIP
TMP
FWAH
YEE!! ♡♡ INCREDIBLE!!
TAKISHIMA!
I MUST...
...BEAT THIS GUY!

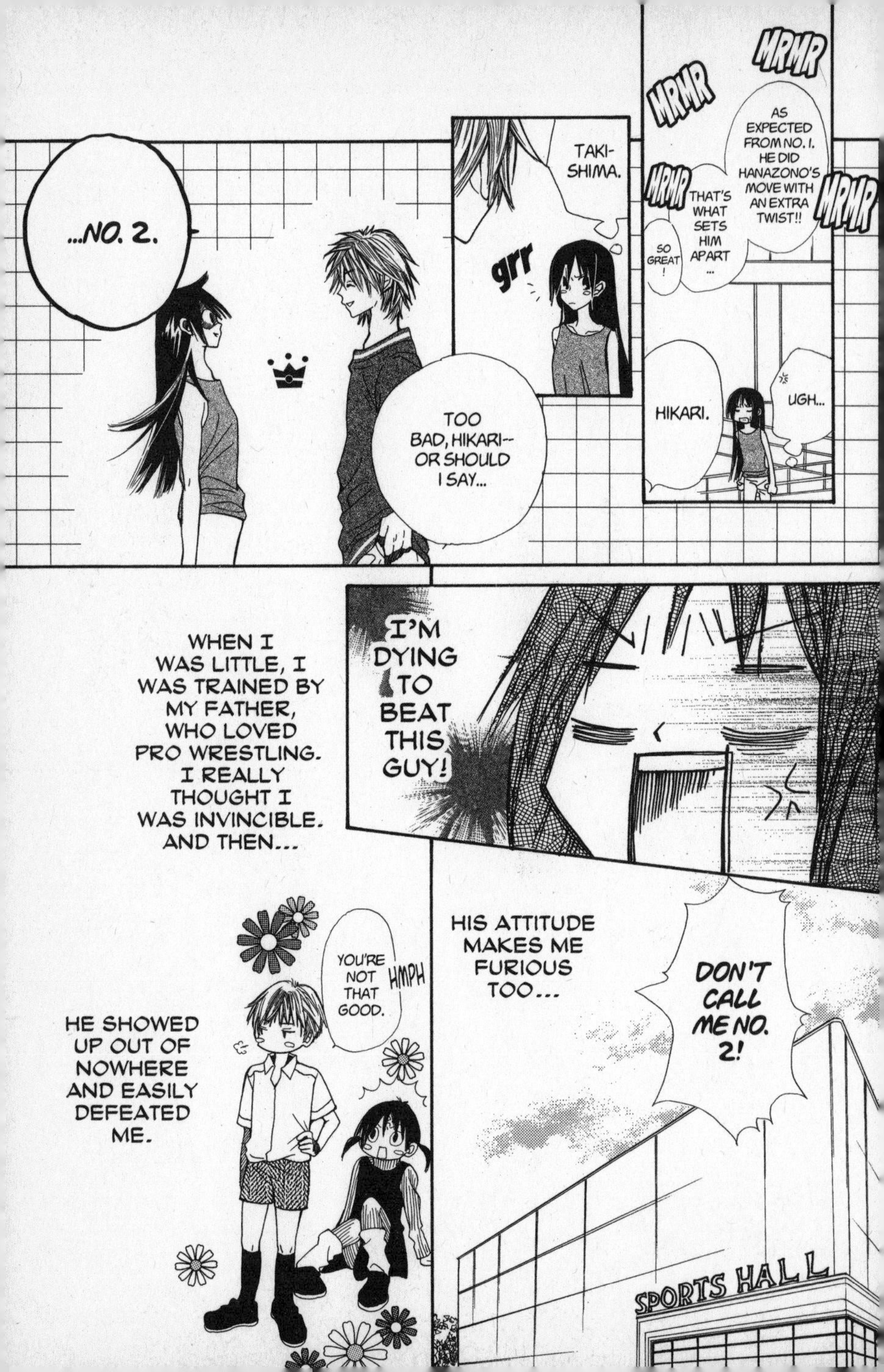
MRMR
MRMR
AS EXPECTED FROM NO. 1. HE DID HANAZONO'S MOVE WITH AN EXTRA TWIST!!
MRMR
THAT'S WHAT SETS HIM APART...
MRMR
SO GREAT!
HIKARI.
UGH...
TAKI-SHIMA.
grr
TOO BAD, HIKARI--OR SHOULD I SAY...
...NO. 2.
I'M DYING TO BEAT THIS GUY!
WHEN I WAS LITTLE, I WAS TRAINED BY MY FATHER, WHO LOVED PRO WRESTLING. I REALLY THOUGHT I WAS INVINCIBLE. AND THEN...
DON'T CALL ME NO. 2!
HIS ATTITUDE MAKES ME FURIOUS TOO...
SPORTS HALL
YOU'RE NOT THAT GOOD.
HMPH
HE SHOWED UP OUT OF NOWHERE AND EASILY DEFEATED ME.

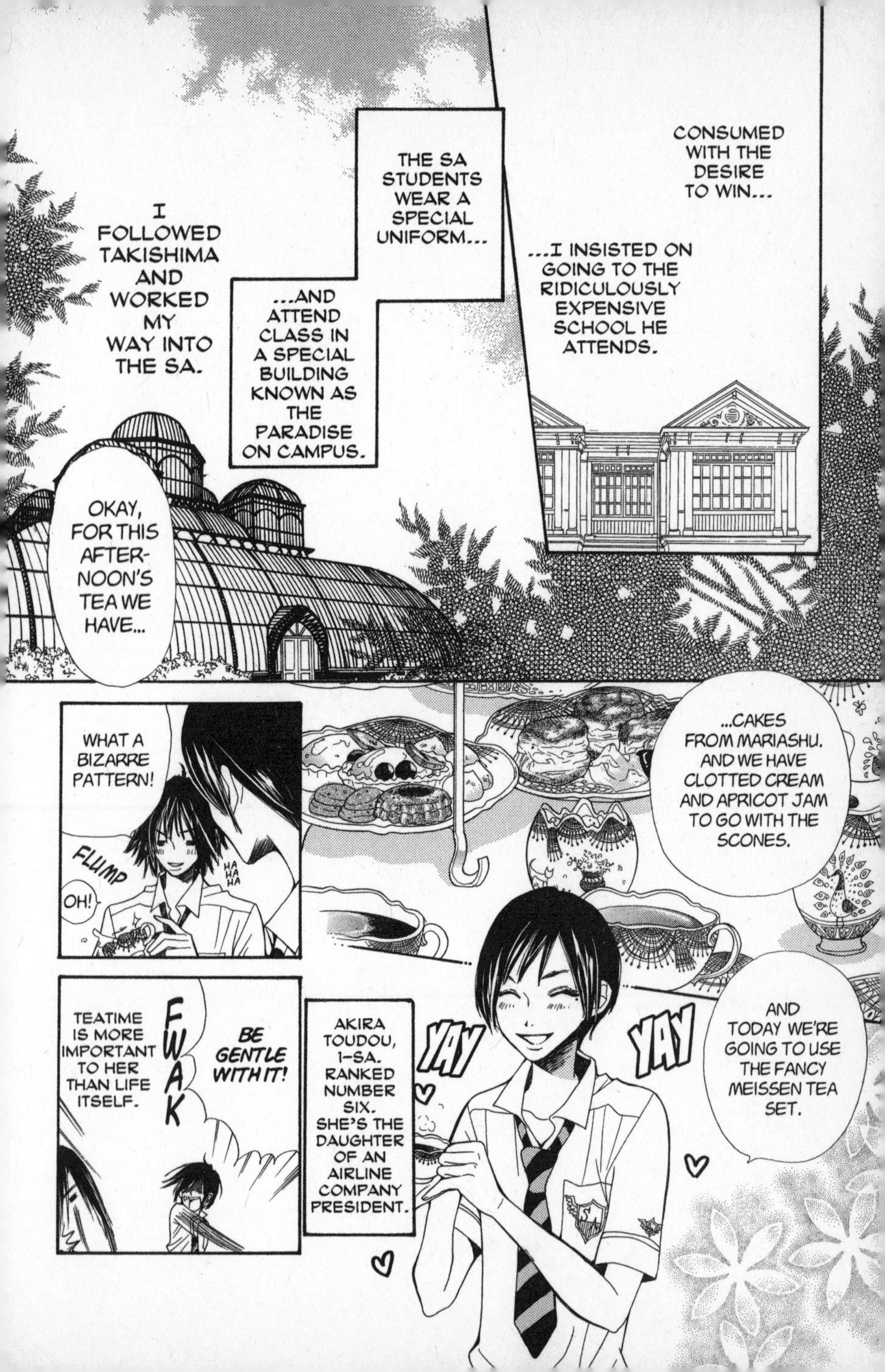
CONSUMED WITH THE DESIRE TO WIN...
...I INSISTED ON GOING TO THE RIDICULOUSLY EXPENSIVE SCHOOL HE ATTENDS.
THE SA STUDENTS WEAR A SPECIAL UNIFORM...
...AND ATTEND CLASS IN A SPECIAL BUILDING KNOWN AS THE PARADISE ON CAMPUS.
I FOLLOWED TAKISHIMA AND WORKED MY WAY INTO THE SA.
OKAY, FOR THIS AFTER-NOON'S TEA WE HAVE...
...CAKES FROM MARIASHU. AND WE HAVE CLOTTED CREAM AND APRICOT JAM TO GO WITH THE SCONES.
AND TODAY WE'RE GOING TO USE THE FANCY MEISSEN TEA SET.
YAY
YAY
AKIRA TOUDOU, 1-SA. RANKED NUMBER SIX. SHE'S THE DAUGHTER OF AN AIRLINE COMPANY PRESIDENT.
WHAT A BIZARRE PATTERN!
HA HA HA
FLUMP
OH!
BE GENTLE WITH IT!
FWAK
TEATIME IS MORE IMPORTANT TO HER THAN LIFE ITSELF.

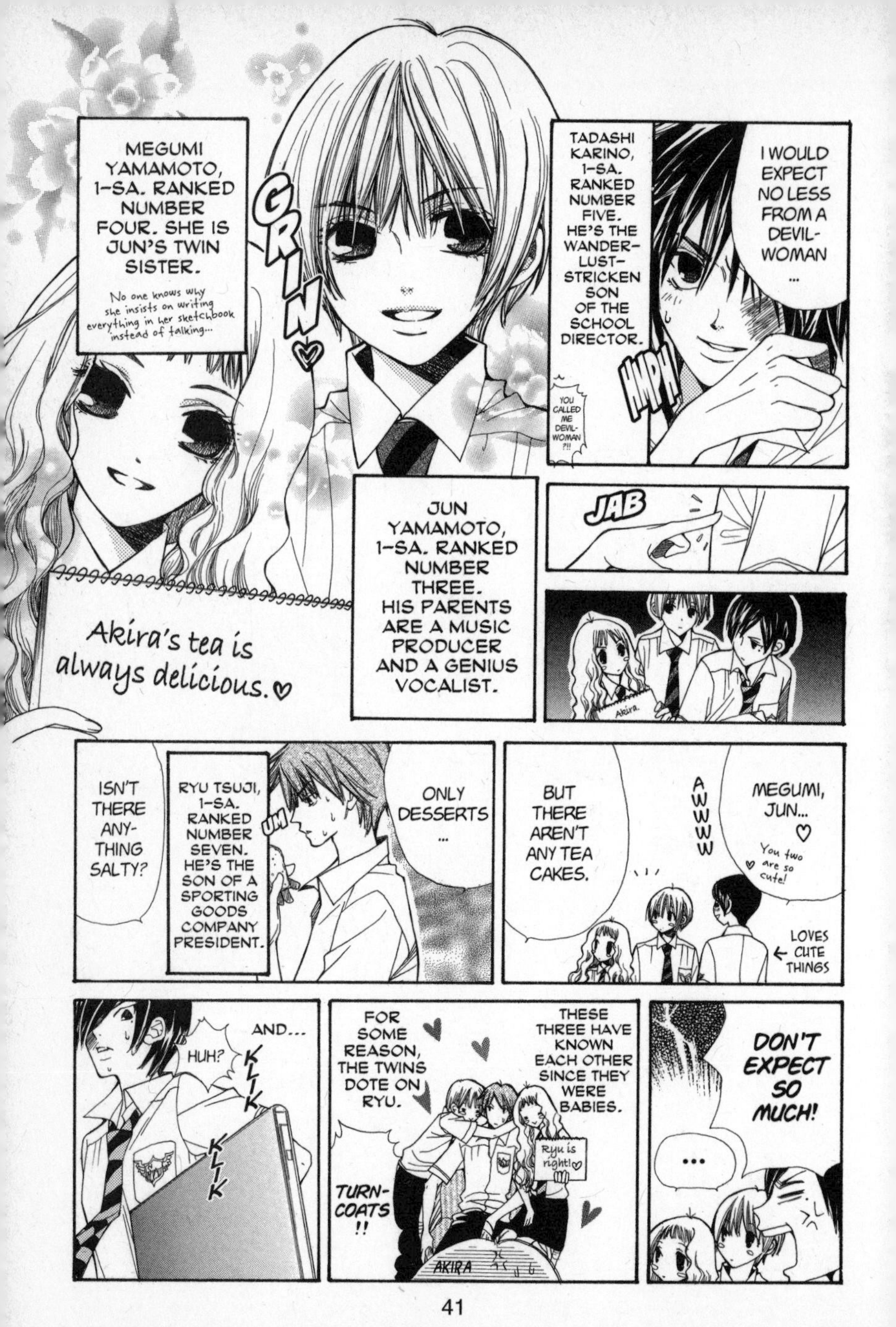
TADASHI KARINO, 1-SA. RANKED NUMBER FIVE. HE'S THE WANDERLUST-STRICKEN SON OF THE SCHOOL DIRECTOR.
I WOULD EXPECT NO LESS FROM A DEVIL-WOMAN ...
HMPH
YOU CALLED ME DEVIL-WOMAN ?!!
GRIN ♡
MEGUMI YAMAMOTO, 1-SA. RANKED NUMBER FOUR. SHE IS JUN'S TWIN SISTER.
No one knows why she insists on writing everything in her sketchbook instead of talking...
JUN YAMAMOTO, 1-SA. RANKED NUMBER THREE. HIS PARENTS ARE A MUSIC PRODUCER AND A GENIUS VOCALIST.
Akira's tea is always delicious. ♡
JAB
Akira.
MEGUMI, JUN... ♡
You two are so cute!
AWWWW
BUT THERE AREN'T ANY TEA CAKES.
LOVES CUTE THINGS
ONLY DESSERTS ...
UM
RYU TSUJI, 1-SA. RANKED NUMBER SEVEN. HE'S THE SON OF A SPORTING GOODS COMPANY PRESIDENT.
ISN'T THERE ANYTHING SALTY?
DON'T EXPECT SO MUCH!
...
THESE THREE HAVE KNOWN EACH OTHER SINCE THEY WERE BABIES.
FOR SOME REASON, THE TWINS DOTE ON RYU.
Ryu is right! ♡
TURNCOATS !!
AKIRA
AND...
HUH?
KLIK
KLIK

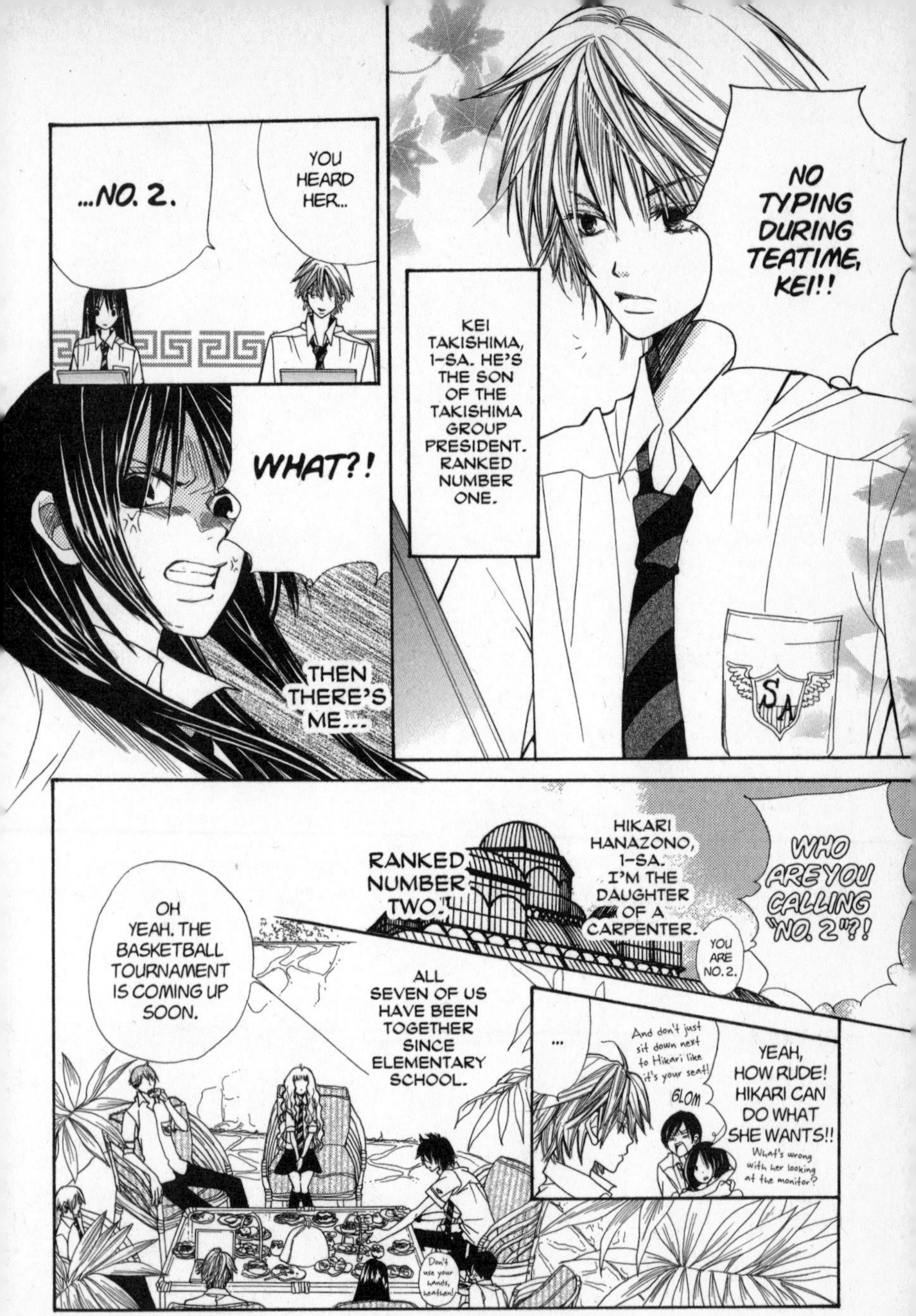
NO TYPING DURING TEATIME, KEI!!
KEI TAKISHIMA, 1-SA. HE'S THE SON OF THE TAKISHIMA GROUP PRESIDENT. RANKED NUMBER ONE.
YOU HEARD HER...
...NO. 2.
WHAT?!
THEN THERE'S ME...
WHO ARE YOU CALLING "NO. 2"?!
HIKARI HANAZONO, 1-SA. I'M THE DAUGHTER OF A CARPENTER.
YOU ARE NO. 2.
RANKED NUMBER TWO.
YEAH, HOW RUDE! HIKARI CAN DO WHAT SHE WANTS!!
What's wrong with her looking at the monitor?
And don't just sit down next to Hikari like it's your seat!
GLOM
...
ALL SEVEN OF US HAVE BEEN TOGETHER SINCE ELEMENTARY SCHOOL.
OH YEAH. THE BASKETBALL TOURNAMENT IS COMING UP SOON.
Don't use your hands, heathen!

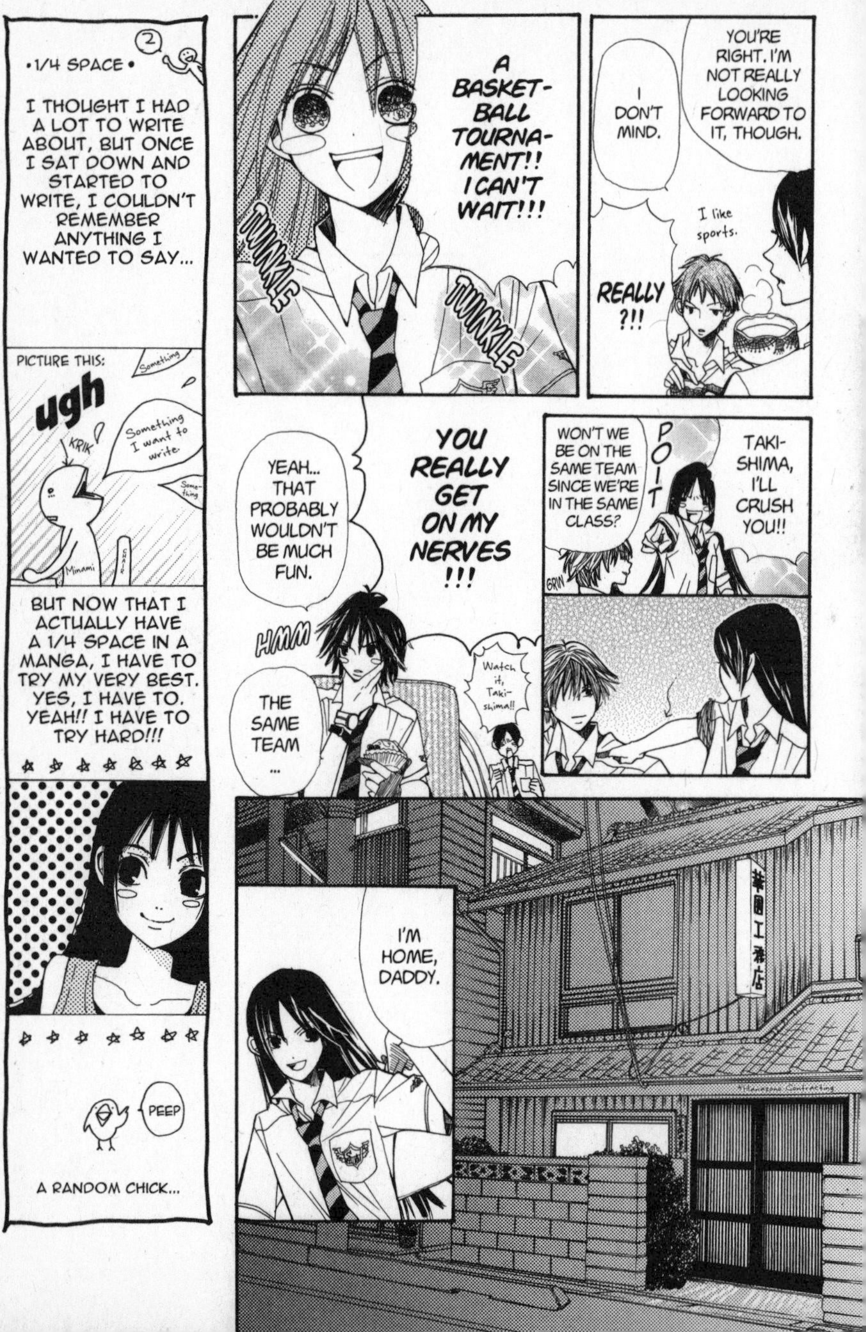
YOU'RE RIGHT. I'M NOT REALLY LOOKING FORWARD TO IT, THOUGH.
I DON'T MIND.
I like sports.
REALLY?!!
A BASKETBALL TOURNAMENT!! I CAN'T WAIT!!!
TWINKLE
TWINKLE
TAKI-SHIMA, I'LL CRUSH YOU!!
POIT
WON'T WE BE ON THE SAME TEAM SINCE WE'RE IN THE SAME CLASS?
GRIN
YOU REALLY GET ON MY NERVES!!!
YEAH... THAT PROBABLY WOULDN'T BE MUCH FUN.
HMM
Watch it, Taki-shima!!
THE SAME TEAM...
I'M HOME, DADDY.
•1/4 SPACE•
②
I THOUGHT I HAD A LOT TO WRITE ABOUT, BUT ONCE I SAT DOWN AND STARTED TO WRITE, I COULDN'T REMEMBER ANYTHING I WANTED TO SAY...
PICTURE THIS:
Something
ugh
KRIK
Something I want to write.
Some-thing
Minami
CHAIR
BUT NOW THAT I ACTUALLY HAVE A 1/4 SPACE IN A MANGA, I HAVE TO TRY MY VERY BEST. YES, I HAVE TO. YEAH!! I HAVE TO TRY HARD!!!
PEEP
A RANDOM CHICK...

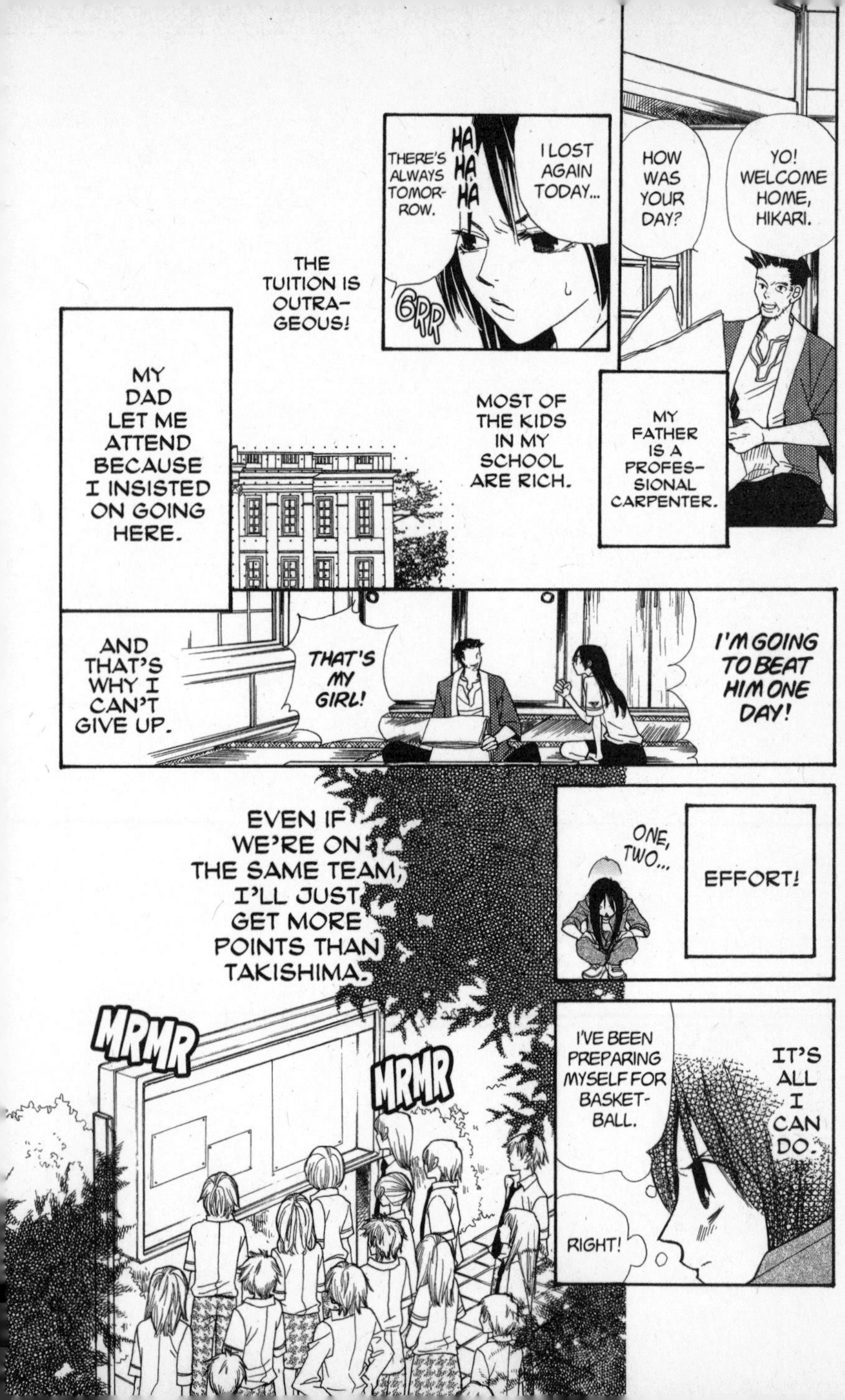
YO! WELCOME HOME, HIKARI.
HOW WAS YOUR DAY?
I LOST AGAIN TODAY...
HA HA HA
THERE'S ALWAYS TOMORROW.
GRR
THE TUITION IS OUTRAGEOUS!
MY FATHER IS A PROFESSIONAL CARPENTER.
MOST OF THE KIDS IN MY SCHOOL ARE RICH.
MY DAD LET ME ATTEND BECAUSE I INSISTED ON GOING HERE.
I'M GOING TO BEAT HIM ONE DAY!
THAT'S MY GIRL!
AND THAT'S WHY I CAN'T GIVE UP.
EFFORT!
ONE, TWO...
EVEN IF WE'RE ON THE SAME TEAM, I'LL JUST GET MORE POINTS THAN TAKISHIMA.
IT'S ALL I CAN DO.
I'VE BEEN PREPARING MYSELF FOR BASKETBALL.
RIGHT!
MRMR
MRMR

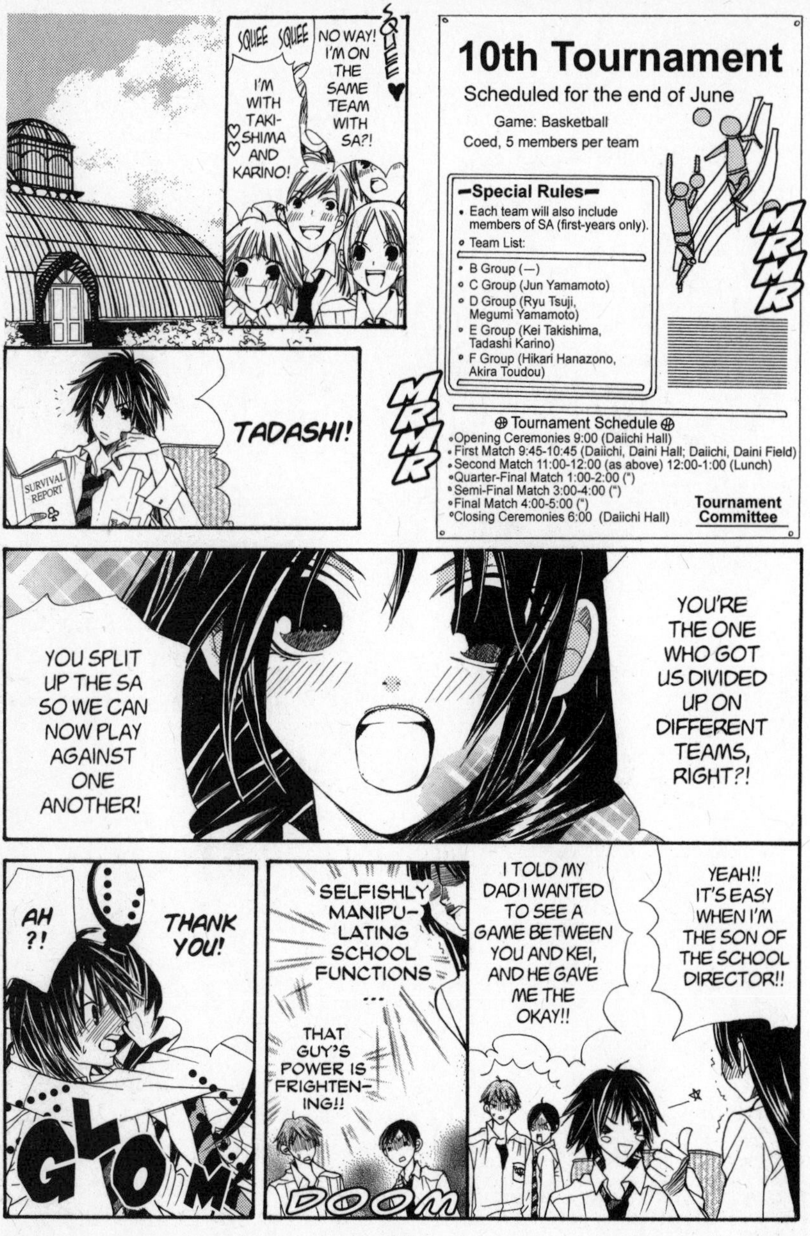
10th Tournament
Scheduled for the end of June
Game: Basketball
Coed, 5 members per team
Special Rules
• Each team will also include members of SA (first-years only).
• Team List:
• B Group (—)
• C Group (Jun Yamamoto)
• D Group (Ryu Tsuji, Megumi Yamamoto)
• E Group (Kei Takishima, Tadashi Karino)
• F Group (Hikari Hanazono, Akira Toudou)
Tournament Schedule
• Opening Ceremonies 9:00 (Daiichi Hall)
• First Match 9:45-10:45 (Daiichi, Daini Hall; Daiichi, Daini Field)
• Second Match 11:00-12:00 (as above) 12:00-1:00 (Lunch)
• Quarter-Final Match 1:00-2:00 (")
• Semi-Final Match 3:00-4:00 (")
• Final Match 4:00-5:00 (")
• Closing Ceremonies 6:00 (Daiichi Hall)
Tournament Committee
MRMR
MRMR
SQUEE
SQUEE SQUEE
NO WAY! I'M ON THE SAME TEAM WITH SA?!
I'M WITH TAKI-SHIMA AND KARINO!
TADASHI!
SURVIVAL REPORT
YOU'RE THE ONE WHO GOT US DIVIDED UP ON DIFFERENT TEAMS, RIGHT?!
YOU SPLIT UP THE SA SO WE CAN NOW PLAY AGAINST ONE ANOTHER!
YEAH!! IT'S EASY WHEN I'M THE SON OF THE SCHOOL DIRECTOR!!
I TOLD MY DAD I WANTED TO SEE A GAME BETWEEN YOU AND KEI, AND HE GAVE ME THE OKAY!!
SELFISHLY MANIPU-LATING SCHOOL FUNCTIONS...
THAT GUY'S POWER IS FRIGHTEN-ING!!
DOOM
THANK YOU!
AH?!
GLOMP

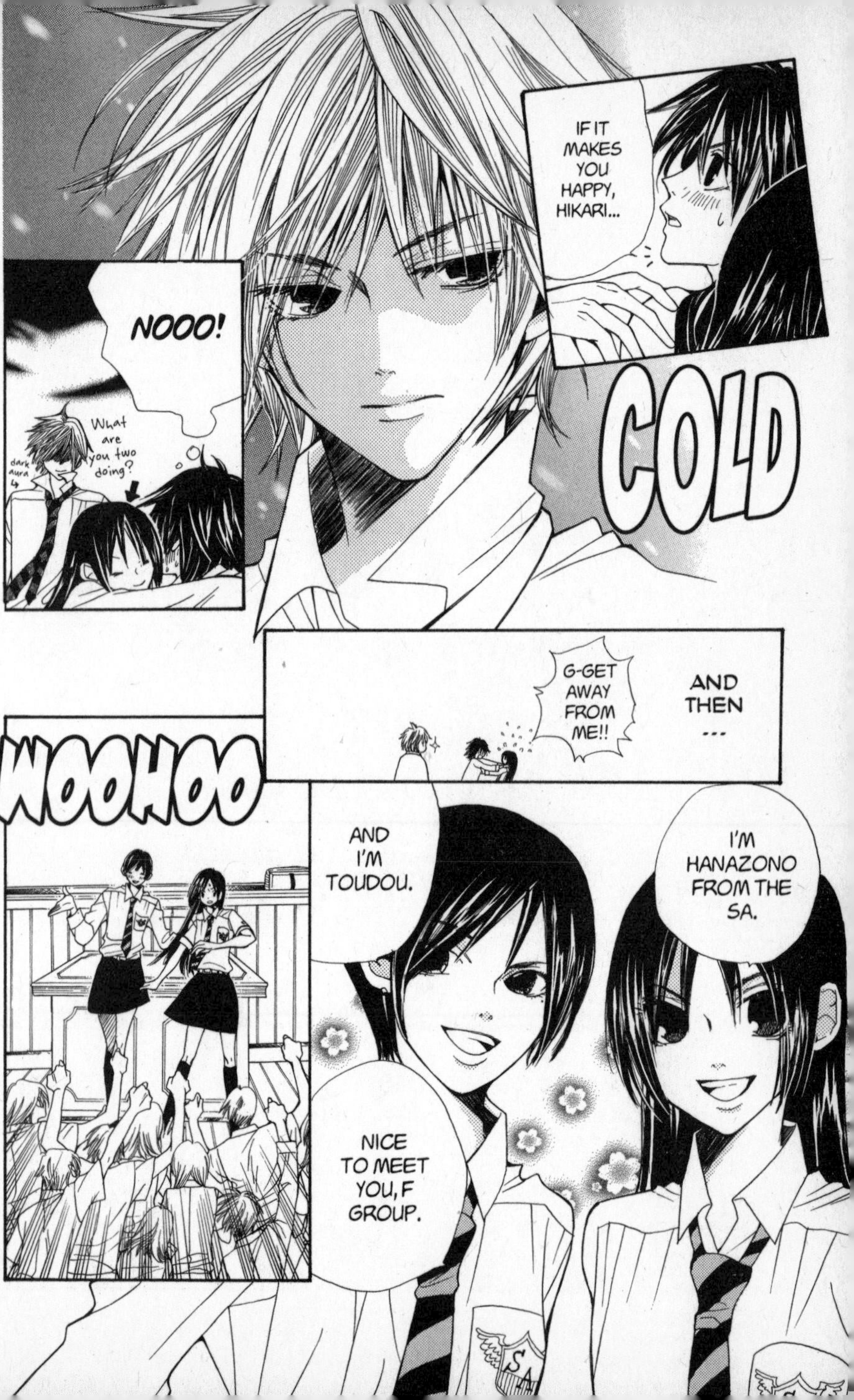
IF IT MAKES YOU HAPPY, HIKARI...
COLD
NOOO!
What are you two doing?
dark aura
AND THEN ...
G-GET AWAY FROM ME!!
I'M HANAZONO FROM THE SA.
AND I'M TOUDOU.
NICE TO MEET YOU, F GROUP.
WOOHOO

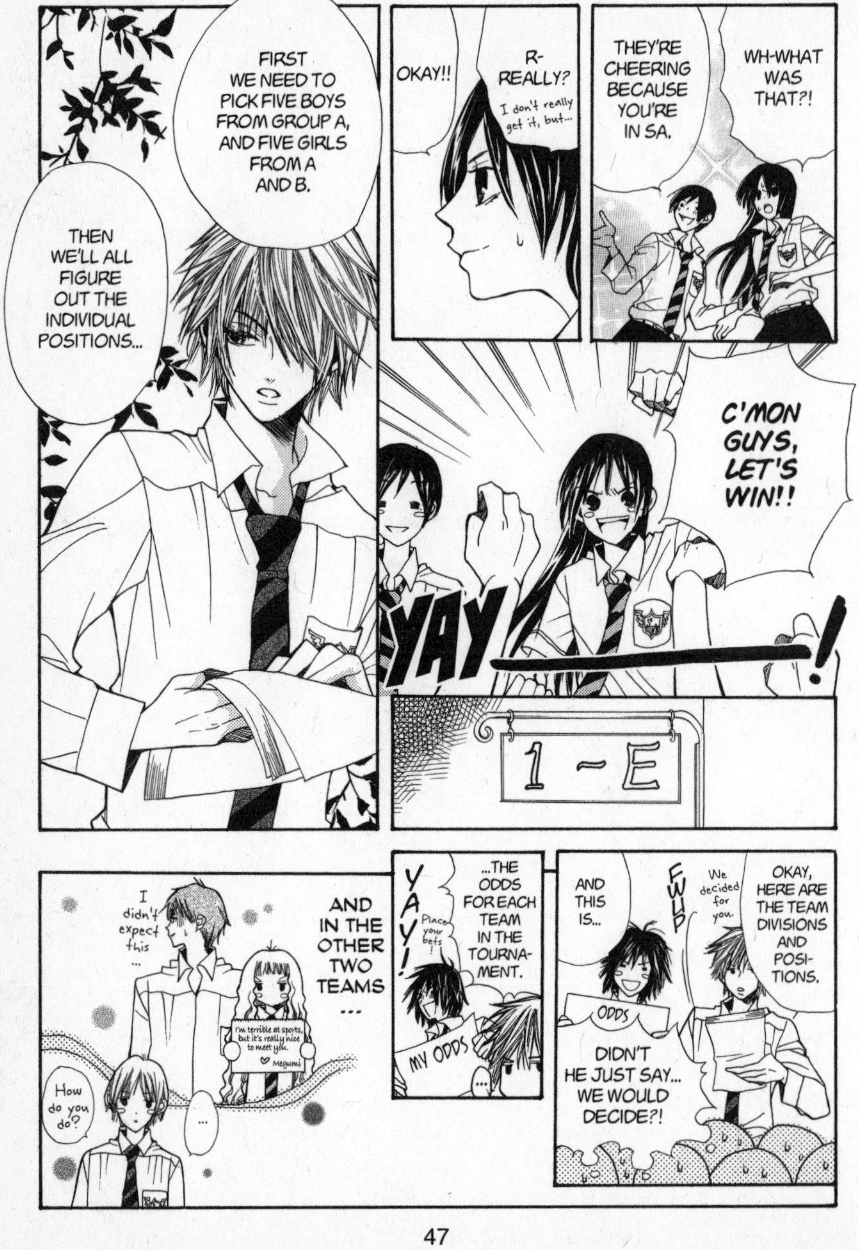
WH-WHAT WAS THAT?!
THEY'RE CHEERING BECAUSE YOU'RE IN SA.
R-REALLY?
I don't really get it, but...
OKAY!!
C'MON GUYS, LET'S WIN!!
YAY—!
1-E
FIRST WE NEED TO PICK FIVE BOYS FROM GROUP A, AND FIVE GIRLS FROM A AND B.
THEN WE'LL ALL FIGURE OUT THE INDIVIDUAL POSITIONS...
OKAY, HERE ARE THE TEAM DIVISIONS AND POSITIONS.
We decided for you.
FWUP
AND THIS IS...
ODDS
DIDN'T HE JUST SAY... WE WOULD DECIDE?!
...THE ODDS FOR EACH TEAM IN THE TOURNAMENT.
YAY!
Place your bets!
MY ODDS
...
AND IN THE OTHER TWO TEAMS...
I didn't expect this...
I'm terrible at sports, but it's really nice to meet you. ♥ Megumi
How do you do?
...

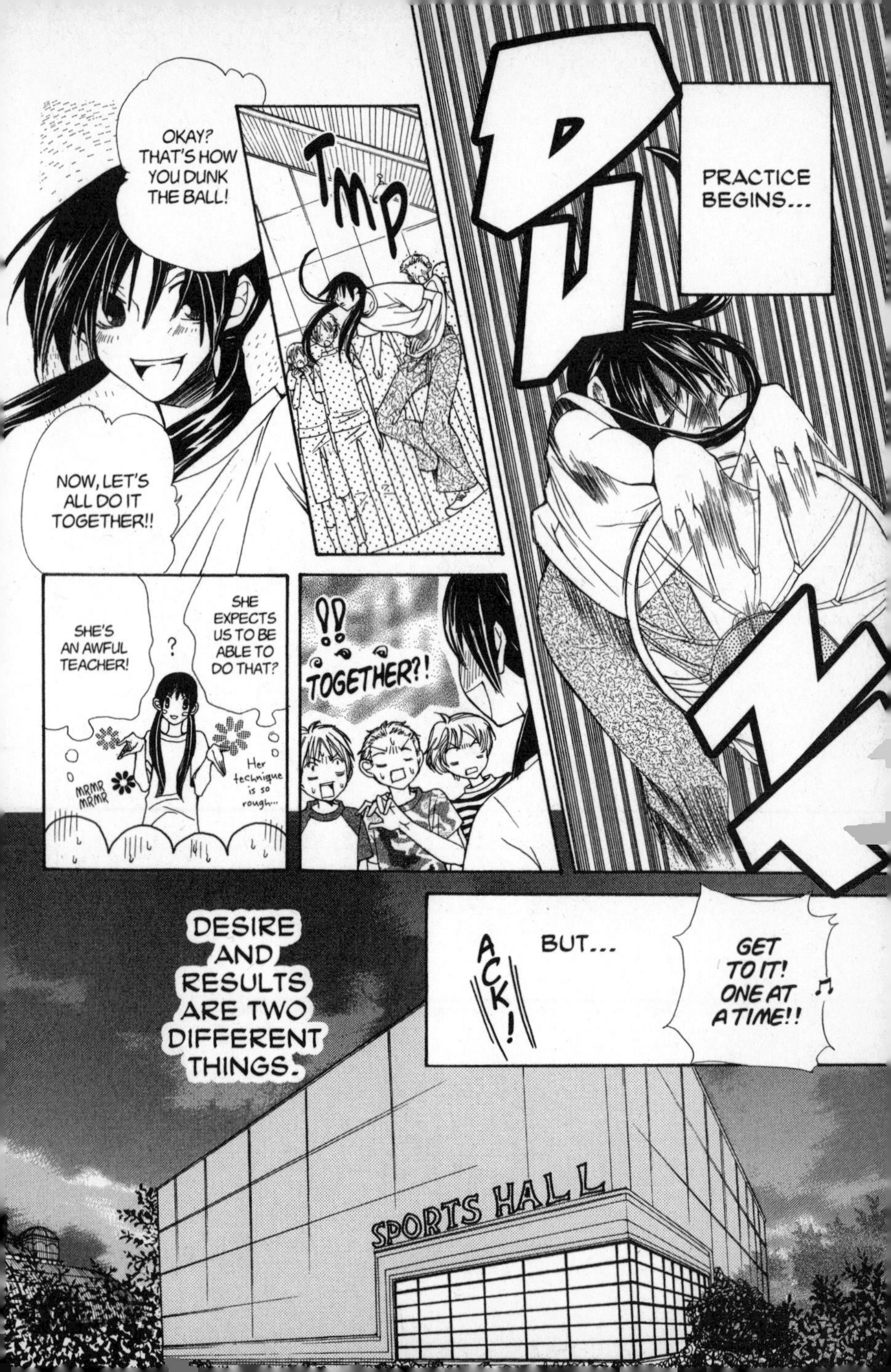
PRACTICE BEGINS...
DUNK
TMP
OKAY? THAT'S HOW YOU DUNK THE BALL!
NOW, LET'S ALL DO IT TOGETHER!!
!!
TOGETHER?!
SHE EXPECTS US TO BE ABLE TO DO THAT?
?
SHE'S AN AWFUL TEACHER!
Her technique is so rough...
MRMR MRMR
GET TO IT! ONE AT A TIME!!
BUT...
ACK!
DESIRE AND RESULTS ARE TWO DIFFERENT THINGS.
SPORTS HALL

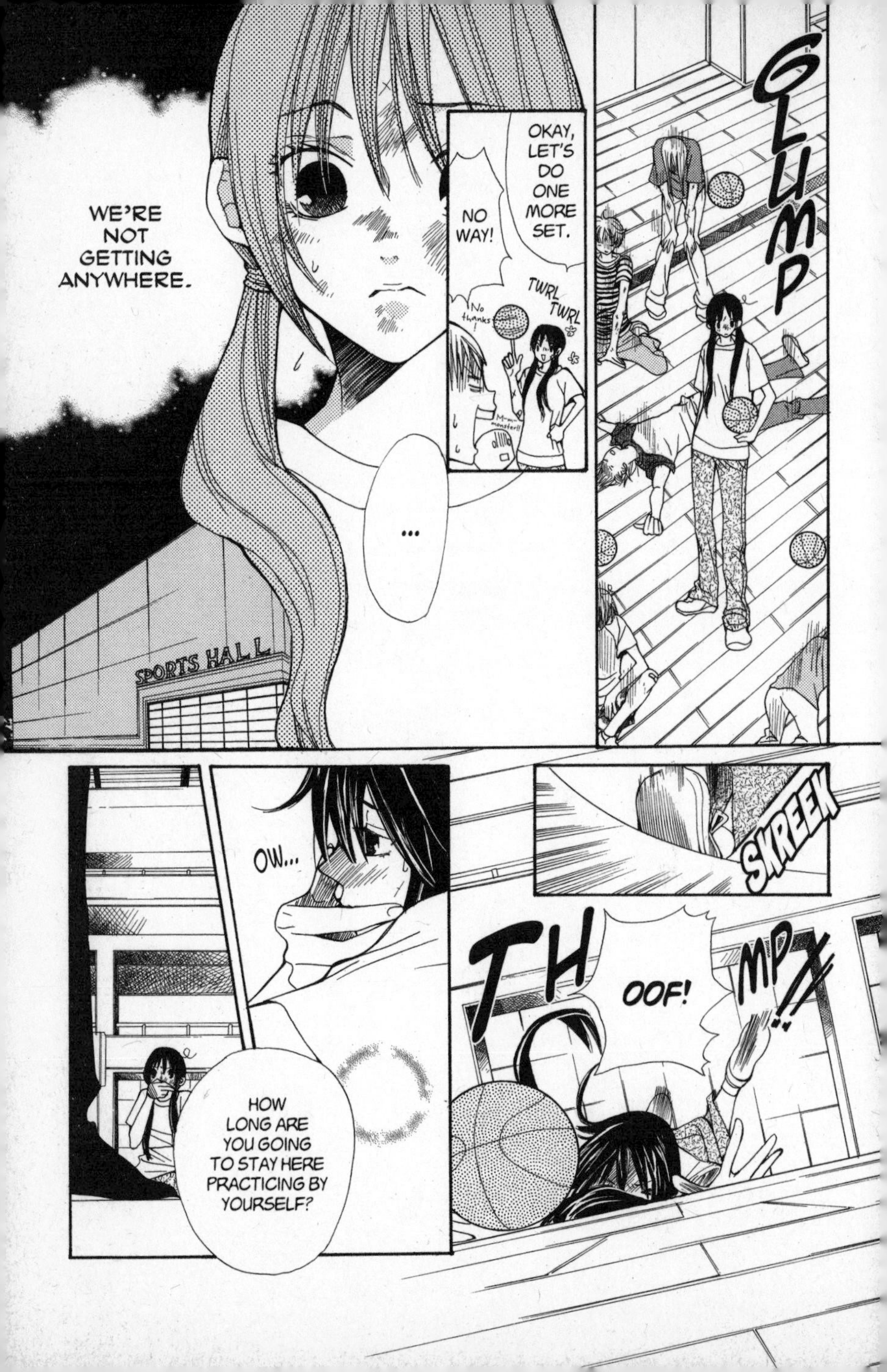
GLUMP
OKAY, LET'S DO ONE MORE SET.
NO WAY!
TWRL TWRL
No thanks!
M-m-monster!!
WE'RE NOT GETTING ANYWHERE.
...
SPORTS HALL
SKREEK
TH MP
OOF!
OW...
HOW LONG ARE YOU GOING TO STAY HERE PRACTICING BY YOURSELF?

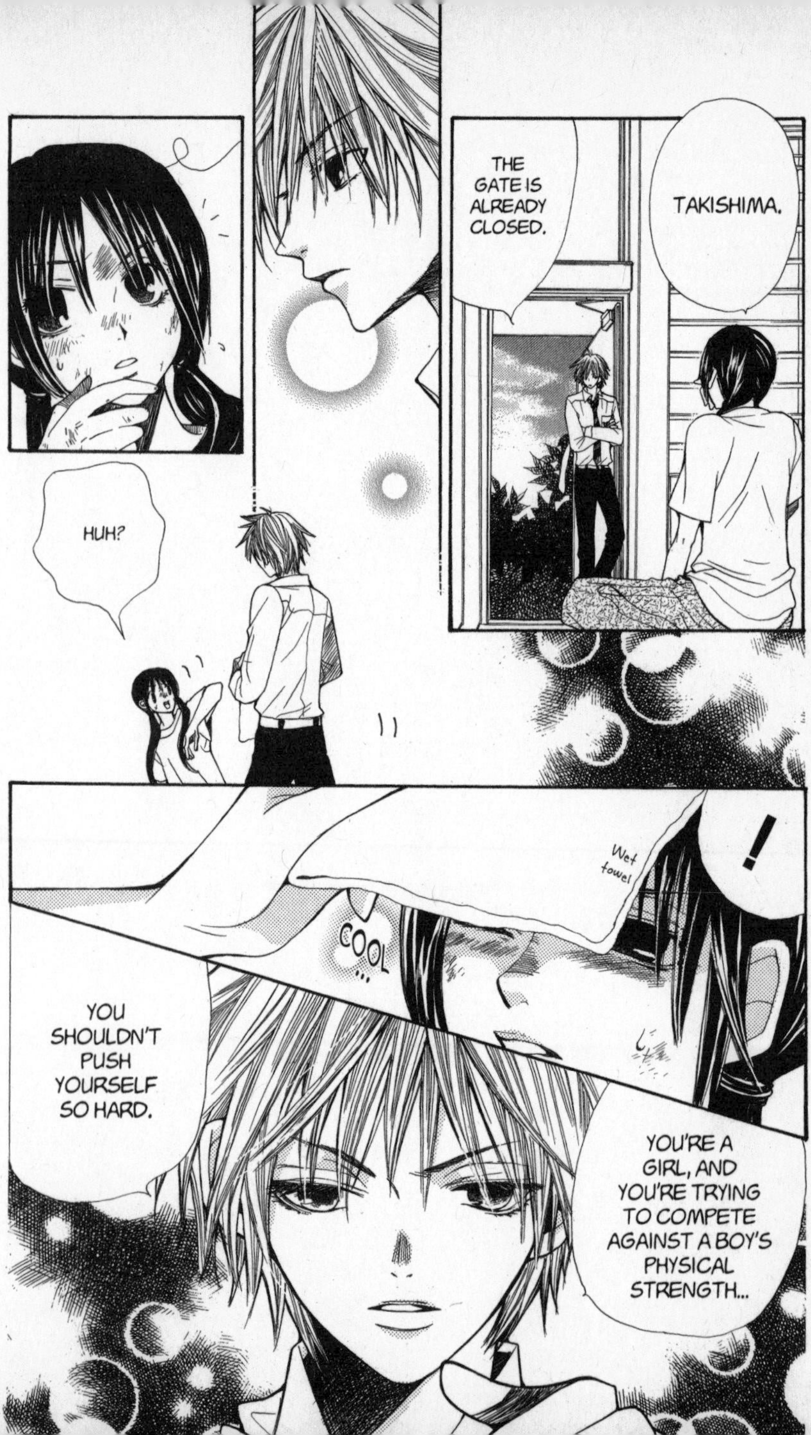
TAKISHIMA.
THE GATE IS ALREADY CLOSED.
HUH?
!
Wet towel
COOL...
YOU'RE A GIRL, AND YOU'RE TRYING TO COMPETE AGAINST A BOY'S PHYSICAL STRENGTH...
YOU SHOULDN'T PUSH YOURSELF SO HARD.

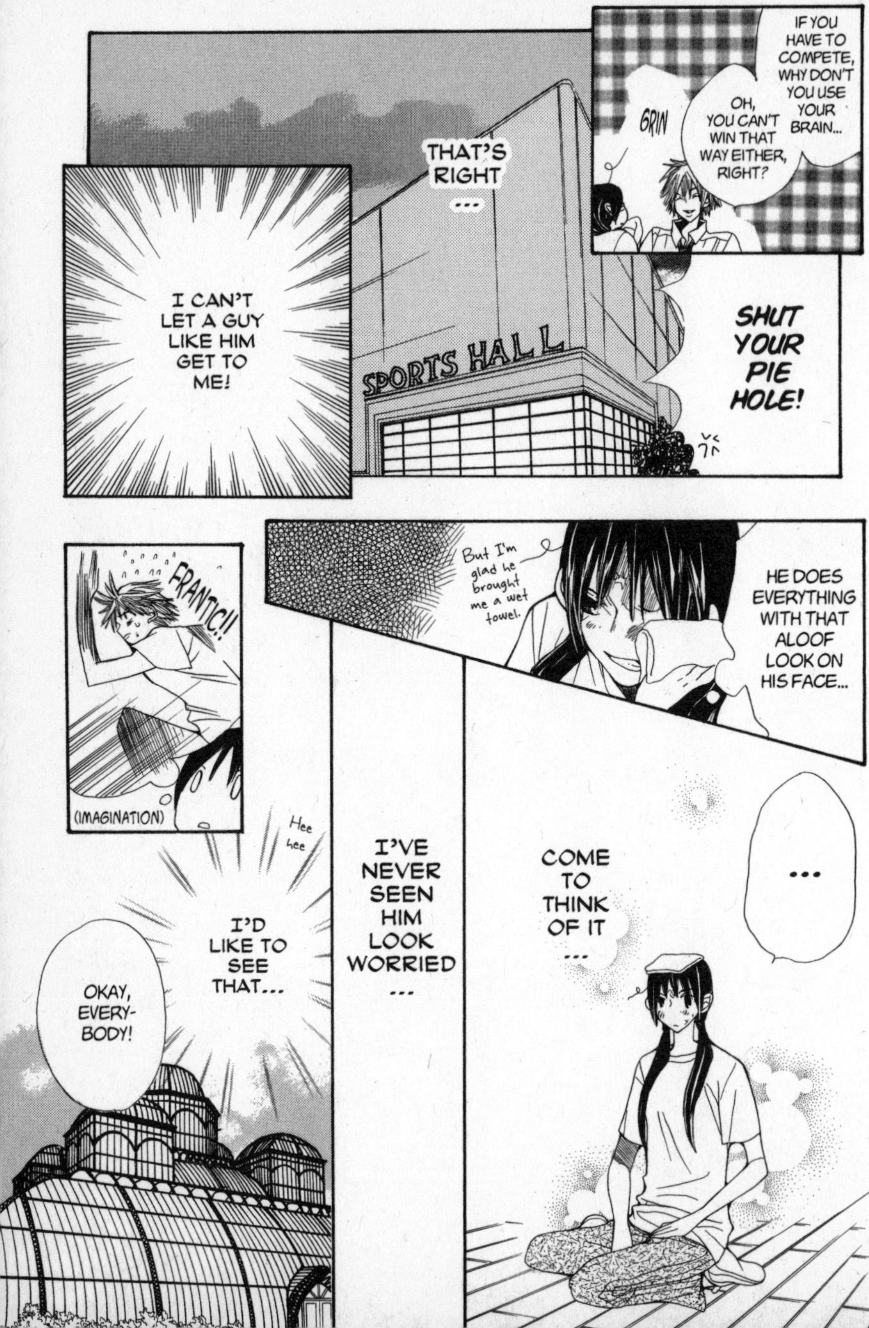
IF YOU HAVE TO COMPETE, WHY DON'T YOU USE YOUR BRAIN...
OH, YOU CAN'T WIN THAT WAY EITHER, RIGHT?
GRIN
SHUT YOUR PIE HOLE!
SPORTS HALL
THAT'S RIGHT...
I CAN'T LET A GUY LIKE HIM GET TO ME!
HE DOES EVERYTHING WITH THAT ALOOF LOOK ON HIS FACE...
But I'm glad he brought me a wet towel.
...
COME TO THINK OF IT...
I'VE NEVER SEEN HIM LOOK WORRIED...
FRANTIC!!
(IMAGINATION)
Hee hee
I'D LIKE TO SEE THAT...
OKAY, EVERY-BODY!

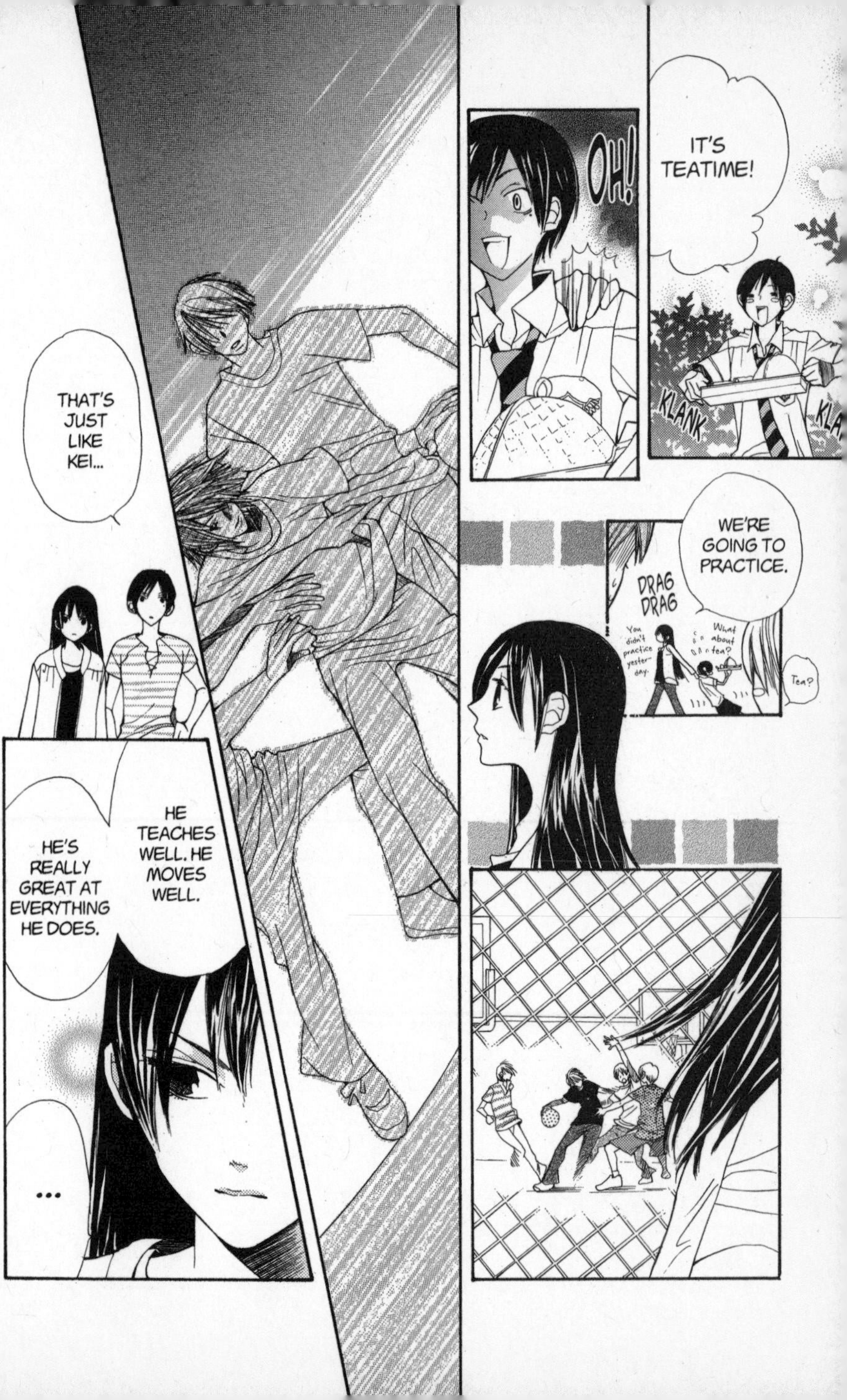
IT'S TEATIME!
KLANK
KLA
OH!
WE'RE GOING TO PRACTICE.
DRAG DRAG
You didn't practice yester-day.
What about tea?
Tea?
THAT'S JUST LIKE KEI...
HE TEACHES WELL. HE MOVES WELL.
HE'S REALLY GREAT AT EVERYTHING HE DOES.
...

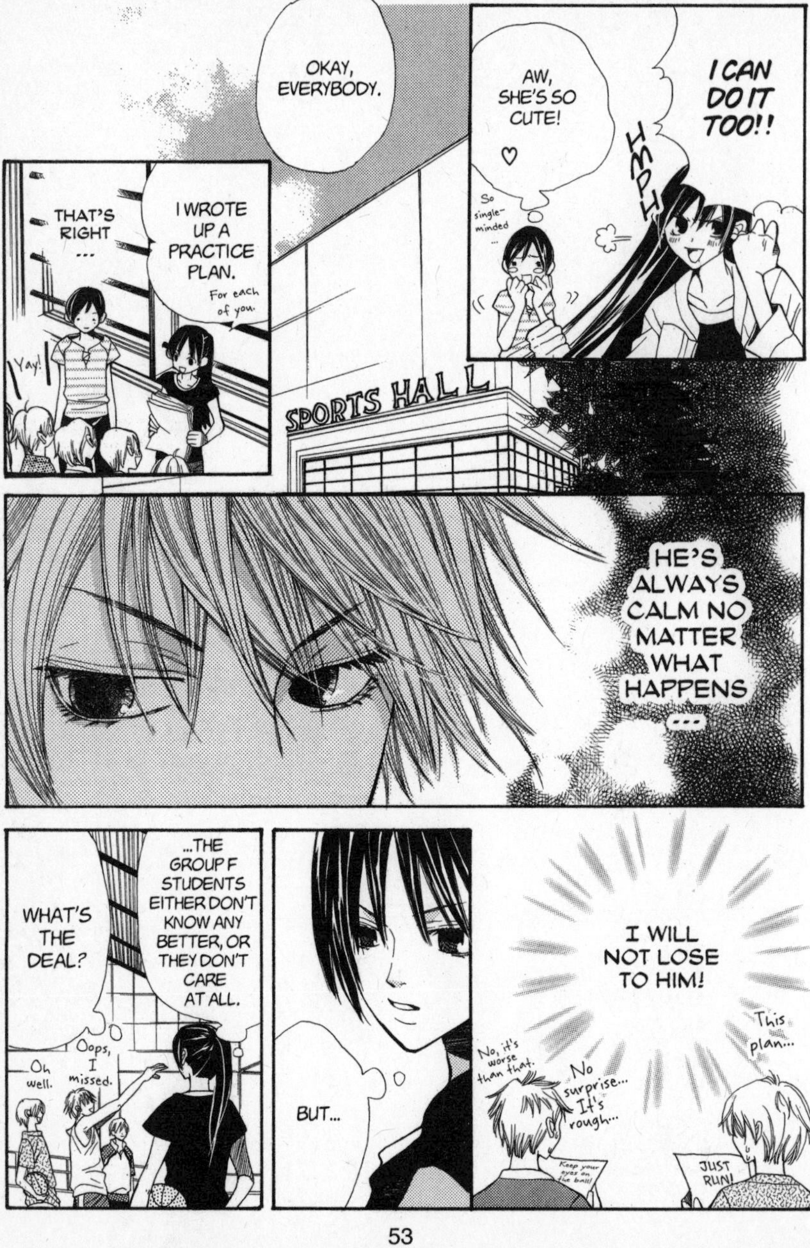
I CAN DO IT TOO!!
HMPH
AW, SHE'S SO CUTE!
♡
So single-minded...
OKAY, EVERYBODY.
I WROTE UP A PRACTICE PLAN.
For each of you.
THAT'S RIGHT...
Yay!
SPORTS HALL
HE'S ALWAYS CALM NO MATTER WHAT HAPPENS...
I WILL NOT LOSE TO HIM!
This plan...
No surprise... It's rough...
No, it's worse than that.
JUST RUN!
Keep your eyes on the ball!
BUT...
...THE GROUP F STUDENTS EITHER DON'T KNOW ANY BETTER, OR THEY DON'T CARE AT ALL.
WHAT'S THE DEAL?
Oops, I missed.
Oh well.

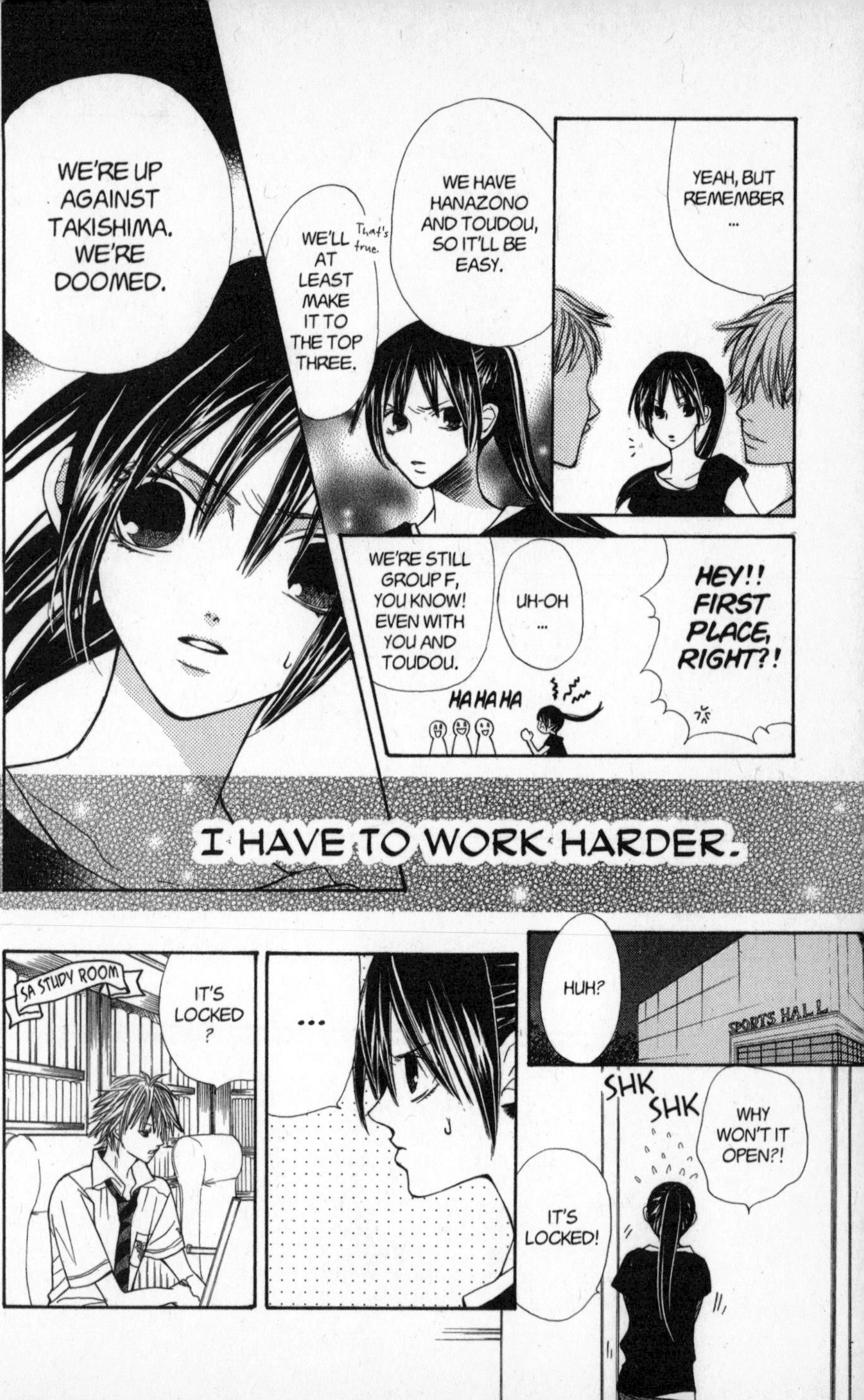
YEAH, BUT REMEMBER ...
WE HAVE HANAZONO AND TOUDOU, SO IT'LL BE EASY.
That's true.
WE'LL AT LEAST MAKE IT TO THE TOP THREE.
WE'RE UP AGAINST TAKISHIMA. WE'RE DOOMED.
HEY!! FIRST PLACE, RIGHT?!
UH-OH ...
WE'RE STILL GROUP F, YOU KNOW! EVEN WITH YOU AND TOUDOU.
HA HA HA
I HAVE TO WORK HARDER.
HUH?
SPORTS HALL
SHK SHK
WHY WON'T IT OPEN?!
IT'S LOCKED!
...
SA STUDY ROOM
IT'S LOCKED?

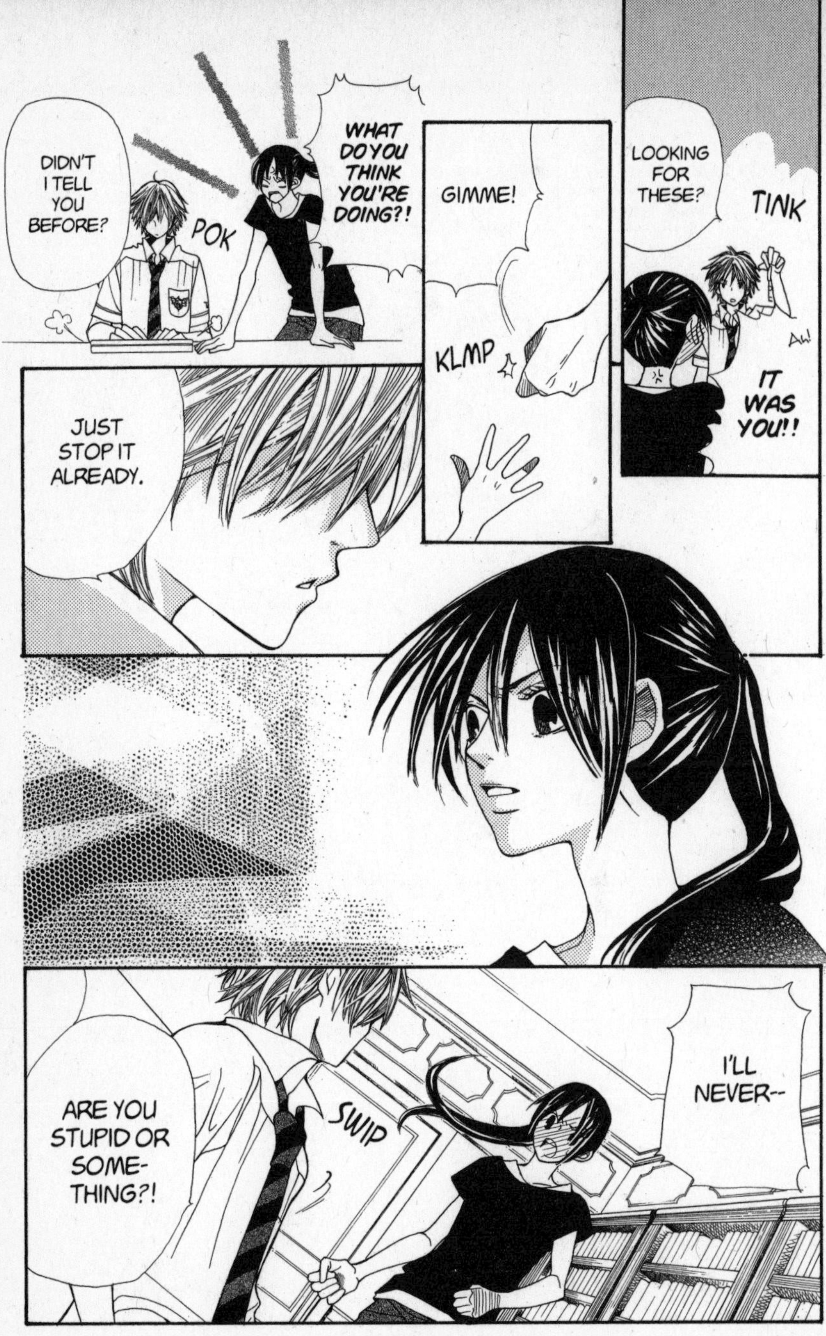
LOOKING FOR THESE?
TINK
Ah!
IT WAS YOU!!
GIMME!
KLMP
WHAT DO YOU THINK YOU'RE DOING?!
DIDN'T I TELL YOU BEFORE?
POK
JUST STOP IT ALREADY.
I'LL NEVER--
SWIP
ARE YOU STUPID OR SOME-THING?!

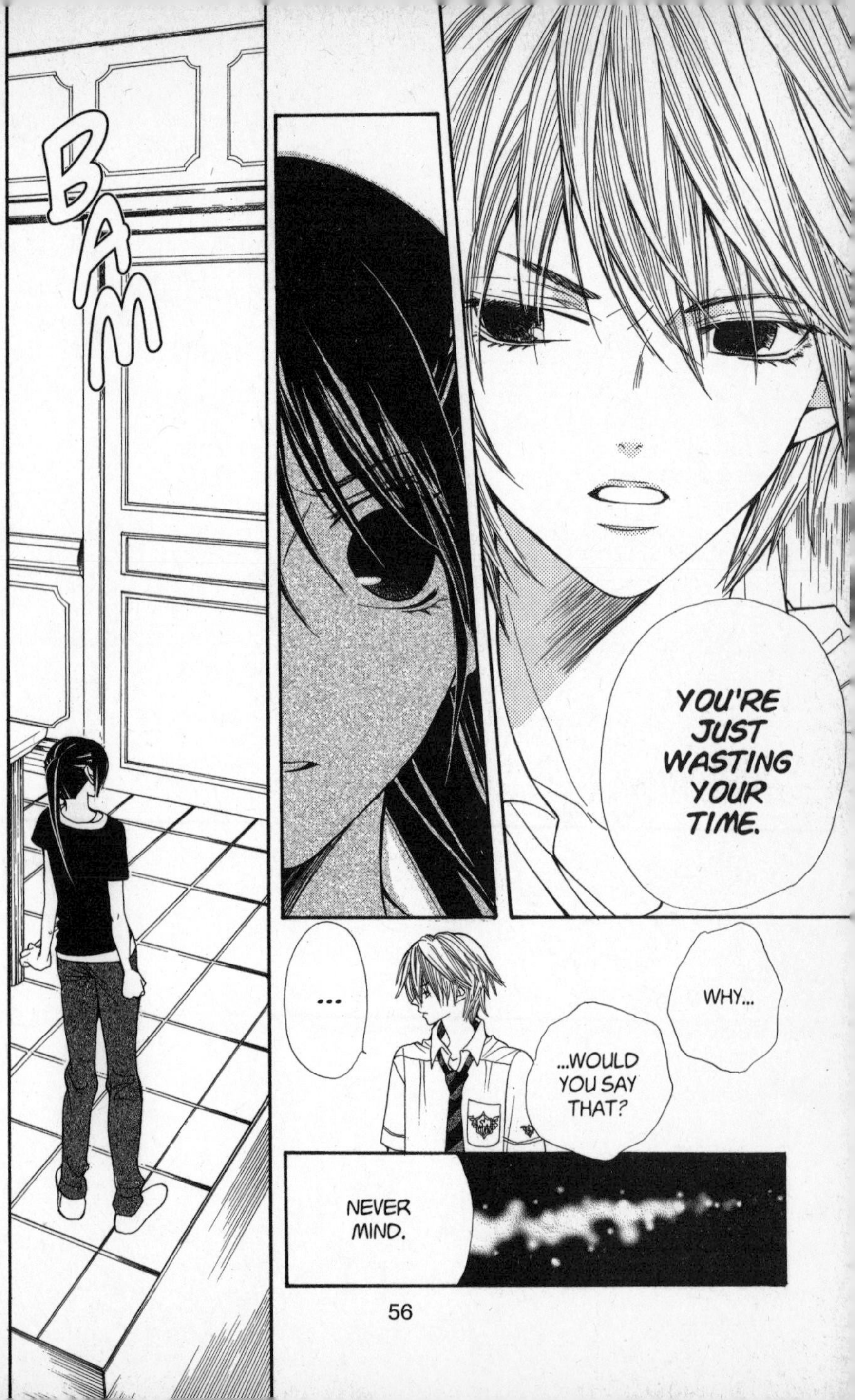
YOU'RE JUST WASTING YOUR TIME.
WHY...
...WOULD YOU SAY THAT?
...
NEVER MIND.
BAM

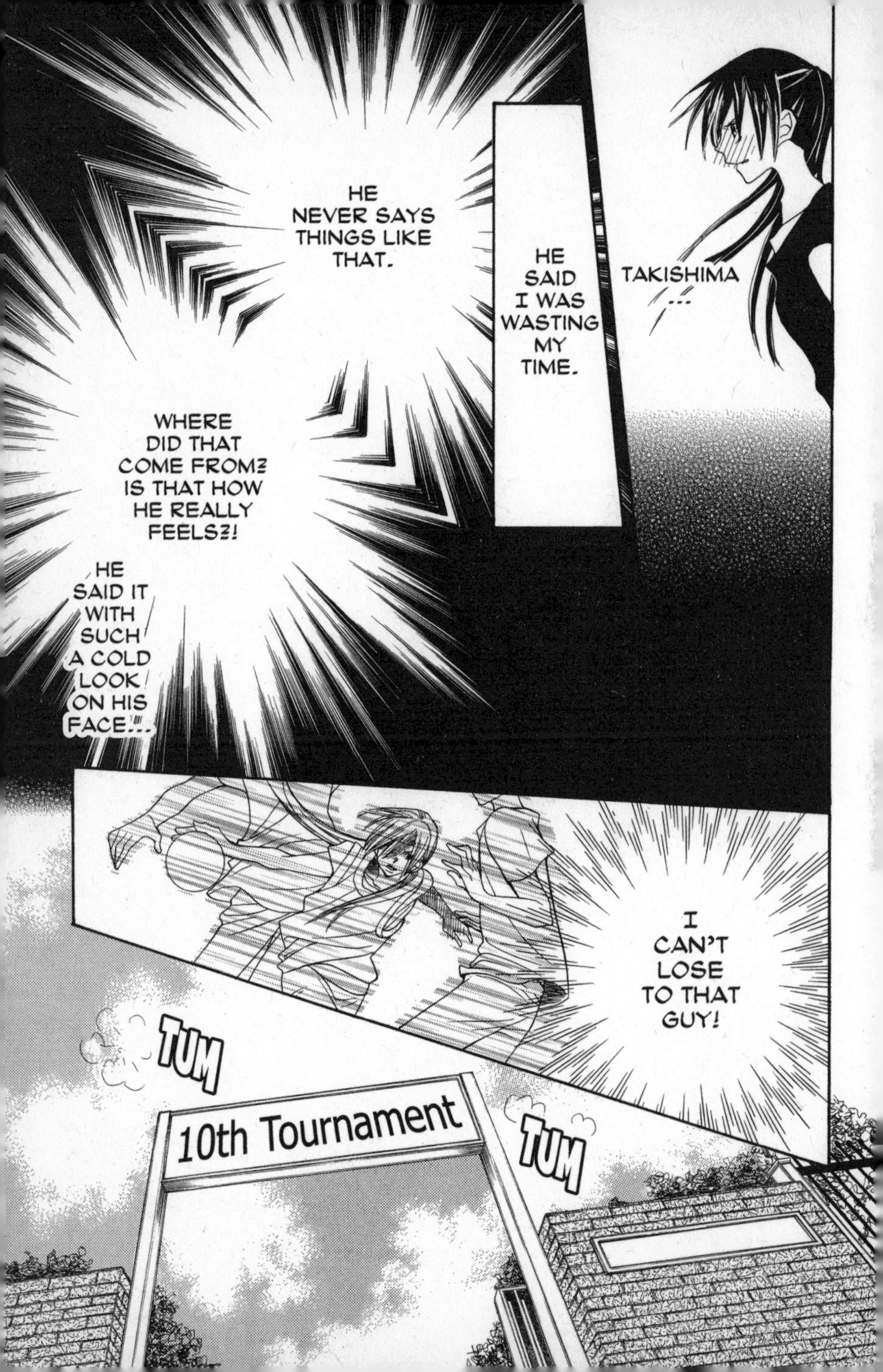
TAKISHIMA...
HE SAID I WAS WASTING MY TIME.
HE NEVER SAYS THINGS LIKE THAT.
WHERE DID THAT COME FROM? IS THAT HOW HE REALLY FEELS?!
HE SAID IT WITH SUCH A COLD LOOK ON HIS FACE...
I CAN'T LOSE TO THAT GUY!
TUM
TUM
10th Tournament

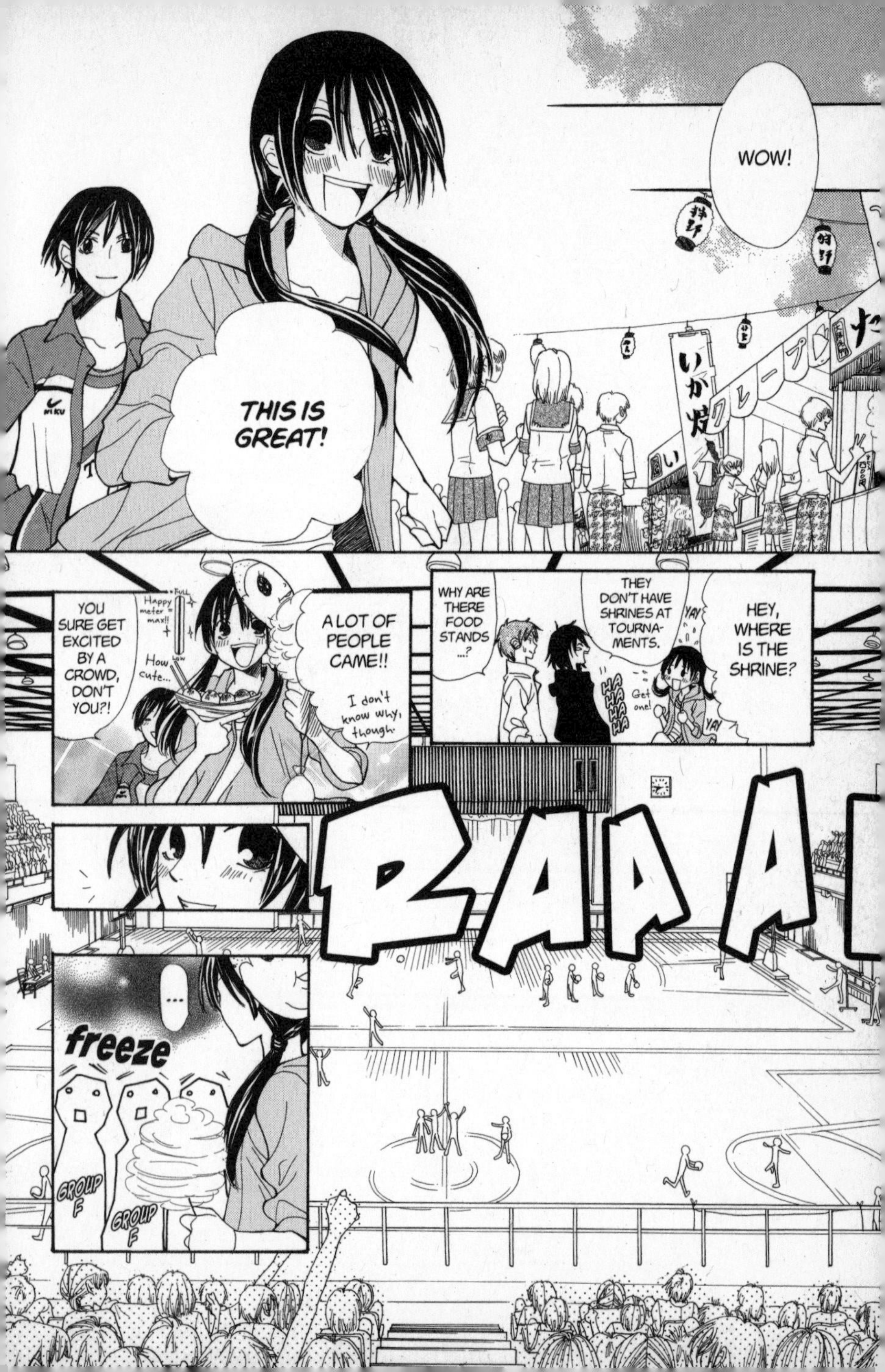
WOW!
THIS IS GREAT!
いか焼
クレープ
HEY, WHERE IS THE SHRINE?
YAY
Get one!
YAY
HA HA HA HA
THEY DON'T HAVE SHRINES AT TOURNAMENTS.
WHY ARE THERE FOOD STANDS ...?
A LOT OF PEOPLE CAME!!
I don't know why, though.
FULL
Happy meter = max!!
LOW
How cute...
YOU SURE GET EXCITED BY A CROWD, DON'T YOU?!
RAAA
...
freeze
GROUP F
GROUP F

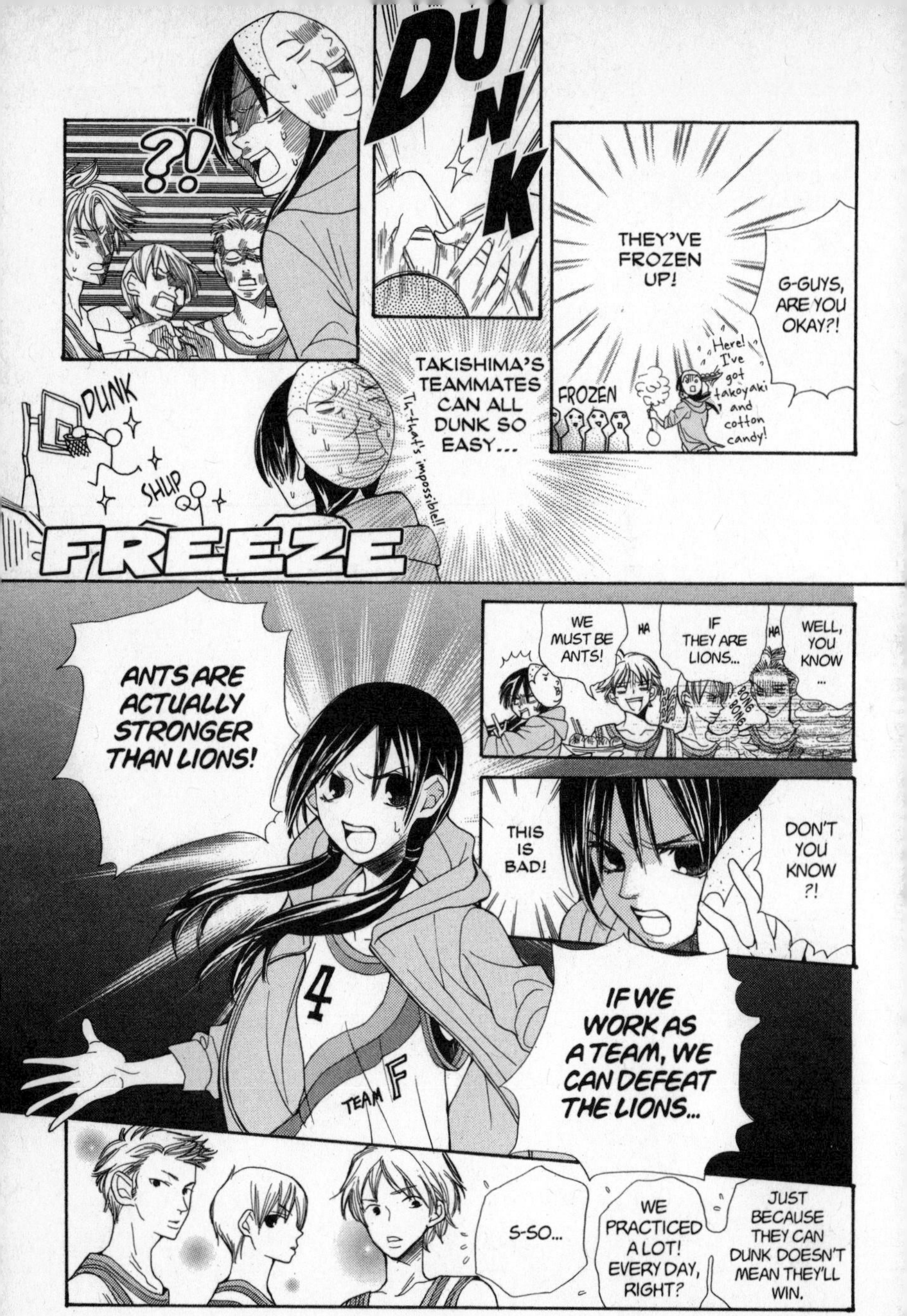
?!
DUNK
G-GUYS, ARE YOU OKAY?!
THEY'VE FROZEN UP!
Here! I've got takoyaki and cotton candy!
FROZEN
Th-that's impossible!!
TAKISHIMA'S TEAMMATES CAN ALL DUNK SO EASY...
DUNK
SHUP
FREEZE
WELL, YOU KNOW ...
HA
IF THEY ARE LIONS...
HA
WE MUST BE ANTS!
BONG BONG
DON'T YOU KNOW ?!
THIS IS BAD!
ANTS ARE ACTUALLY STRONGER THAN LIONS!
IF WE WORK AS A TEAM, WE CAN DEFEAT THE LIONS...
4
TEAM F
JUST BECAUSE THEY CAN DUNK DOESN'T MEAN THEY'LL WIN.
WE PRACTICED A LOT! EVERY DAY, RIGHT?
S-SO...

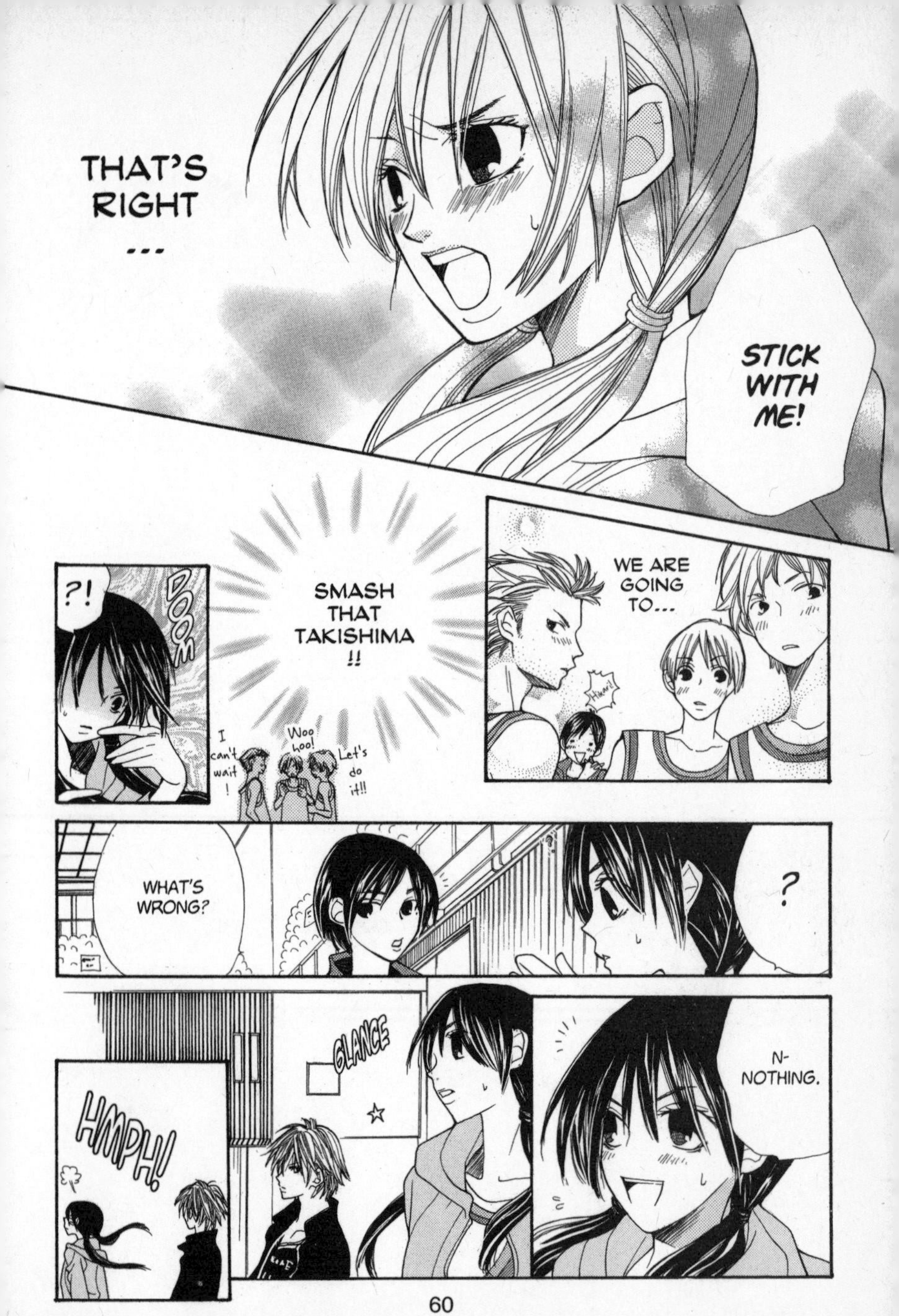
THAT'S RIGHT ...
STICK WITH ME!
WE ARE GOING TO...
Hikari!
SMASH THAT TAKISHIMA !!
I can't wait!
Woo hoo!
Let's do it!!
?!
DOOM
?
WHAT'S WRONG?
N-NOTHING.
GLANCE
HMPH!

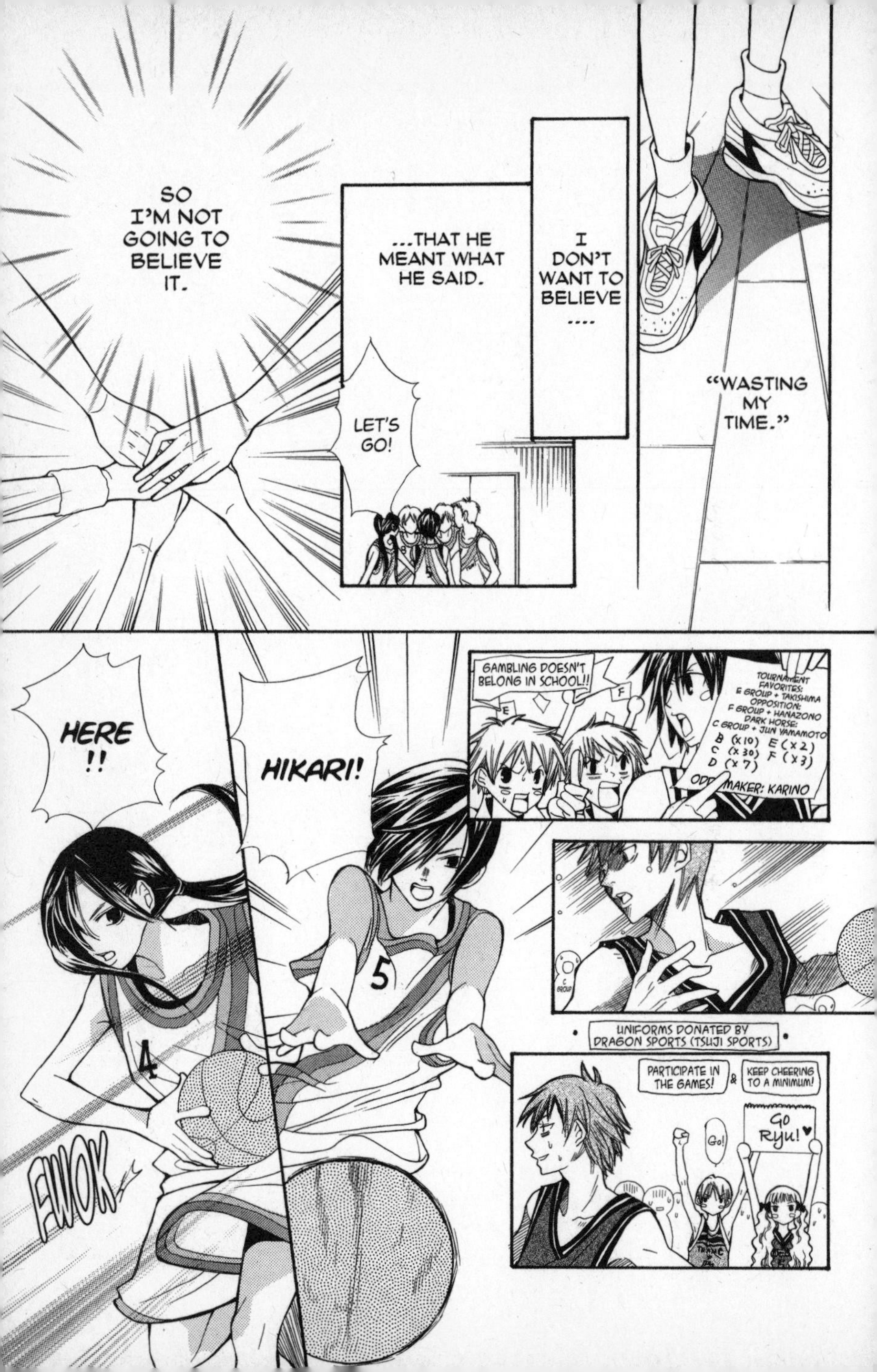
"WASTING MY TIME."
I DON'T WANT TO BELIEVE ....
...THAT HE MEANT WHAT HE SAID.
LET'S GO!
SO I'M NOT GOING TO BELIEVE IT.
GAMBLING DOESN'T BELONG IN SCHOOL!!
E
F
TOURNAMENT FAVORITES: E GROUP + TAKISHIMA
OPPOSITION: F GROUP + HANAZONO
DARK HORSE: C GROUP + JUN YAMAMOTO
B (x10) E (x2)
C (x30) F (x3)
D (x7)
ODD MAKER: KARINO
C GROUP
UNIFORMS DONATED BY DRAGON SPORTS (TSUJI SPORTS)
PARTICIPATE IN THE GAMES!
&
KEEP CHEERING TO A MINIMUM!
Go!
Go Ryu!♥
HIKARI!
HERE!!
FWOK

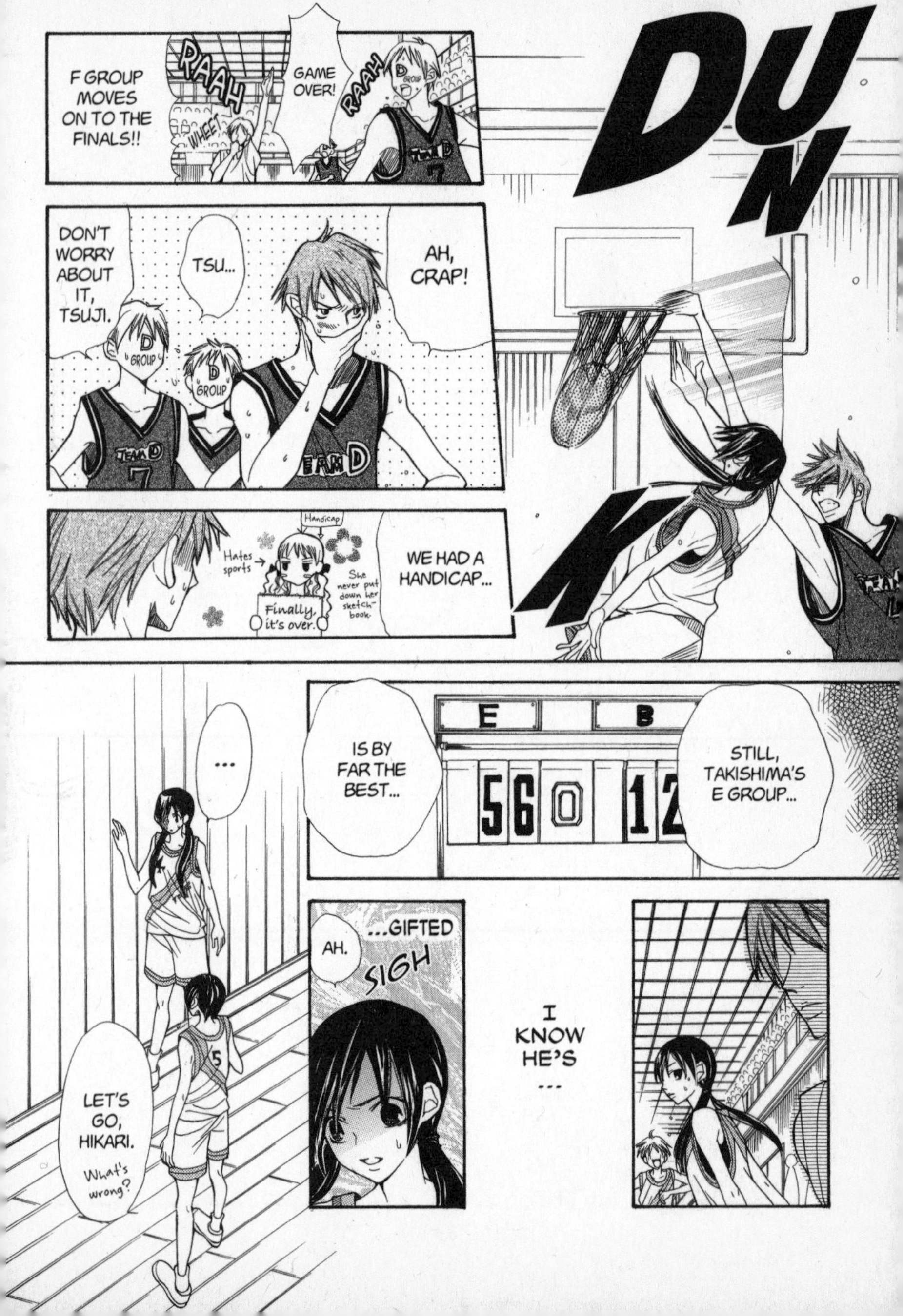
DUN
K
RAAAH
GAME OVER!
RAAAH
F GROUP MOVES ON TO THE FINALS!!
WHEET
AH, CRAP!
TSU...
DON'T WORRY ABOUT IT, TSUJI.
WE HAD A HANDICAP...
Handicap
She never put down her sketchbook.
Hates sports
Finally, it's over.
STILL, TAKISHIMA'S E GROUP...
E
B
56
0
12
IS BY FAR THE BEST...
I KNOW HE'S ...
...GIFTED
SIGH
AH.
...
LET'S GO, HIKARI.
What's wrong?

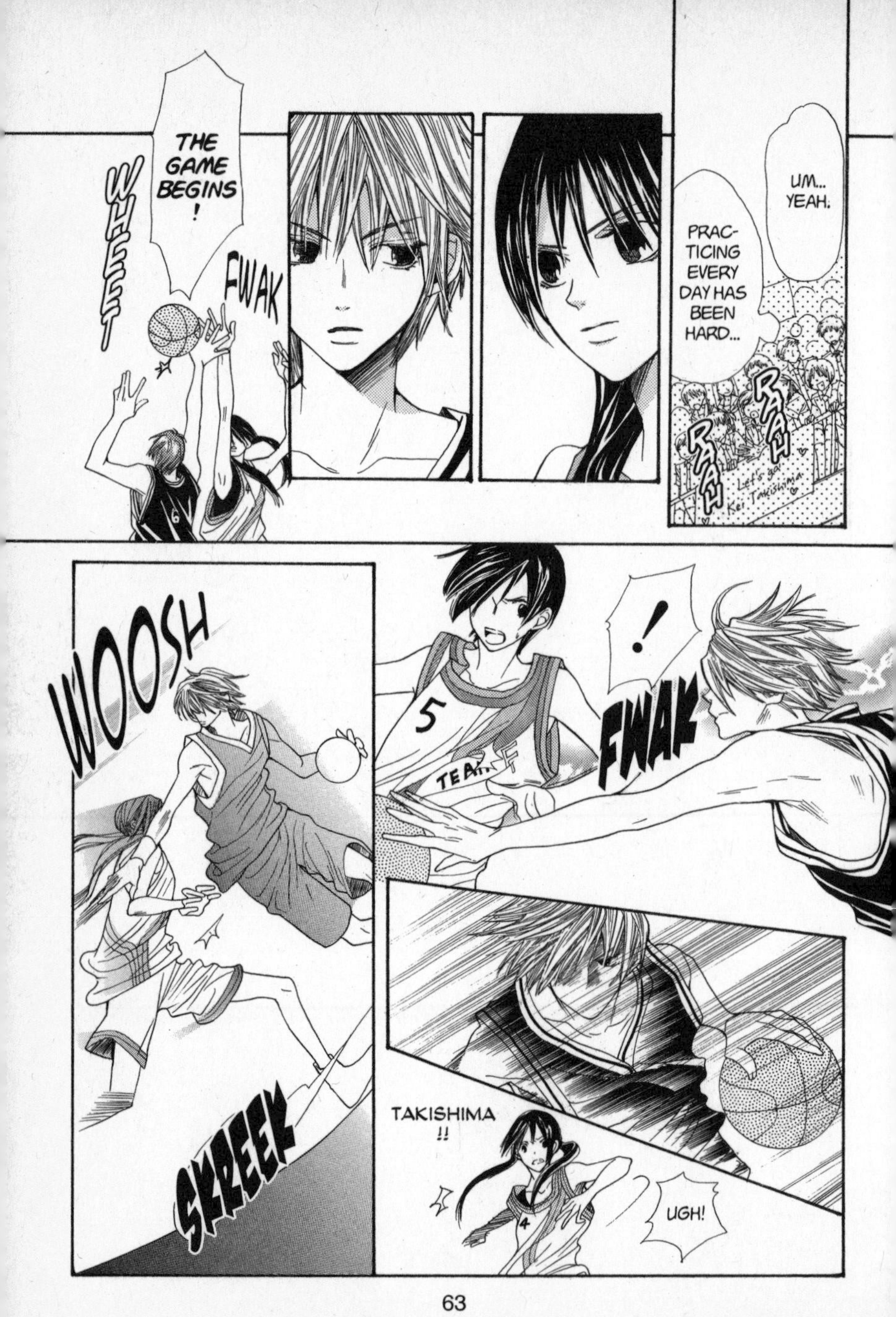
UM... YEAH.
PRAC-TICING EVERY DAY HAS BEEN HARD...
RAAH
RAAH
RAAH
Let's go! Kei Takishima
THE GAME BEGINS!
WHEET
FWAK
!
FWAK
TEAM F
TAKISHIMA!!
UGH!
WOOSH
SKREEK

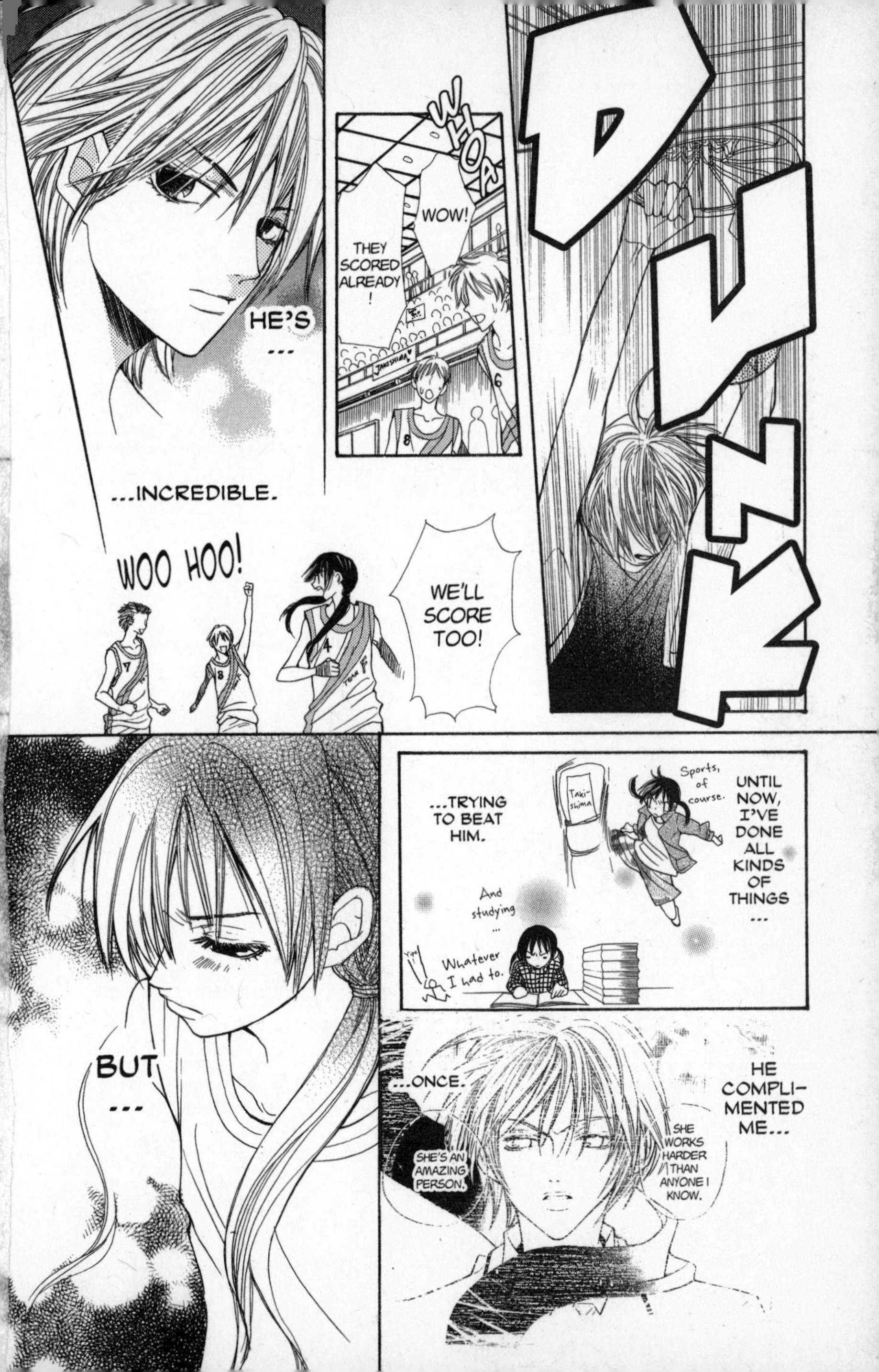
DUNK
WHOA
WOW!
THEY SCORED ALREADY!
HE'S...
...INCREDIBLE.
WE'LL SCORE TOO!
WOO HOO!
UNTIL NOW, I'VE DONE ALL KINDS OF THINGS...
Sports, of course.
...TRYING TO BEAT HIM.
And studying...
Whatever I had to.
HE COMPLIMENTED ME...
SHE WORKS HARDER THAN ANYONE I KNOW.
SHE'S AN AMAZING PERSON.
...ONCE.
BUT...

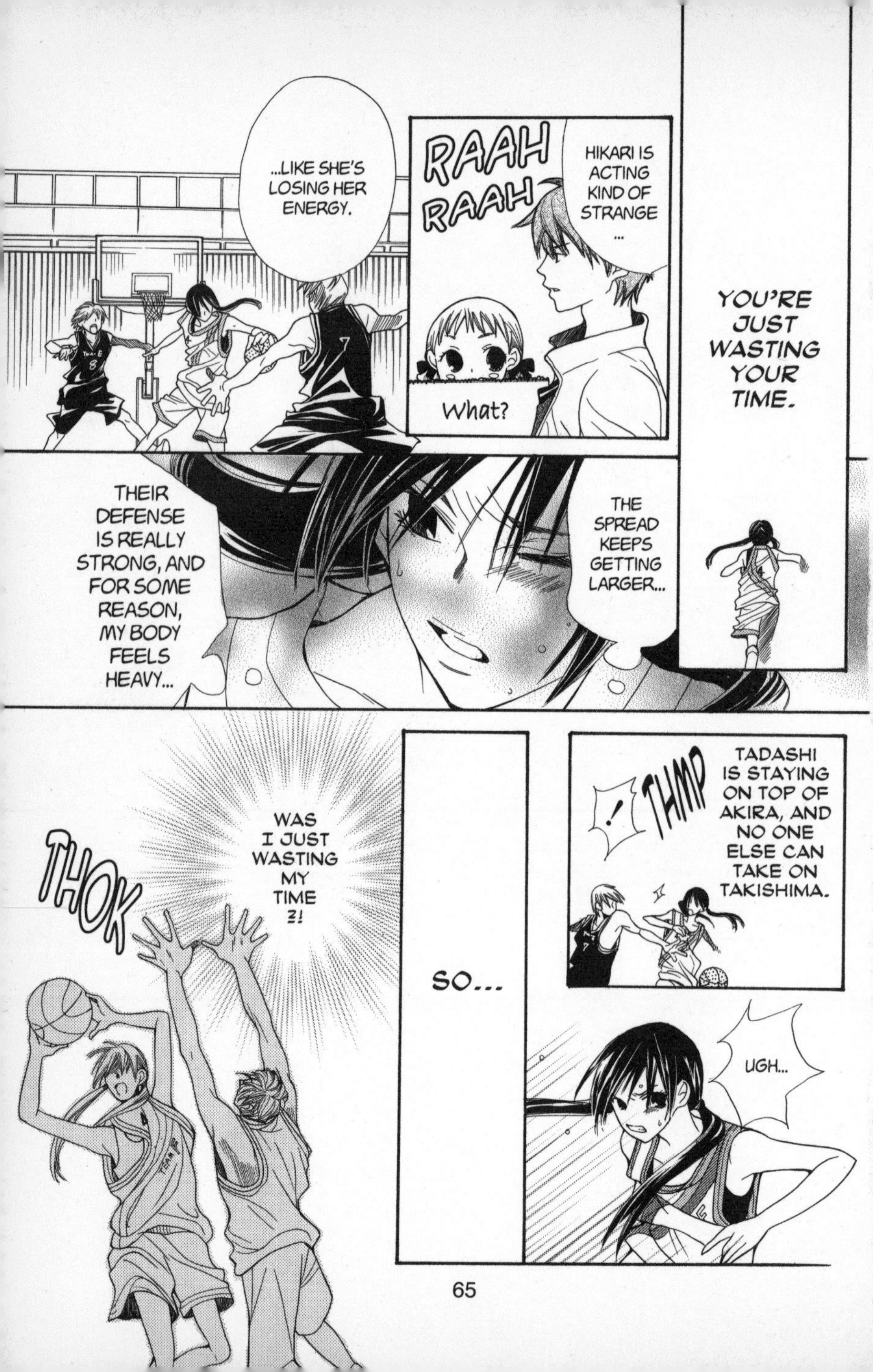

YOU'RE JUST WASTING YOUR TIME.
HIKARI IS ACTING KIND OF STRANGE ...
RAAH RAAH
What?
...LIKE SHE'S LOSING HER ENERGY.
THE SPREAD KEEPS GETTING LARGER...
THEIR DEFENSE IS REALLY STRONG, AND FOR SOME REASON, MY BODY FEELS HEAVY...
TADASHI IS STAYING ON TOP OF AKIRA, AND NO ONE ELSE CAN TAKE ON TAKISHIMA.
THMP
!
UGH...
SO...
WAS I JUST WASTING MY TIME ?!
THOK

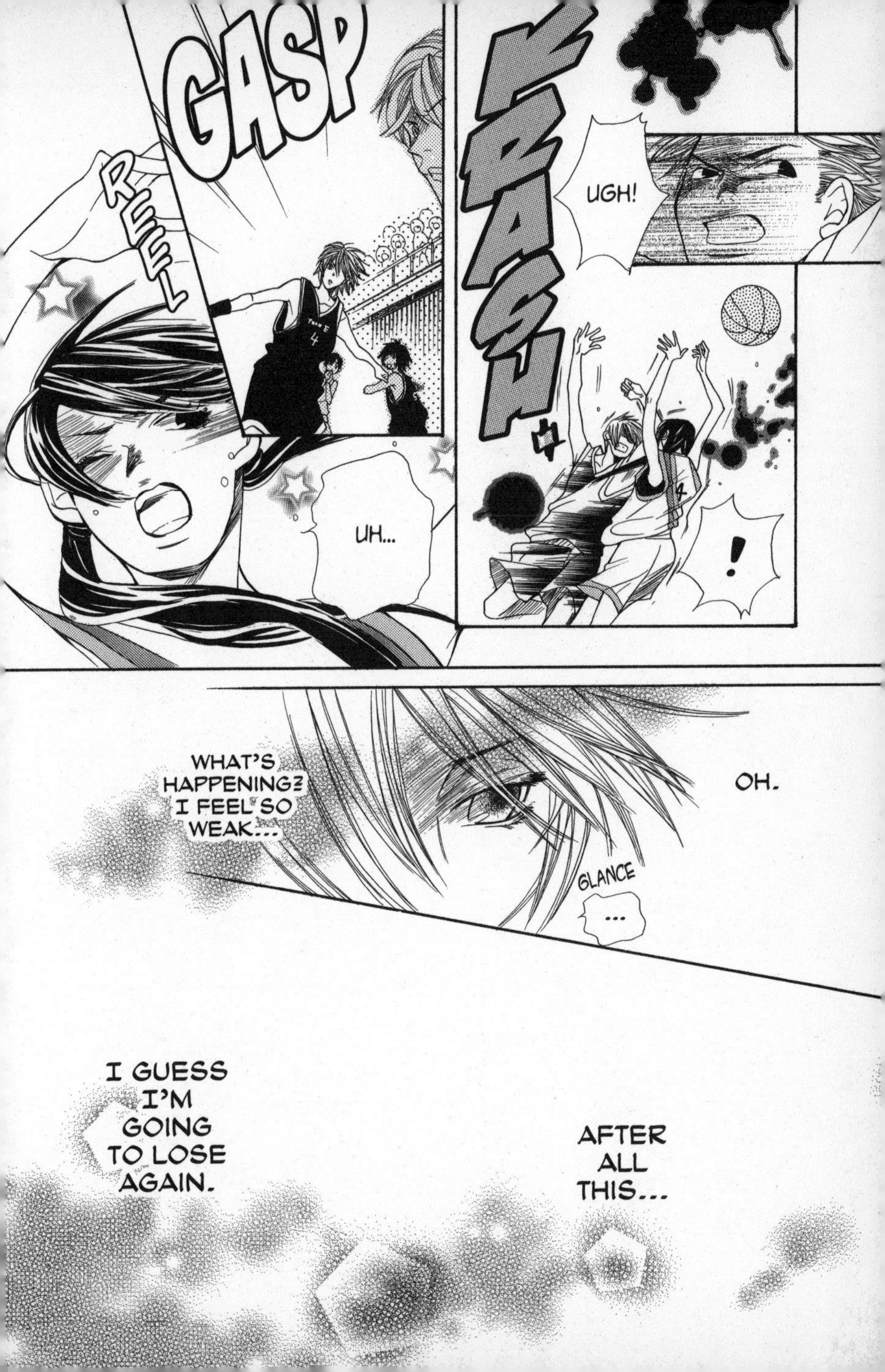
KRASH
UGH!
!
GASP
REEL
UH...
OH.
WHAT'S HAPPENING? I FEEL SO WEAK...
GLANCE
...
AFTER ALL THIS...
I GUESS I'M GOING TO LOSE AGAIN.

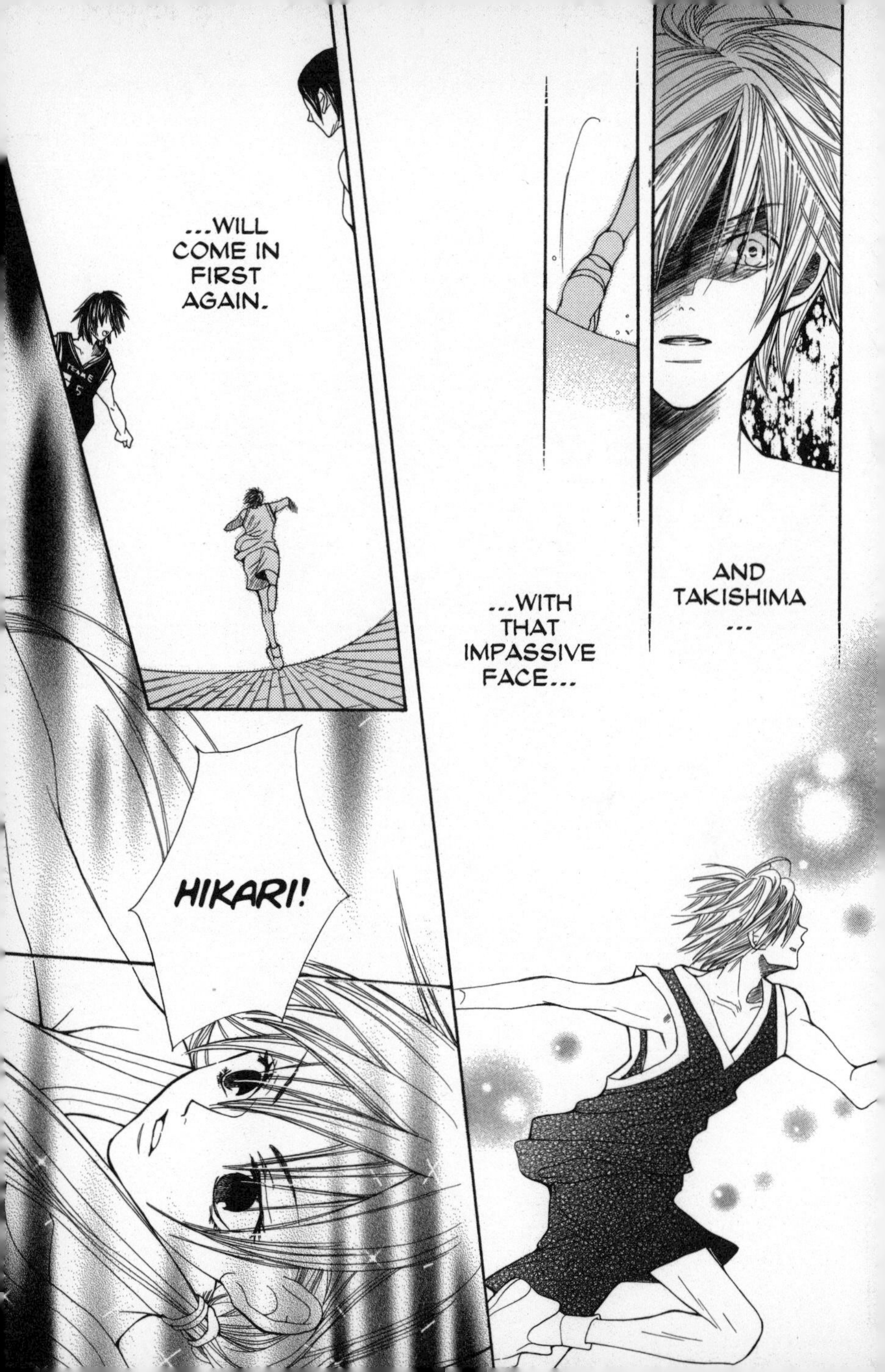
AND TAKISHIMA...
...WITH THAT IMPASSIVE FACE...
...WILL COME IN FIRST AGAIN.
HIKARI!

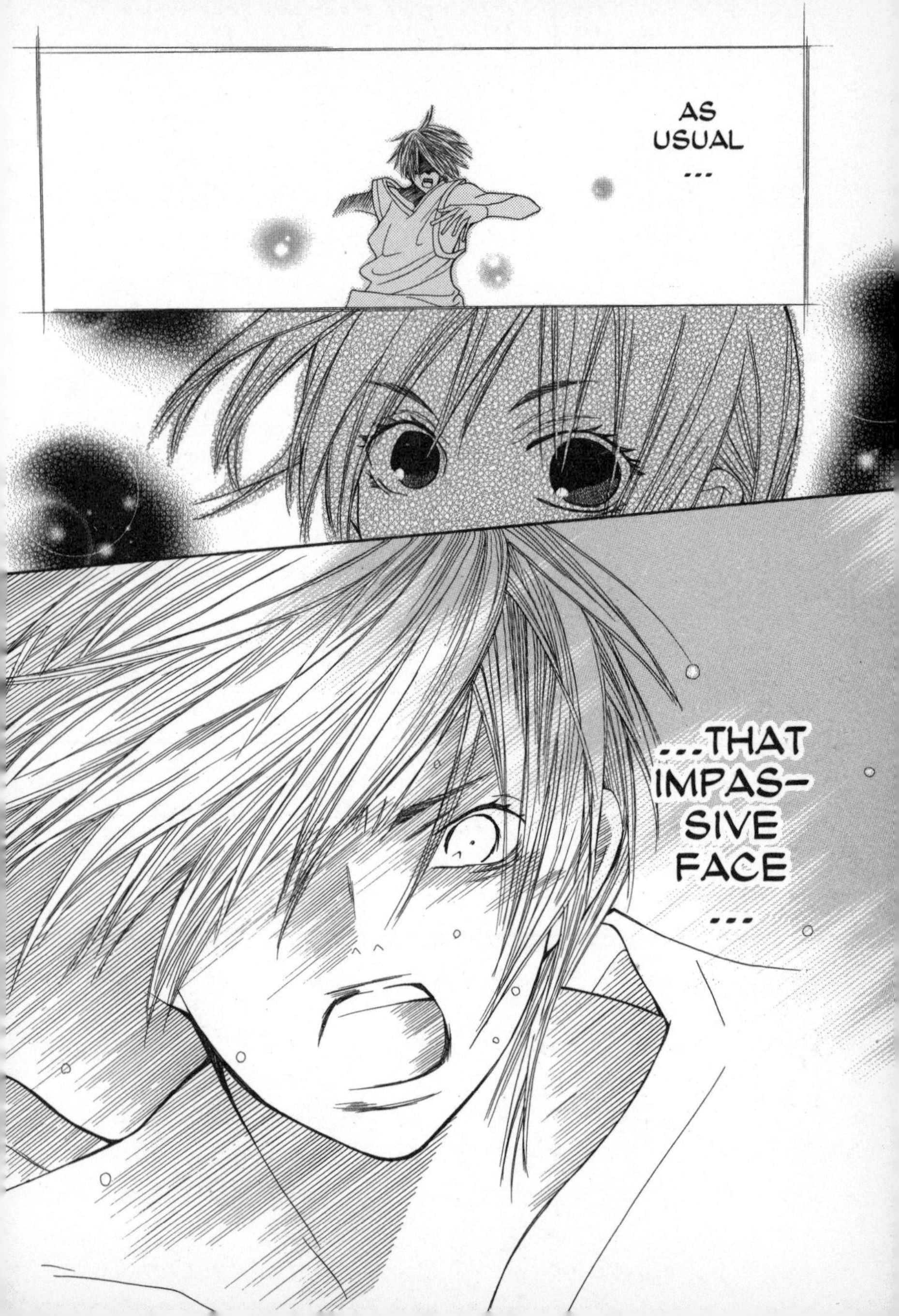
AS USUAL ...
...THAT IMPAS- SIVE FACE ...

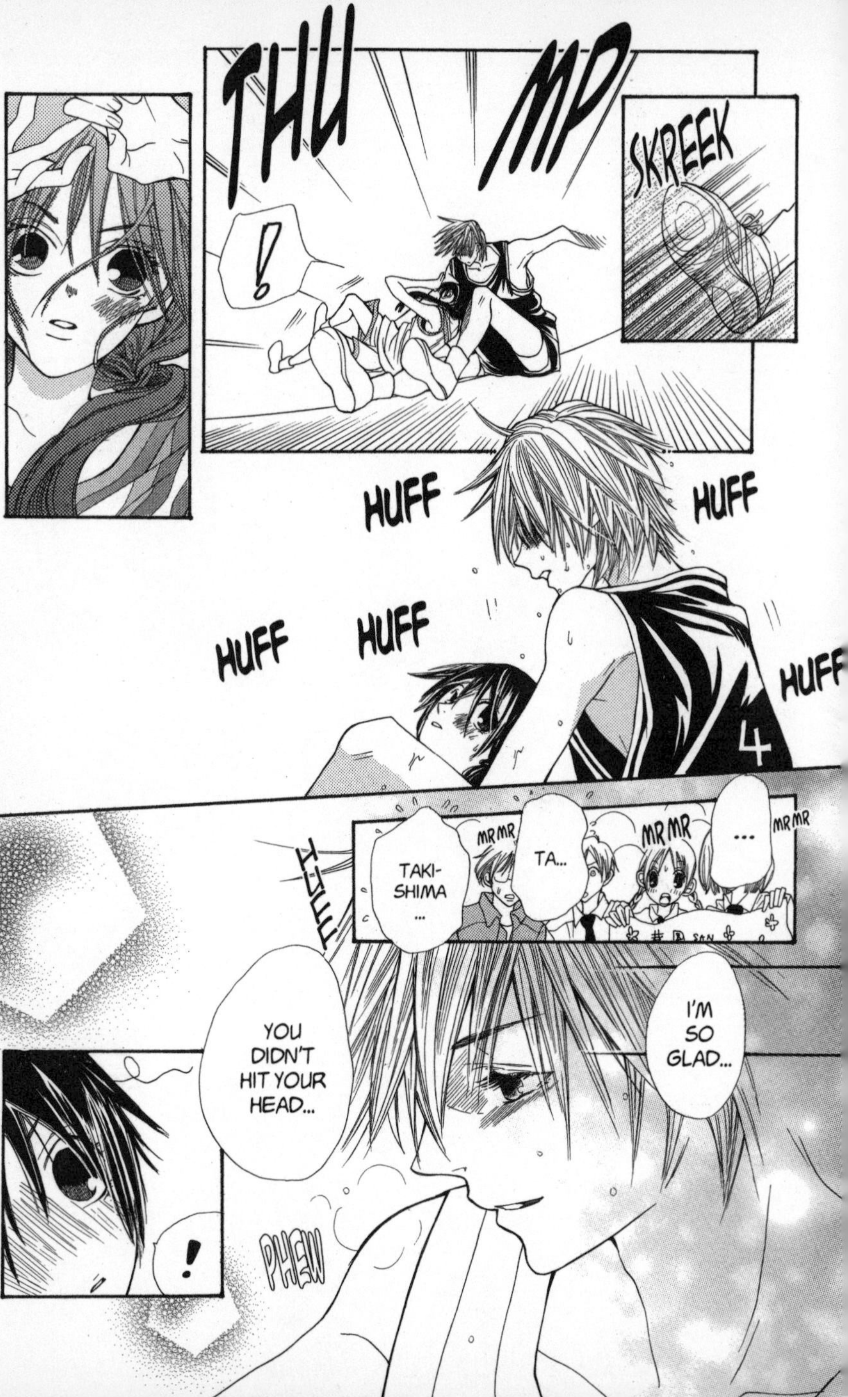
SKREEK
THUMP
!
HUFF
HUFF
HUFF
HUFF
HUFF
...
MR MR
MR MR
TA...
MR MR
TAKI-SHIMA ...
HUFF
I'M SO GLAD...
YOU DIDN'T HIT YOUR HEAD...
PHEW
!

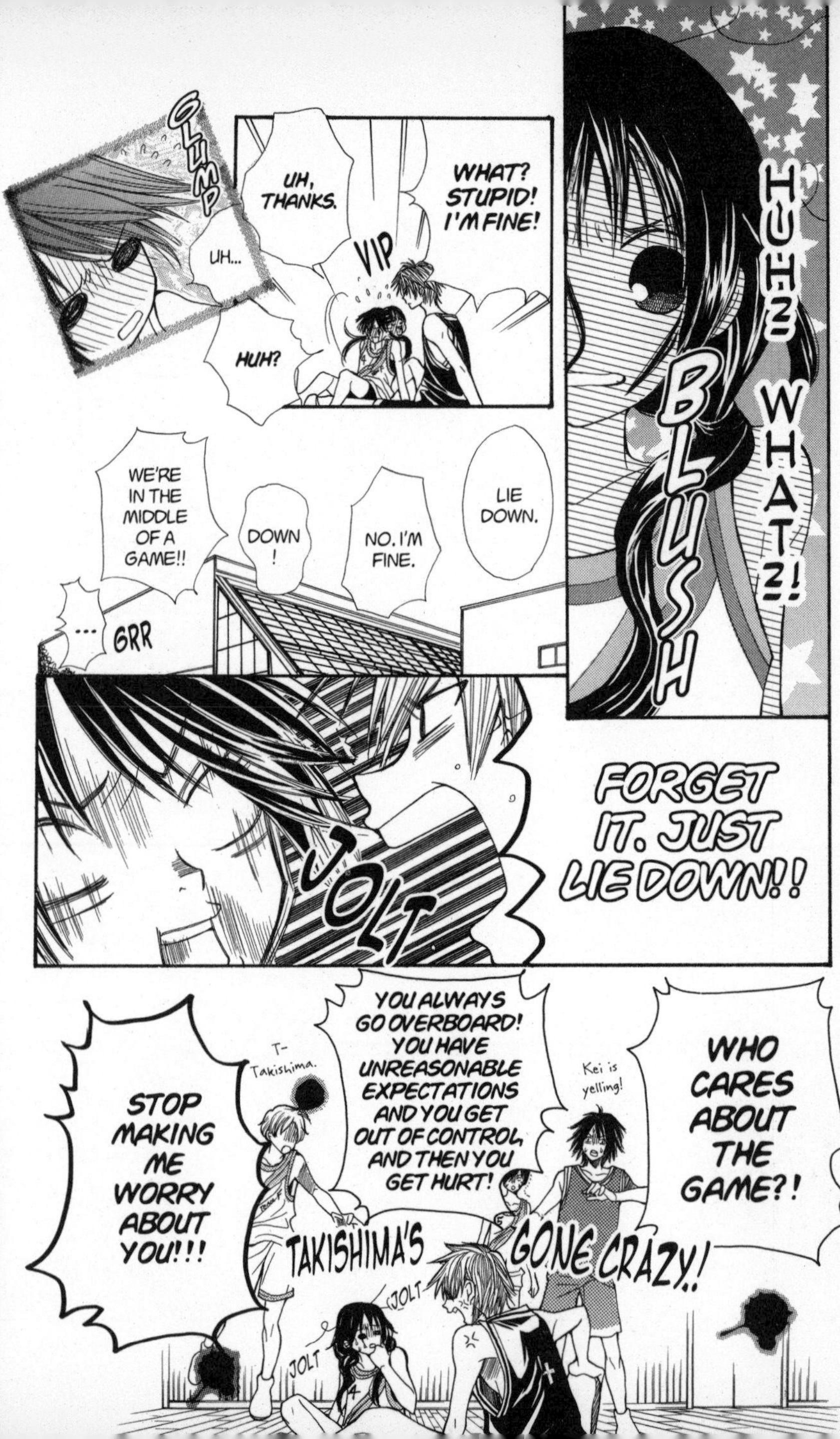
HUH?! WHAT?!
BLUSH
WHAT? STUPID! I'M FINE!
VIP
UH, THANKS.
HUH?
GLUMP
UH...
LIE DOWN.
NO. I'M FINE.
DOWN!
WE'RE IN THE MIDDLE OF A GAME!!
... GRR
FORGET IT. JUST LIE DOWN!!
JOLT
WHO CARES ABOUT THE GAME?!
Kei is yelling!
YOU ALWAYS GO OVERBOARD! YOU HAVE UNREASONABLE EXPECTATIONS AND YOU GET OUT OF CONTROL, AND THEN YOU GET HURT!
T-Takishima.
STOP MAKING ME WORRY ABOUT YOU!!!
TAKISHIMA'S GONE CRAZY!
JOLT
JOLT

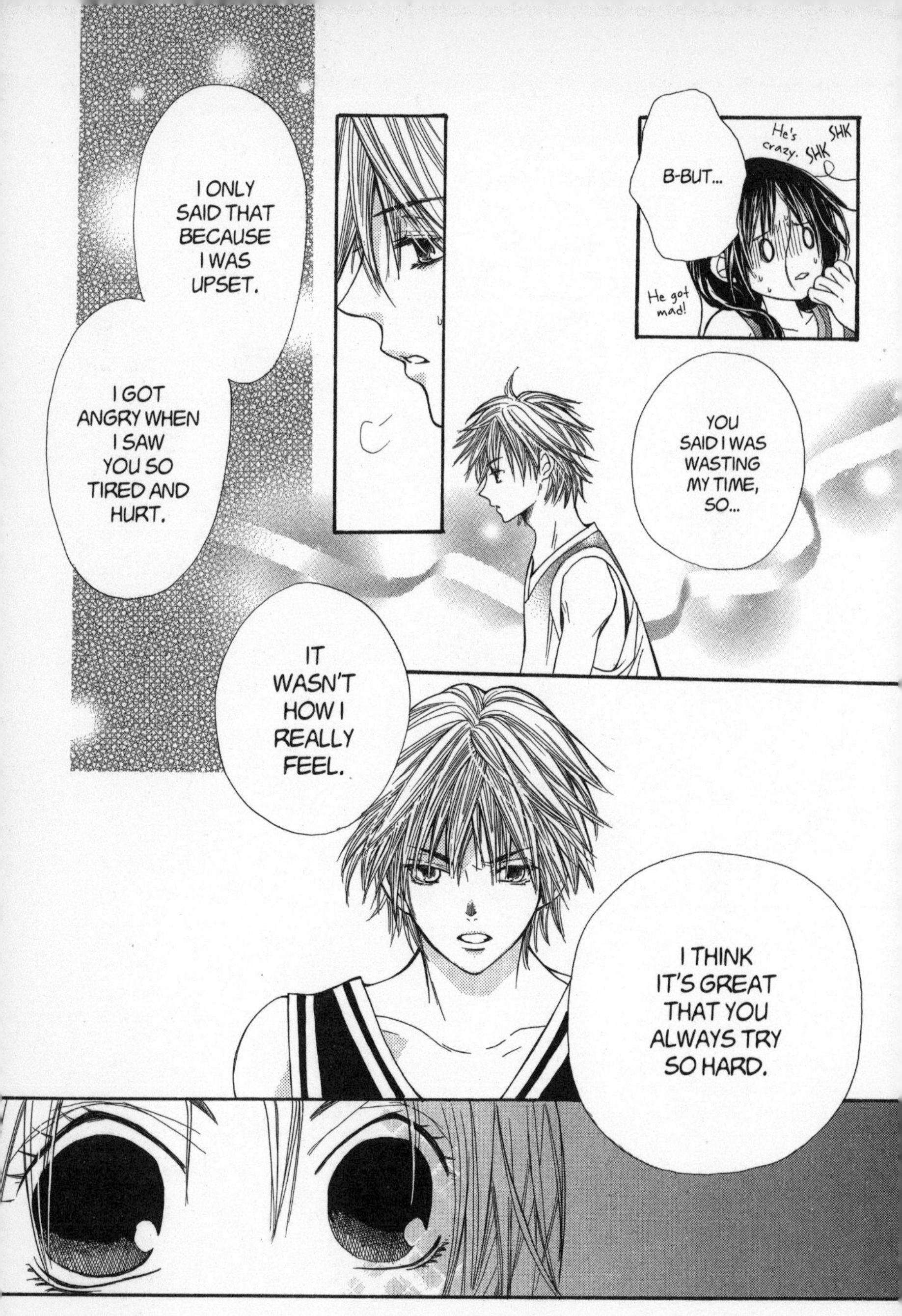
B-BUT...
He's crazy.
SHK SHK
He got mad!
YOU SAID I WAS WASTING MY TIME, SO...
I ONLY SAID THAT BECAUSE I WAS UPSET.
I GOT ANGRY WHEN I SAW YOU SO TIRED AND HURT.
IT WASN'T HOW I REALLY FEEL.
I THINK IT'S GREAT THAT YOU ALWAYS TRY SO HARD.

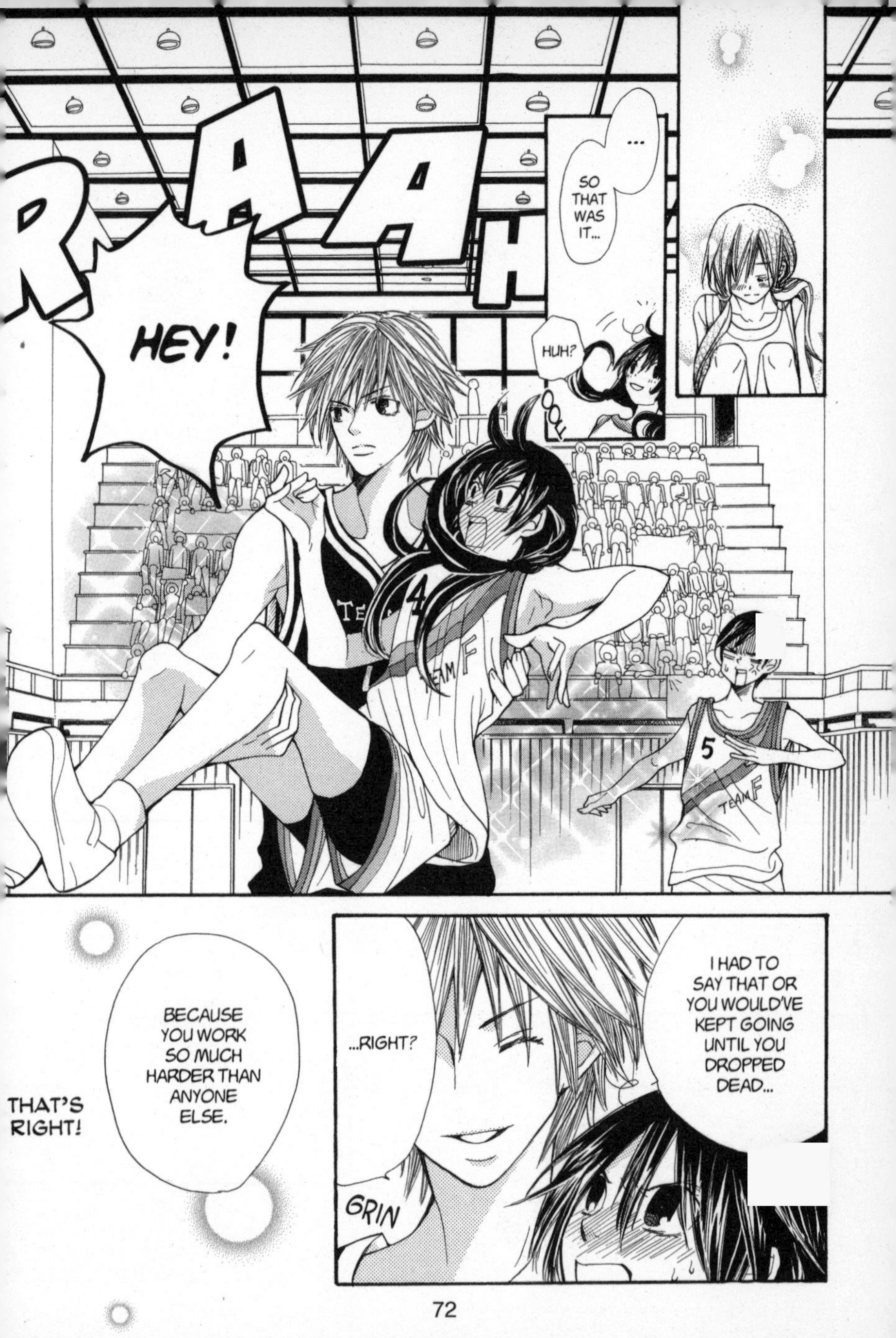
...
SO THAT WAS IT...
HUH?
RAAH
HEY!
I HAD TO SAY THAT OR YOU WOULD'VE KEPT GOING UNTIL YOU DROPPED DEAD...
...RIGHT?
GRIN
BECAUSE YOU WORK SO MUCH HARDER THAN ANYONE ELSE.
THAT'S RIGHT!

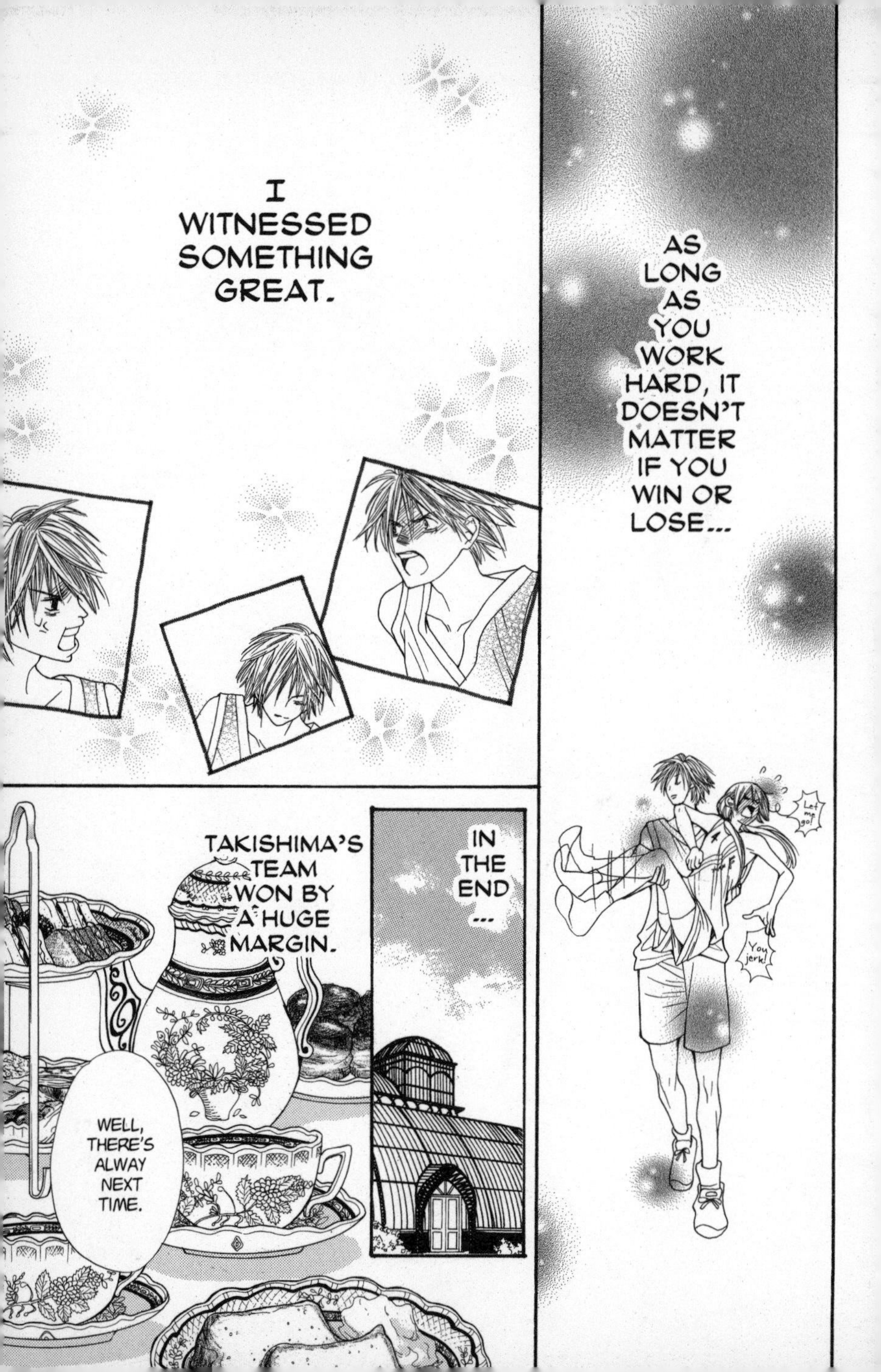
AS LONG AS YOU WORK HARD, IT DOESN'T MATTER IF YOU WIN OR LOSE...
Let me go!
You jerk!
I WITNESSED SOMETHING GREAT.
IN THE END ...
TAKISHIMA'S TEAM WON BY A HUGE MARGIN.
WELL, THERE'S ALWAY NEXT TIME.

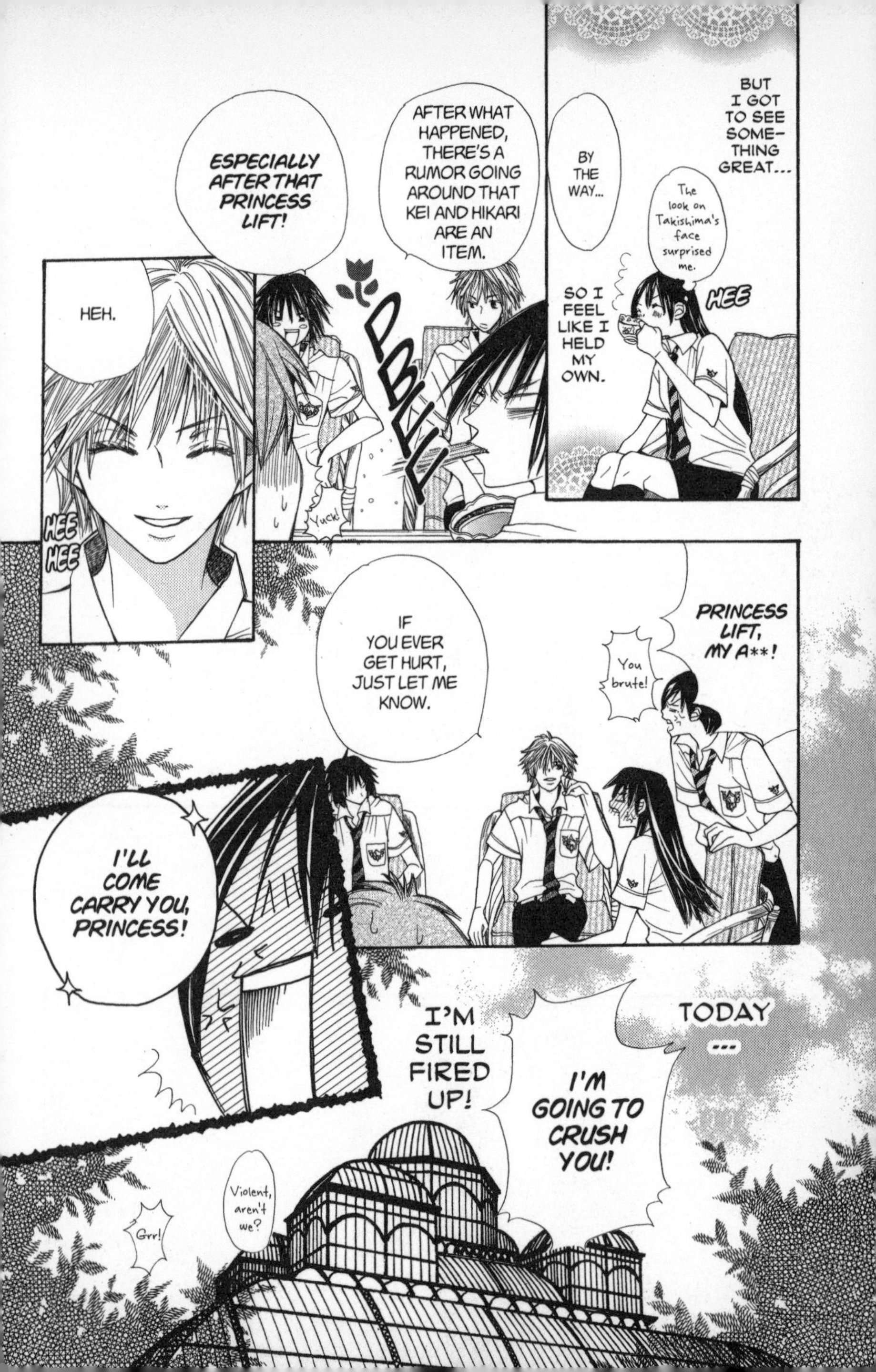
BUT I GOT TO SEE SOME-THING GREAT...
BY THE WAY...
The look on Takishima's face surprised me.
HEE
SO I FEEL LIKE I HELD MY OWN.
AFTER WHAT HAPPENED, THERE'S A RUMOR GOING AROUND THAT KEI AND HIKARI ARE AN ITEM.
ESPECIALLY AFTER THAT PRINCESS LIFT!
PBLLL
Yuck!
HEH.
HEE HEE
PRINCESS LIFT, MY A**!
You brute!
IF YOU EVER GET HURT, JUST LET ME KNOW.
I'LL COME CARRY YOU, PRINCESS!
TODAY...
I'M GOING TO CRUSH YOU!
I'M STILL FIRED UP!
Violent, aren't we?
Grr!

Chapter 3

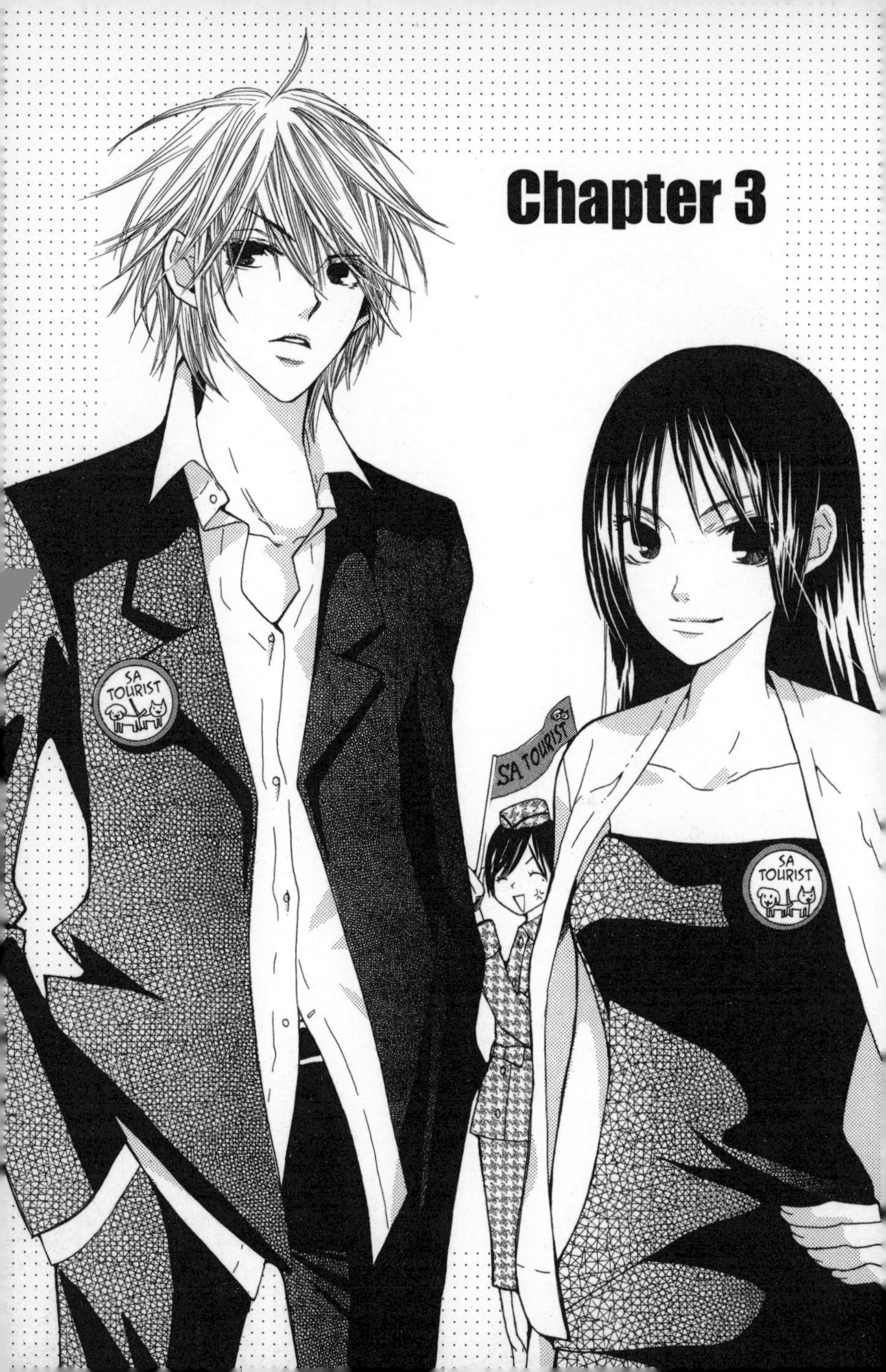
SA TOURIST
SA TOURIST
SA TOURIST

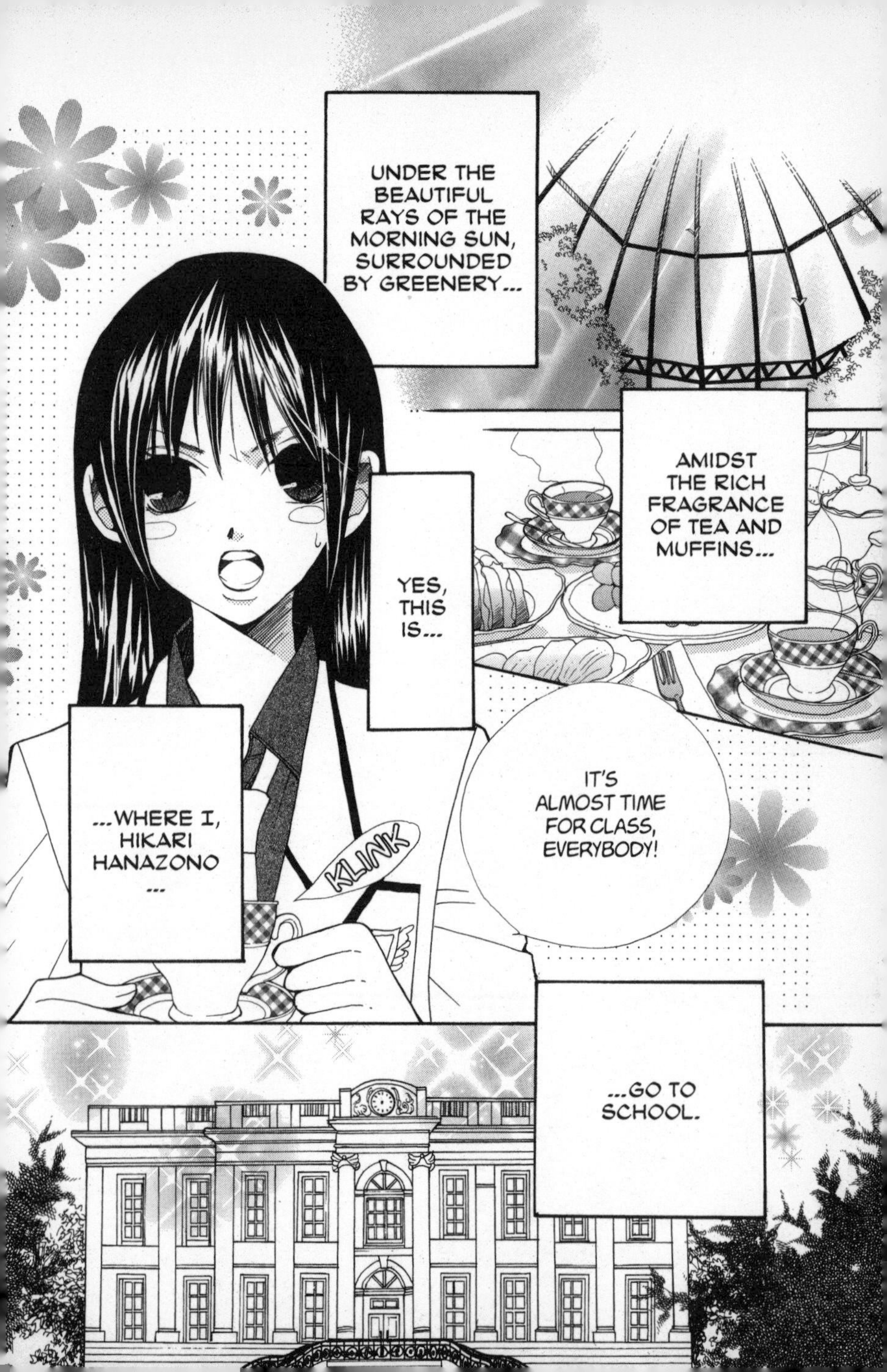
UNDER THE BEAUTIFUL RAYS OF THE MORNING SUN, SURROUNDED BY GREENERY...
AMIDST THE RICH FRAGRANCE OF TEA AND MUFFINS...
YES, THIS IS...
IT'S ALMOST TIME FOR CLASS, EVERYBODY!
KLINK
...WHERE I, HIKARI HANAZONO ...
...GO TO SCHOOL.

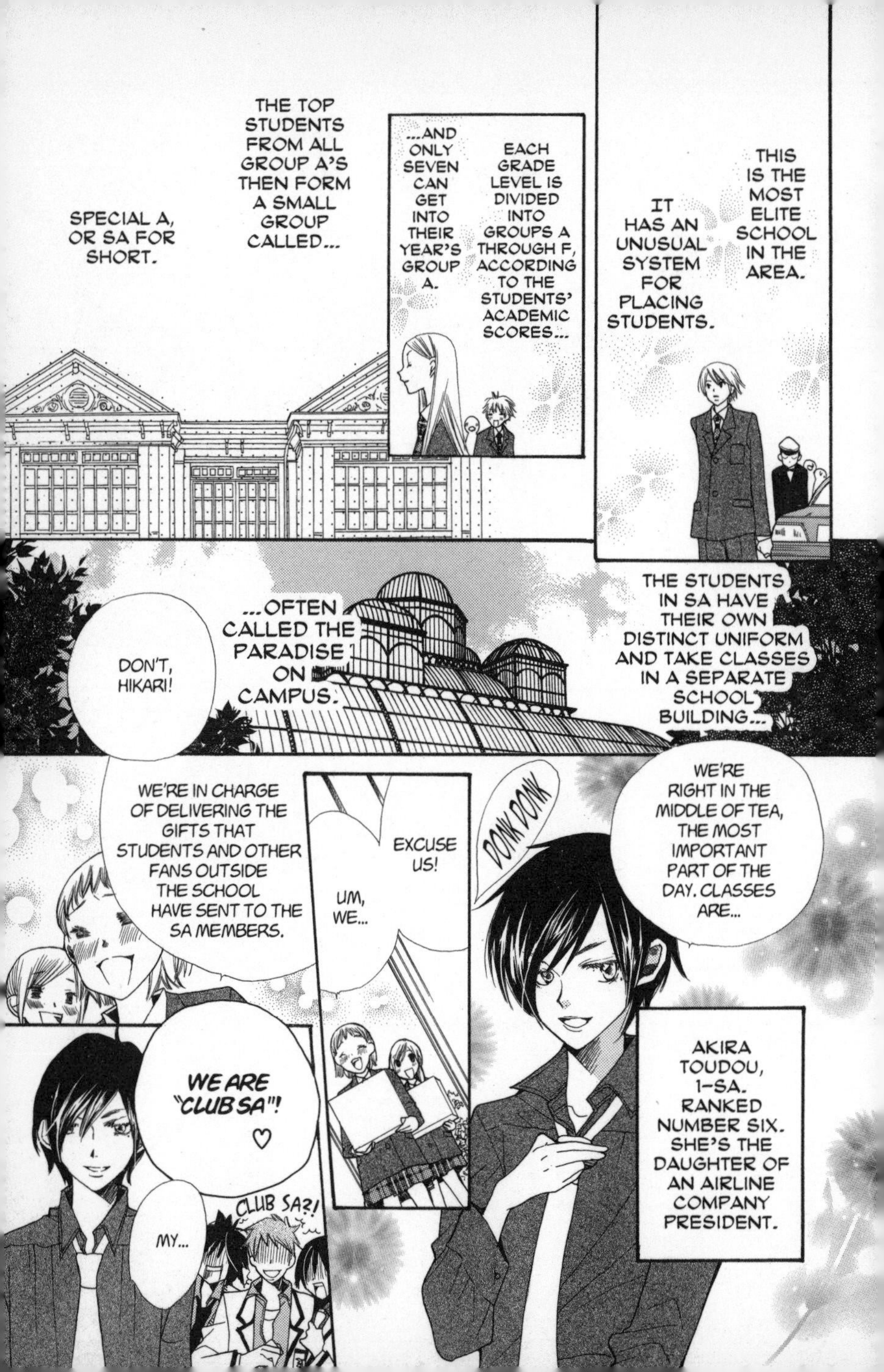
THIS IS THE MOST ELITE SCHOOL IN THE AREA.
IT HAS AN UNUSUAL SYSTEM FOR PLACING STUDENTS.
EACH GRADE LEVEL IS DIVIDED INTO GROUPS A THROUGH F, ACCORDING TO THE STUDENTS' ACADEMIC SCORES...
...AND ONLY SEVEN CAN GET INTO THEIR YEAR'S GROUP A.
THE TOP STUDENTS FROM ALL GROUP A'S THEN FORM A SMALL GROUP CALLED...
SPECIAL A, OR SA FOR SHORT.
THE STUDENTS IN SA HAVE THEIR OWN DISTINCT UNIFORM AND TAKE CLASSES IN A SEPARATE SCHOOL BUILDING...
...OFTEN CALLED THE PARADISE ON CAMPUS.
DON'T, HIKARI!
WE'RE RIGHT IN THE MIDDLE OF TEA, THE MOST IMPORTANT PART OF THE DAY. CLASSES ARE...
DONK DONK
AKIRA TOUDOU, 1-SA. RANKED NUMBER SIX. SHE'S THE DAUGHTER OF AN AIRLINE COMPANY PRESIDENT.
EXCUSE US!
UM, WE...
WE'RE IN CHARGE OF DELIVERING THE GIFTS THAT STUDENTS AND OTHER FANS OUTSIDE THE SCHOOL HAVE SENT TO THE SA MEMBERS.
WE ARE "CLUB SA"! ♥
CLUB SA?!
MY...

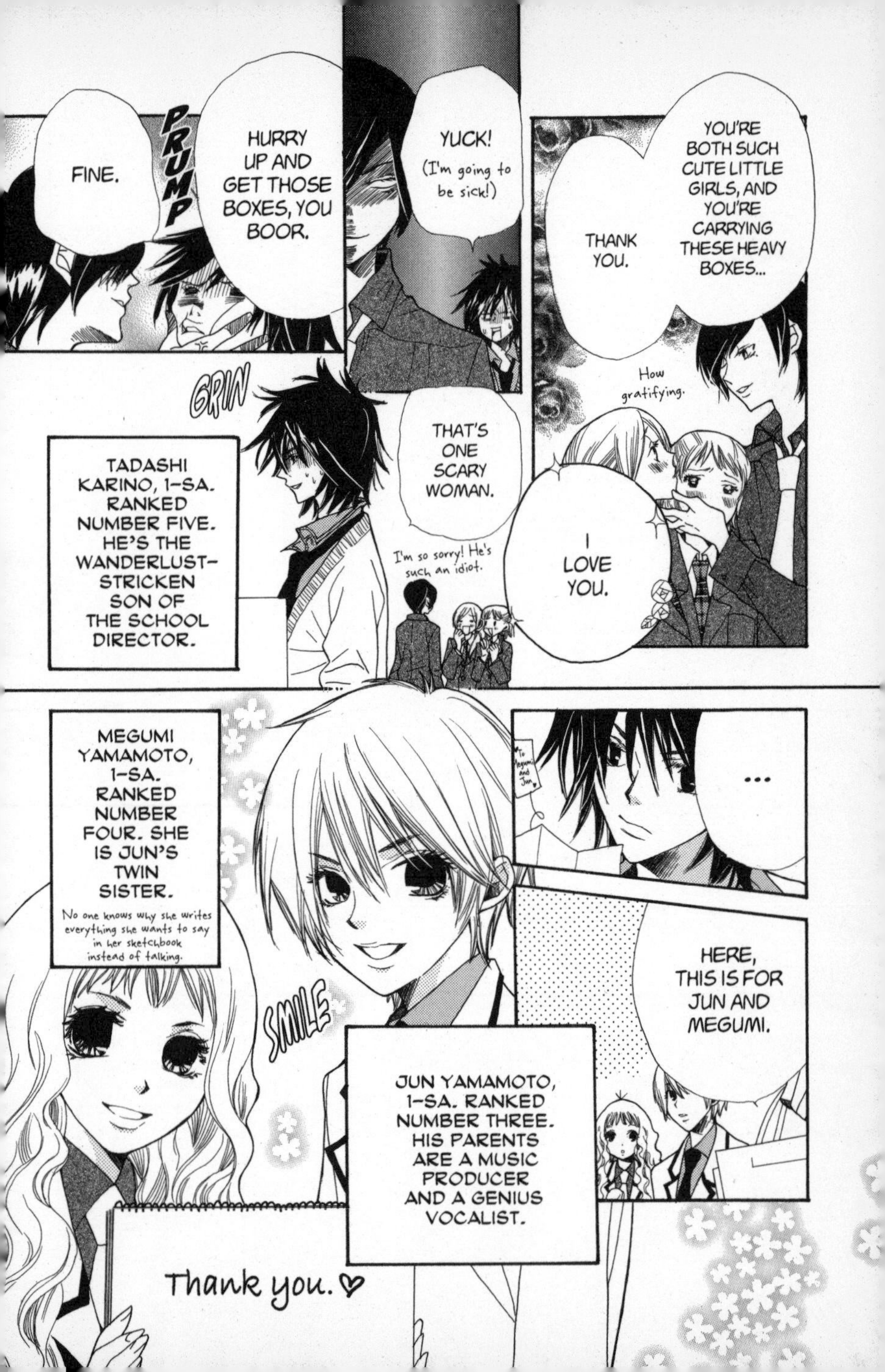
YOU'RE BOTH SUCH CUTE LITTLE GIRLS, AND YOU'RE CARRYING THESE HEAVY BOXES...
THANK YOU.
How gratifying.
I LOVE YOU.
YUCK!
(I'm going to be sick!)
HURRY UP AND GET THOSE BOXES, YOU BOOR.
PRUMP
FINE.
THAT'S ONE SCARY WOMAN.
I'm so sorry! He's such an idiot.
GRIN
TADASHI KARINO, 1-SA. RANKED NUMBER FIVE. HE'S THE WANDERLUST-STRICKEN SON OF THE SCHOOL DIRECTOR.
...
HERE, THIS IS FOR JUN AND MEGUMI.
JUN YAMAMOTO, 1-SA. RANKED NUMBER THREE. HIS PARENTS ARE A MUSIC PRODUCER AND A GENIUS VOCALIST.
SMILE
MEGUMI YAMAMOTO, 1-SA. RANKED NUMBER FOUR. SHE IS JUN'S TWIN SISTER.
No one knows why she writes everything she wants to say in her sketchbook instead of talking.
Thank you. ♡

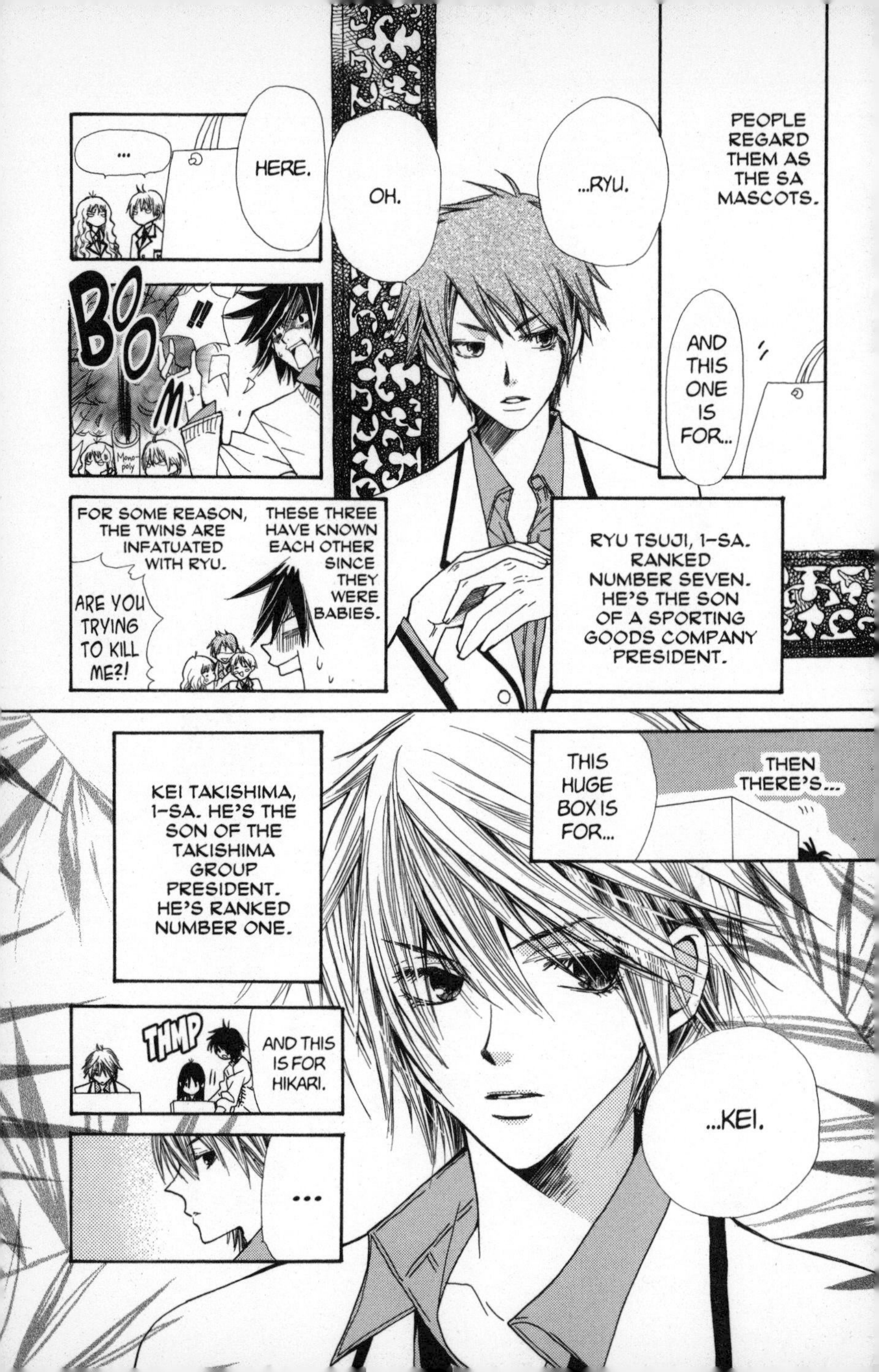
PEOPLE REGARD THEM AS THE SA MASCOTS.
AND THIS ONE IS FOR...
...RYU.
OH.
HERE.
...
BOOM!!
Mono-poly
RYU TSUJI, 1-SA. RANKED NUMBER SEVEN. HE'S THE SON OF A SPORTING GOODS COMPANY PRESIDENT.
THESE THREE HAVE KNOWN EACH OTHER SINCE THEY WERE BABIES.
FOR SOME REASON, THE TWINS ARE INFATUATED WITH RYU.
ARE YOU TRYING TO KILL ME?!
THEN THERE'S...
THIS HUGE BOX IS FOR...
KEI TAKISHIMA, 1-SA. HE'S THE SON OF THE TAKISHIMA GROUP PRESIDENT. HE'S RANKED NUMBER ONE.
...KEI.
AND THIS IS FOR HIKARI.
THMP
...

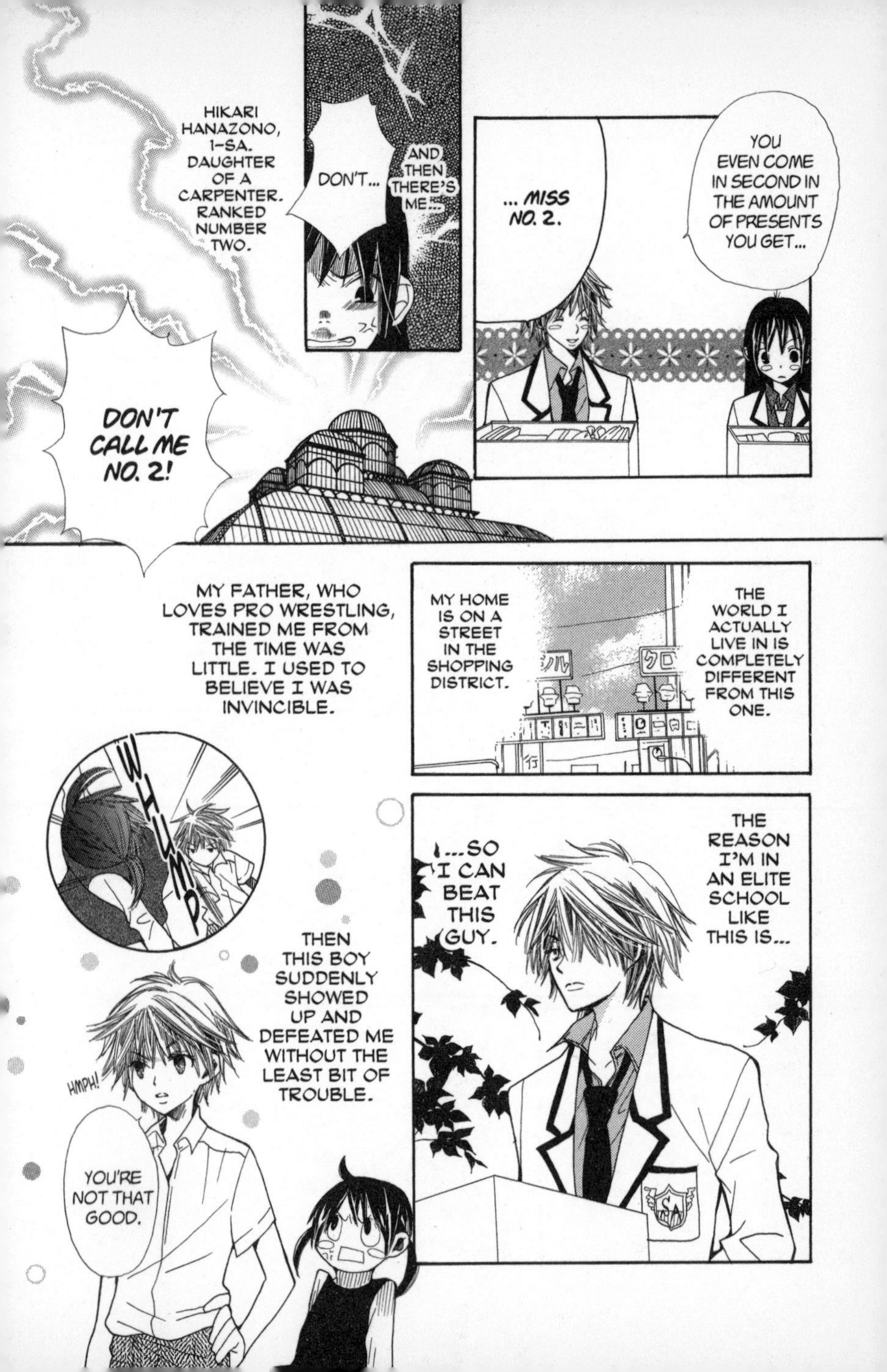
YOU EVEN COME IN SECOND IN THE AMOUNT OF PRESENTS YOU GET...
... MISS NO. 2.
AND THEN THERE'S ME...
DON'T...
HIKARI HANAZONO, 1-SA. DAUGHTER OF A CARPENTER. RANKED NUMBER TWO.
DON'T CALL ME NO. 2!
THE WORLD I ACTUALLY LIVE IN IS COMPLETELY DIFFERENT FROM THIS ONE.
MY HOME IS ON A STREET IN THE SHOPPING DISTRICT.
MY FATHER, WHO LOVES PRO WRESTLING, TRAINED ME FROM THE TIME WAS LITTLE. I USED TO BELIEVE I WAS INVINCIBLE.
THE REASON I'M IN AN ELITE SCHOOL LIKE THIS IS...
...SO I CAN BEAT THIS GUY.
WHUMP
THEN THIS BOY SUDDENLY SHOWED UP AND DEFEATED ME WITHOUT THE LEAST BIT OF TROUBLE.
HMPH!
YOU'RE NOT THAT GOOD.

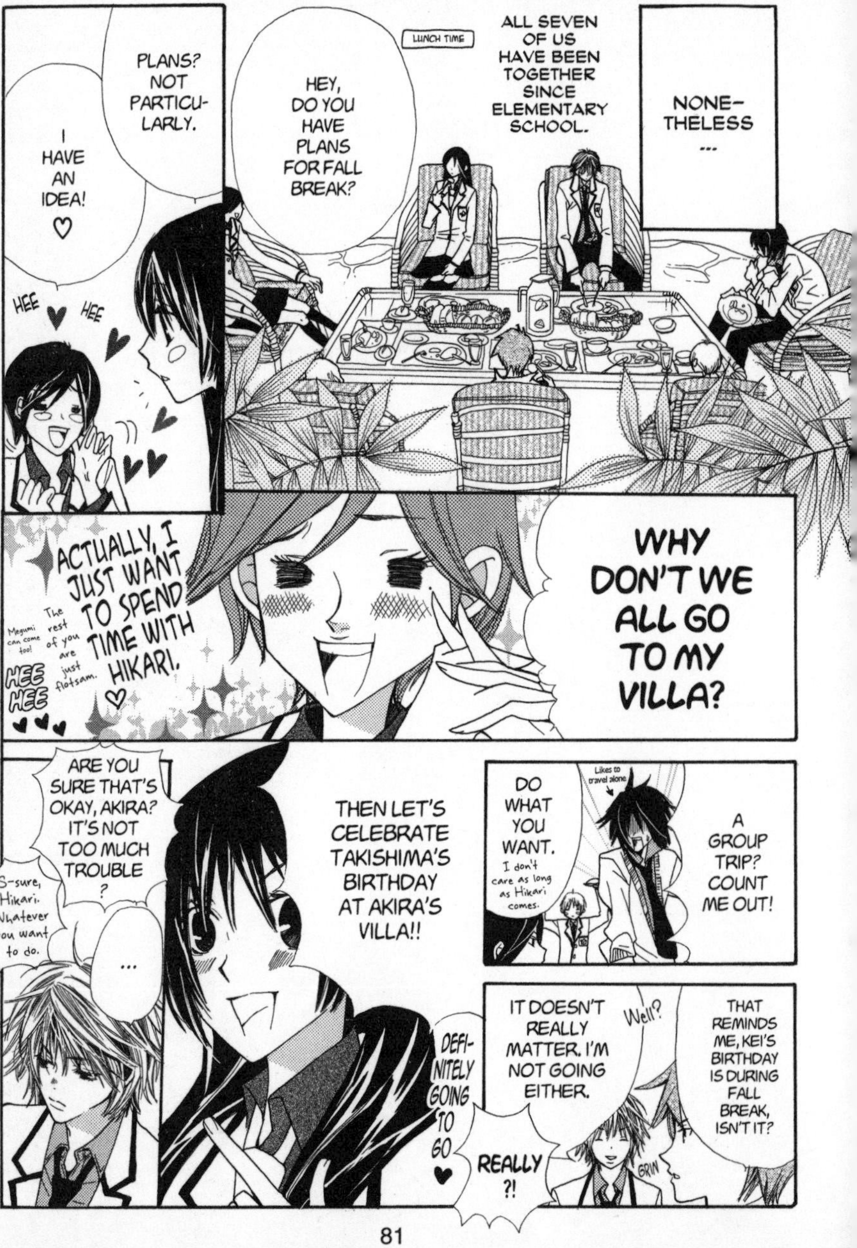
NONE-THELESS ...
ALL SEVEN OF US HAVE BEEN TOGETHER SINCE ELEMENTARY SCHOOL.
LUNCH TIME
HEY, DO YOU HAVE PLANS FOR FALL BREAK?
PLANS? NOT PARTICU-LARLY.
I HAVE AN IDEA! ♡
HEE HEE
WHY DON'T WE ALL GO TO MY VILLA?
ACTUALLY, I JUST WANT TO SPEND TIME WITH HIKARI. ♡
The rest of you are just flotsam.
Megumi can come too!
HEE HEE
A GROUP TRIP? COUNT ME OUT!
Likes to travel alone
DO WHAT YOU WANT.
I don't care as long as Hikari comes.
THAT REMINDS ME, KEI'S BIRTHDAY IS DURING FALL BREAK, ISN'T IT?
Well?
GRIN
IT DOESN'T REALLY MATTER. I'M NOT GOING EITHER.
REALLY ?!
DEFI-NITELY GOING TO GO ♥
THEN LET'S CELEBRATE TAKISHIMA'S BIRTHDAY AT AKIRA'S VILLA!!
ARE YOU SURE THAT'S OKAY, AKIRA? IT'S NOT TOO MUCH TROUBLE?
...
S-sure, Hikari. Whatever you want to do.

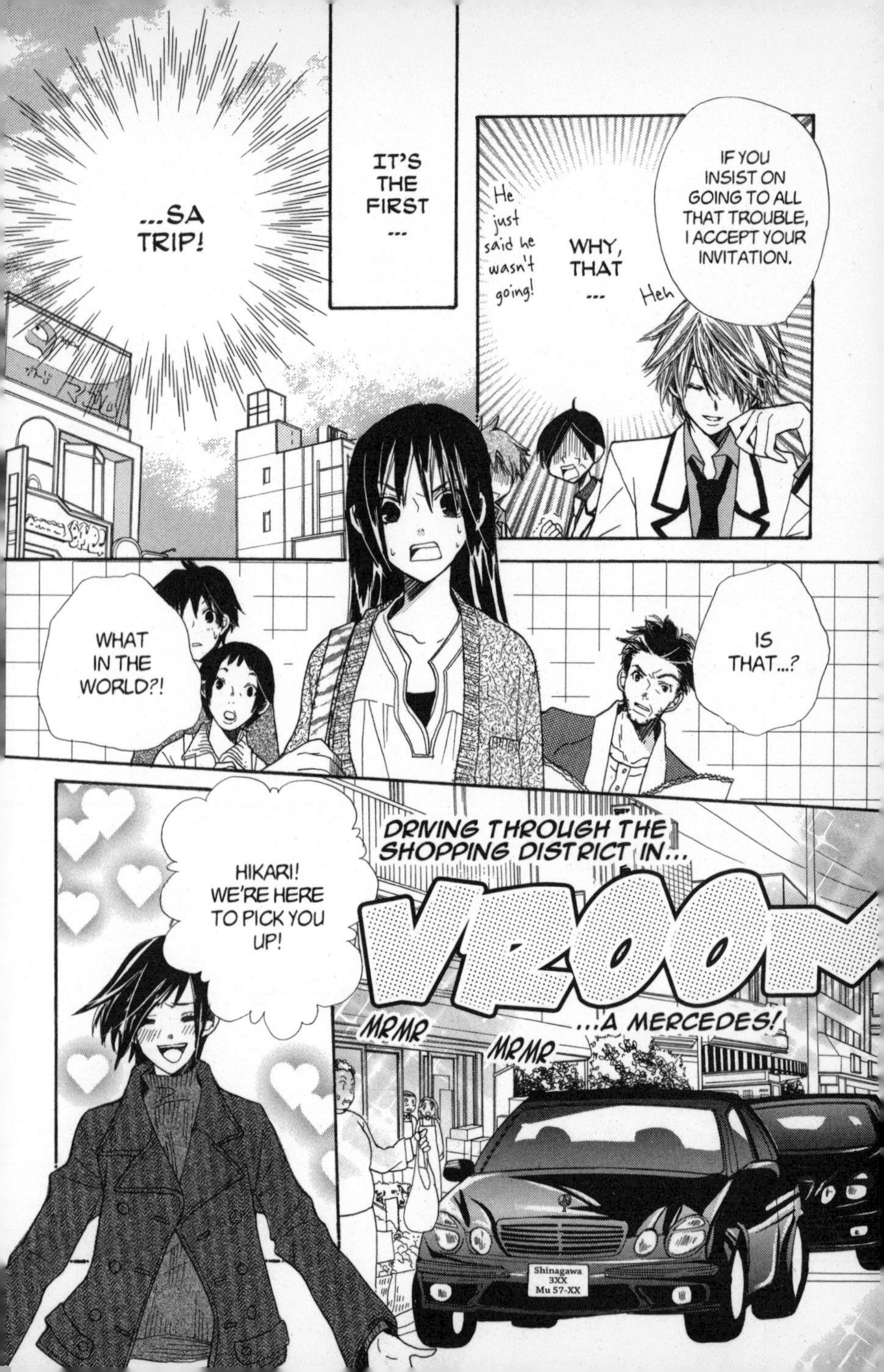
IF YOU INSIST ON GOING TO ALL THAT TROUBLE, I ACCEPT YOUR INVITATION.
Heh
WHY, THAT ...
He just said he wasn't going!
IT'S THE FIRST ...
...SA TRIP!
IS THAT...?
WHAT IN THE WORLD?!
DRIVING THROUGH THE SHOPPING DISTRICT IN...
VROOM
...A MERCEDES!
MRMR
MRMR
Shinagawa 3XX Mu 57-XX
HIKARI! WE'RE HERE TO PICK YOU UP!

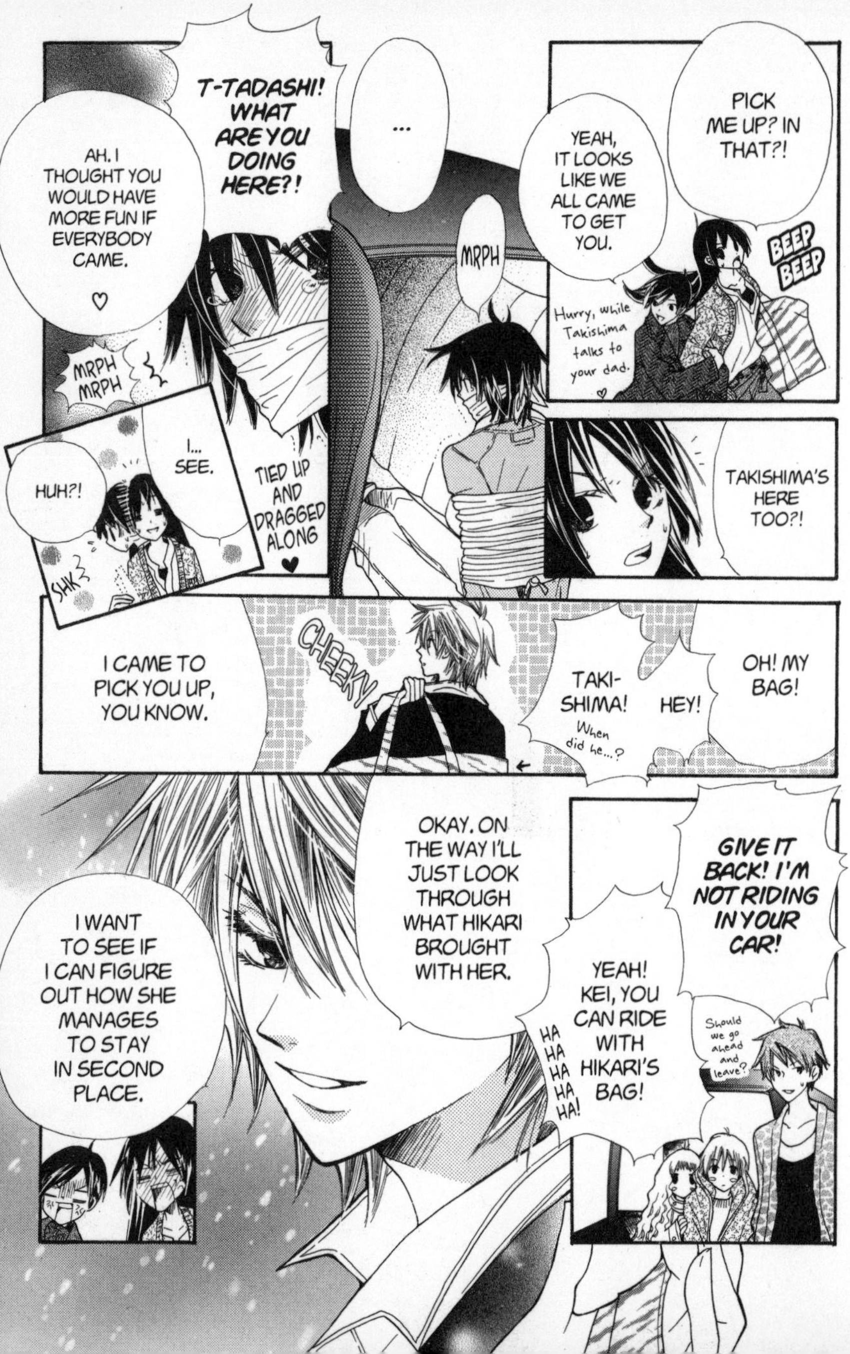
PICK ME UP? IN THAT?!
YEAH, IT LOOKS LIKE WE ALL CAME TO GET YOU.
BEEP BEEP
Hurry, while Takishima talks to your dad. ♡
TAKISHIMA'S HERE TOO?!
...
MRPH
T-TADASHI! WHAT ARE YOU DOING HERE?!
AH. I THOUGHT YOU WOULD HAVE MORE FUN IF EVERYBODY CAME. ♡
MRPH MRPH
TIED UP AND DRAGGED ALONG ♥
I... SEE.
HUH?!
SHK
OH! MY BAG!
HEY!
TAKI-SHIMA!
When did he...?
CHEEKY
I CAME TO PICK YOU UP, YOU KNOW.
GIVE IT BACK! I'M NOT RIDING IN YOUR CAR!
Should we go ahead and leave?
YEAH! KEI, YOU CAN RIDE WITH HIKARI'S BAG!
HA HA HA HA HA HA!
OKAY. ON THE WAY I'LL JUST LOOK THROUGH WHAT HIKARI BROUGHT WITH HER.
I WANT TO SEE IF I CAN FIGURE OUT HOW SHE MANAGES TO STAY IN SECOND PLACE.

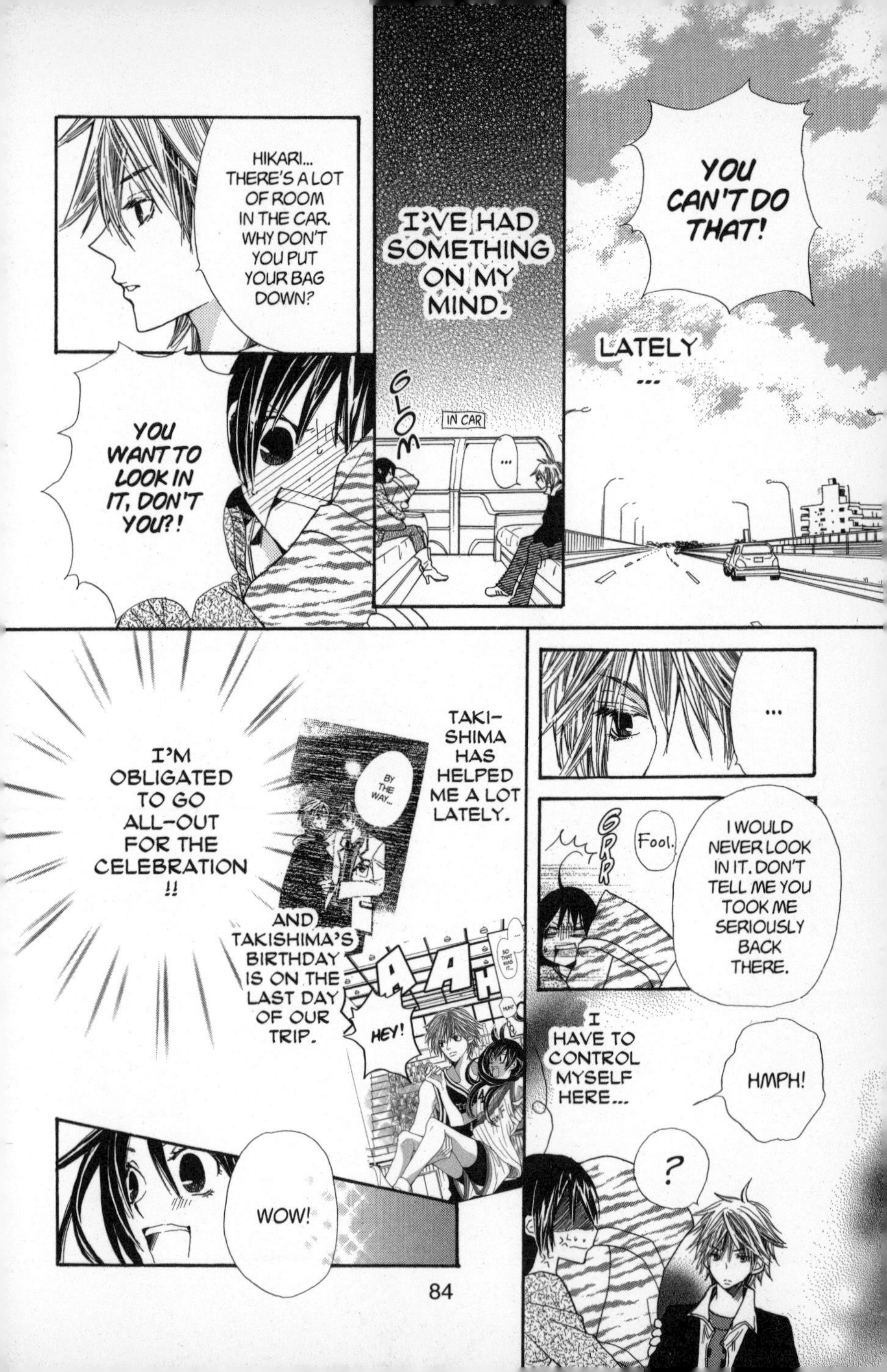
YOU CAN'T DO THAT!
LATELY ...
I'VE HAD SOMETHING ON MY MIND.
GLOM
IN CAR
...
HIKARI... THERE'S A LOT OF ROOM IN THE CAR. WHY DON'T YOU PUT YOUR BAG DOWN?
YOU WANT TO LOOK IN IT, DON'T YOU?!
...
GRR
Fool.
I WOULD NEVER LOOK IN IT. DON'T TELL ME YOU TOOK ME SERIOUSLY BACK THERE.
I HAVE TO CONTROL MYSELF HERE...
HMPH!
?
TAKI-SHIMA HAS HELPED ME A LOT LATELY.
BY THE WAY...
AND TAKISHIMA'S BIRTHDAY IS ON THE LAST DAY OF OUR TRIP.
AAH
HEY!
I'M OBLIGATED TO GO ALL-OUT FOR THE CELEBRATION !!
WOW!

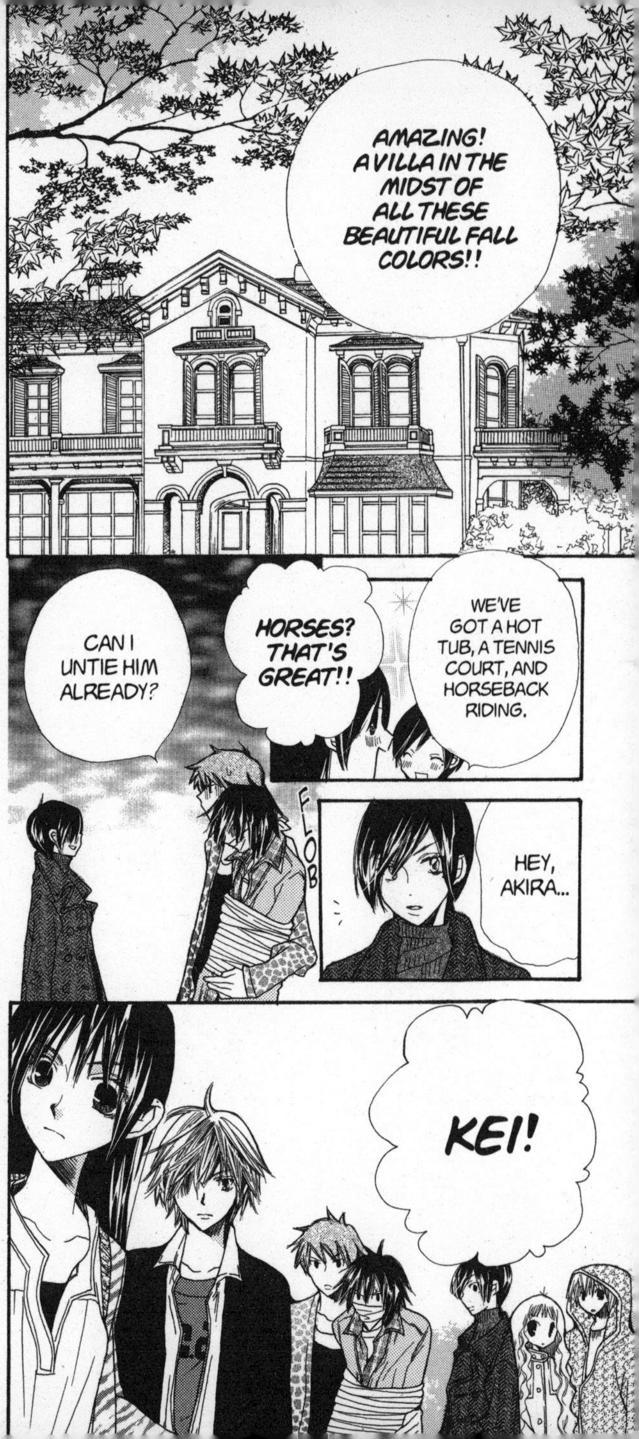
AMAZING! A VILLA IN THE MIDST OF ALL THESE BEAUTIFUL FALL COLORS!!
WE'VE GOT A HOT TUB, A TENNIS COURT, AND HORSEBACK RIDING.
HORSES? THAT'S GREAT!!
HEY, AKIRA...
CAN I UNTIE HIM ALREADY?
FLOB
KEI!

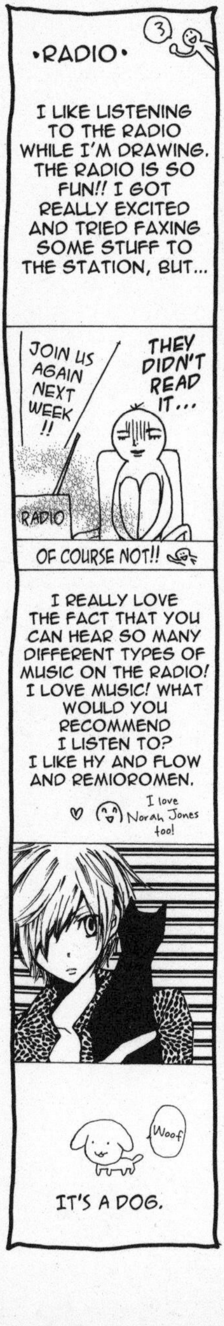
3
•RADIO•
I LIKE LISTENING TO THE RADIO WHILE I'M DRAWING. THE RADIO IS SO FUN!! I GOT REALLY EXCITED AND TRIED FAXING SOME STUFF TO THE STATION, BUT...
THEY DIDN'T READ IT...
JOIN US AGAIN NEXT WEEK !!
RADIO
OF COURSE NOT!!
I REALLY LOVE THE FACT THAT YOU CAN HEAR SO MANY DIFFERENT TYPES OF MUSIC ON THE RADIO! I LOVE MUSIC! WHAT WOULD YOU RECOMMEND I LISTEN TO? I LIKE HY AND FLOW AND REMIOROMEN.
I love Norah Jones too!
Woof
IT'S A DOG.

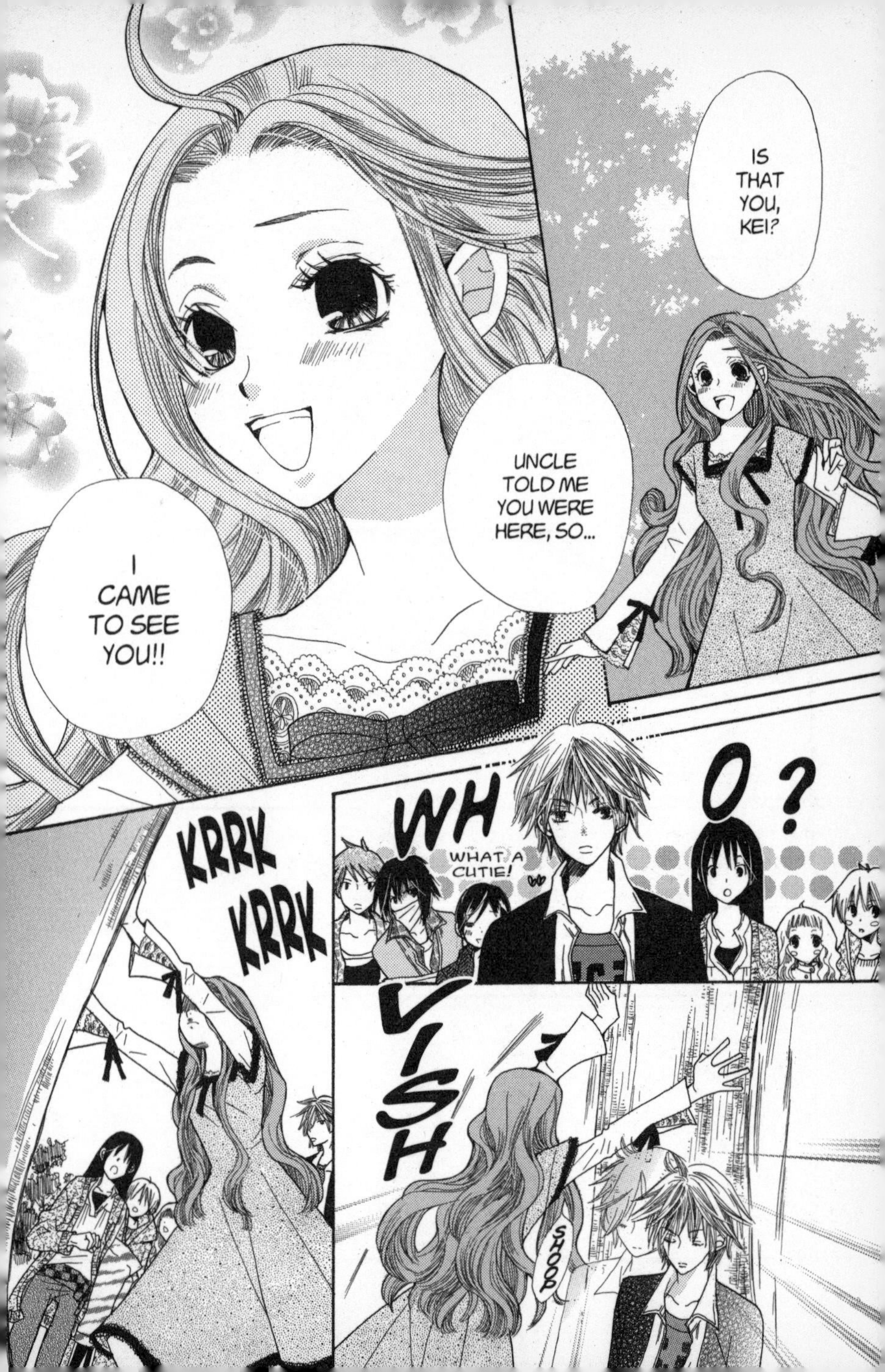
IS THAT YOU, KEI?
UNCLE TOLD ME YOU WERE HERE, SO...
I CAME TO SEE YOU!!
WHO?
WHAT A CUTIE!
VISH
SHOOP
KRRK KRRK

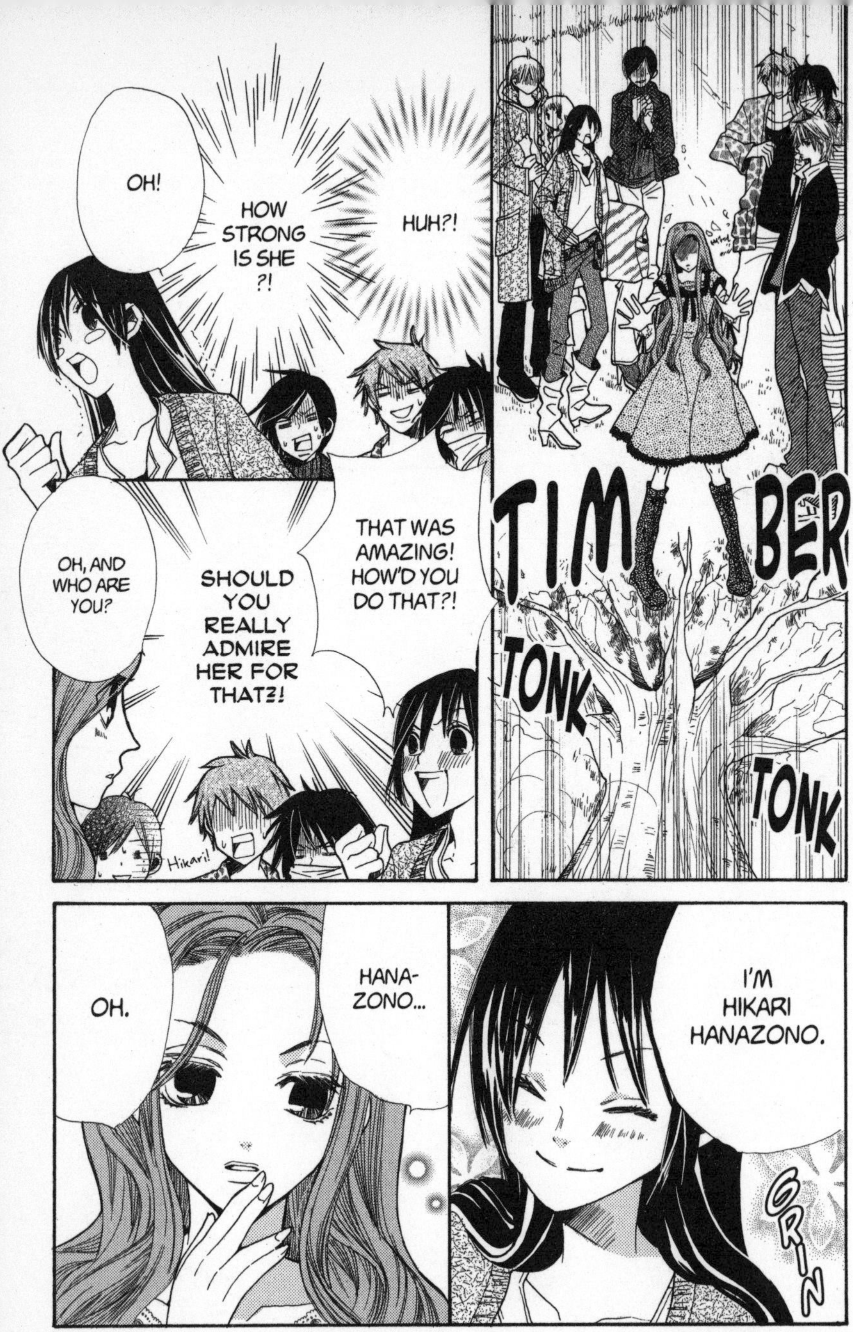
TIMBER
TONK
TONK
HUH?!
HOW STRONG IS SHE ?!
OH!
THAT WAS AMAZING! HOW'D YOU DO THAT?!
SHOULD YOU REALLY ADMIRE HER FOR THAT?!
OH, AND WHO ARE YOU?
Hikari!
I'M HIKARI HANAZONO.
GRIN
HANA-ZONO...
OH.

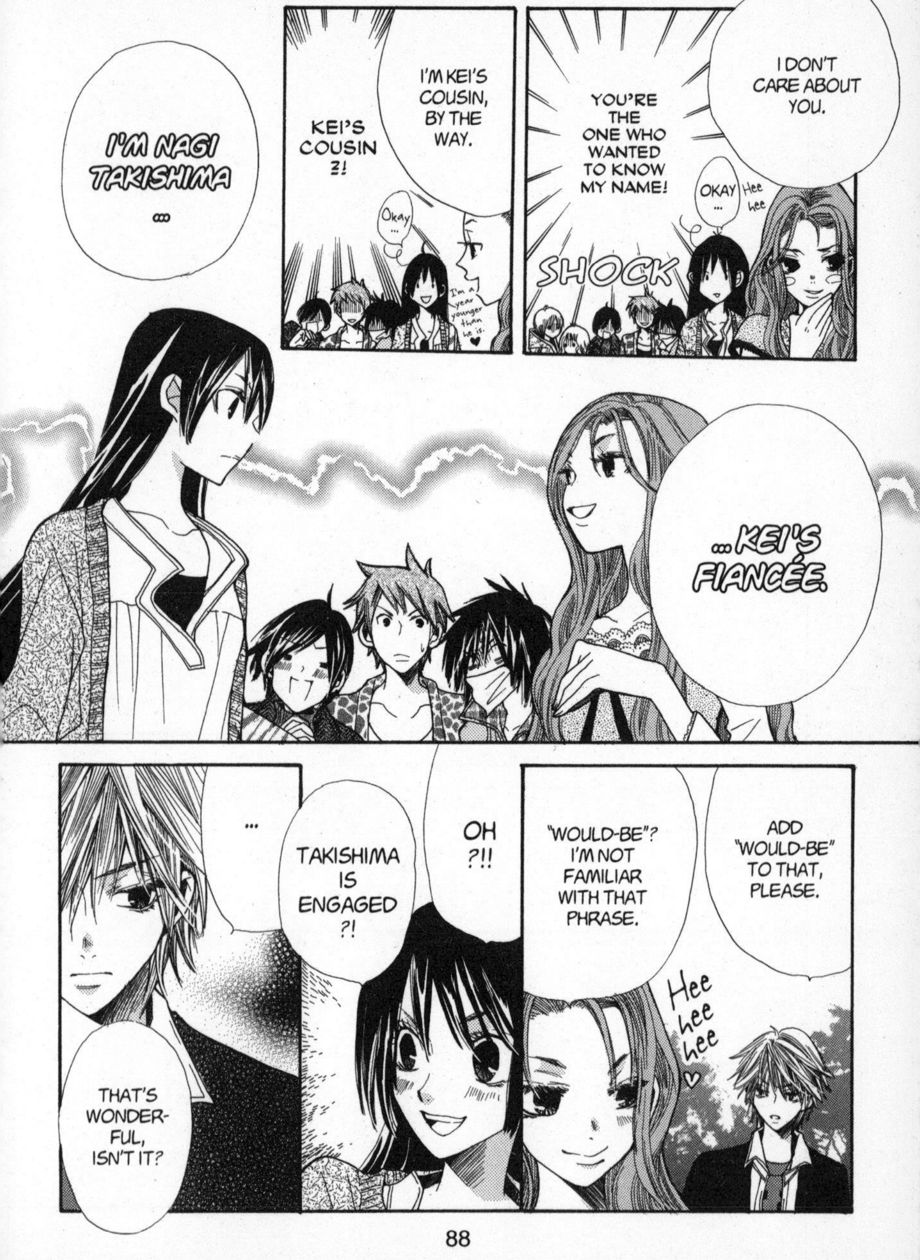
I DON'T CARE ABOUT YOU.
YOU'RE THE ONE WHO WANTED TO KNOW MY NAME!
OKAY ...
Hee hee
SHOCK
I'M KEI'S COUSIN, BY THE WAY.
KEI'S COUSIN ?!
Okay ...
I'm a year younger than he is. ♥
I'M NAGI TAKISHIMA ...
...KEI'S FIANCÉE.
ADD "WOULD-BE" TO THAT, PLEASE.
"WOULD-BE"? I'M NOT FAMILIAR WITH THAT PHRASE.
Hee hee hee ♥
OH ?!!
TAKISHIMA IS ENGAGED ?!
...
THAT'S WONDER-FUL, ISN'T IT?

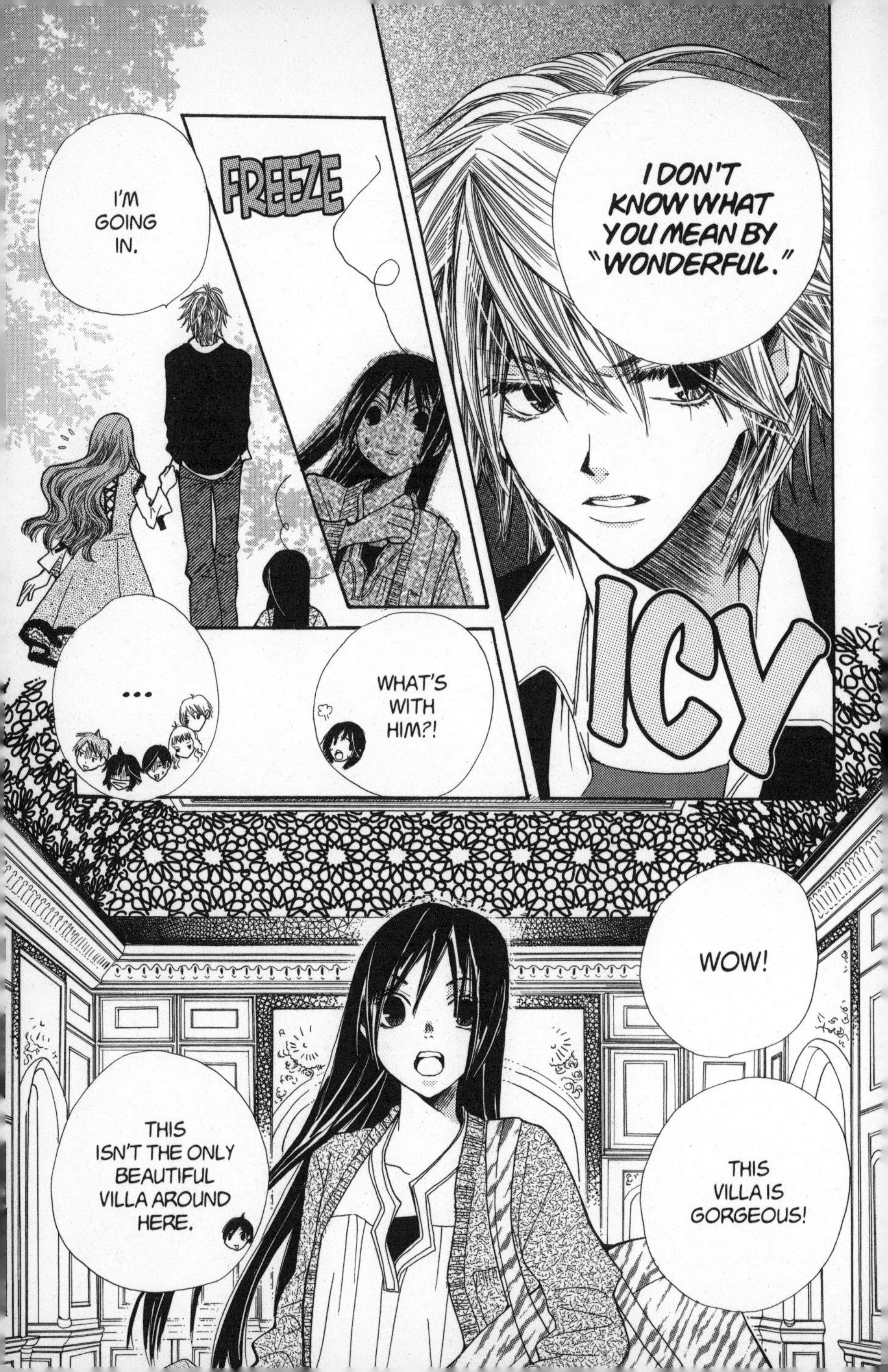

I DON'T KNOW WHAT YOU MEAN BY "WONDERFUL."
ICY
FREEZE
I'M GOING IN.
WHAT'S WITH HIM?!
...
WOW!
THIS VILLA IS GORGEOUS!
THIS ISN'T THE ONLY BEAUTIFUL VILLA AROUND HERE.

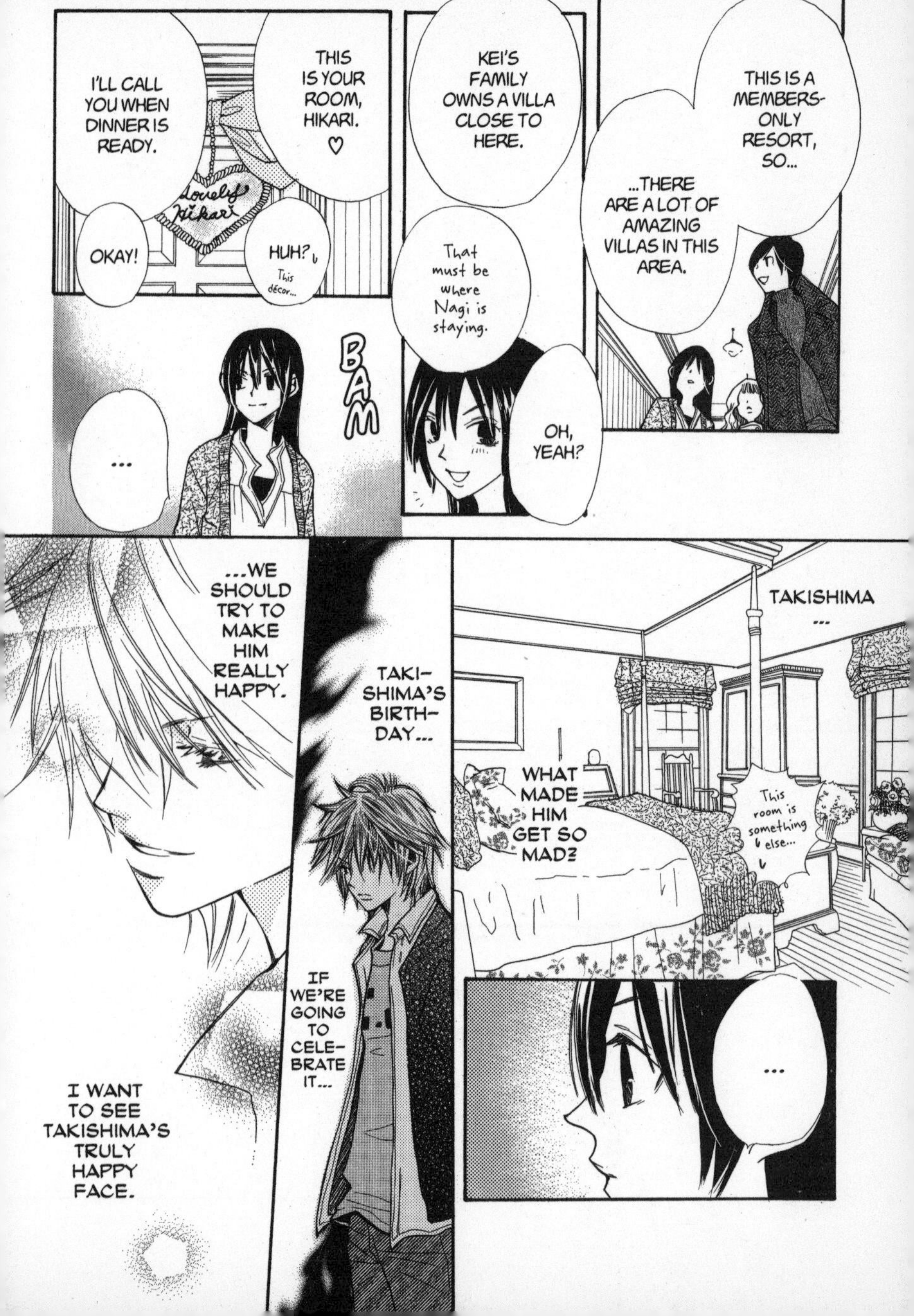
THIS IS A MEMBERS-ONLY RESORT, SO...
...THERE ARE A LOT OF AMAZING VILLAS IN THIS AREA.
KEI'S FAMILY OWNS A VILLA CLOSE TO HERE.
That must be where Nagi is staying.
OH, YEAH?
THIS IS YOUR ROOM, HIKARI. ♡
I'LL CALL YOU WHEN DINNER IS READY.
Lovely Hikari
HUH?
This décor...
OKAY!
BAM
...
TAKISHIMA...
This room is something else...
WHAT MADE HIM GET SO MAD?
...
TAKISHIMA'S BIRTHDAY...
IF WE'RE GOING TO CELEBRATE IT...
...WE SHOULD TRY TO MAKE HIM REALLY HAPPY.
I WANT TO SEE TAKISHIMA'S TRULY HAPPY FACE.

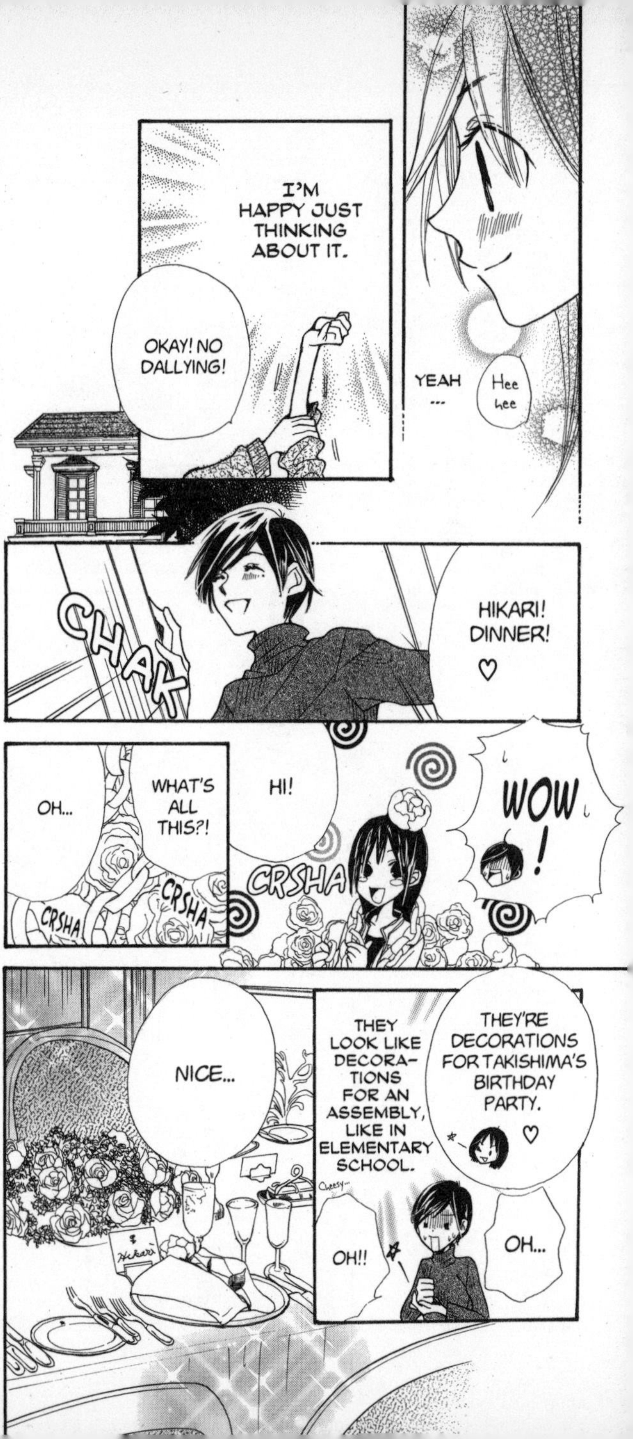
YEAH ...
Hee hee
I'M HAPPY JUST THINKING ABOUT IT.
OKAY! NO DALLYING!
HIKARI! DINNER! ♡
CHAK
WOW!
HI!
CRSHA
WHAT'S ALL THIS?!
OH...
CRSHA
CRSHA
THEY'RE DECORATIONS FOR TAKISHIMA'S BIRTHDAY PARTY. ♡
OH...
THEY LOOK LIKE DECORATIONS FOR AN ASSEMBLY, LIKE IN ELEMENTARY SCHOOL.
Cheesy...
OH!!
NICE...
Hikari

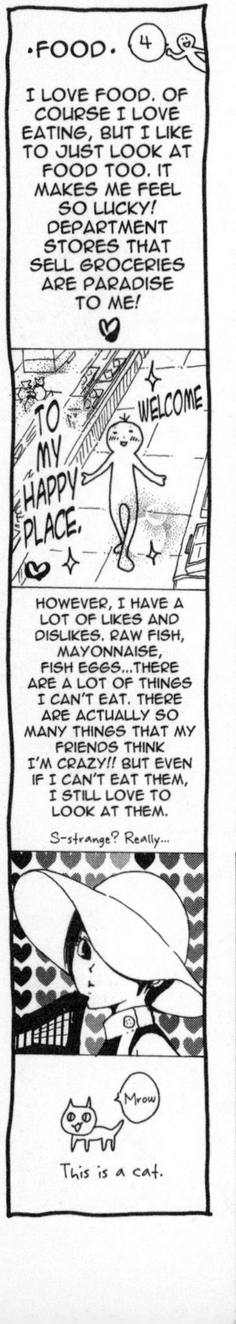
•FOOD• 4
I LOVE FOOD. OF COURSE I LOVE EATING, BUT I LIKE TO JUST LOOK AT FOOD TOO. IT MAKES ME FEEL SO LUCKY! DEPARTMENT STORES THAT SELL GROCERIES ARE PARADISE TO ME! ♥
WELCOME
TO MY HAPPY PLACE.
HOWEVER, I HAVE A LOT OF LIKES AND DISLIKES. RAW FISH, MAYONNAISE, FISH EGGS...THERE ARE A LOT OF THINGS I CAN'T EAT. THERE ARE ACTUALLY SO MANY THINGS THAT MY FRIENDS THINK I'M CRAZY!! BUT EVEN IF I CAN'T EAT THEM, I STILL LOVE TO LOOK AT THEM.
S-strange? Really...
Mrow
This is a cat.

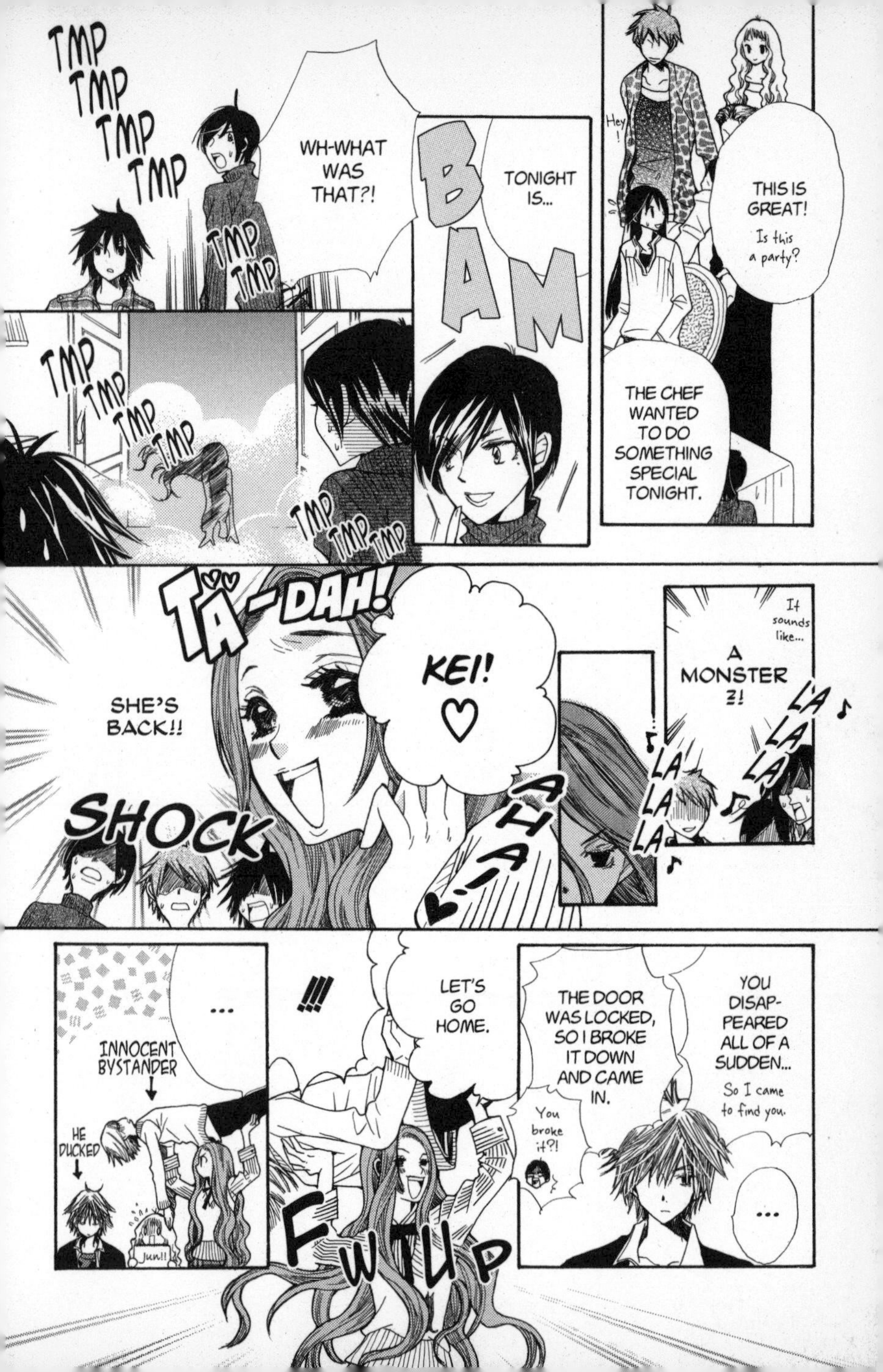
Hey!
THIS IS GREAT!
Is this a party?
THE CHEF WANTED TO DO SOMETHING SPECIAL TONIGHT.
BAM
TONIGHT IS...
TMP TMP TMP TMP
WH-WHAT WAS THAT?!
TMP TMP
TMP TMP TMP TMP
TMP TMP TMP
It sounds like...
A MONSTER?!
LA LA LA
LA LA LA
TA-DAH!
KEI! ♥
SHE'S BACK!!
AHAHA ♥
SHOCK
YOU DISAPPEARED ALL OF A SUDDEN...
So I came to find you.
THE DOOR WAS LOCKED, SO I BROKE IT DOWN AND CAME IN.
You broke it?!
...
LET'S GO HOME.
!!!
FWUP
...
INNOCENT BYSTANDER
HE DUCKED
Jun!!

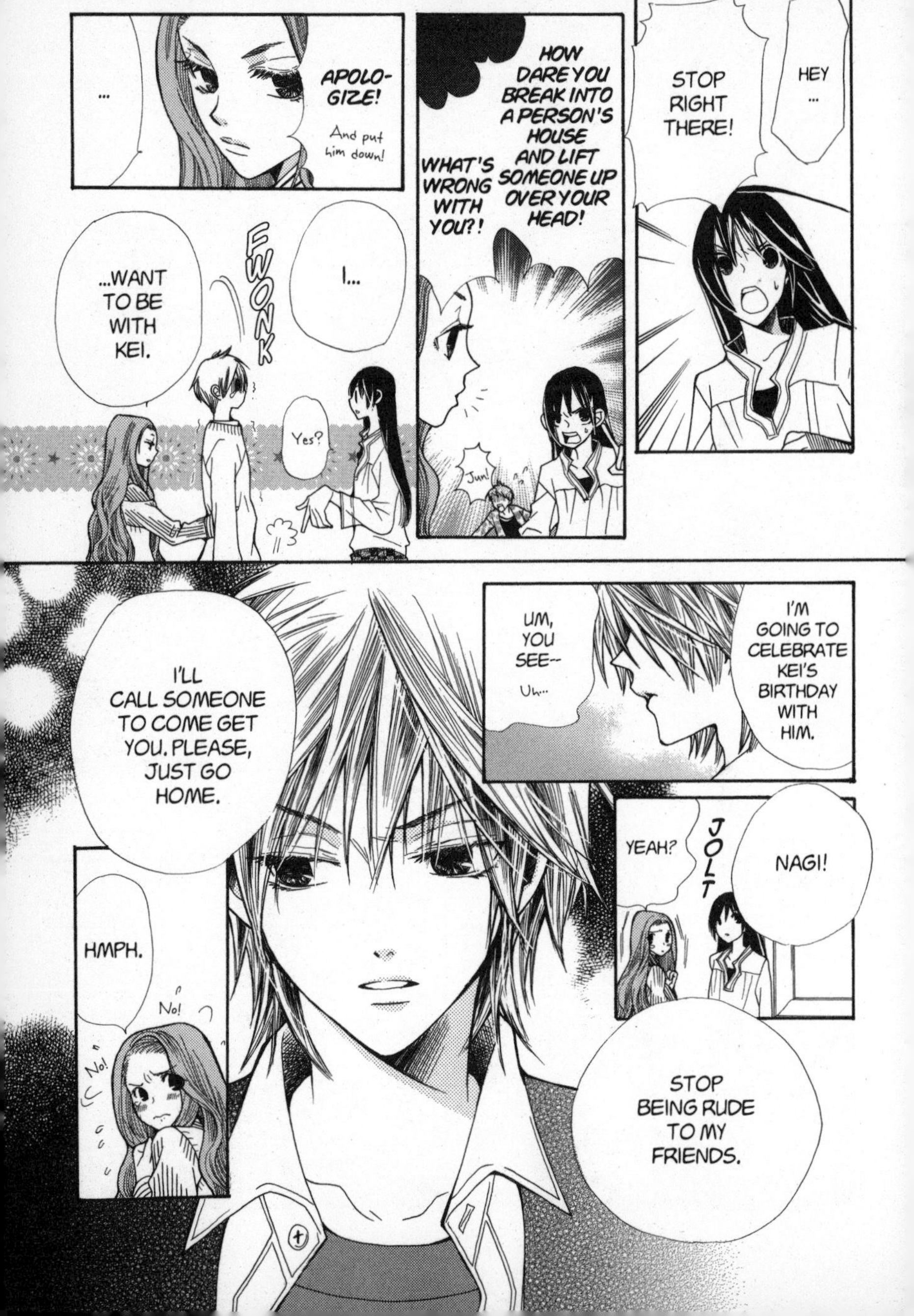
HEY ...
STOP RIGHT THERE!
HOW DARE YOU BREAK INTO A PERSON'S HOUSE AND LIFT SOMEONE UP OVER YOUR HEAD!
WHAT'S WRONG WITH YOU?!
Jun!
APOLO-GIZE!
And put him down!
...
I...
FWONK
...WANT TO BE WITH KEI.
Yes?
I'M GOING TO CELEBRATE KEI'S BIRTHDAY WITH HIM.
UM, YOU SEE--
Uh...
NAGI!
JOLT
YEAH?
STOP BEING RUDE TO MY FRIENDS.
I'LL CALL SOMEONE TO COME GET YOU. PLEASE, JUST GO HOME.
HMPH.
No!
No!

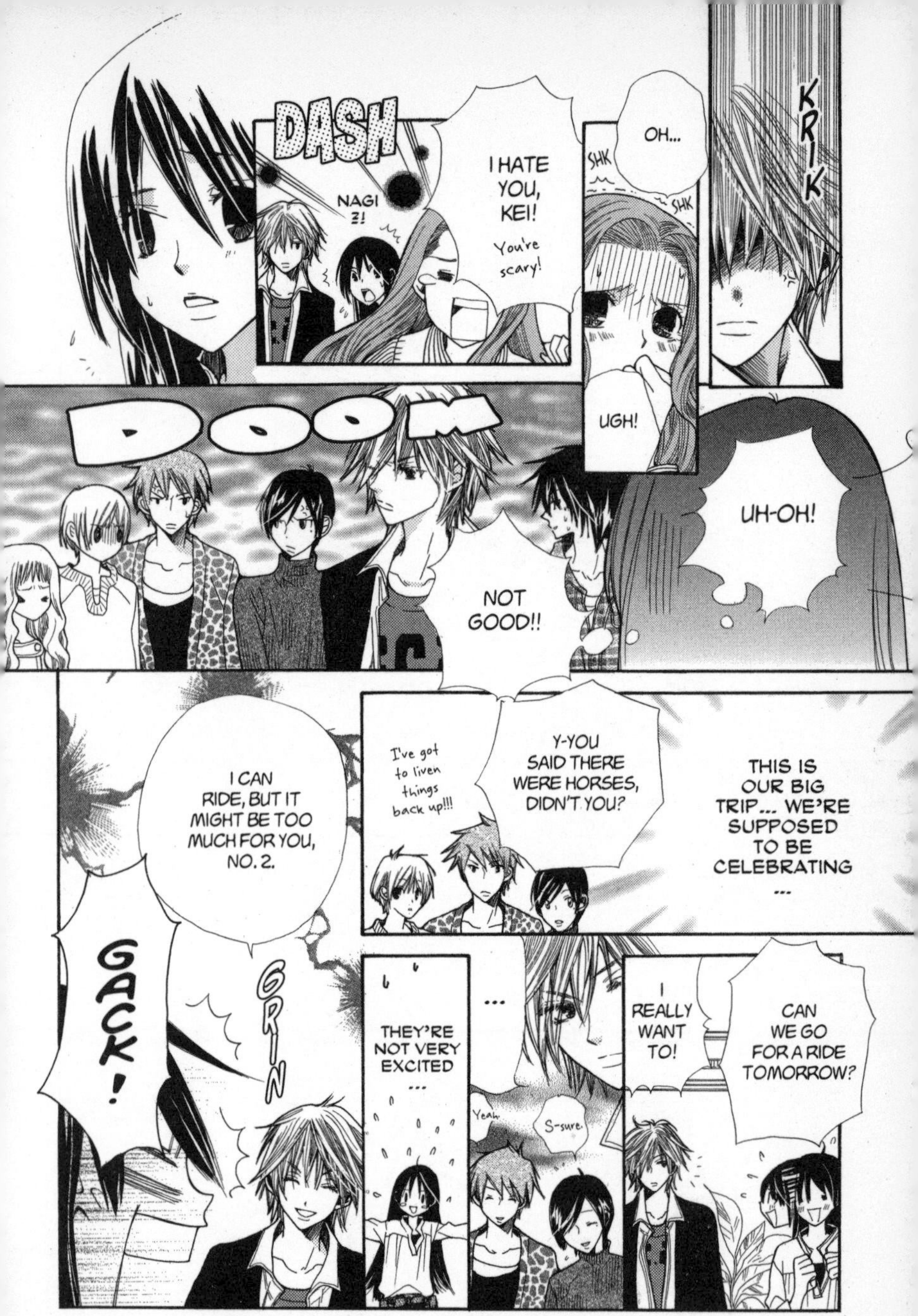
KRIK
OH...
SHK
SHK
UGH!
DASH
I HATE YOU, KEI!
You're scary!
NAGI Z!
UH-OH!
NOT GOOD!!
DOOM
THIS IS OUR BIG TRIP... WE'RE SUPPOSED TO BE CELEBRATING ...
Y-YOU SAID THERE WERE HORSES, DIDN'T YOU?
I've got to liven things back up!!!
CAN WE GO FOR A RIDE TOMORROW?
I REALLY WANT TO!
...
S-sure.
Yeah
THEY'RE NOT VERY EXCITED ...
I CAN RIDE, BUT IT MIGHT BE TOO MUCH FOR YOU, NO. 2.
GRIN
GACK!

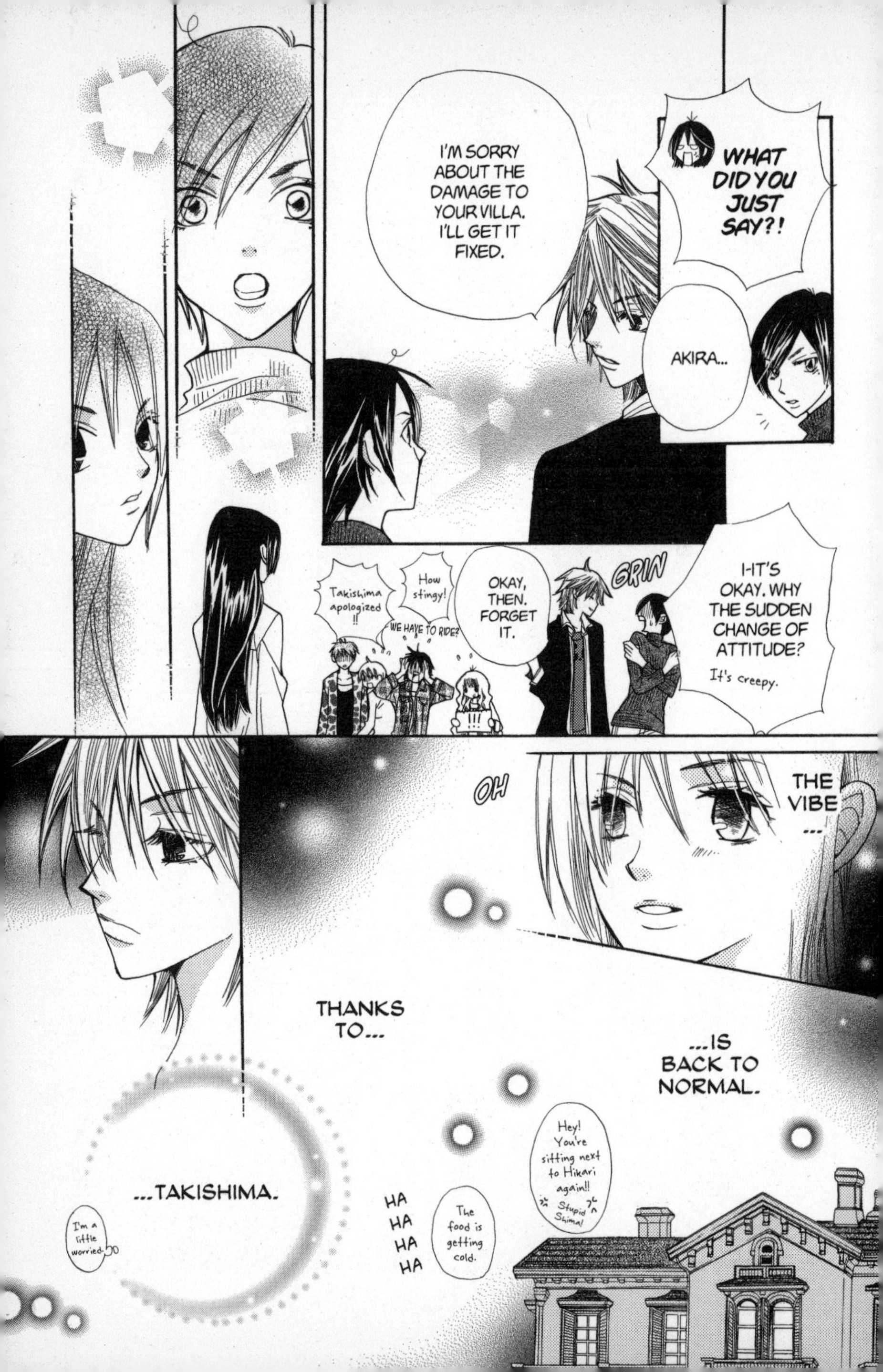
WHAT DID YOU JUST SAY?!
AKIRA...
I'M SORRY ABOUT THE DAMAGE TO YOUR VILLA. I'LL GET IT FIXED.
I-IT'S OKAY. WHY THE SUDDEN CHANGE OF ATTITUDE?
It's creepy.
GRIN
OKAY, THEN. FORGET IT.
How stingy!
WE HAVE TO RIDE?
Takishima apologized!!
THE VIBE...
OH
...IS BACK TO NORMAL.
THANKS TO...
Hey! You're sitting next to Hikari again!!
Stupid Shima!
The food is getting cold.
HA HA HA HA
...TAKISHIMA.
I'm a little worried.

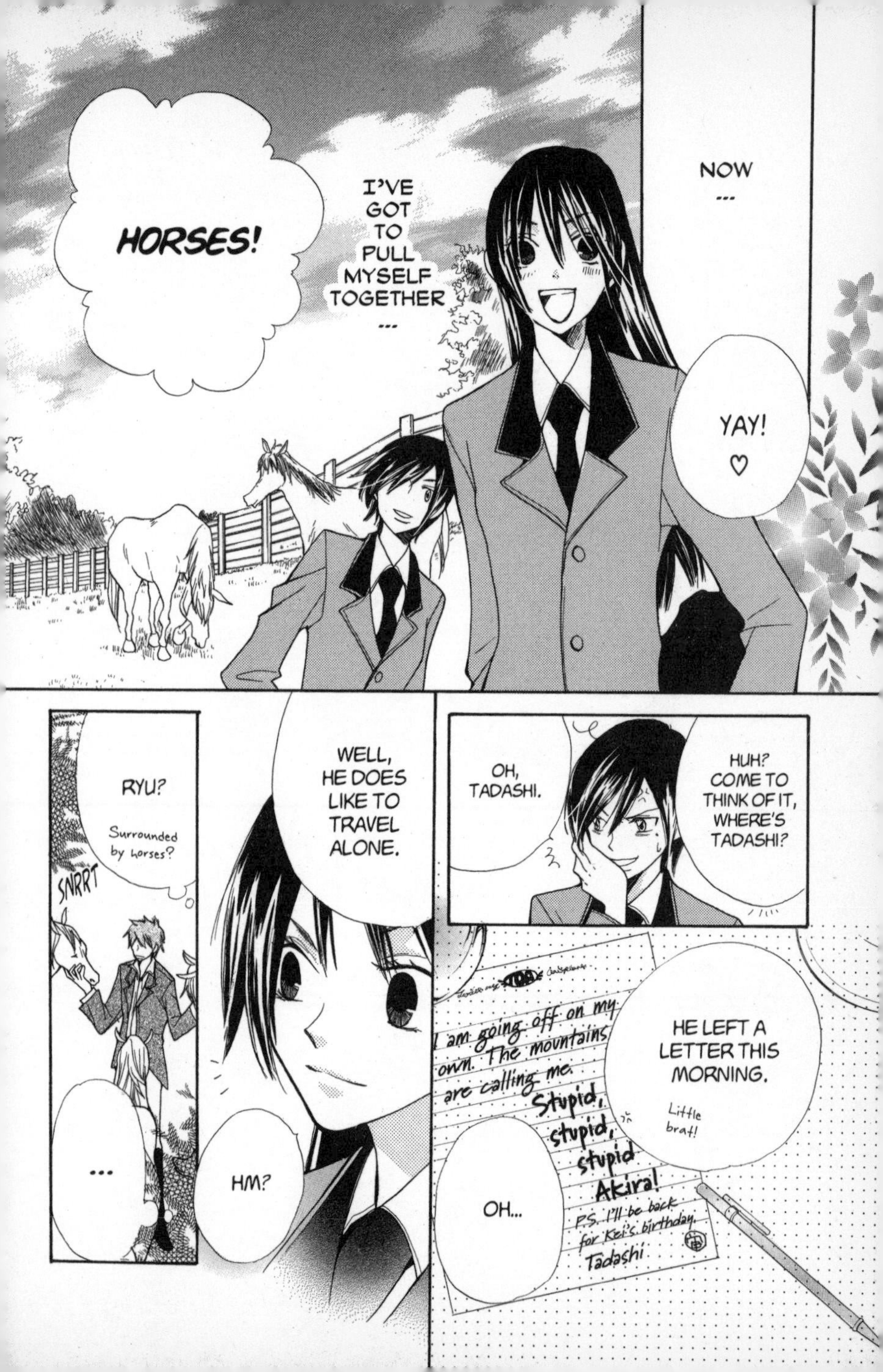
NOW ---
YAY! ♡
I'VE GOT TO PULL MYSELF TOGETHER ---
HORSES!
HUH? COME TO THINK OF IT, WHERE'S TADASHI?
OH, TADASHI.
HE LEFT A LETTER THIS MORNING.
Little brat!
I am going off on my own. The mountains are calling me.
Stupid, stupid, stupid Akira!
P.S. I'll be back for Kei's birthday.
Tadashi
OH...
WELL, HE DOES LIKE TO TRAVEL ALONE.
HM?
RYU?
Surrounded by horses?
SNRRT
...

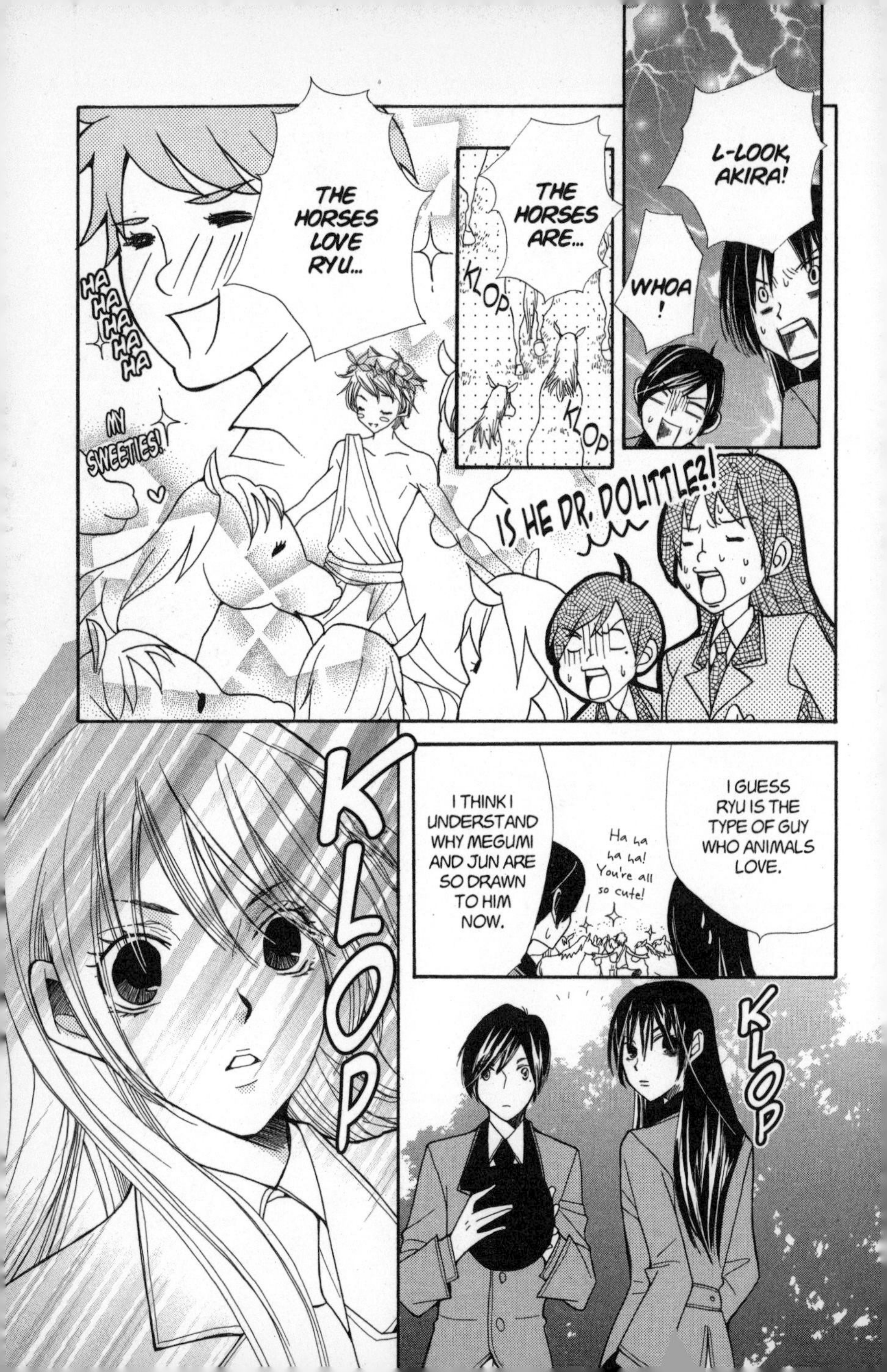
L-LOOK, AKIRA!
WHOA!
THE HORSES ARE...
KLOP
KLOP
THE HORSES LOVE RYU...
IS HE DR. DOLITTLE?!
HA HA HA HA HA HA
MY SWEETIES!
I GUESS RYU IS THE TYPE OF GUY WHO ANIMALS LOVE.
Ha ha ha ha! You're all so cute!
I THINK I UNDERSTAND WHY MEGUMI AND JUN ARE SO DRAWN TO HIM NOW.
KLOP
KLOP

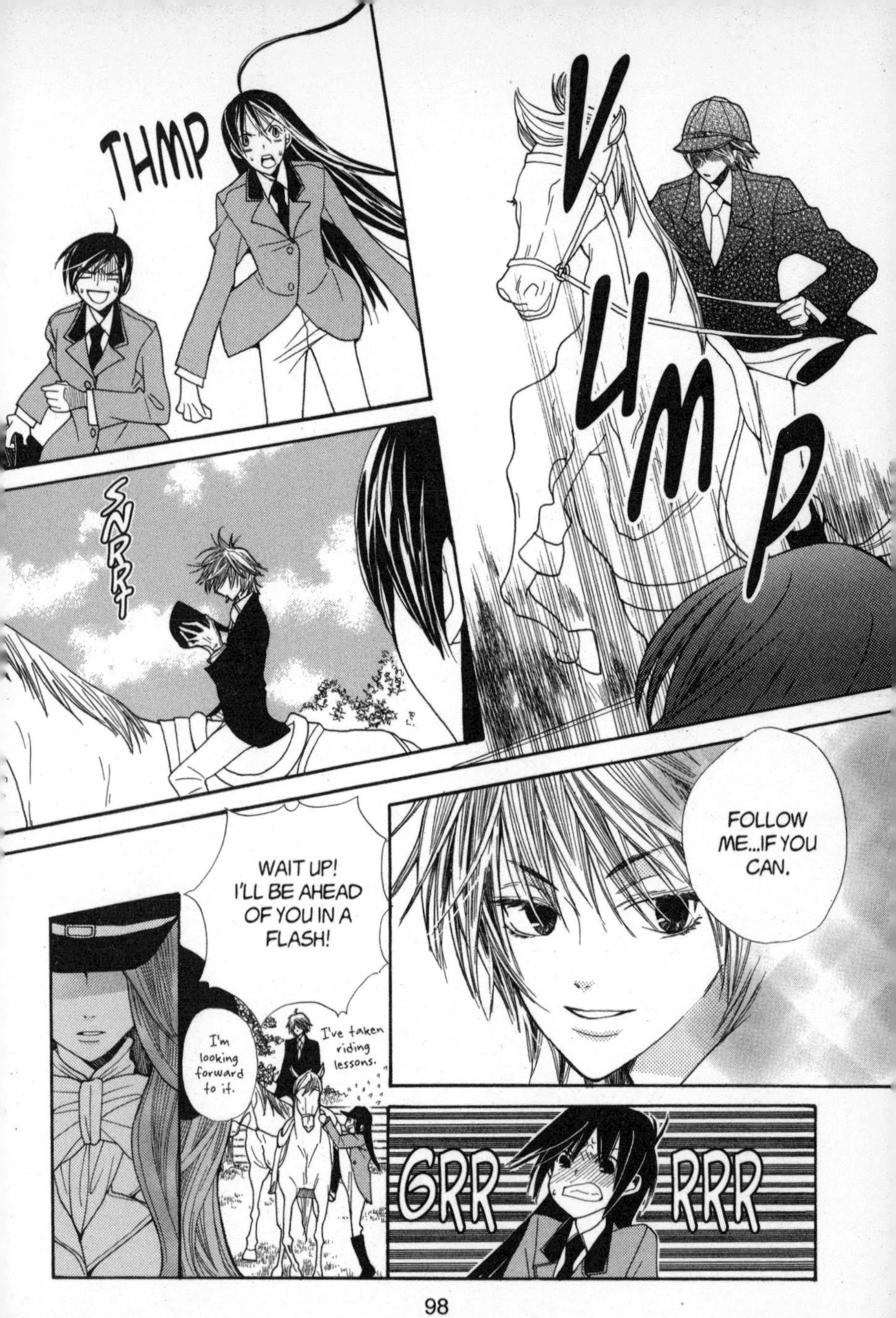
VUMP
THMP
SNRRT
FOLLOW ME...IF YOU CAN.
GRR RRR
WAIT UP! I'LL BE AHEAD OF YOU IN A FLASH!
I've taken riding lessons.
I'm looking forward to it.

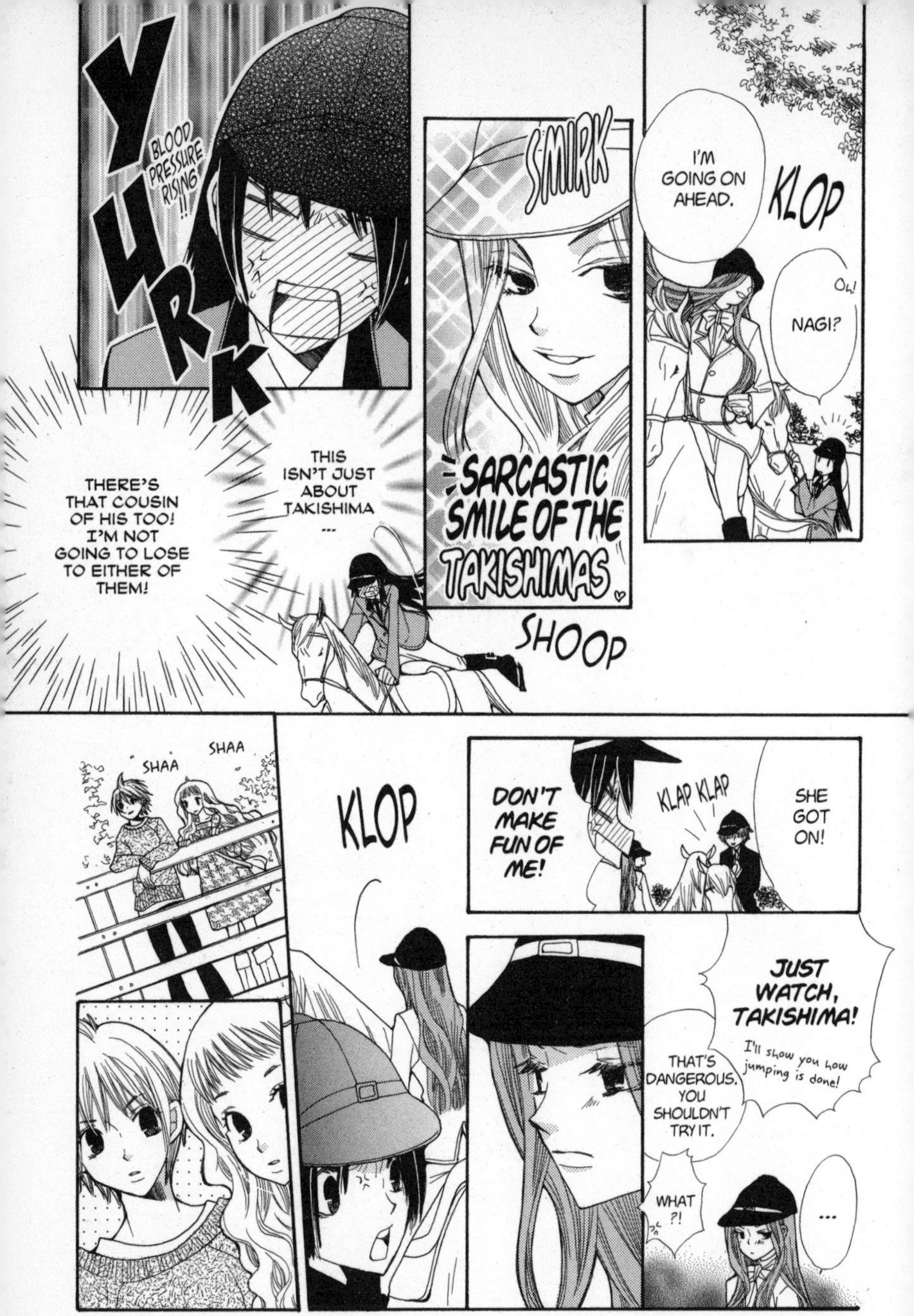
I'M GOING ON AHEAD.
KLOP
OH! NAGI?
SMIRK
SARCASTIC SMILE OF THE TAKISHIMAS ♡
YURK
BLOOD PRESSURE RISING!!
THIS ISN'T JUST ABOUT TAKISHIMA...
THERE'S THAT COUSIN OF HIS TOO! I'M NOT GOING TO LOSE TO EITHER OF THEM!
SHOOP
SHE GOT ON!
KLAP KLAP
DON'T MAKE FUN OF ME!
JUST WATCH, TAKISHIMA!
I'll show you how jumping is done!
THAT'S DANGEROUS. YOU SHOULDN'T TRY IT.
WHAT?!
...
KLOP
SHAA
SHAA

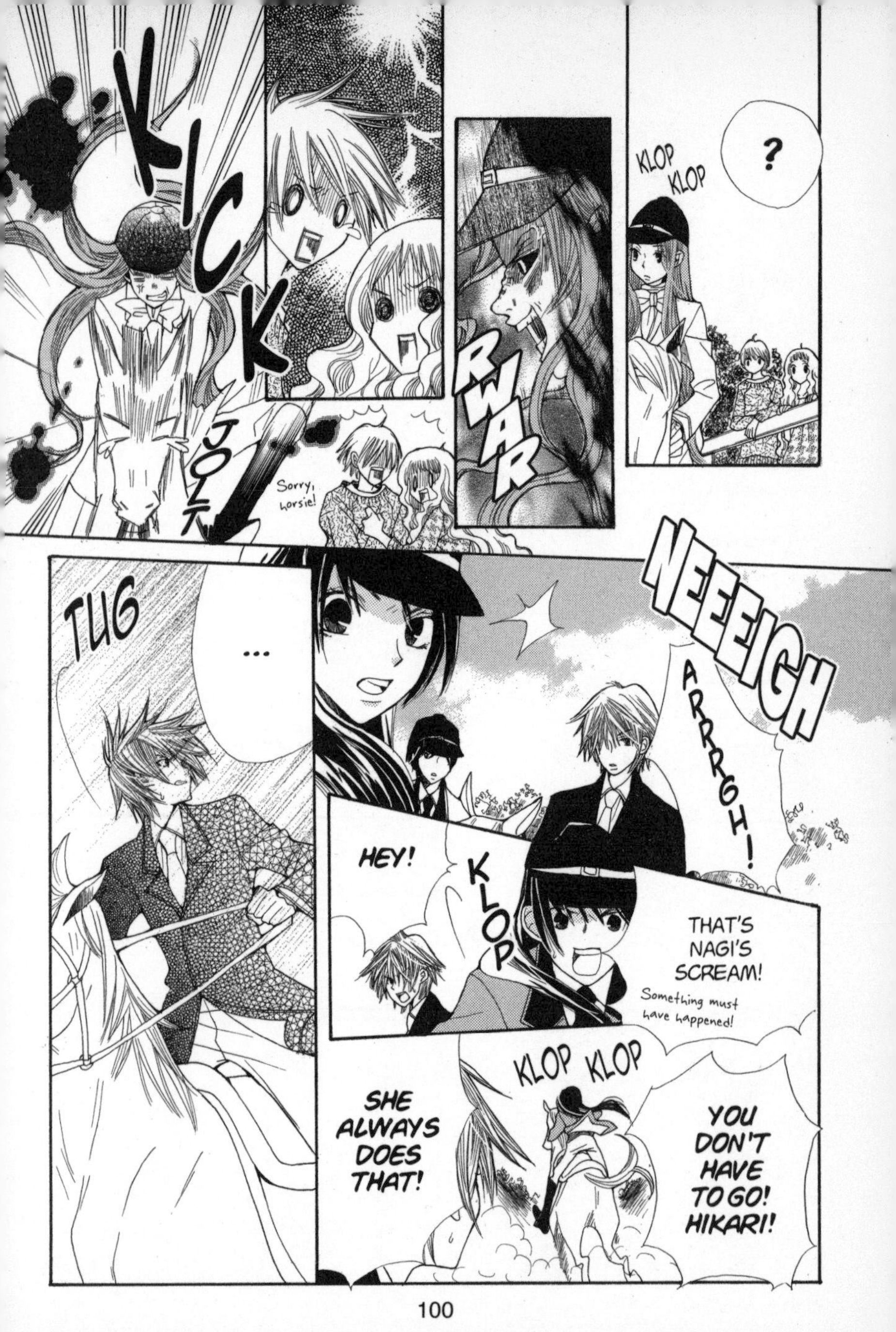

KLOP KLOP
?
RWAR
Sorry, horsie!
KICK
JOLT
NEEEIGH
ARRRGH!
THAT'S NAGI'S SCREAM!
Something must have happened!
KLOP
HEY!
YOU DON'T HAVE TO GO! HIKARI!
KLOP KLOP
SHE ALWAYS DOES THAT!
TUG
...

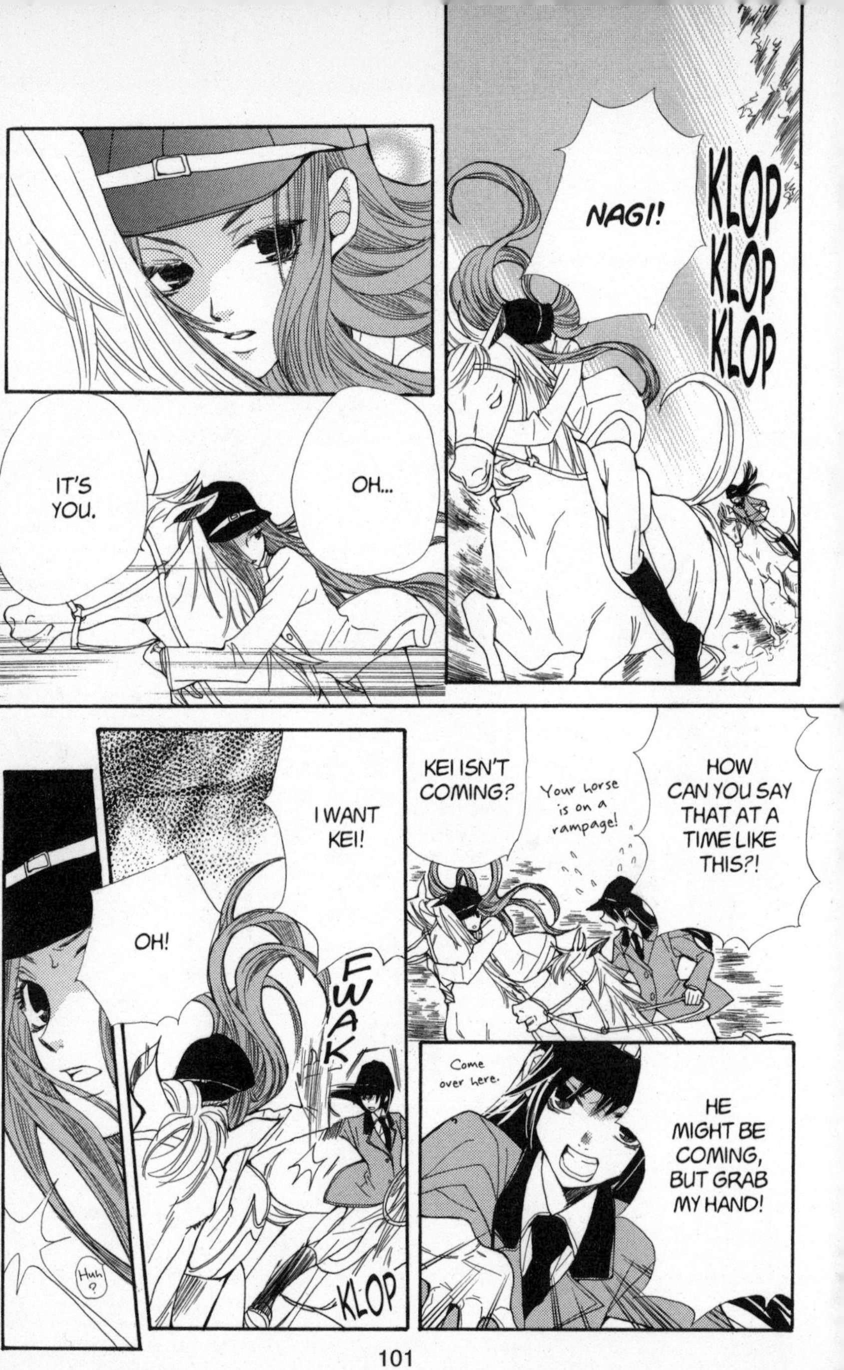
NAGI!
KLOP KLOP KLOP
OH...
IT'S YOU.
HOW CAN YOU SAY THAT AT A TIME LIKE THIS?!
Your horse is on a rampage!
KEI ISN'T COMING?
HE MIGHT BE COMING, BUT GRAB MY HAND!
Come over here.
I WANT KEI!
FWAK
KLOP
OH!
Huh?

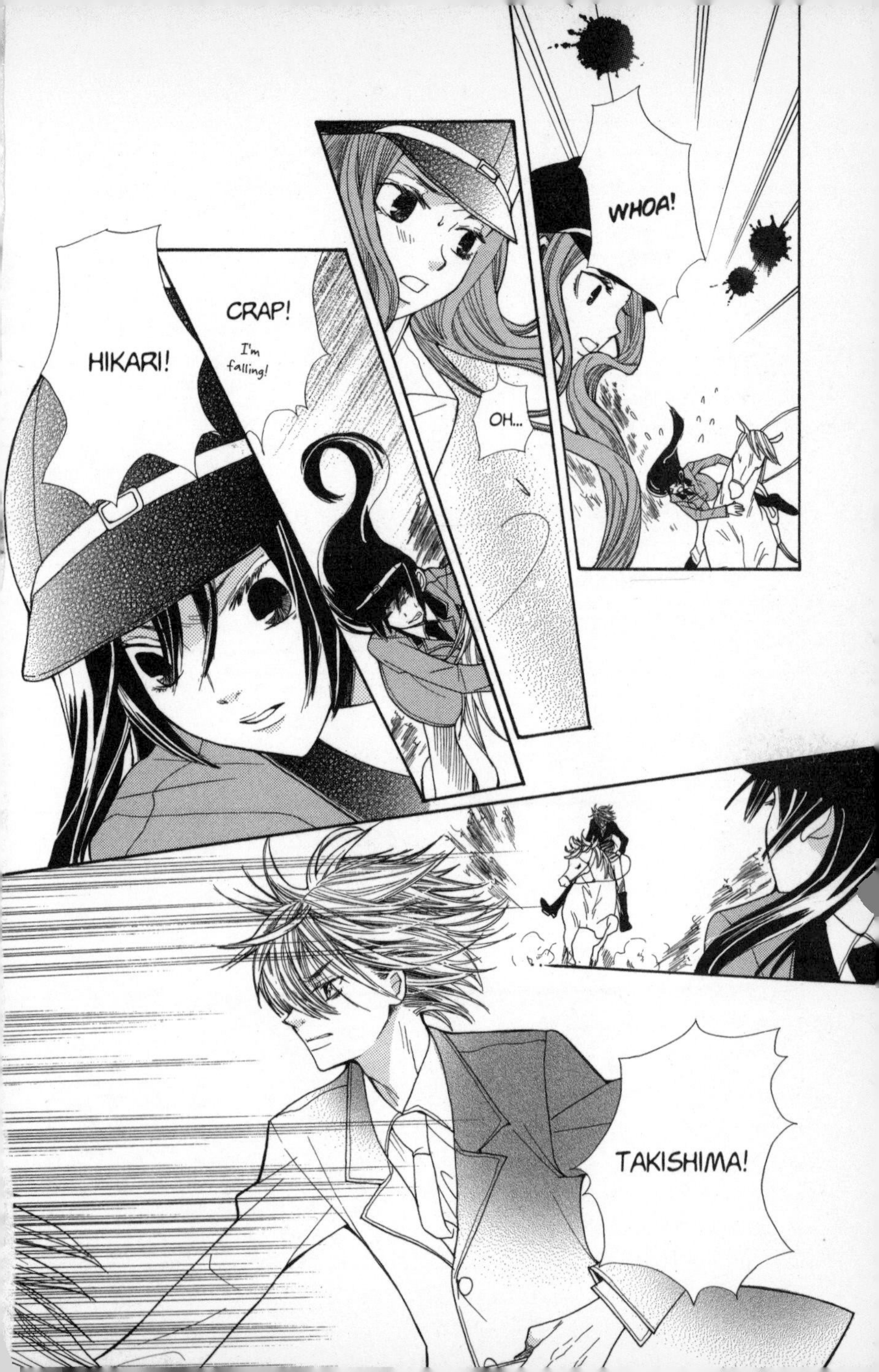
WHOA!
OH...
CRAP!
I'm falling!
HIKARI!
TAKISHIMA!

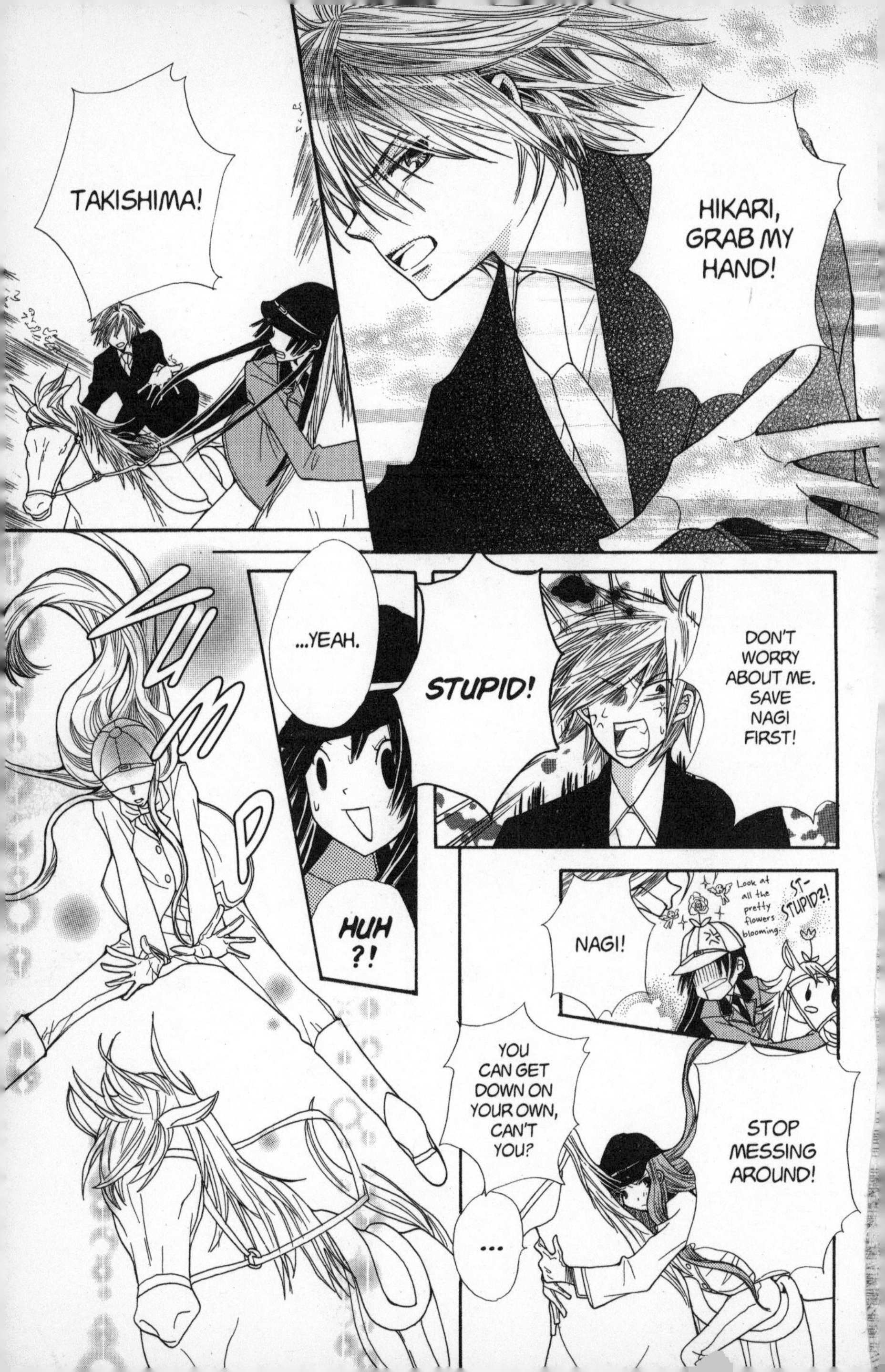
HIKARI, GRAB MY HAND!
TAKISHIMA!
DON'T WORRY ABOUT ME. SAVE NAGI FIRST!
STUPID!
...YEAH.
HUH?!
NAGI!
ST-STUPID?!
Look at all the pretty flowers blooming.
STOP MESSING AROUND!
YOU CAN GET DOWN ON YOUR OWN, CAN'T YOU?
...
VUMP

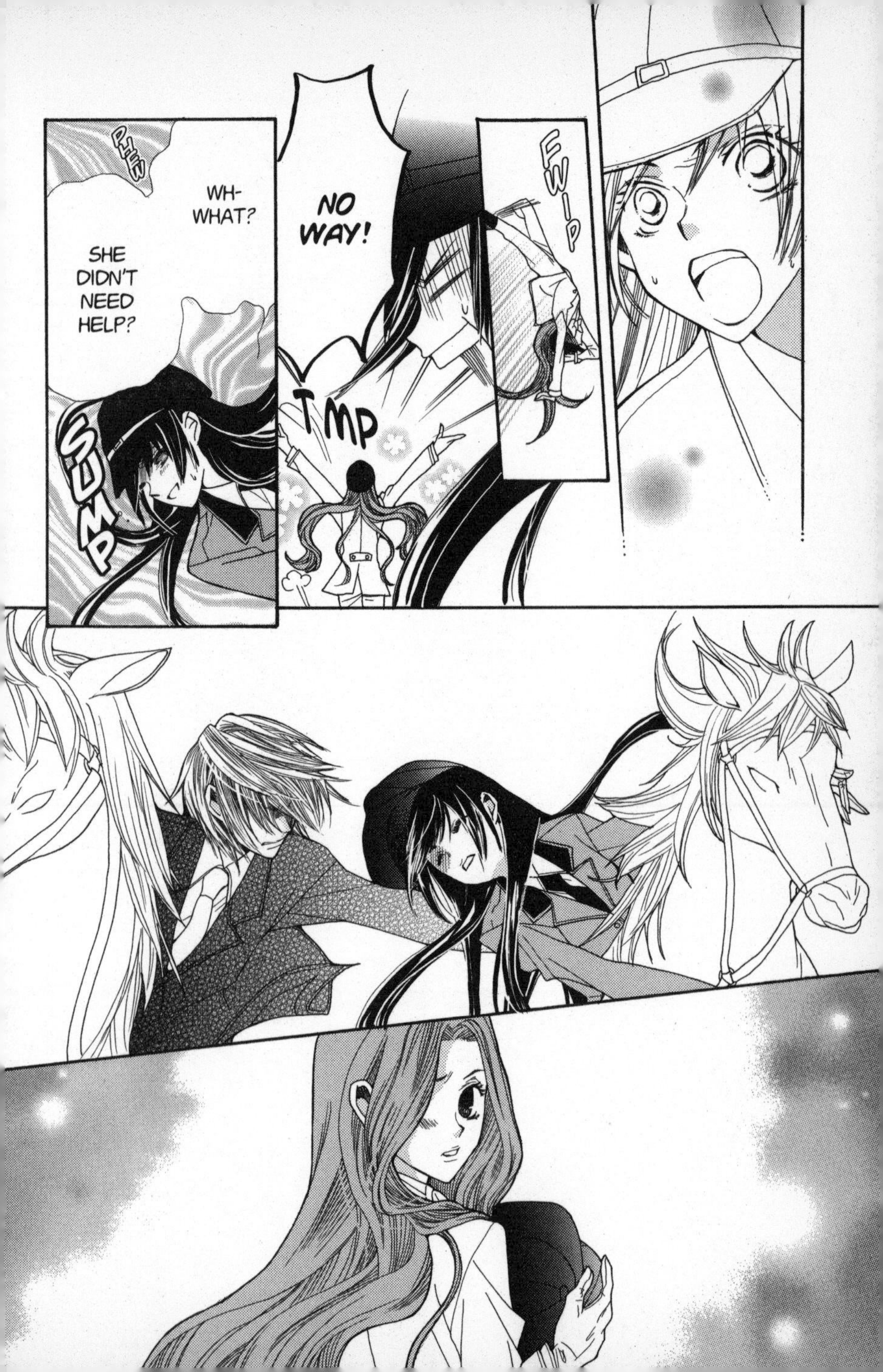
FWIP
NO WAY!
TMP
PHEW
WH-WHAT?
SHE DIDN'T NEED HELP?
SUMP

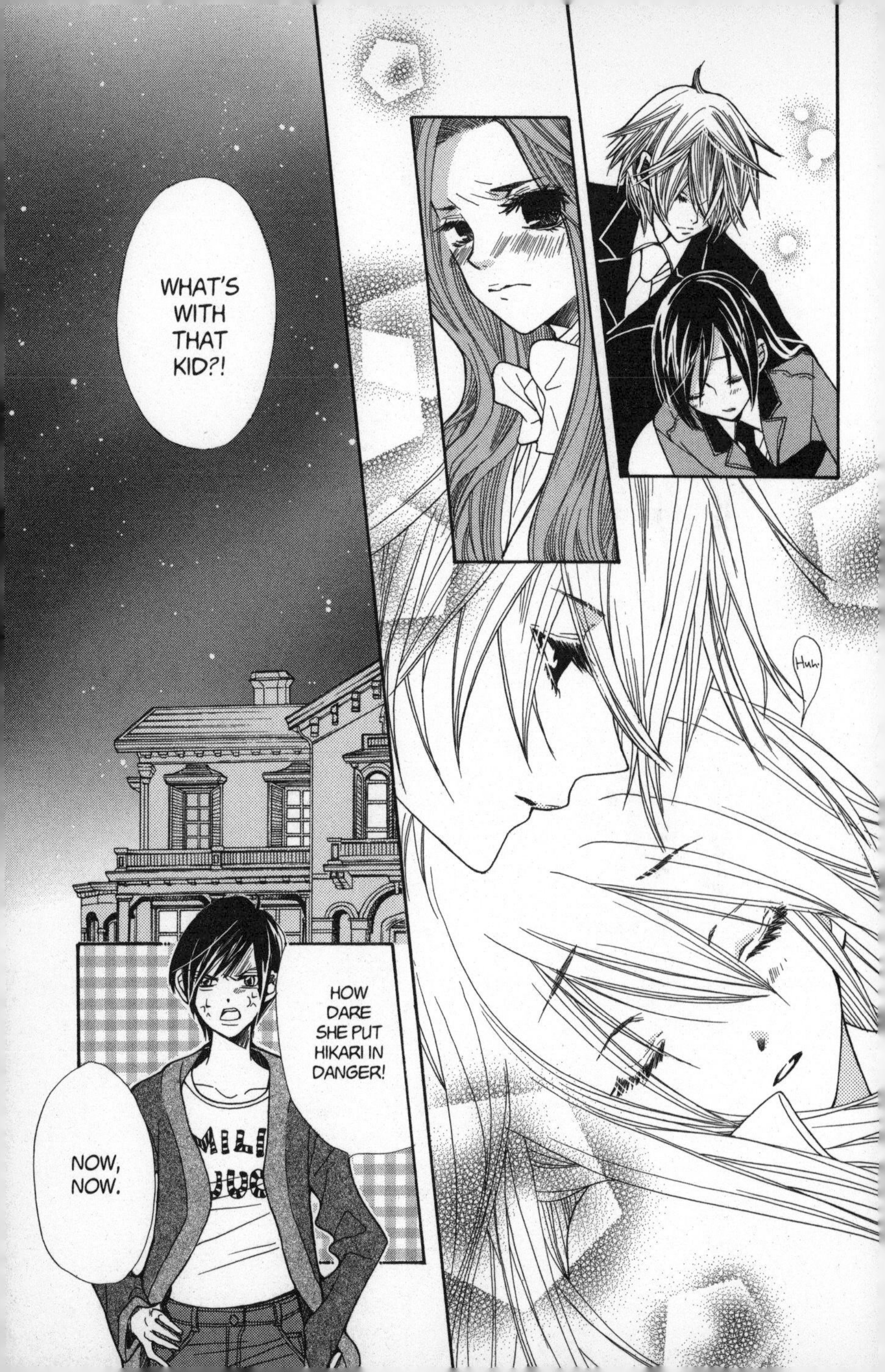
Huh.
WHAT'S WITH THAT KID?!
HOW DARE SHE PUT HIKARI IN DANGER!
NOW, NOW.

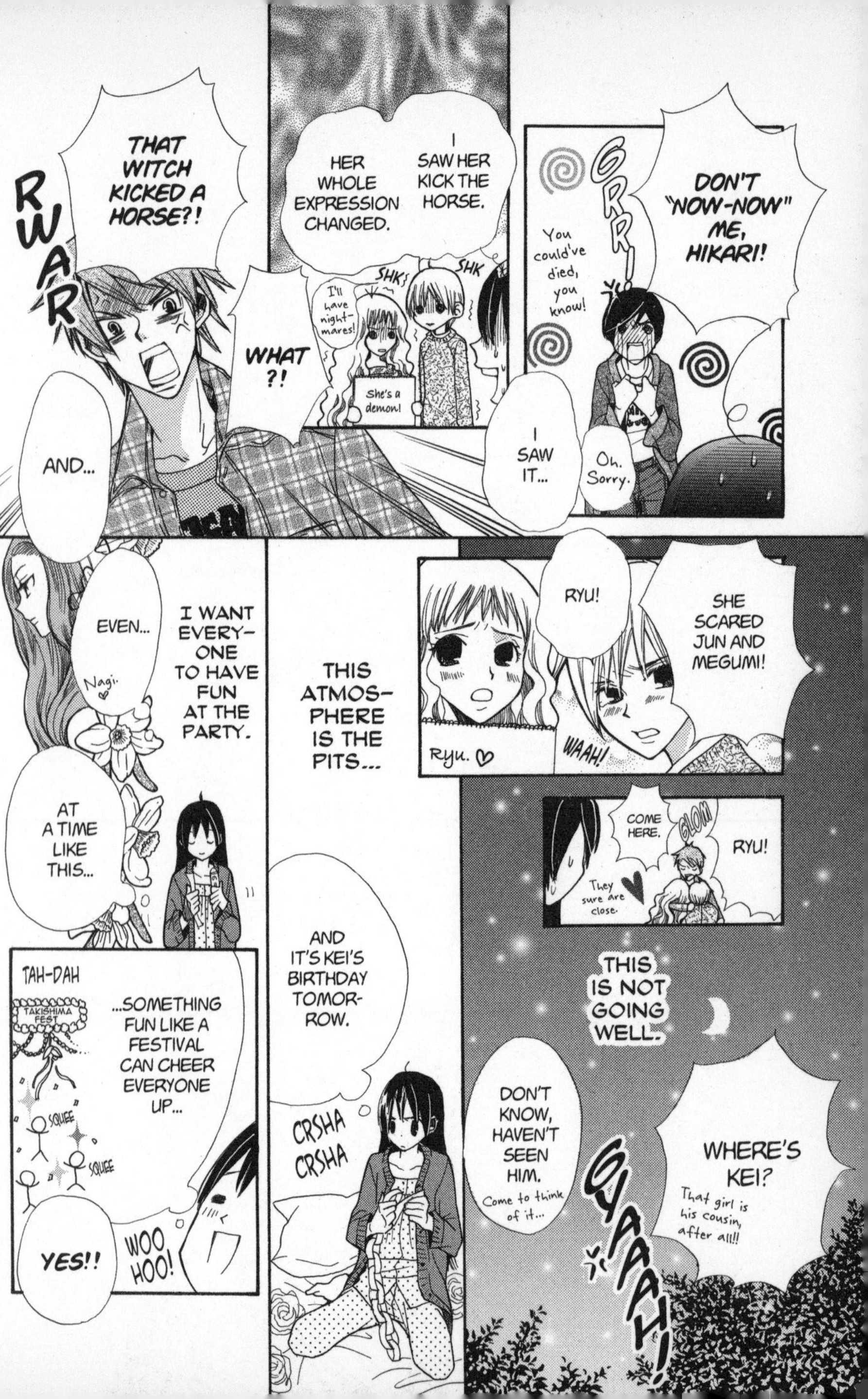
DON'T "NOW-NOW" ME, HIKARI!
GRRR!
You could've died, you know!
I SAW IT...
Oh. Sorry.
I SAW HER KICK THE HORSE.
HER WHOLE EXPRESSION CHANGED.
SHK
SHK
I'll have night-mares!
She's a demon!
WHAT?!
RWAR
THAT WITCH KICKED A HORSE?!
AND...
RYU!
SHE SCARED JUN AND MEGUMI!
WAAH!
Ryu. ♡
RYU!
COME HERE.
GLOM
They sure are close.
THIS ATMOS-PHERE IS THE PITS...
I WANT EVERY-ONE TO HAVE FUN AT THE PARTY.
EVEN...
Nagi. ♡
AT A TIME LIKE THIS...
THIS IS NOT GOING WELL.
WHERE'S KEI?
That girl is his cousin, after all!!
DON'T KNOW, HAVEN'T SEEN HIM.
Come to think of it...
GYAAAH!
AND IT'S KEI'S BIRTHDAY TOMOR-ROW.
CRSHA CRSHA
TAH-DAH
TAKISHIMA FEST
...SOMETHING FUN LIKE A FESTIVAL CAN CHEER EVERYONE UP...
SQUEE
SQUEE
WOO HOO!
YES!!

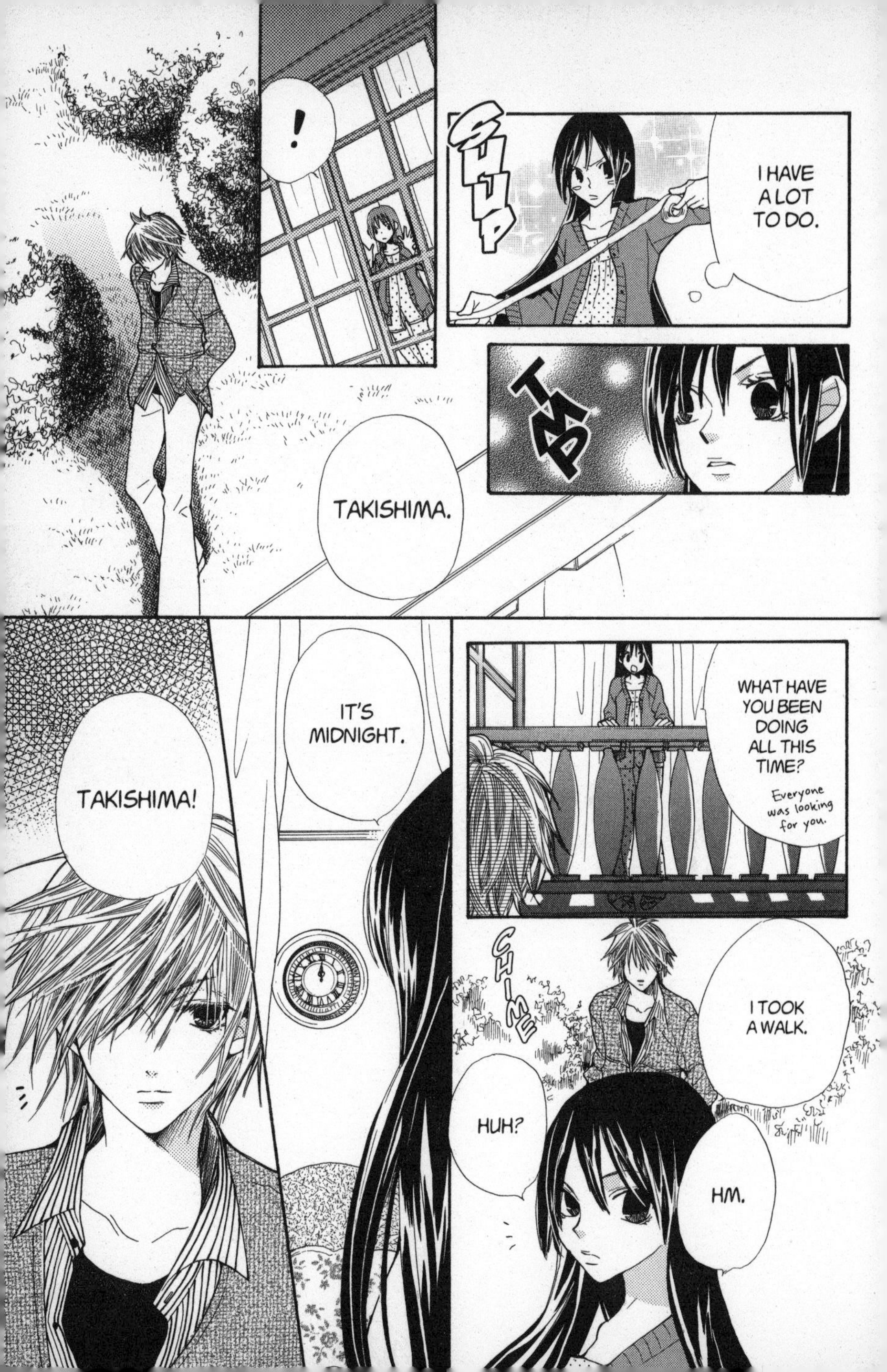
SHUP
I HAVE A LOT TO DO.
TMP
!
TAKISHIMA.
WHAT HAVE YOU BEEN DOING ALL THIS TIME?
Everyone was looking for you.
CHIME
I TOOK A WALK.
HUH?
HM.
IT'S MIDNIGHT.
TAKISHIMA!

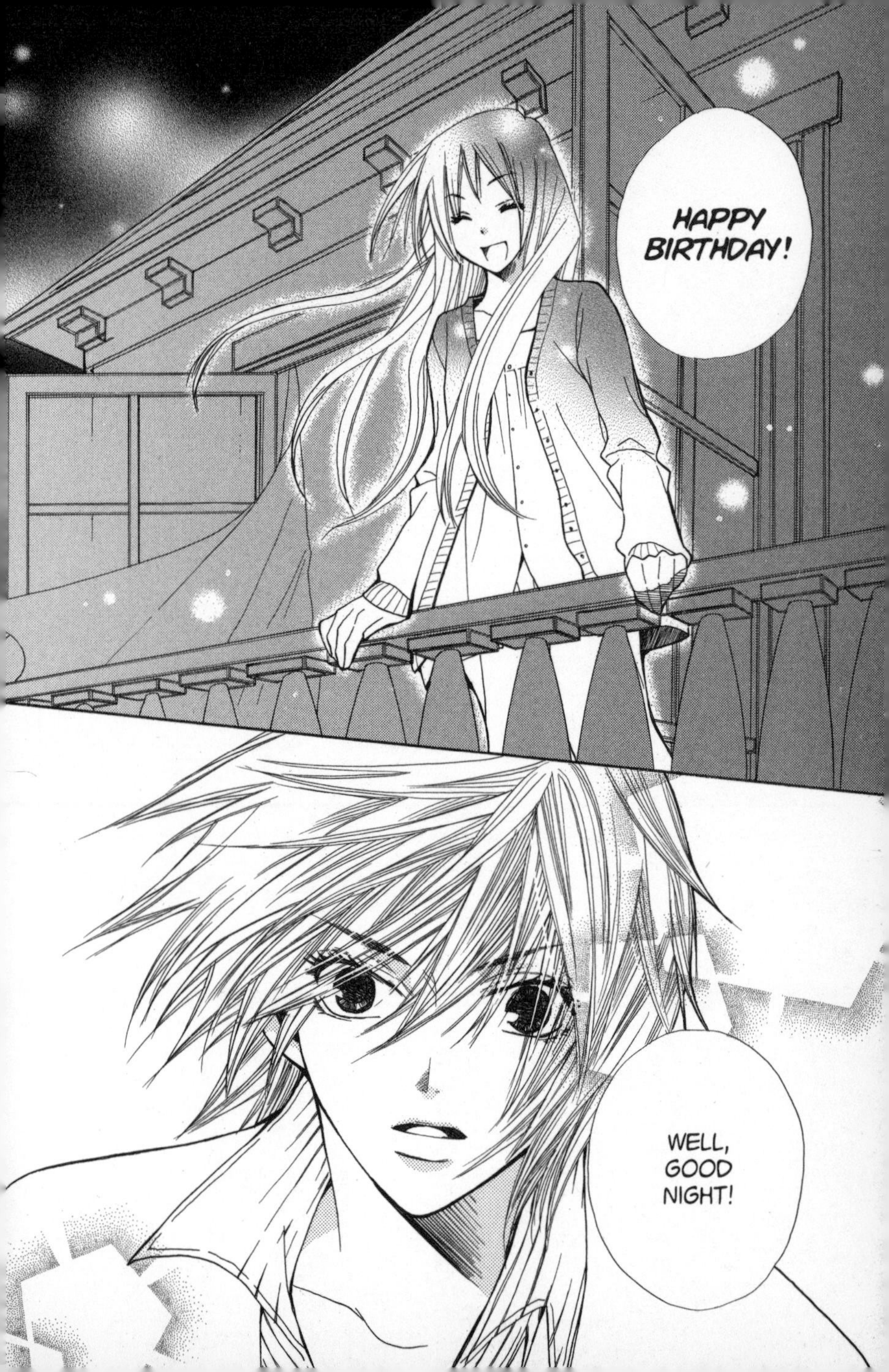
HAPPY BIRTHDAY!
WELL, GOOD NIGHT!

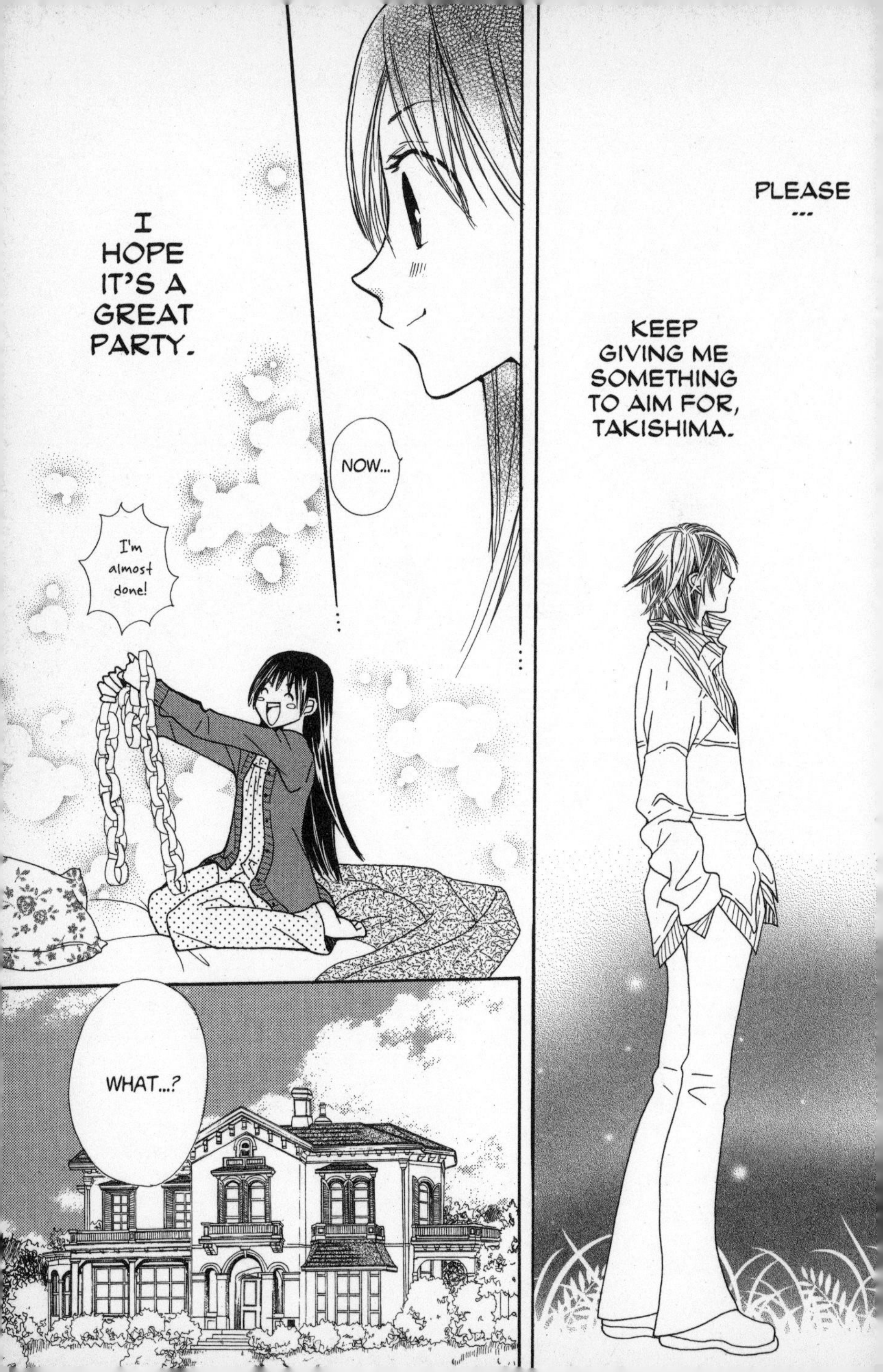
PLEASE ...
KEEP GIVING ME SOMETHING TO AIM FOR, TAKISHIMA.
NOW...
I HOPE IT'S A GREAT PARTY.
I'm almost done!
WHAT...?

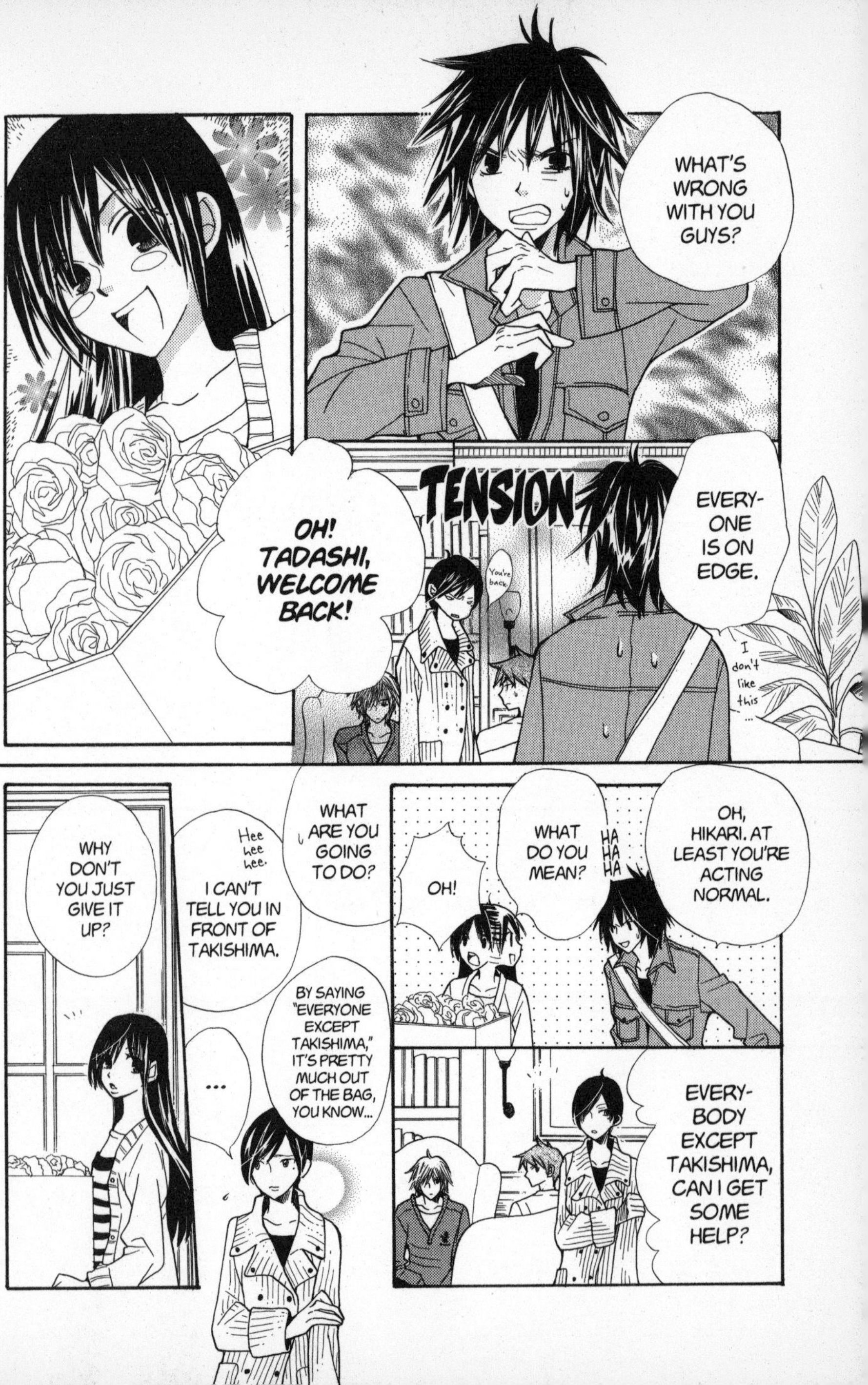
WHAT'S WRONG WITH YOU GUYS?
TENSION
EVERY-ONE IS ON EDGE.
You're back.
I don't like this...
OH! TADASHI, WELCOME BACK!
OH, HIKARI. AT LEAST YOU'RE ACTING NORMAL.
HA HA HA
WHAT DO YOU MEAN?
OH!
EVERY-BODY EXCEPT TAKISHIMA, CAN I GET SOME HELP?
WHAT ARE YOU GOING TO DO?
Hee hee hee.
I CAN'T TELL YOU IN FRONT OF TAKISHIMA.
WHY DON'T YOU JUST GIVE IT UP?
BY SAYING "EVERYONE EXCEPT TAKISHIMA," IT'S PRETTY MUCH OUT OF THE BAG, YOU KNOW...
...

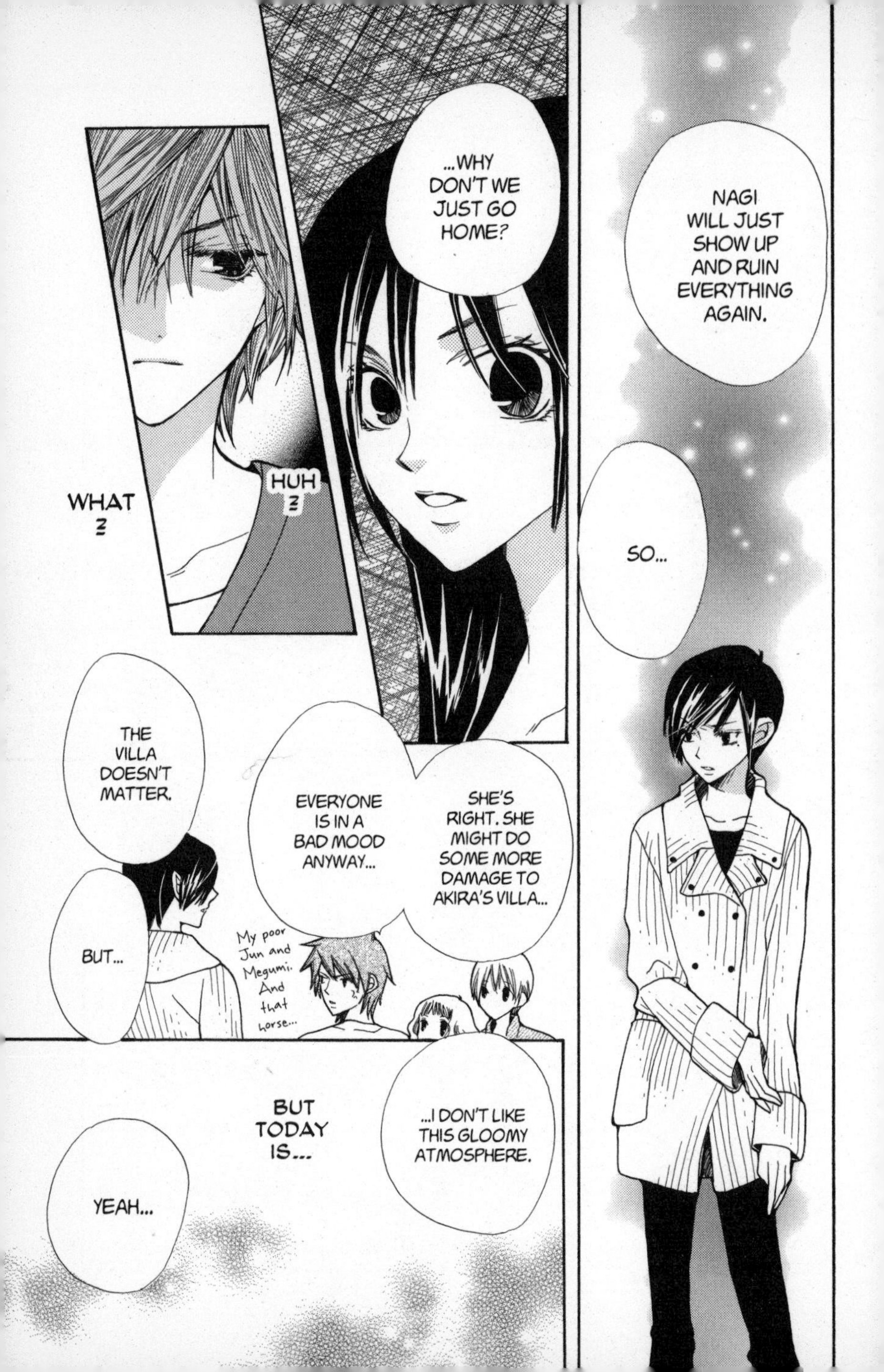
NAGI WILL JUST SHOW UP AND RUIN EVERYTHING AGAIN.
SO...
...WHY DON'T WE JUST GO HOME?
HUH?
WHAT?
SHE'S RIGHT. SHE MIGHT DO SOME MORE DAMAGE TO AKIRA'S VILLA...
EVERYONE IS IN A BAD MOOD ANYWAY...
THE VILLA DOESN'T MATTER.
My poor Jun and Megumi. And that horse...
BUT...
...I DON'T LIKE THIS GLOOMY ATMOSPHERE.
BUT TODAY IS...
YEAH...

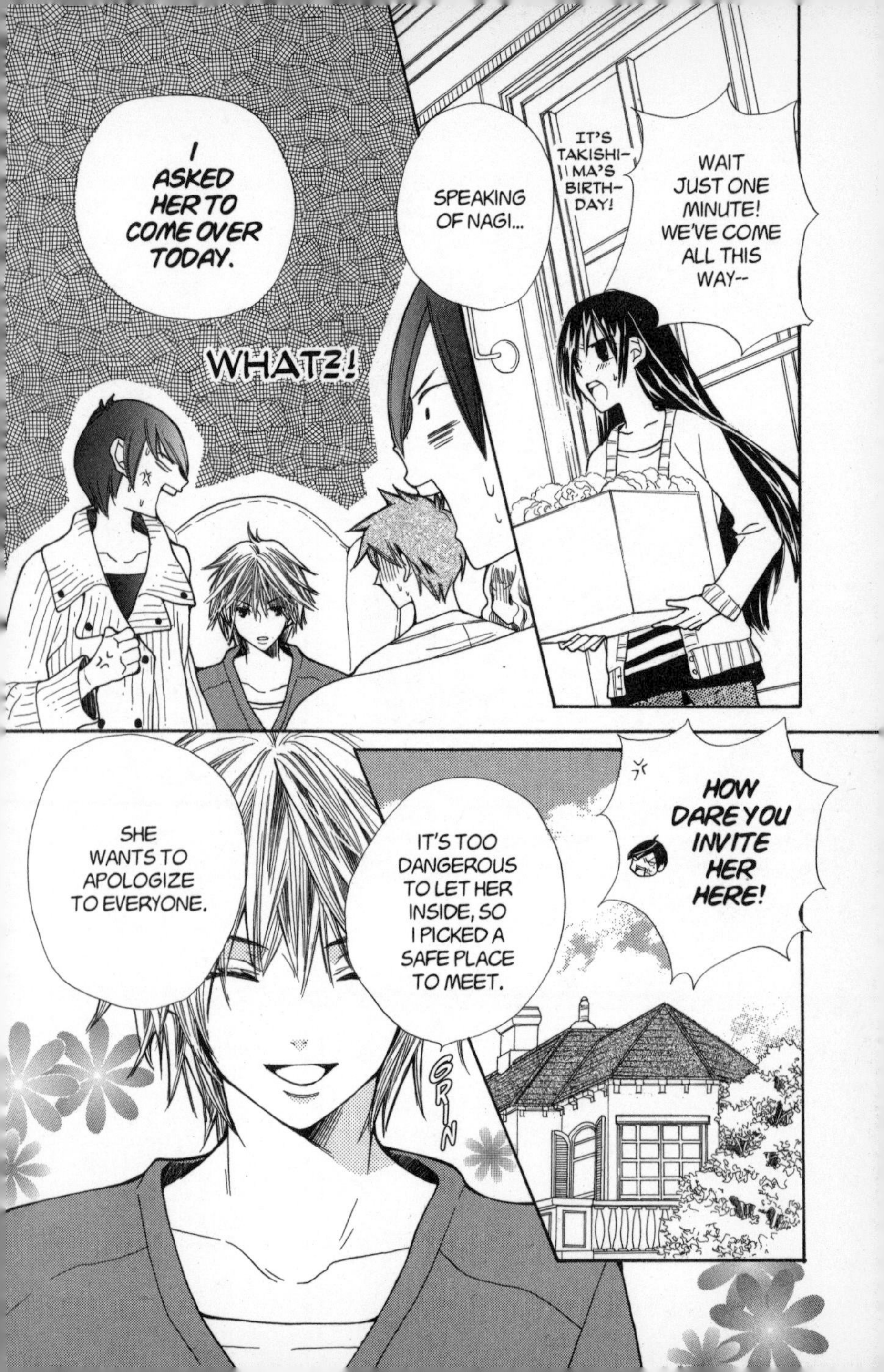
WAIT JUST ONE MINUTE! WE'VE COME ALL THIS WAY--
IT'S TAKISHIMA'S BIRTHDAY!
SPEAKING OF NAGI...
I ASKED HER TO COME OVER TODAY.
WHAT?!
HOW DARE YOU INVITE HER HERE!
IT'S TOO DANGEROUS TO LET HER INSIDE, SO I PICKED A SAFE PLACE TO MEET.
SHE WANTS TO APOLOGIZE TO EVERYONE.
GRIN

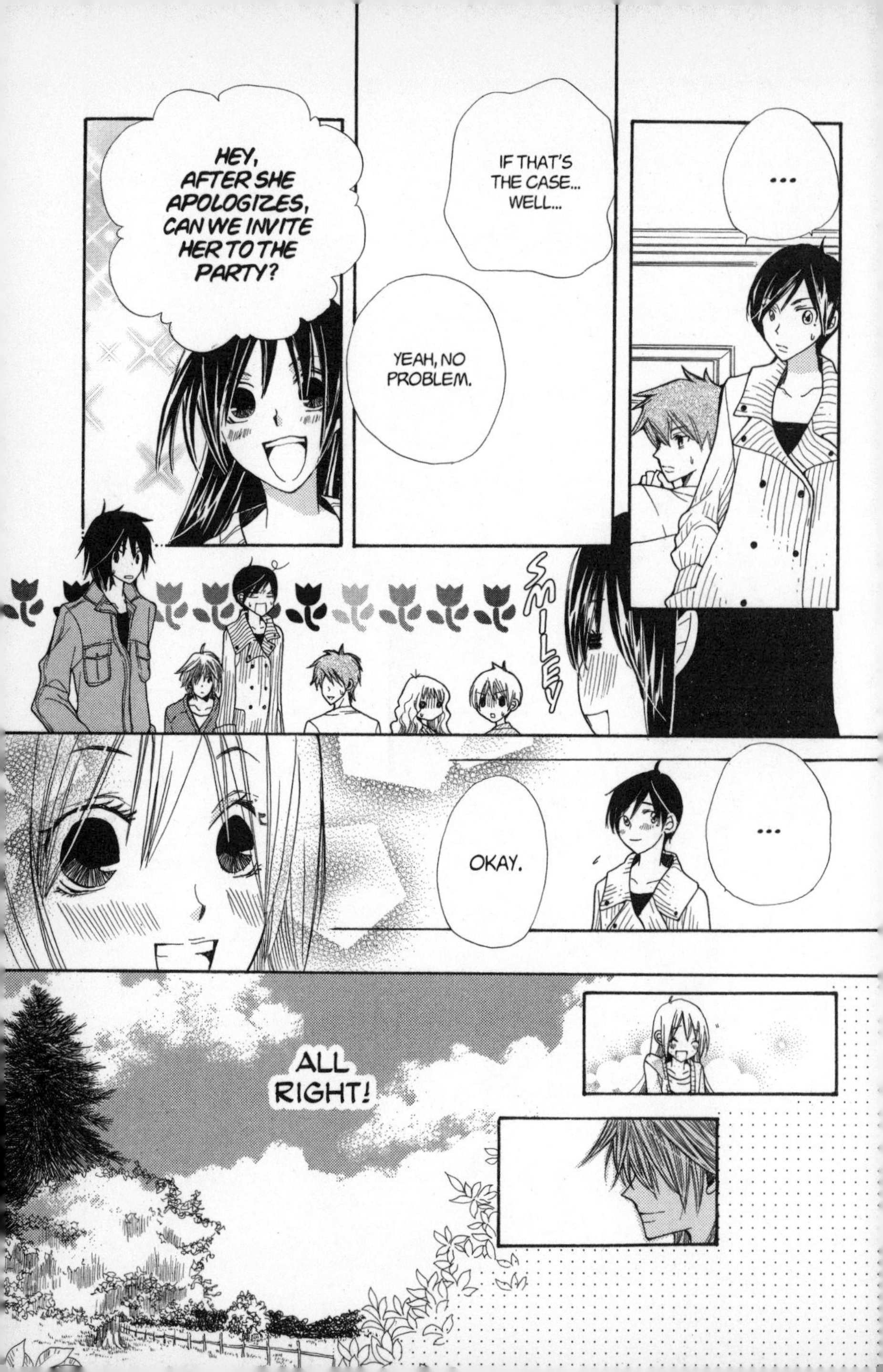
...
IF THAT'S THE CASE... WELL...
YEAH, NO PROBLEM.
HEY, AFTER SHE APOLOGIZES, CAN WE INVITE HER TO THE PARTY?
SMILEY
...
OKAY.
ALL RIGHT!

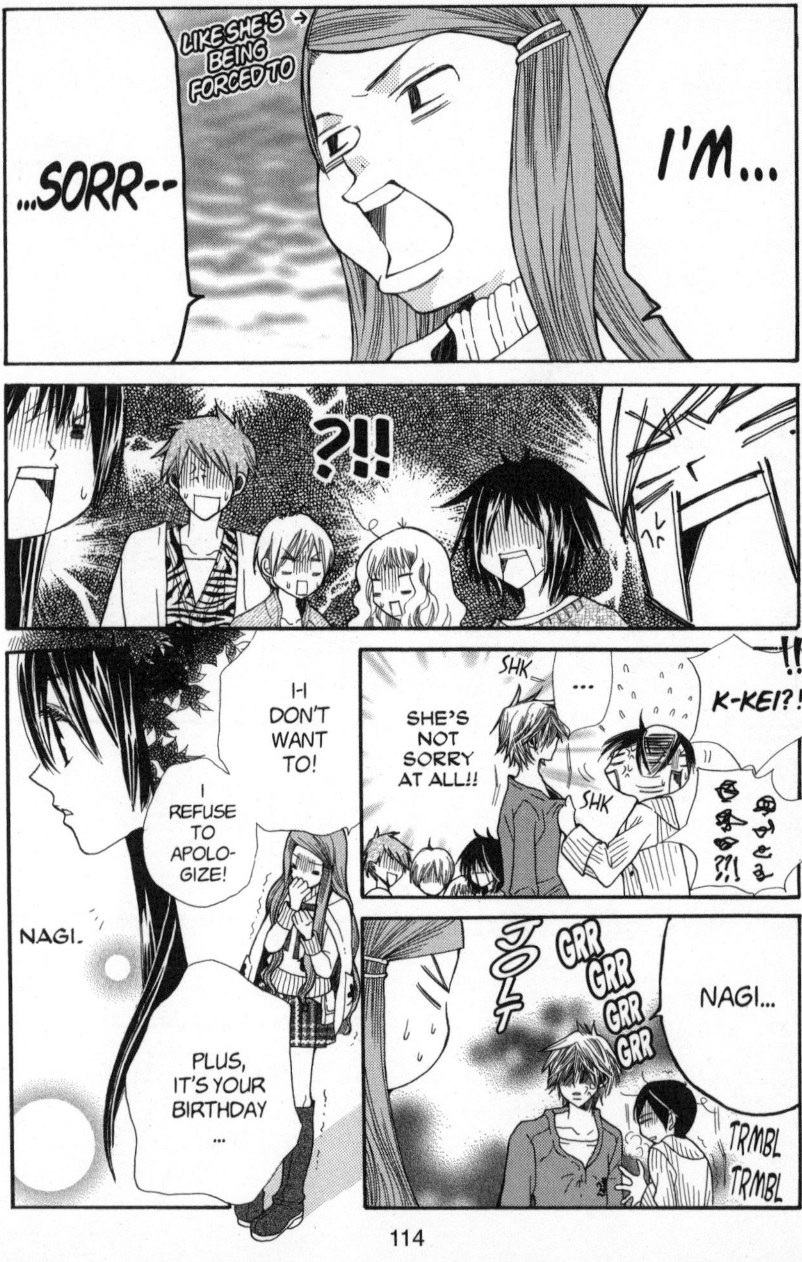
I'M...
LIKE SHE'S BEING FORCED TO
...SORR--
?!!
—!!
K-KEI?!
SHK
...
SHE'S NOT SORRY AT ALL!!
SHK
NAGI...
GRR GRR GRR GRR
JOLT
TRMBL TRMBL
I-I DON'T WANT TO!
I REFUSE TO APOLOGIZE!
NAGI.
PLUS, IT'S YOUR BIRTHDAY ...

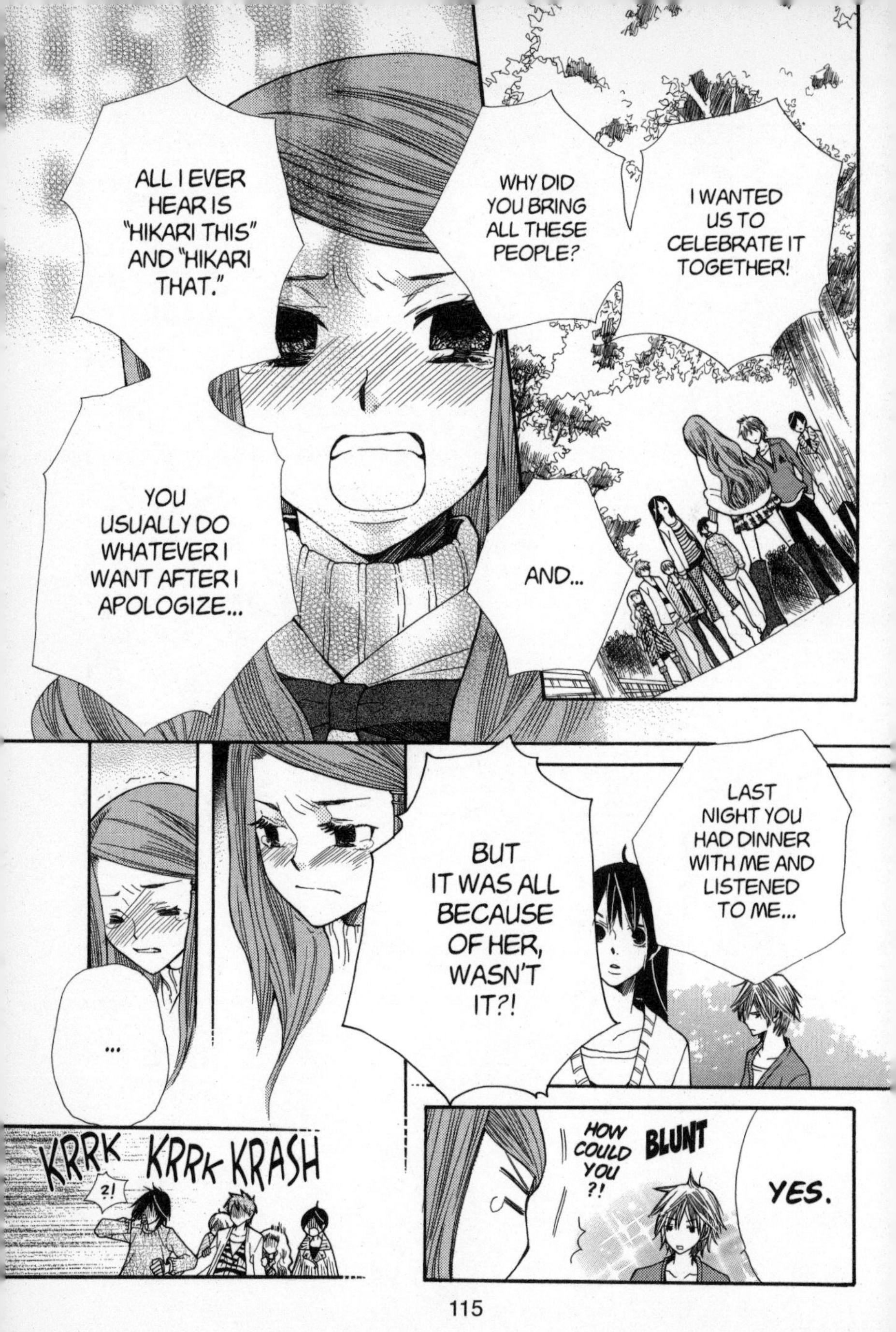
I WANTED US TO CELEBRATE IT TOGETHER!
WHY DID YOU BRING ALL THESE PEOPLE?
AND...
ALL I EVER HEAR IS "HIKARI THIS" AND "HIKARI THAT."
YOU USUALLY DO WHATEVER I WANT AFTER I APOLOGIZE...
LAST NIGHT YOU HAD DINNER WITH ME AND LISTENED TO ME...
BUT IT WAS ALL BECAUSE OF HER, WASN'T IT?!
...
YES.
BLUNT
HOW COULD YOU ?!
KRRK KRRK KRASH
?!

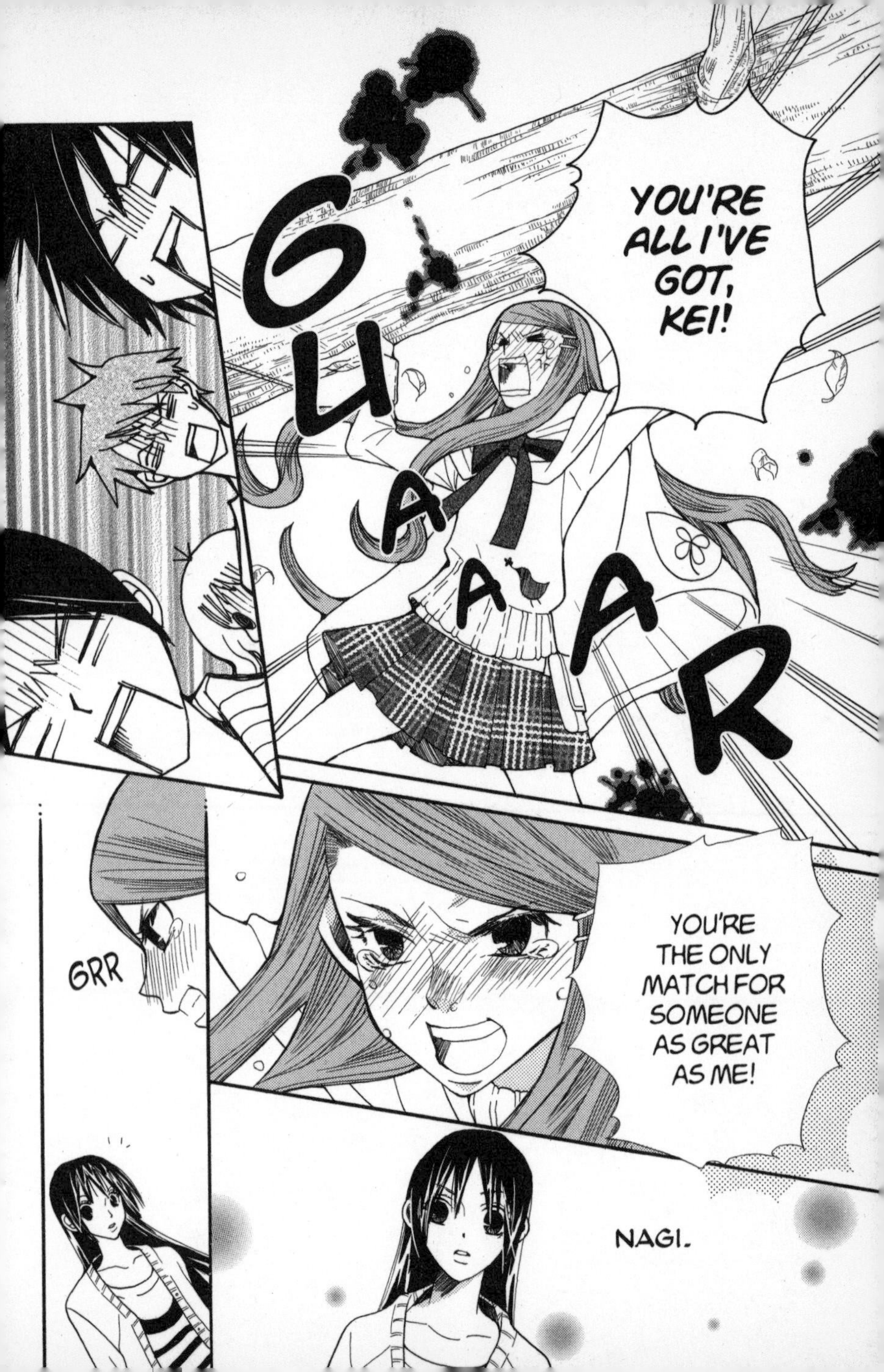
YOU'RE ALL I'VE GOT, KEI!
GUAAAR
YOU'RE THE ONLY MATCH FOR SOMEONE AS GREAT AS ME!
GRR
NAGI.

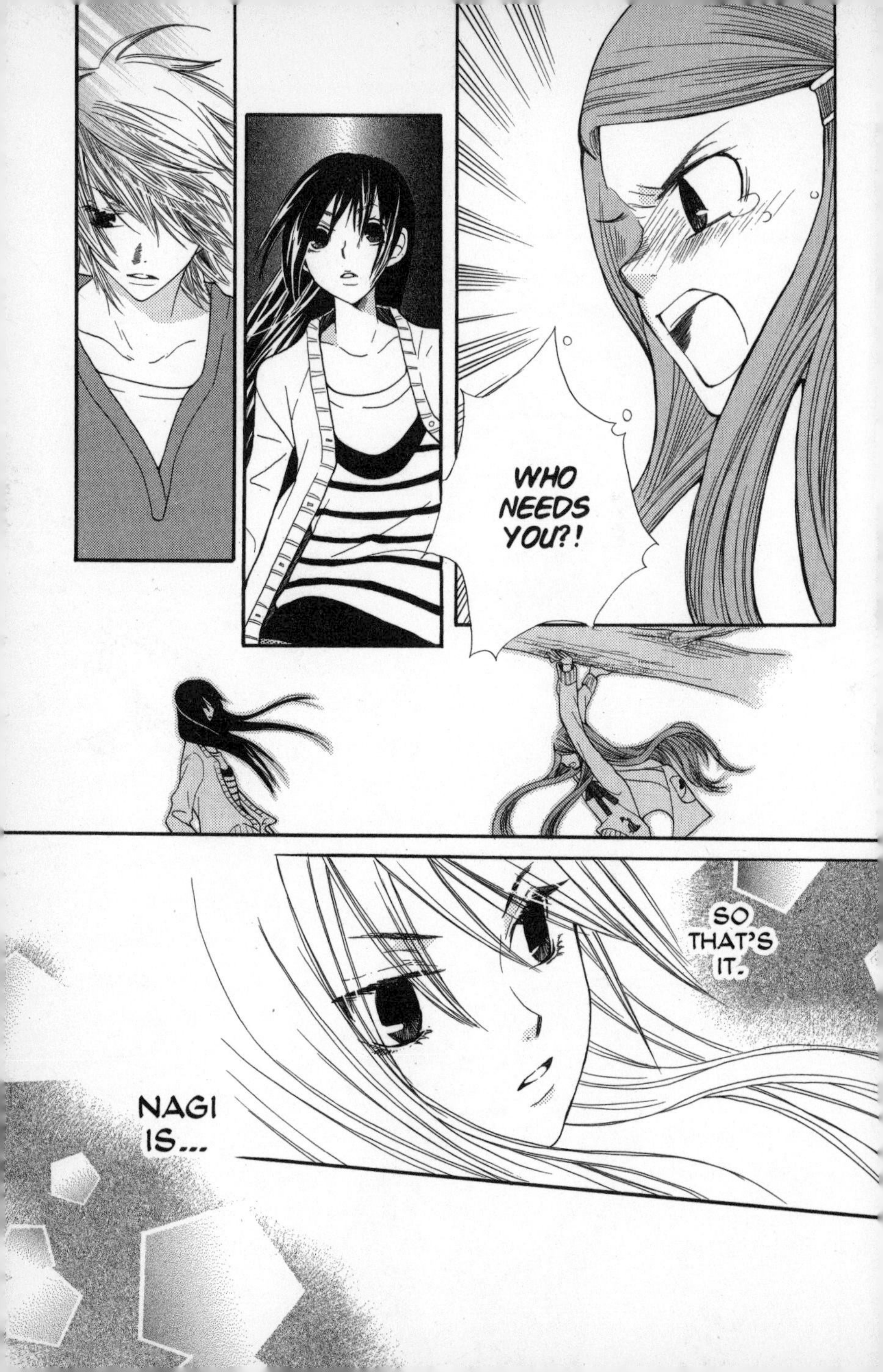
WHO NEEDS YOU?!
SO THAT'S IT.
NAGI IS...

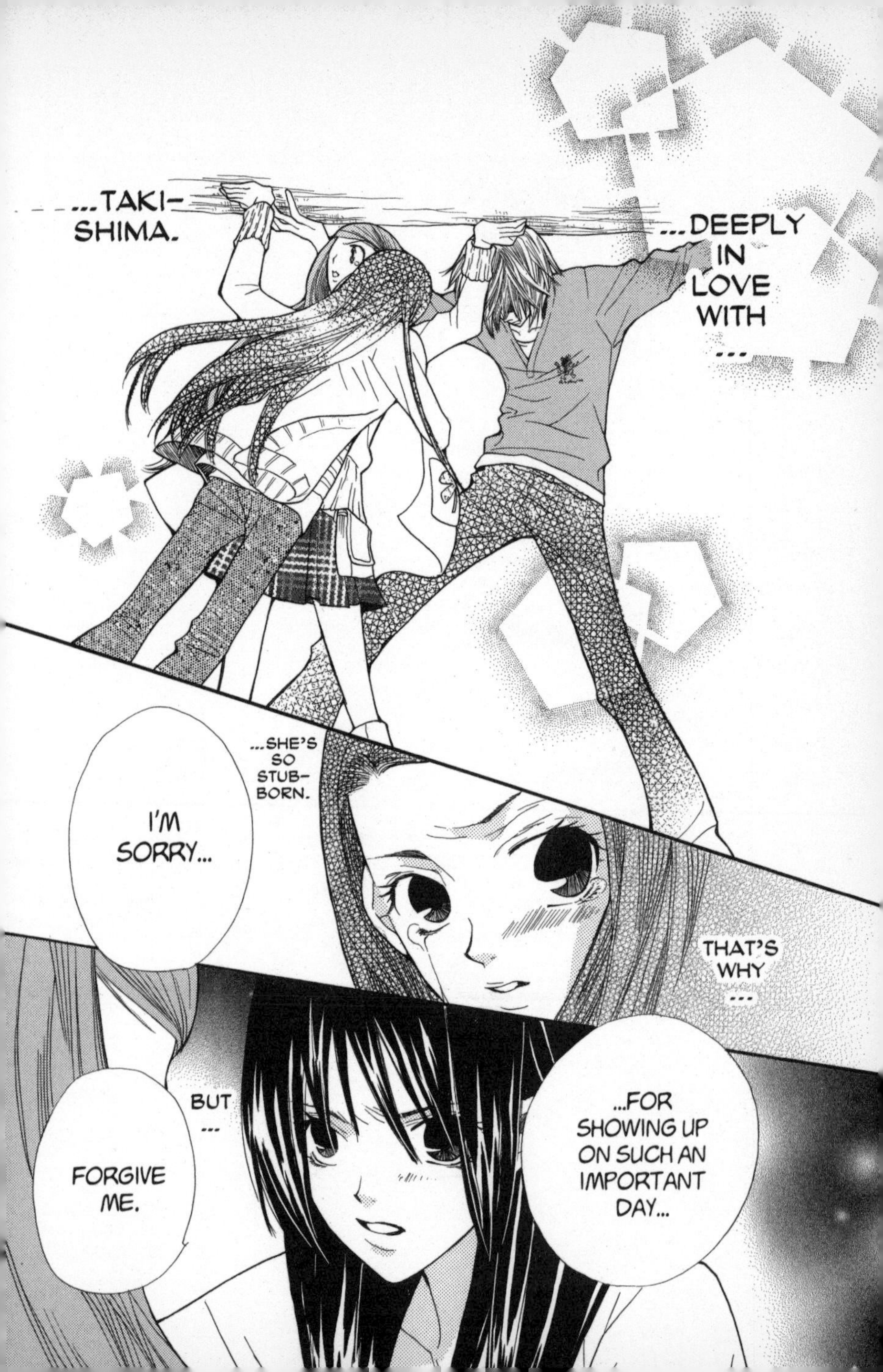
...DEEPLY IN LOVE WITH ...
...TAKI-SHIMA.
...SHE'S SO STUB-BORN.
THAT'S WHY ...
I'M SORRY...
...FOR SHOWING UP ON SUCH AN IMPORTANT DAY...
BUT ...
FORGIVE ME.

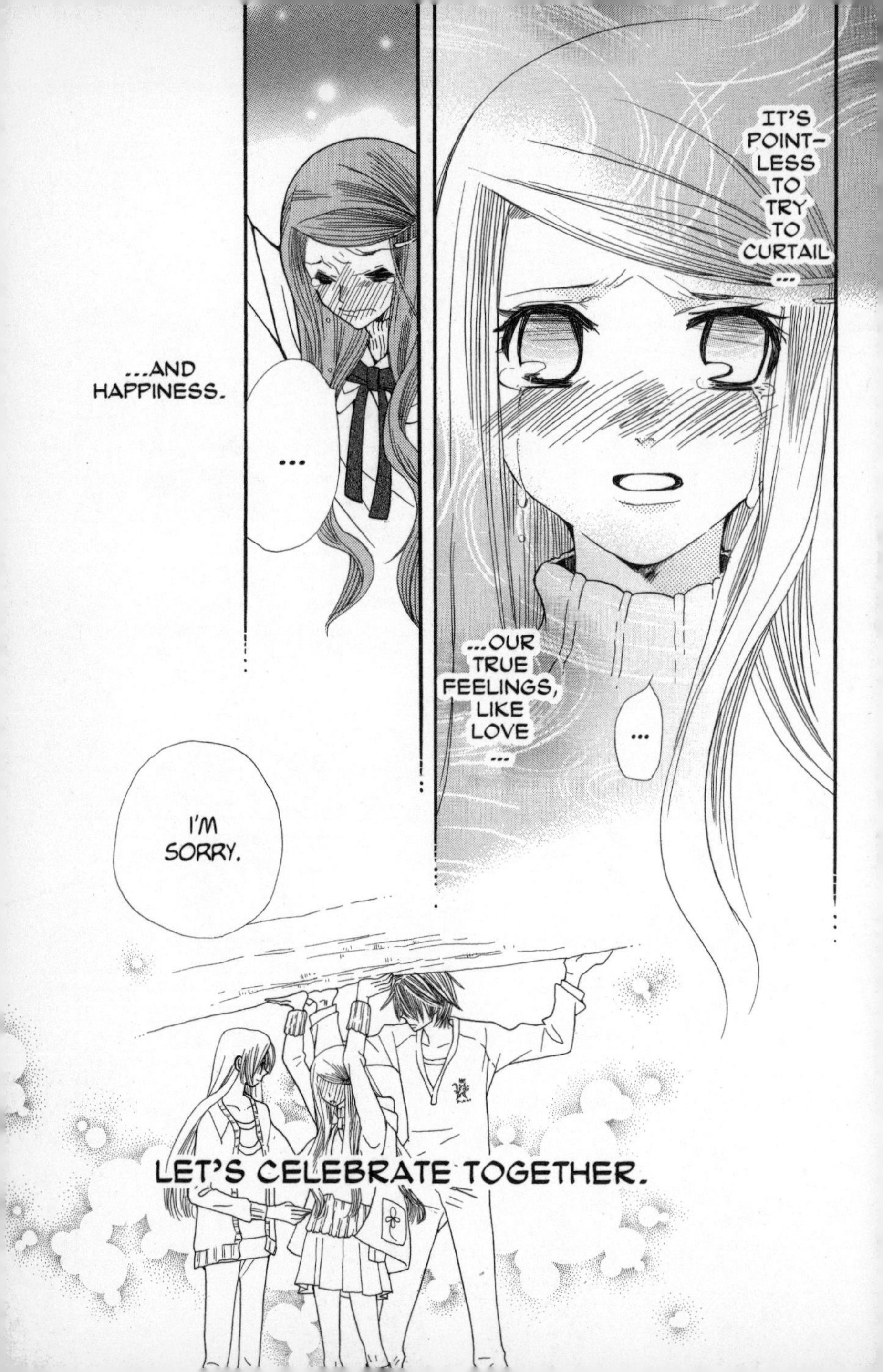
IT'S POINTLESS TO TRY TO CURTAIL...
...OUR TRUE FEELINGS, LIKE LOVE...
...
...
...AND HAPPINESS.
I'M SORRY.
LET'S CELEBRATE TOGETHER.

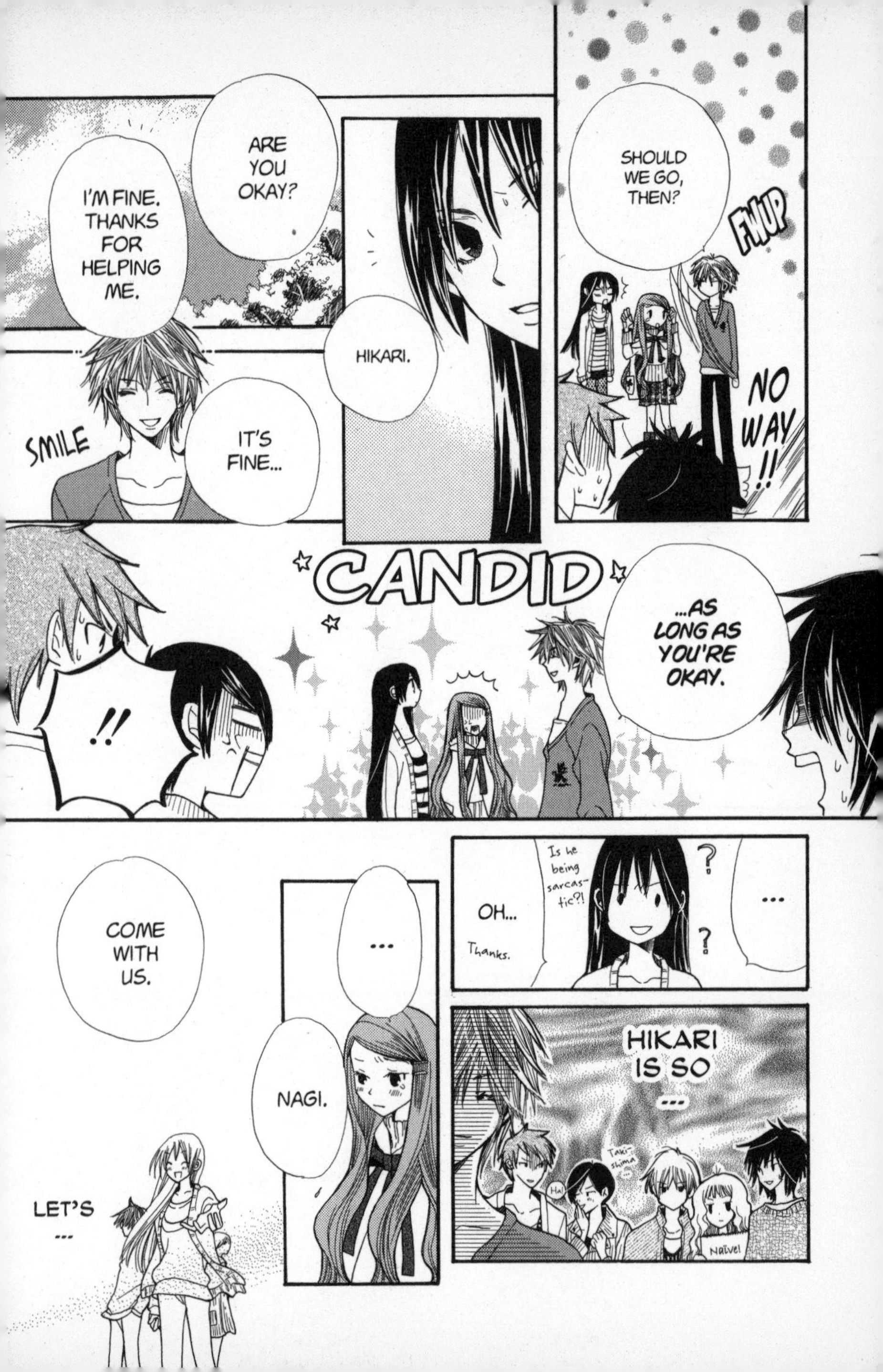
SHOULD WE GO, THEN?
FWUP
NO WAY!!
HIKARI.
ARE YOU OKAY?
I'M FINE. THANKS FOR HELPING ME.
IT'S FINE...
SMILE
...AS LONG AS YOU'RE OKAY.
CANDID
!!
...
?
?
Is he being sarcastic?!
OH...
Thanks.
HIKARI IS SO ...
Taki-shima ...
Ha!
Naive!
...
NAGI.
COME WITH US.
LET'S ...

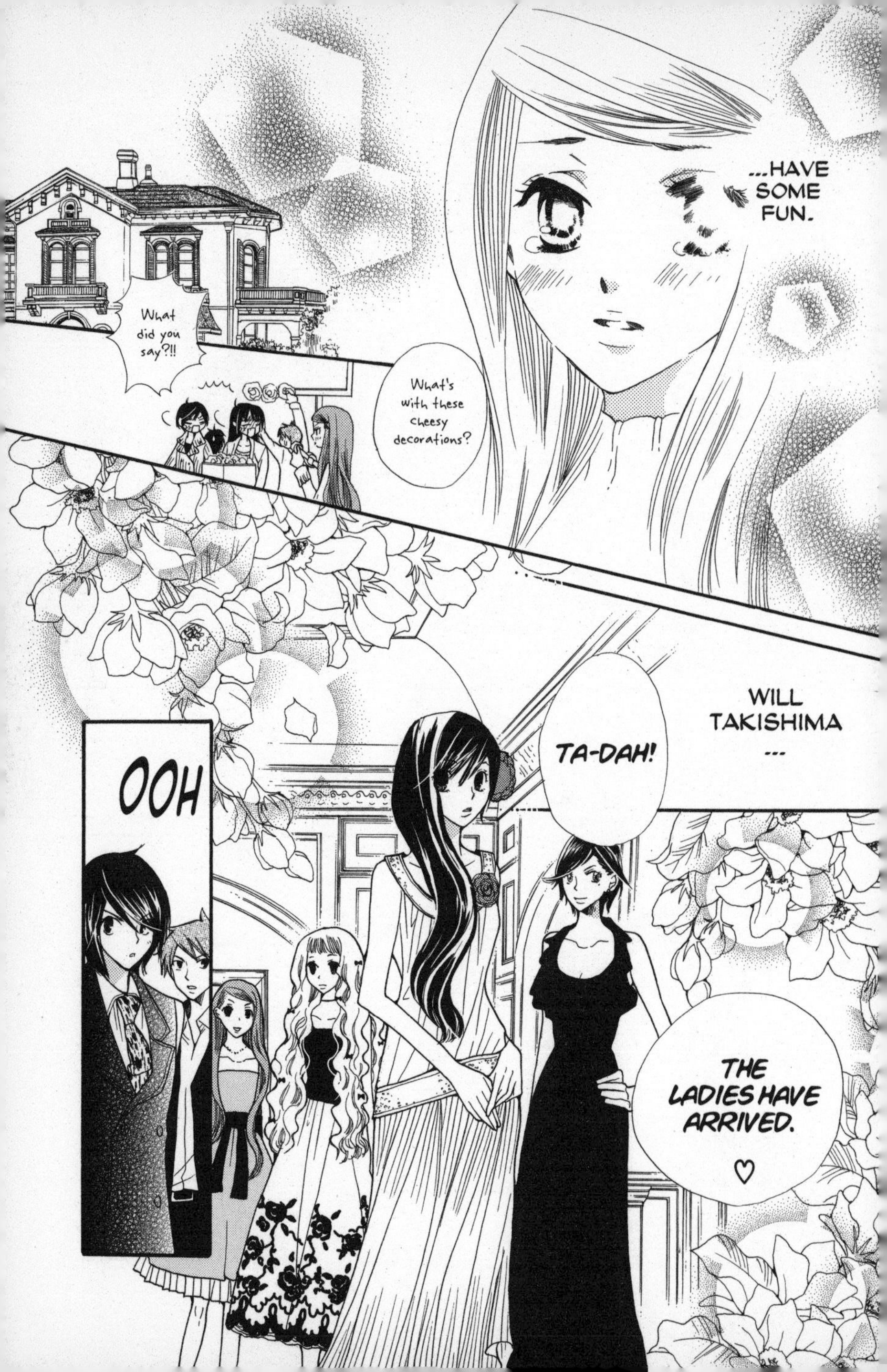
...HAVE SOME FUN.
What's with these cheesy decorations?
What did you say?!!
WILL TAKISHIMA ---
TA-DAH!
THE LADIES HAVE ARRIVED. ♡
OOH

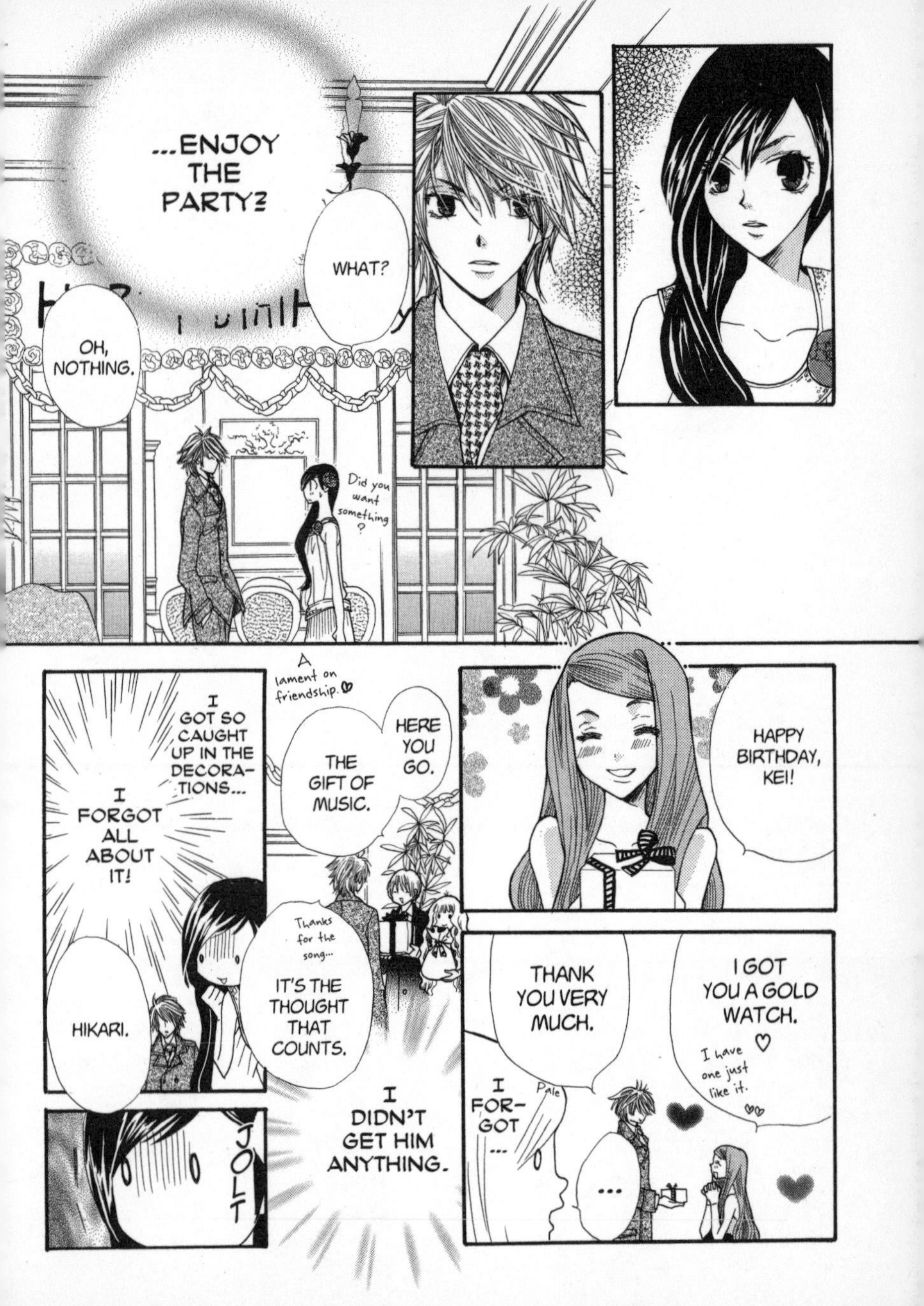
...ENJOY THE PARTY?
WHAT?
OH, NOTHING.
Did you want something?
HAPPY BIRTHDAY, KEI!
I GOT YOU A GOLD WATCH.
I have one just like it.
THANK YOU VERY MUCH.
Pale
I FOR-GOT...
...
A lament on friendship.
HERE YOU GO.
THE GIFT OF MUSIC.
I GOT SO CAUGHT UP IN THE DECORA-TIONS...
I FORGOT ALL ABOUT IT!
Thanks for the song...
IT'S THE THOUGHT THAT COUNTS.
HIKARI.
I DIDN'T GET HIM ANYTHING.
JOLT

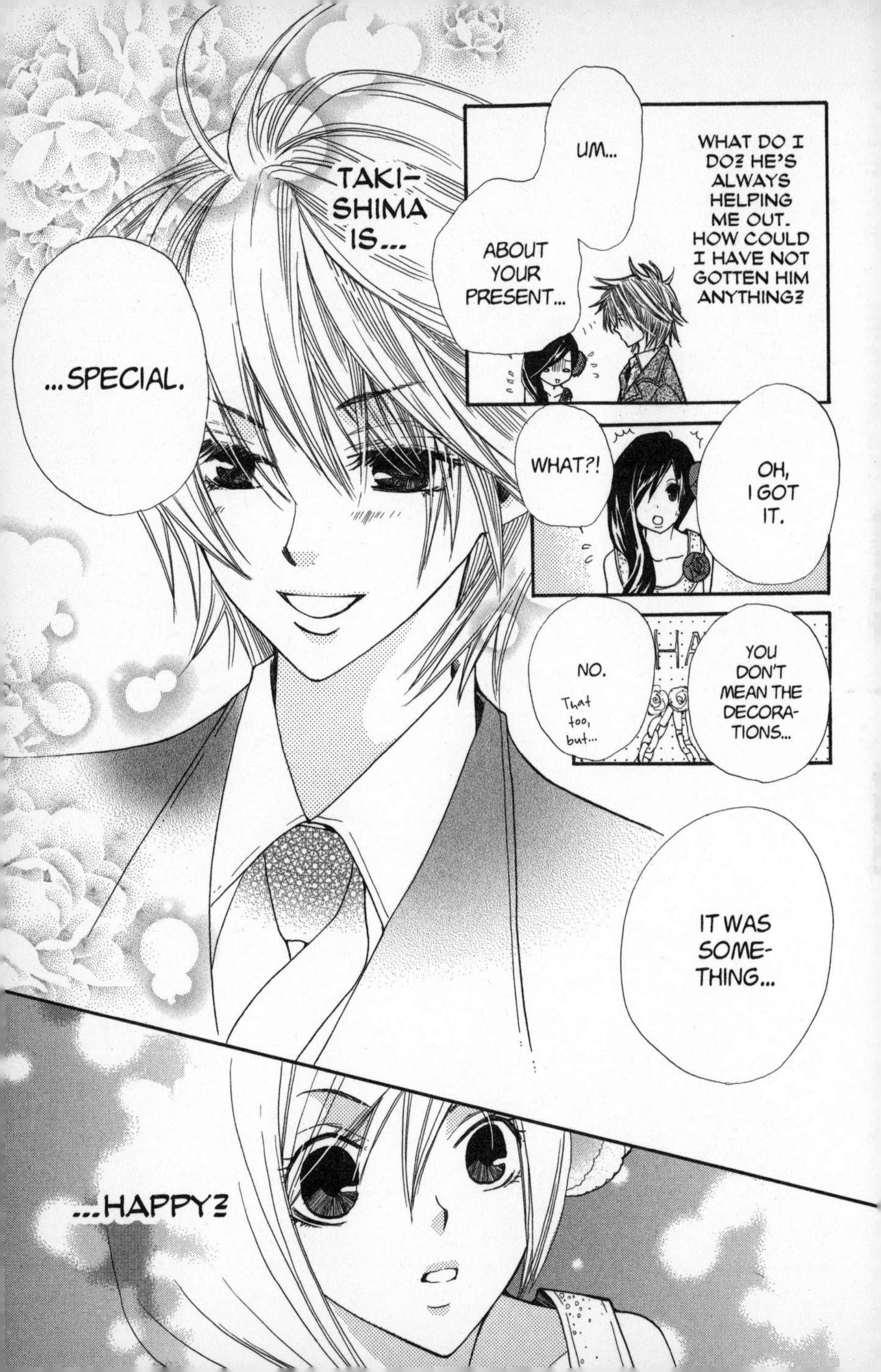
WHAT DO I DO? HE'S ALWAYS HELPING ME OUT. HOW COULD I HAVE NOT GOTTEN HIM ANYTHING?
UM...
ABOUT YOUR PRESENT...
OH, I GOT IT.
WHAT?!
YOU DON'T MEAN THE DECORATIONS...
NO.
That too, but...
IT WAS SOMETHING...
TAKI-SHIMA IS...
...SPECIAL.
...HAPPY?

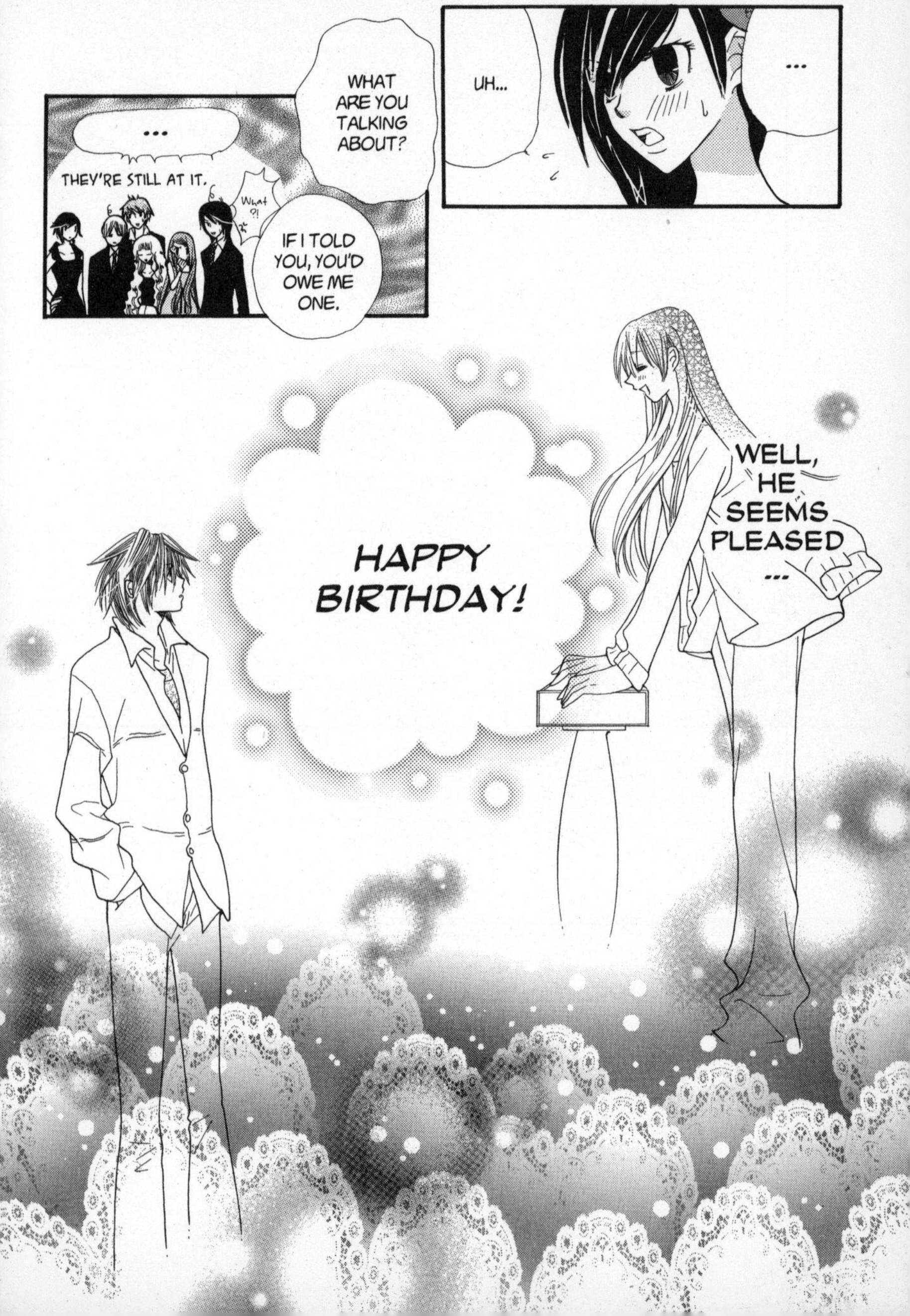
...
UH...
WHAT ARE YOU TALKING ABOUT?
...
THEY'RE STILL AT IT.
What ?!
IF I TOLD YOU, YOU'D OWE ME ONE.
WELL, HE SEEMS PLEASED ...
HAPPY BIRTHDAY!

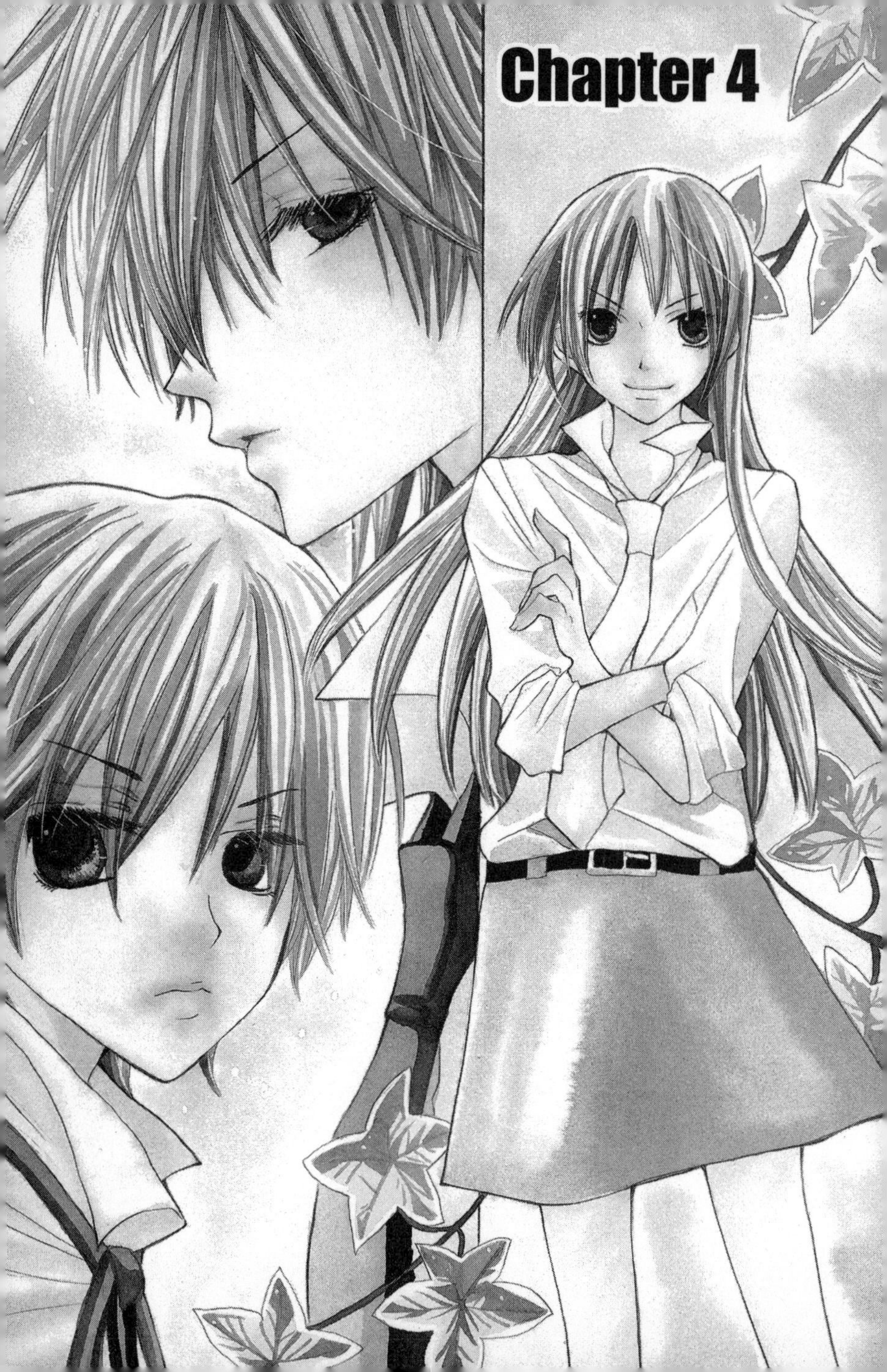
Chapter 4

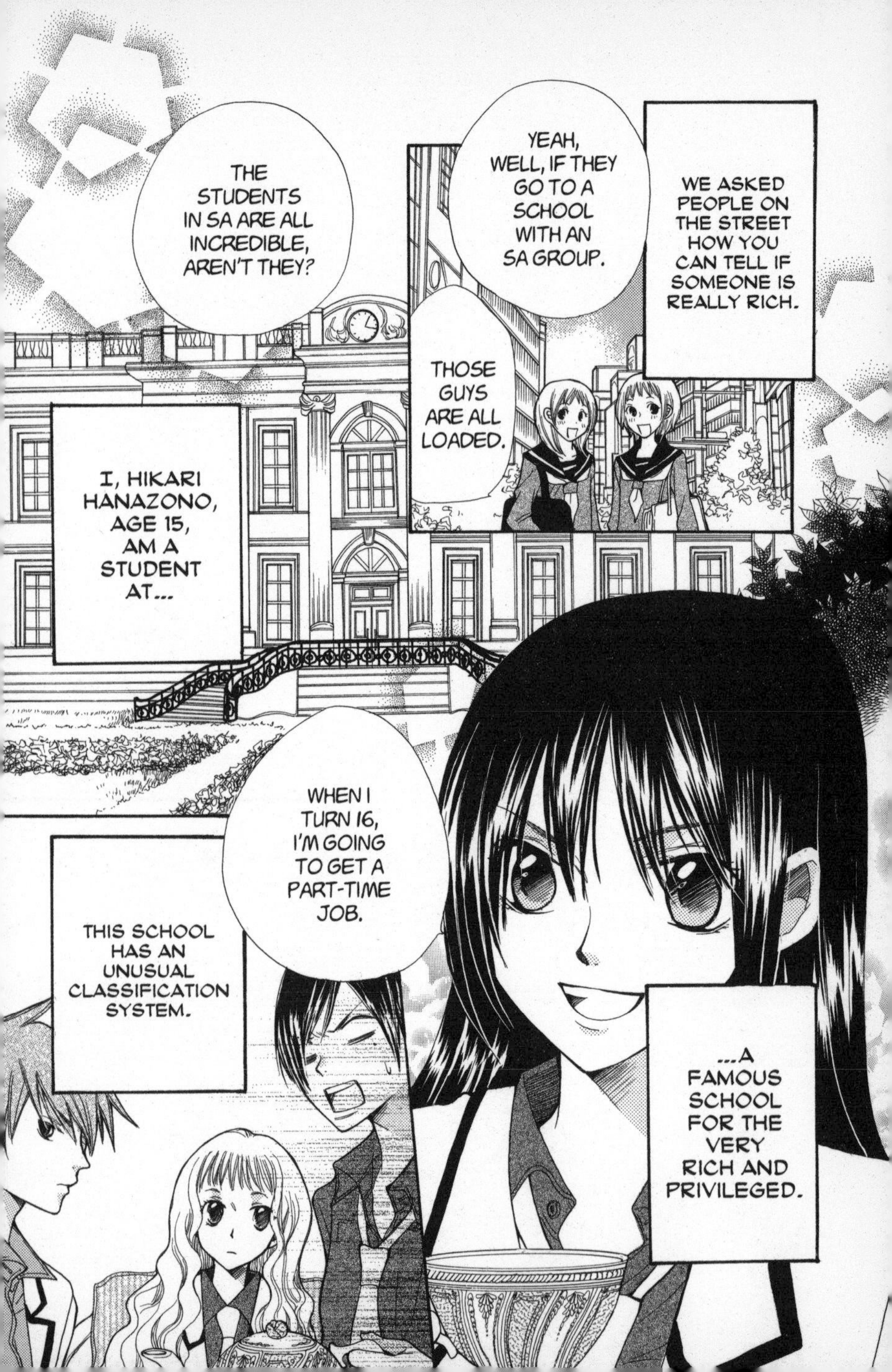
WE ASKED PEOPLE ON THE STREET HOW YOU CAN TELL IF SOMEONE IS REALLY RICH.
YEAH, WELL, IF THEY GO TO A SCHOOL WITH AN SA GROUP.
THOSE GUYS ARE ALL LOADED.
THE STUDENTS IN SA ARE ALL INCREDIBLE, AREN'T THEY?
I, HIKARI HANAZONO, AGE 15, AM A STUDENT AT...
...A FAMOUS SCHOOL FOR THE VERY RICH AND PRIVILEGED.
WHEN I TURN 16, I'M GOING TO GET A PART-TIME JOB.
THIS SCHOOL HAS AN UNUSUAL CLASSIFICATION SYSTEM.

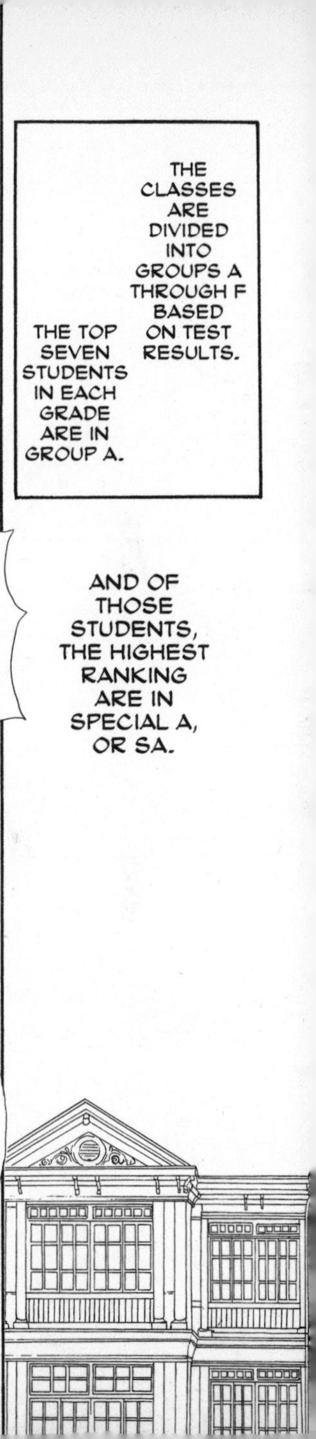
THE CLASSES ARE DIVIDED INTO GROUPS A THROUGH F BASED ON TEST RESULTS.
THE TOP SEVEN STUDENTS IN EACH GRADE ARE IN GROUP A.
AND OF THOSE STUDENTS, THE HIGHEST RANKING ARE IN SPECIAL A, OR SA.

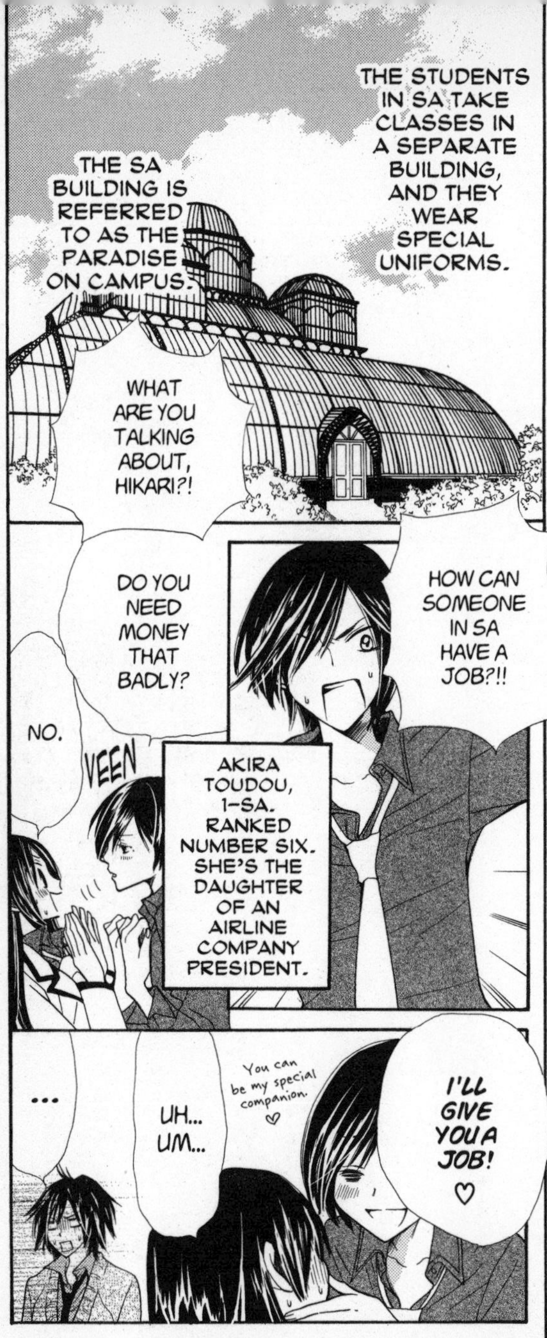
THE STUDENTS IN SA TAKE CLASSES IN A SEPARATE BUILDING, AND THEY WEAR SPECIAL UNIFORMS.
THE SA BUILDING IS REFERRED TO AS THE PARADISE ON CAMPUS.
WHAT ARE YOU TALKING ABOUT, HIKARI?!
HOW CAN SOMEONE IN SA HAVE A JOB?!!
AKIRA TOUDOU, 1-SA. RANKED NUMBER SIX. SHE'S THE DAUGHTER OF AN AIRLINE COMPANY PRESIDENT.
DO YOU NEED MONEY THAT BADLY?
NO.
VEEN
I'LL GIVE YOU A JOB! ♡
You can be my special companion. ♡
UH... UM...
...

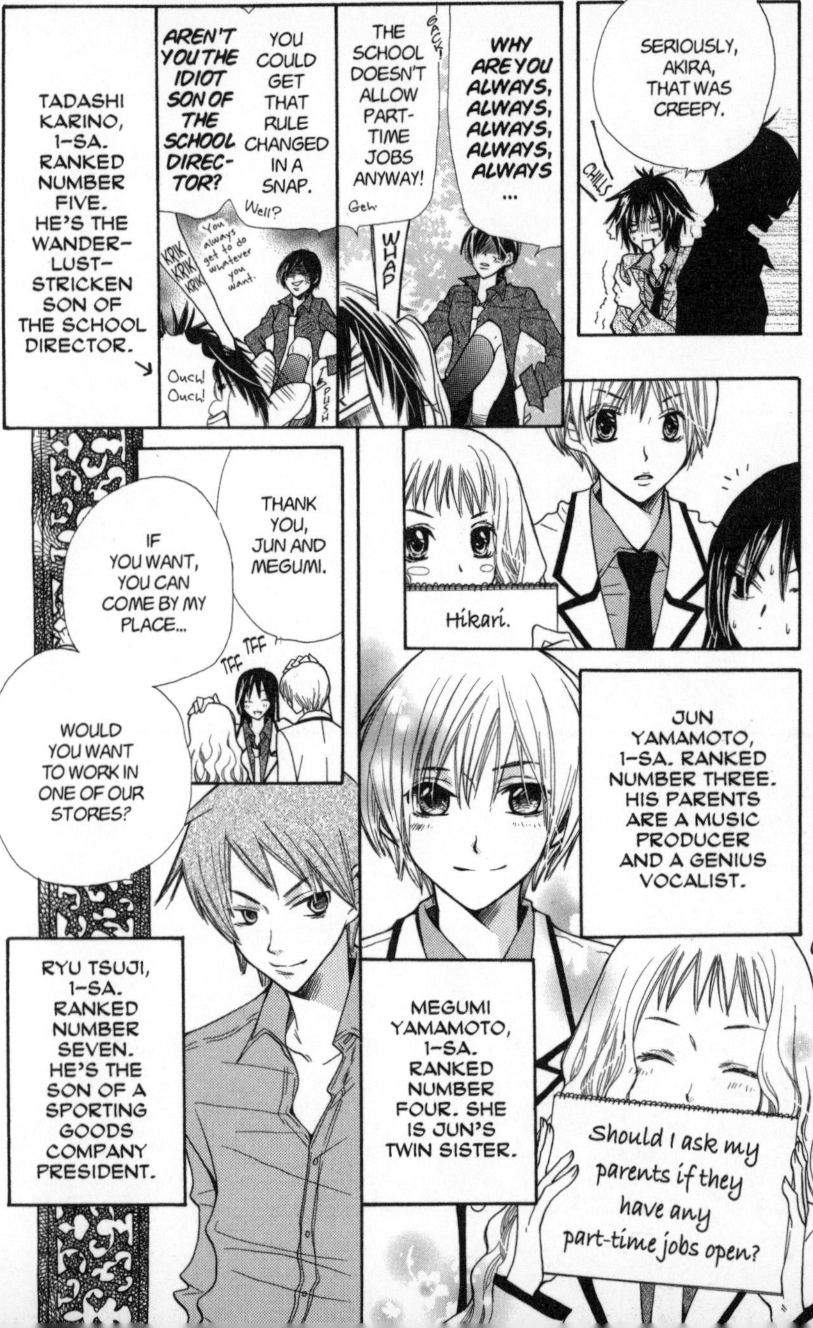
SERIOUSLY, AKIRA, THAT WAS CREEPY.
CHILLS
WHY ARE YOU ALWAYS, ALWAYS, ALWAYS, ALWAYS, ALWAYS ...
GACK!
THE SCHOOL DOESN'T ALLOW PART-TIME JOBS ANYWAY!
Geh
WHAP
YOU COULD GET THAT RULE CHANGED IN A SNAP.
AREN'T YOU THE IDIOT SON OF THE SCHOOL DIRECTOR?
Well?
You always get to do whatever you want.
KRIK KRIK KRIK
PUSH
Ouch! Ouch!
TADASHI KARINO, 1-SA. RANKED NUMBER FIVE. HE'S THE WANDERLUST-STRICKEN SON OF THE SCHOOL DIRECTOR.
Hikari.
JUN YAMAMOTO, 1-SA. RANKED NUMBER THREE. HIS PARENTS ARE A MUSIC PRODUCER AND A GENIUS VOCALIST.
THANK YOU, JUN AND MEGUMI.
IF YOU WANT, YOU CAN COME BY MY PLACE...
TFF TFF
WOULD YOU WANT TO WORK IN ONE OF OUR STORES?
GRIN
Should I ask my parents if they have any part-time jobs open?
MEGUMI YAMAMOTO, 1-SA. RANKED NUMBER FOUR. SHE IS JUN'S TWIN SISTER.
RYU TSUJI, 1-SA. RANKED NUMBER SEVEN. HE'S THE SON OF A SPORTING GOODS COMPANY PRESIDENT.

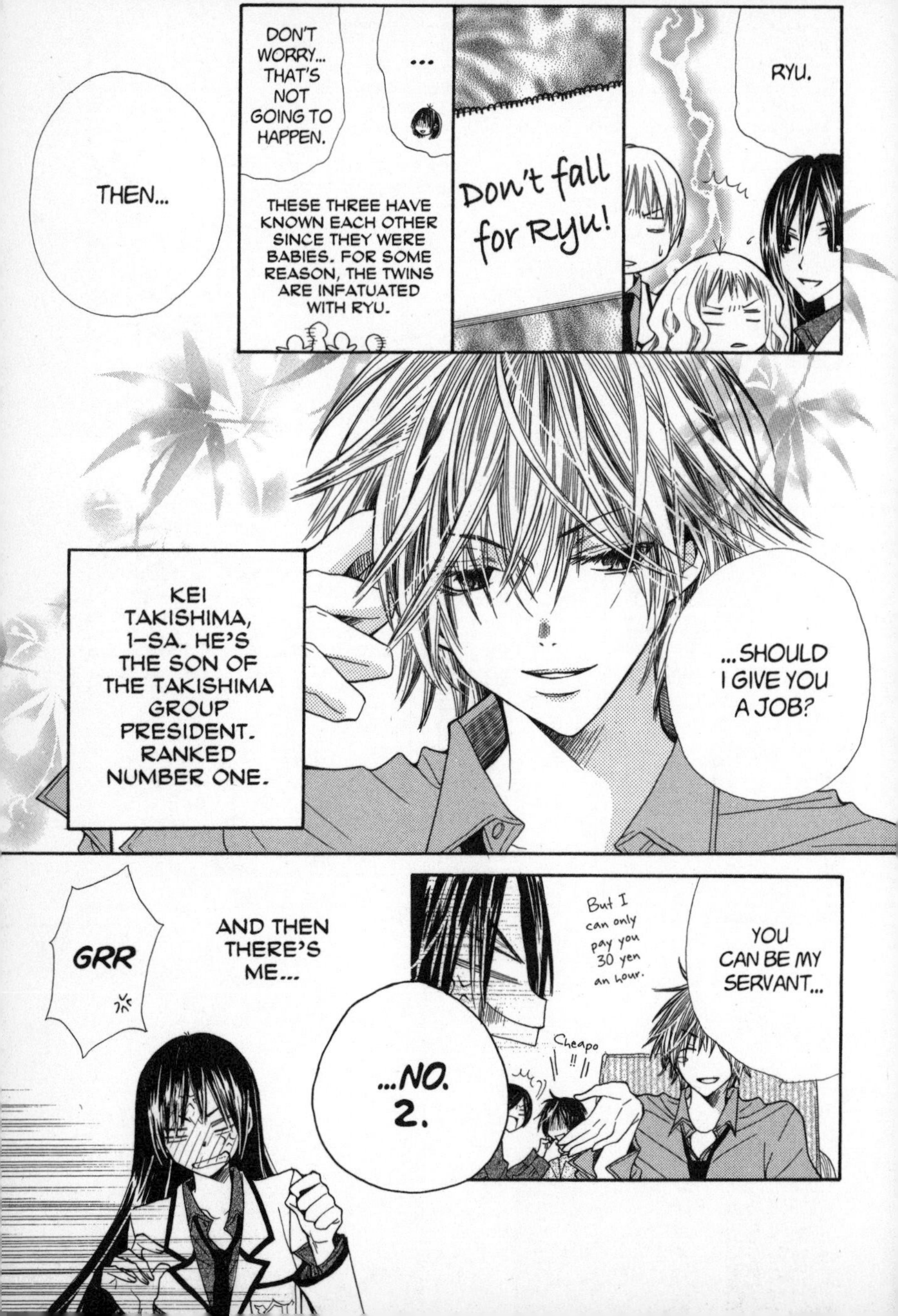
RYU.
Don't fall for Ryu!
...
DON'T WORRY... THAT'S NOT GOING TO HAPPEN.
THESE THREE HAVE KNOWN EACH OTHER SINCE THEY WERE BABIES. FOR SOME REASON, THE TWINS ARE INFATUATED WITH RYU.
THEN...
...SHOULD I GIVE YOU A JOB?
KEI TAKISHIMA, 1-SA. HE'S THE SON OF THE TAKISHIMA GROUP PRESIDENT. RANKED NUMBER ONE.
YOU CAN BE MY SERVANT...
But I can only pay you 30 yen an hour.
Cheapo !!
...NO. 2.
AND THEN THERE'S ME...
GRR

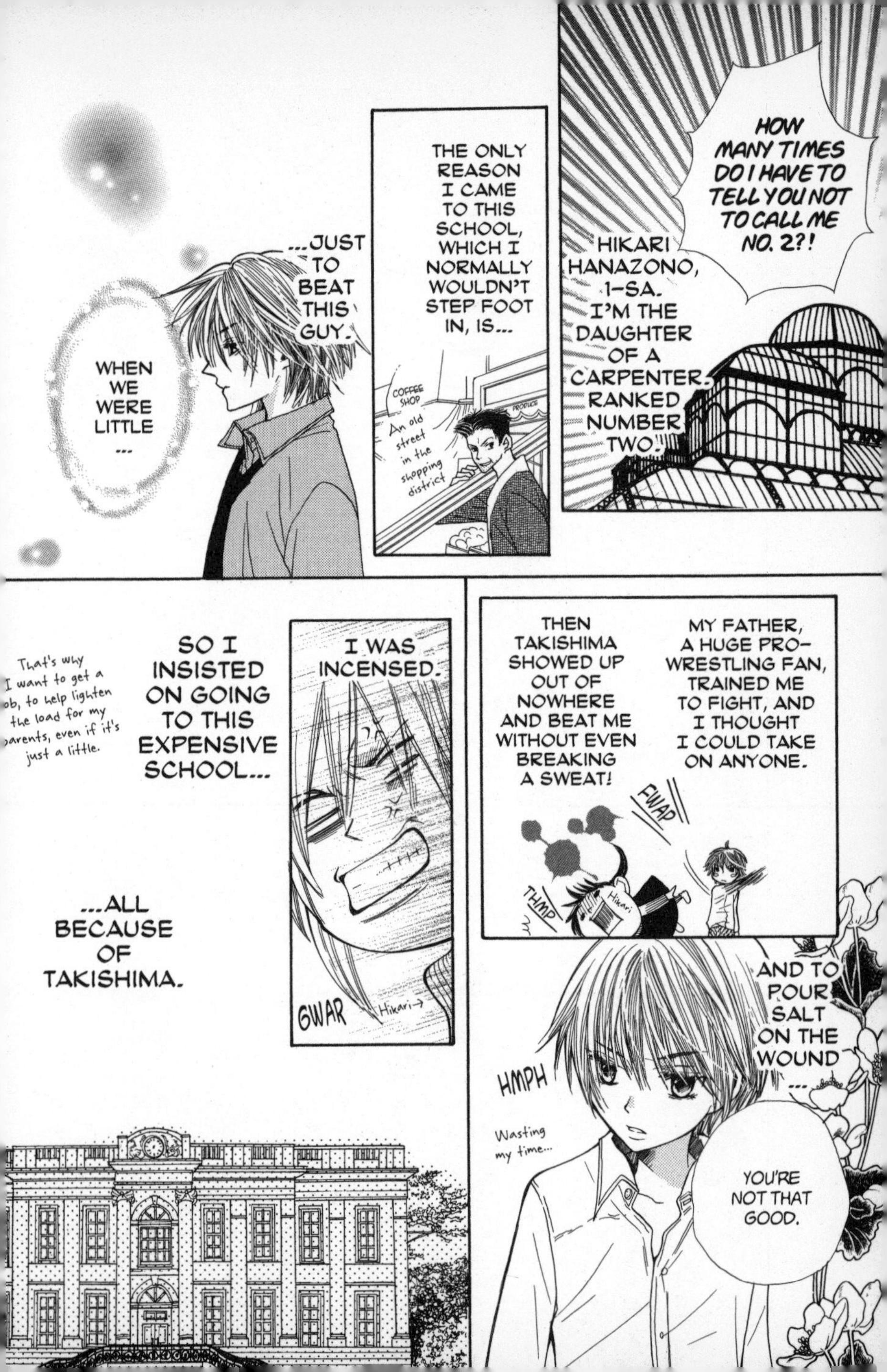
HOW MANY TIMES DO I HAVE TO TELL YOU NOT TO CALL ME NO. 2?!
HIKARI HANAZONO, 1-SA. I'M THE DAUGHTER OF A CARPENTER. RANKED NUMBER TWO.
THE ONLY REASON I CAME TO THIS SCHOOL, WHICH I NORMALLY WOULDN'T STEP FOOT IN, IS...
COFFEE SHOP
PRODUCE
An old street in the shopping district
...JUST TO BEAT THIS GUY.
WHEN WE WERE LITTLE ...
MY FATHER, A HUGE PRO-WRESTLING FAN, TRAINED ME TO FIGHT, AND I THOUGHT I COULD TAKE ON ANYONE.
THEN TAKISHIMA SHOWED UP OUT OF NOWHERE AND BEAT ME WITHOUT EVEN BREAKING A SWEAT!
FWAP
THMP
Hikari
AND TO POUR SALT ON THE WOUND...
HMPH
Wasting my time...
YOU'RE NOT THAT GOOD.
I WAS INCENSED.
GWAR
Hikari→
SO I INSISTED ON GOING TO THIS EXPENSIVE SCHOOL...
That's why I want to get a ob, to help lighten the load for my arents, even if it's just a little.
...ALL BECAUSE OF TAKISHIMA.

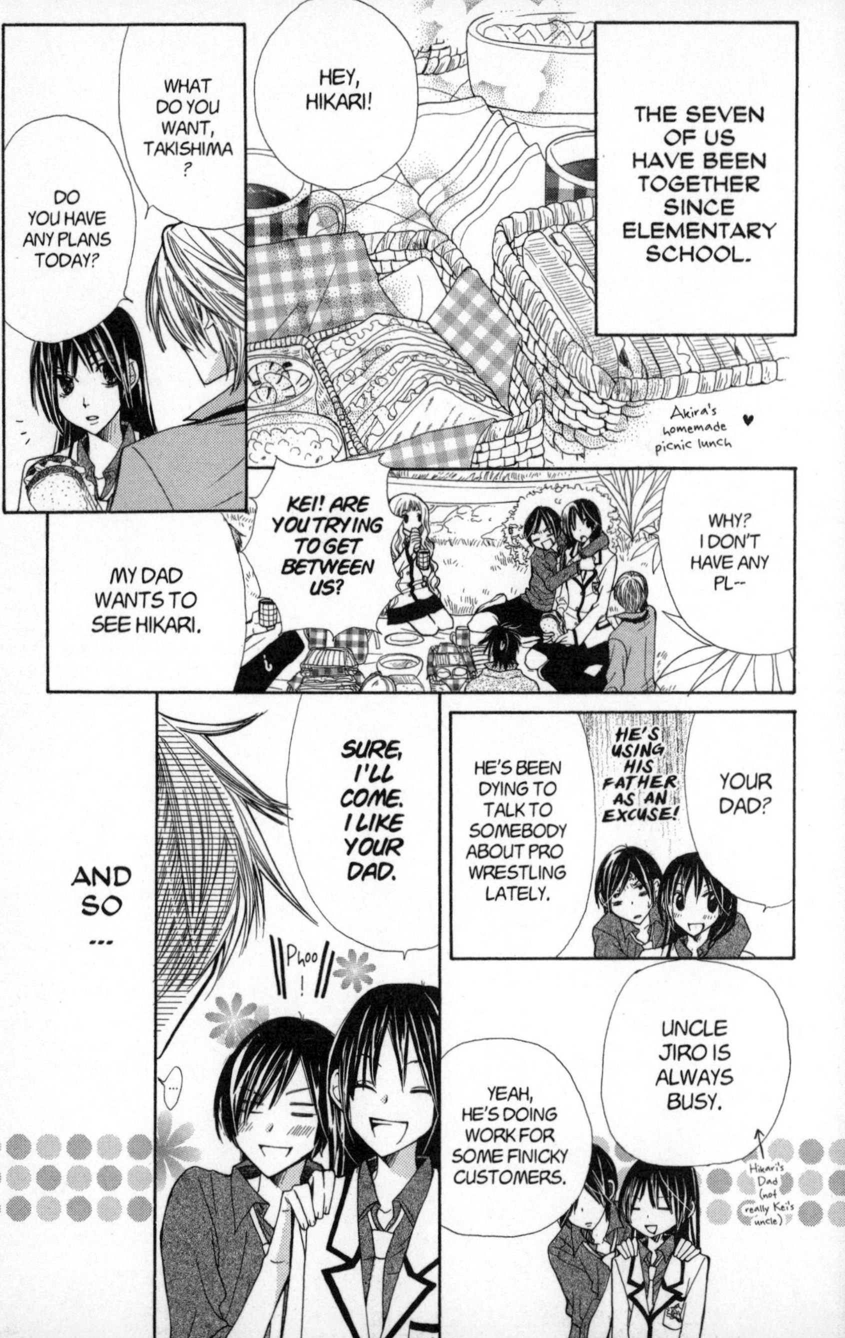
THE SEVEN OF US HAVE BEEN TOGETHER SINCE ELEMENTARY SCHOOL.
Akira's homemade picnic lunch ♥
HEY, HIKARI!
WHAT DO YOU WANT, TAKISHIMA?
DO YOU HAVE ANY PLANS TODAY?
WHY? I DON'T HAVE ANY PL--
KEI! ARE YOU TRYING TO GET BETWEEN US?
MY DAD WANTS TO SEE HIKARI.
YOUR DAD?
HE'S USING HIS FATHER AS AN EXCUSE!
HE'S BEEN DYING TO TALK TO SOMEBODY ABOUT PRO WRESTLING LATELY.
UNCLE JIRO IS ALWAYS BUSY.
Hikari's Dad (not really Kei's uncle)
YEAH, HE'S DOING WORK FOR SOME FINICKY CUSTOMERS.
SURE, I'LL COME. I LIKE YOUR DAD.
Phoo!
...
AND SO ...

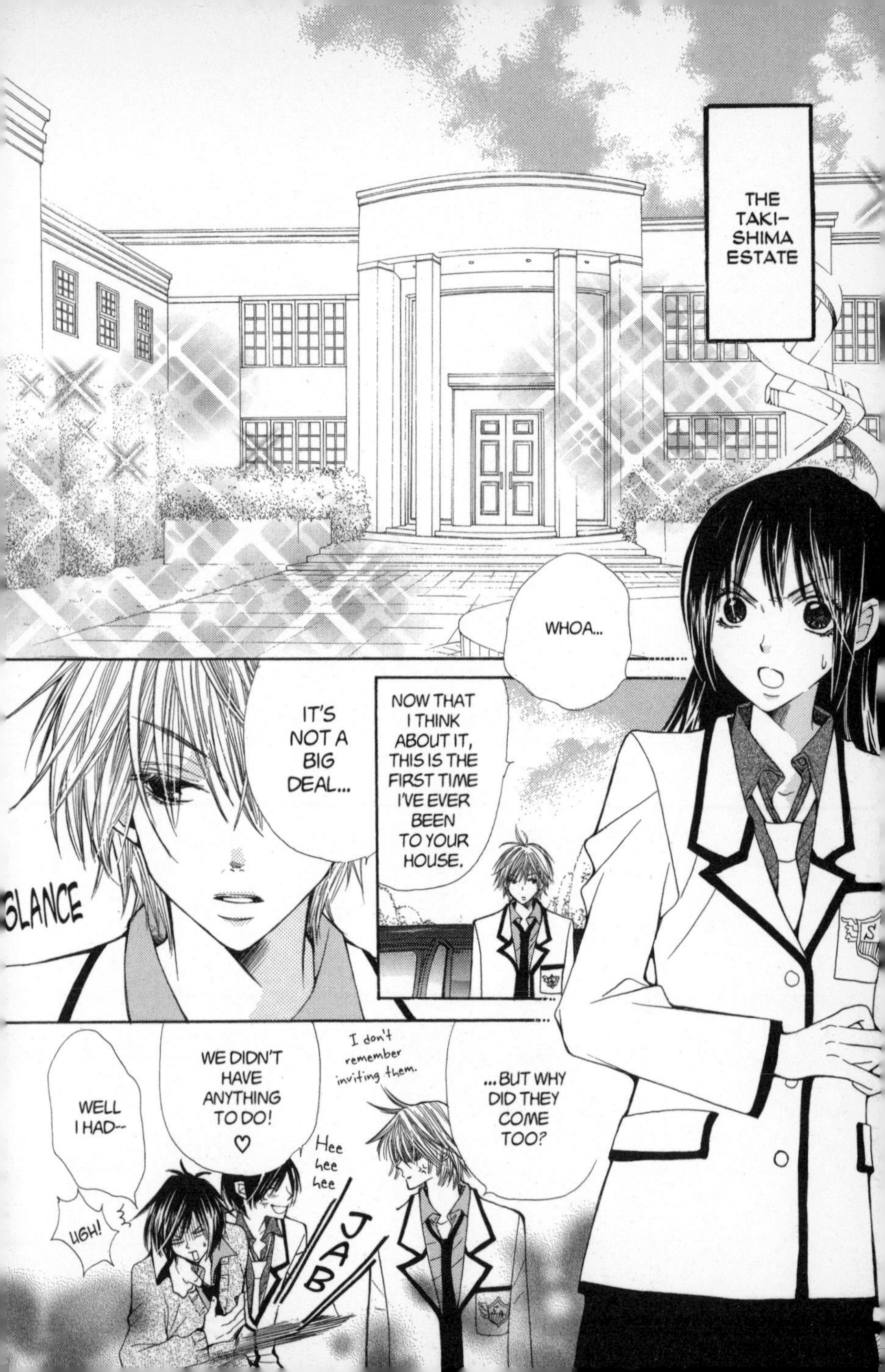
THE TAKI-SHIMA ESTATE
WHOA...
NOW THAT I THINK ABOUT IT, THIS IS THE FIRST TIME I'VE EVER BEEN TO YOUR HOUSE.
IT'S NOT A BIG DEAL...
GLANCE
...BUT WHY DID THEY COME TOO?
I don't remember inviting them.
WE DIDN'T HAVE ANYTHING TO DO! ♡
Hee hee hee
JAB
WELL I HAD--
UGH!

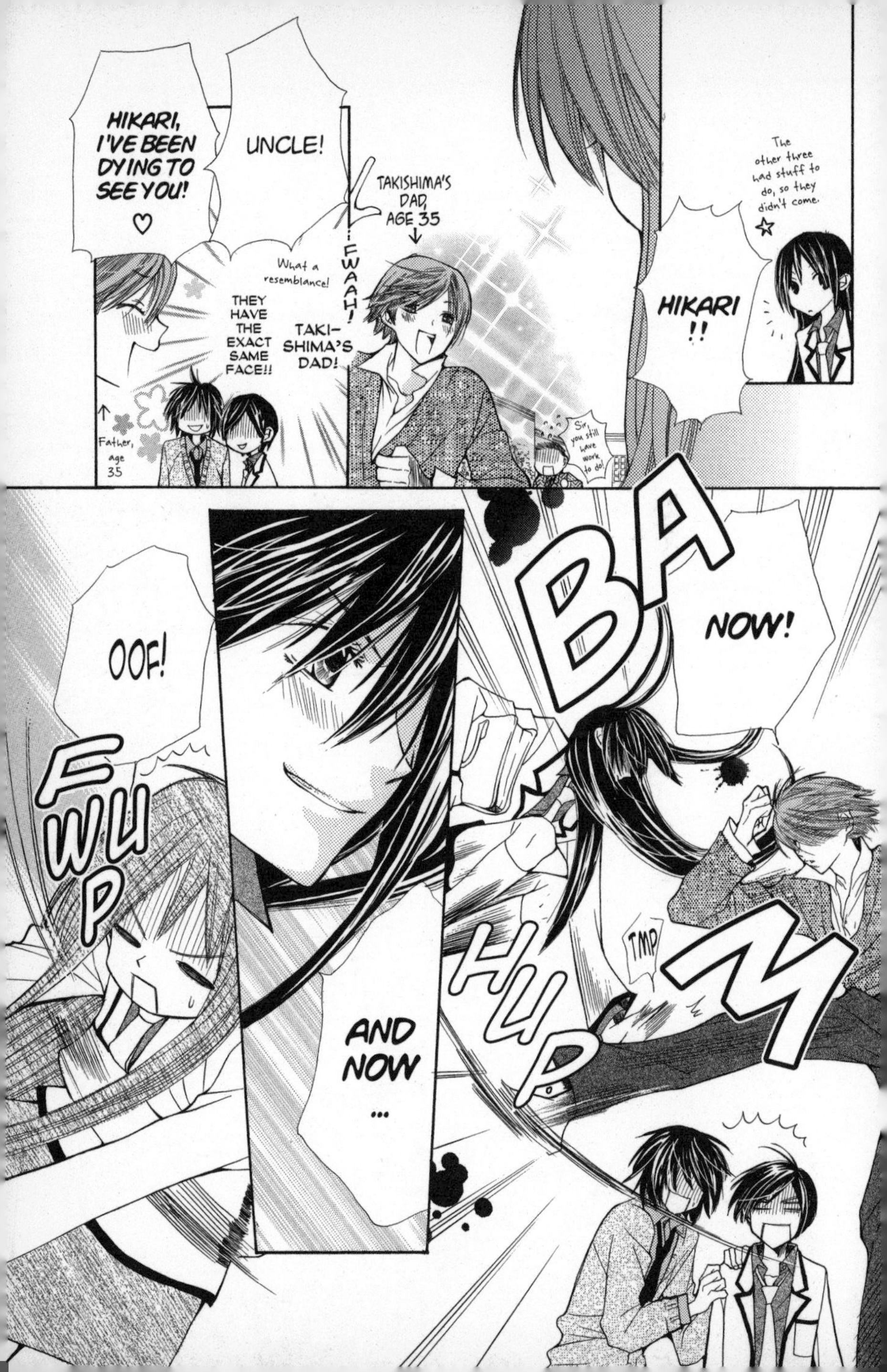
HIKARI!!
The other three had stuff to do, so they didn't come. ☆
HIKARI, I'VE BEEN DYING TO SEE YOU! ♡
UNCLE!
TAKISHIMA'S DAD, AGE 35
FWAAAH!
Sir, you still have work to do!
TAKI-SHIMA'S DAD!
What a resemblance!
THEY HAVE THE EXACT SAME FACE!!
Father, age 35
BAM
NOW!
HUP
TMP
AND NOW ...
OOF!
FWUP

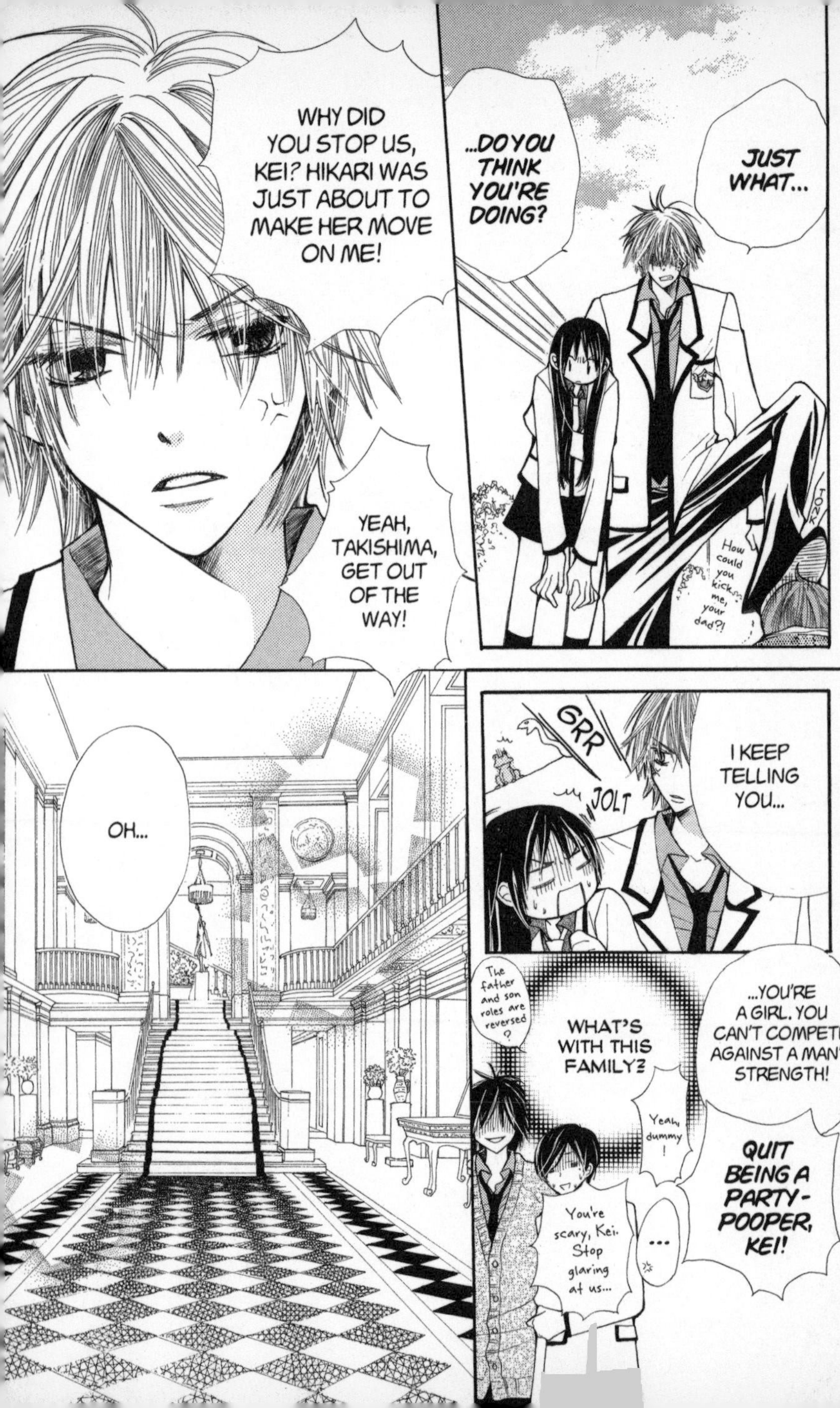
JUST WHAT...
...DO YOU THINK YOU'RE DOING?
TONK
How could you kick me, your dad?!
WHY DID YOU STOP US, KEI? HIKARI WAS JUST ABOUT TO MAKE HER MOVE ON ME!
YEAH, TAKISHIMA, GET OUT OF THE WAY!
GRR
I KEEP TELLING YOU...
JOLT
...YOU'RE A GIRL. YOU CAN'T COMPETE AGAINST A MAN'S STRENGTH!
QUIT BEING A PARTY-POOPER, KEI!
WHAT'S WITH THIS FAMILY?
The father and son roles are reversed?
Yeah, dummy!
...
You're scary, Kei. Stop glaring at us...
OH...

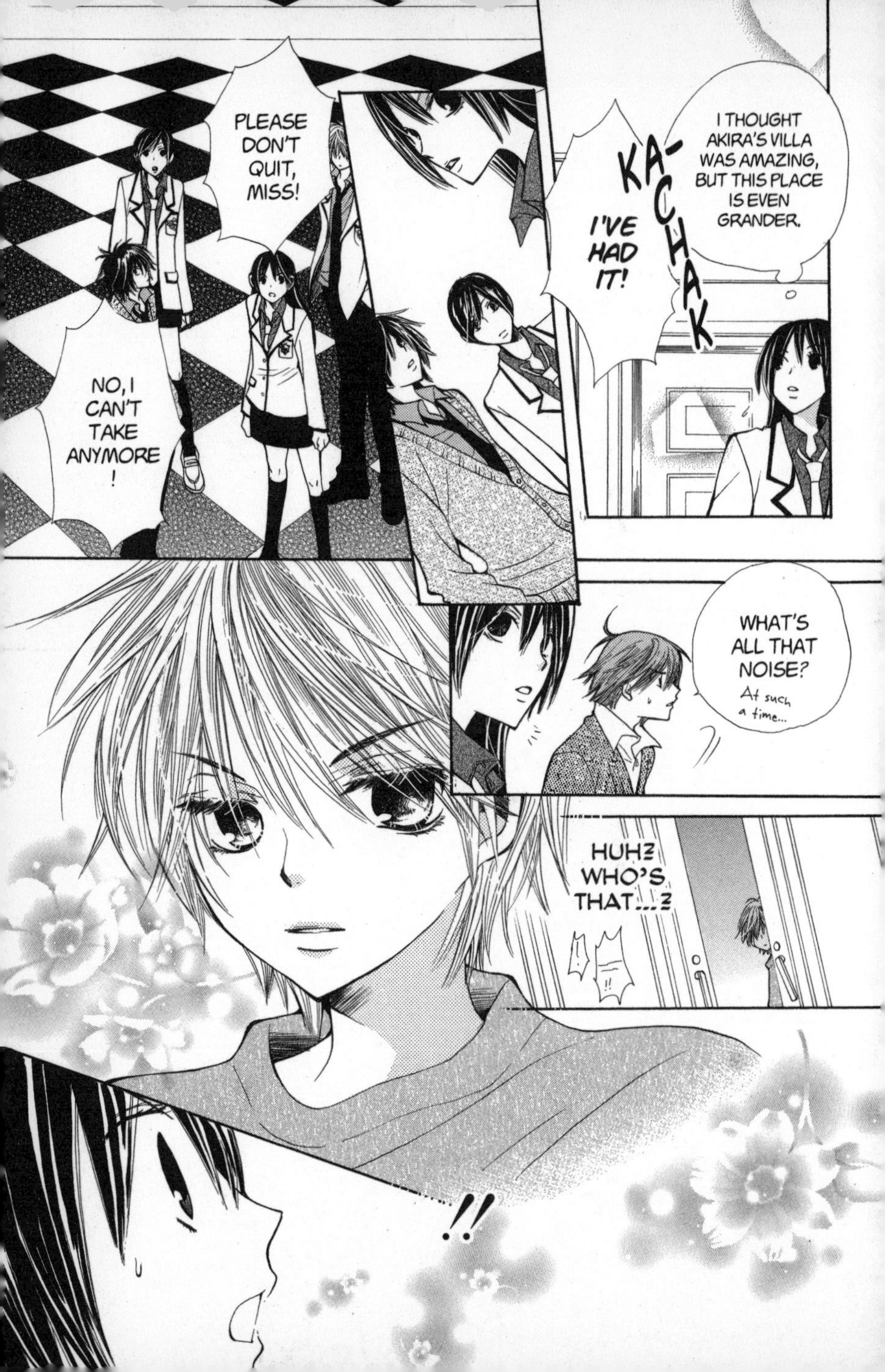
I THOUGHT AKIRA'S VILLA WAS AMAZING, BUT THIS PLACE IS EVEN GRANDER.
KA-CHAK
I'VE HAD IT!
PLEASE DON'T QUIT, MISS!
NO, I CAN'T TAKE ANYMORE!
WHAT'S ALL THAT NOISE?
At such a time...
HUH? WHO'S THAT...?
......!!

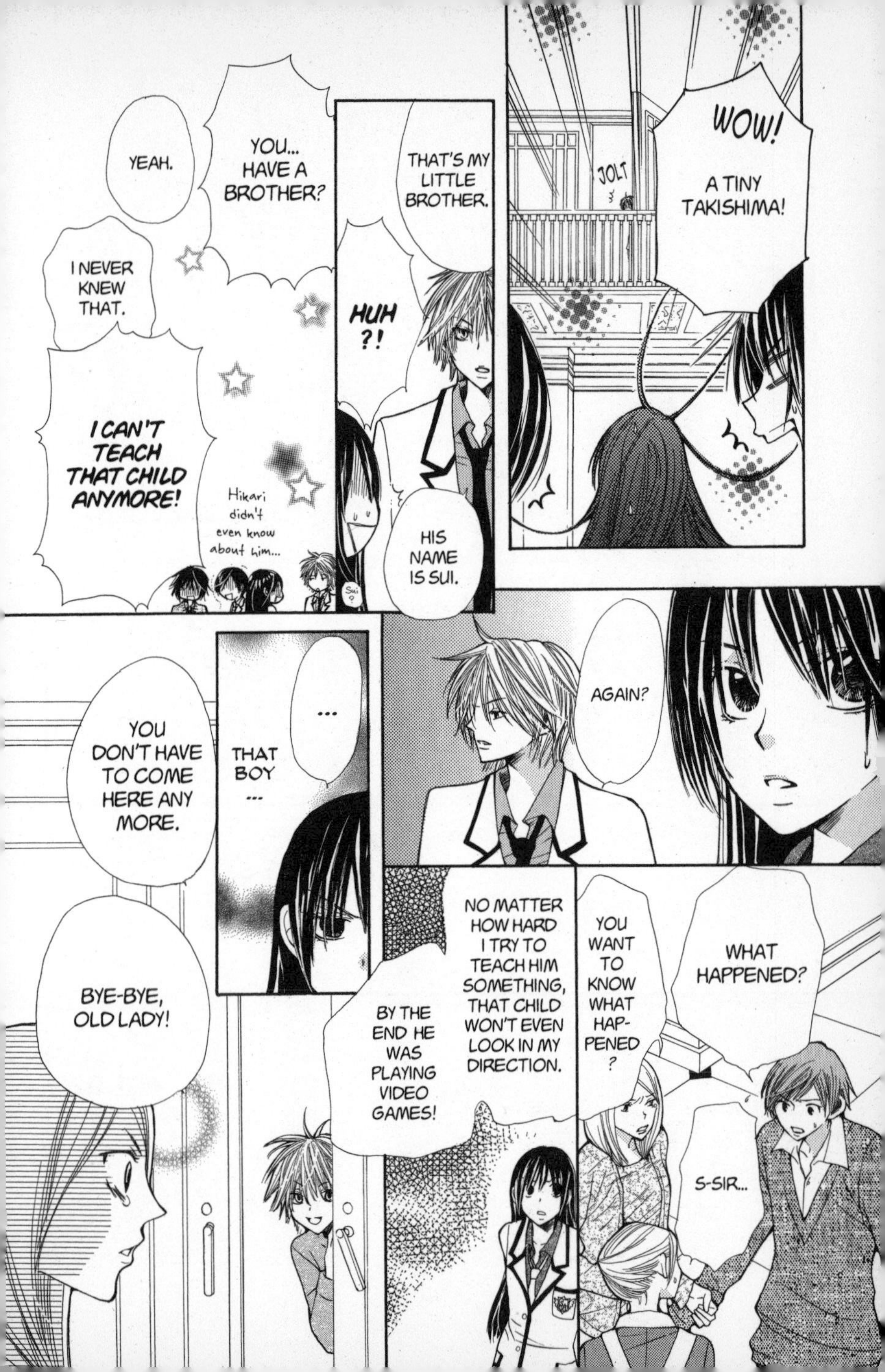
WOW!
JOLT
A TINY TAKISHIMA!
THAT'S MY LITTLE BROTHER.
HUH?!
HIS NAME IS SUI.
YOU... HAVE A BROTHER?
YEAH.
I NEVER KNEW THAT.
I CAN'T TEACH THAT CHILD ANYMORE!
Hikari didn't even know about him...
Sui?
AGAIN?
WHAT HAPPENED?
YOU WANT TO KNOW WHAT HAP-PENED?
NO MATTER HOW HARD I TRY TO TEACH HIM SOMETHING, THAT CHILD WON'T EVEN LOOK IN MY DIRECTION.
BY THE END HE WAS PLAYING VIDEO GAMES!
S-SIR...
...
THAT BOY ...
YOU DON'T HAVE TO COME HERE ANY MORE.
BYE-BYE, OLD LADY!

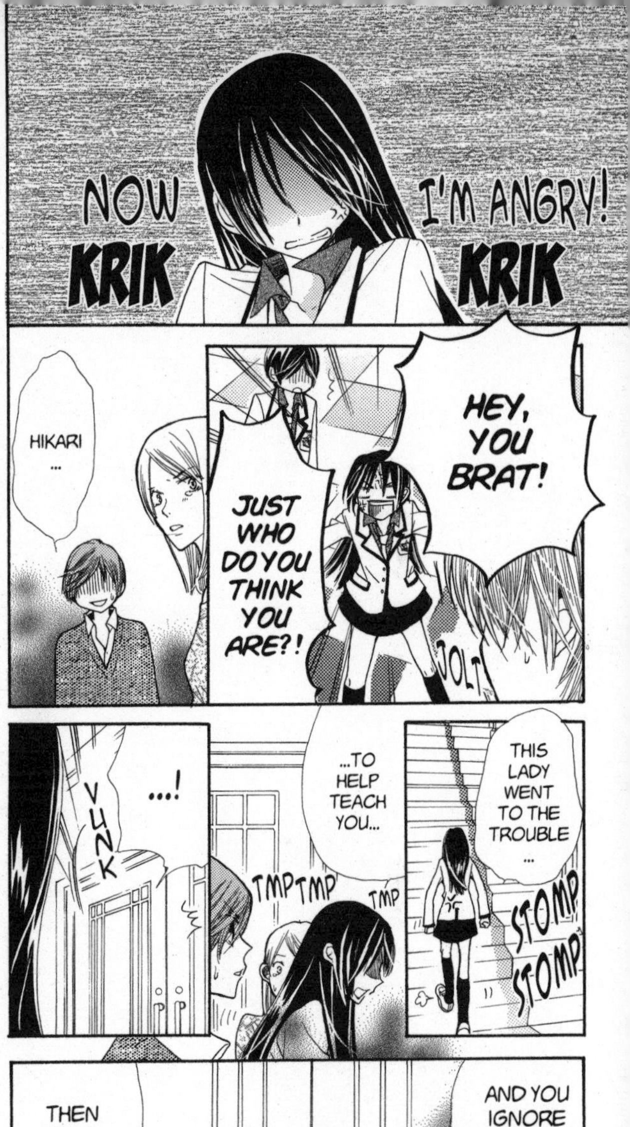
NOW I'M ANGRY!
KRIK KRIK
HEY, YOU BRAT!
JUST WHO DO YOU THINK YOU ARE?!
JOLT
HIKARI ...
THIS LADY WENT TO THE TROUBLE ...
STOMP STOMP
...TO HELP TEACH YOU...
TMP TMP TMP
...!
VUNK
AND YOU IGNORE HER TO PLAY VIDEO GAMES?!
THEN YOU MOCK HER?

⑤ ·THIS AND THAT·

THIS IS MY LAST 1/4 SPACE FOR THIS VOLUME. THANK YOU SO MUCH FOR READING THIS SECTION!

AND I REALLY, REALLY WANT TO THANK YOU FOR PICKING THIS BOOK! I'M SO GLAD THAT YOU EVEN LOOKED AT IT!!

I STILL HAVE A WHOLE LOT TO LEARN, BUT IF YOU ENJOYED IT, EVEN JUST A LITTLE BIT... THAT MAKES ME HAPPY.

IF YOU WANT TO, PLEASE...LET ME KNOW WHAT YOU THOUGHT!

MY ADDRESS:
MAKI MINAMI
C/O SA EDITOR
P.O. BOX 77010
SAN FRANCISCO,
CA 94107

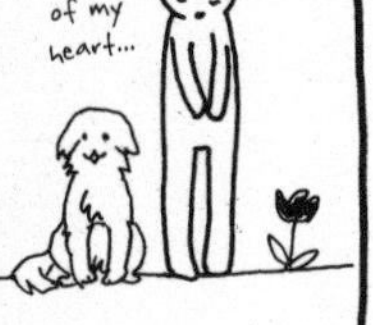
From the bottom of my heart...
And so...
maki minami

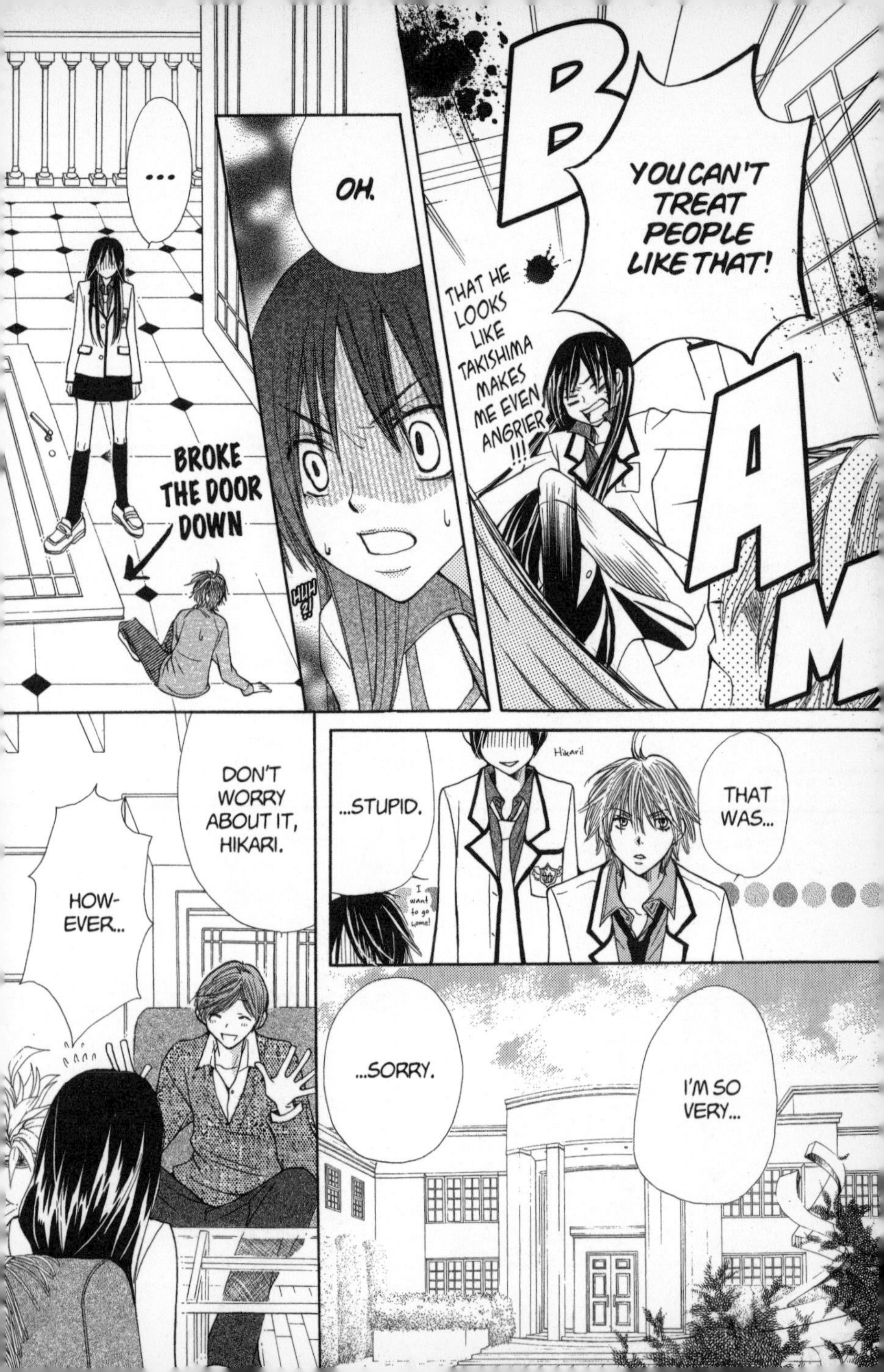
BAM
YOU CAN'T TREAT PEOPLE LIKE THAT!
THAT HE LOOKS LIKE TAKISHIMA MAKES ME EVEN ANGRIER!!!
OH.
HUH?!
...
BROKE THE DOOR DOWN
THAT WAS...
Hikari!
...STUPID.
I want to go home!
I'M SO VERY...
...SORRY.
DON'T WORRY ABOUT IT, HIKARI.
HOW-EVER...

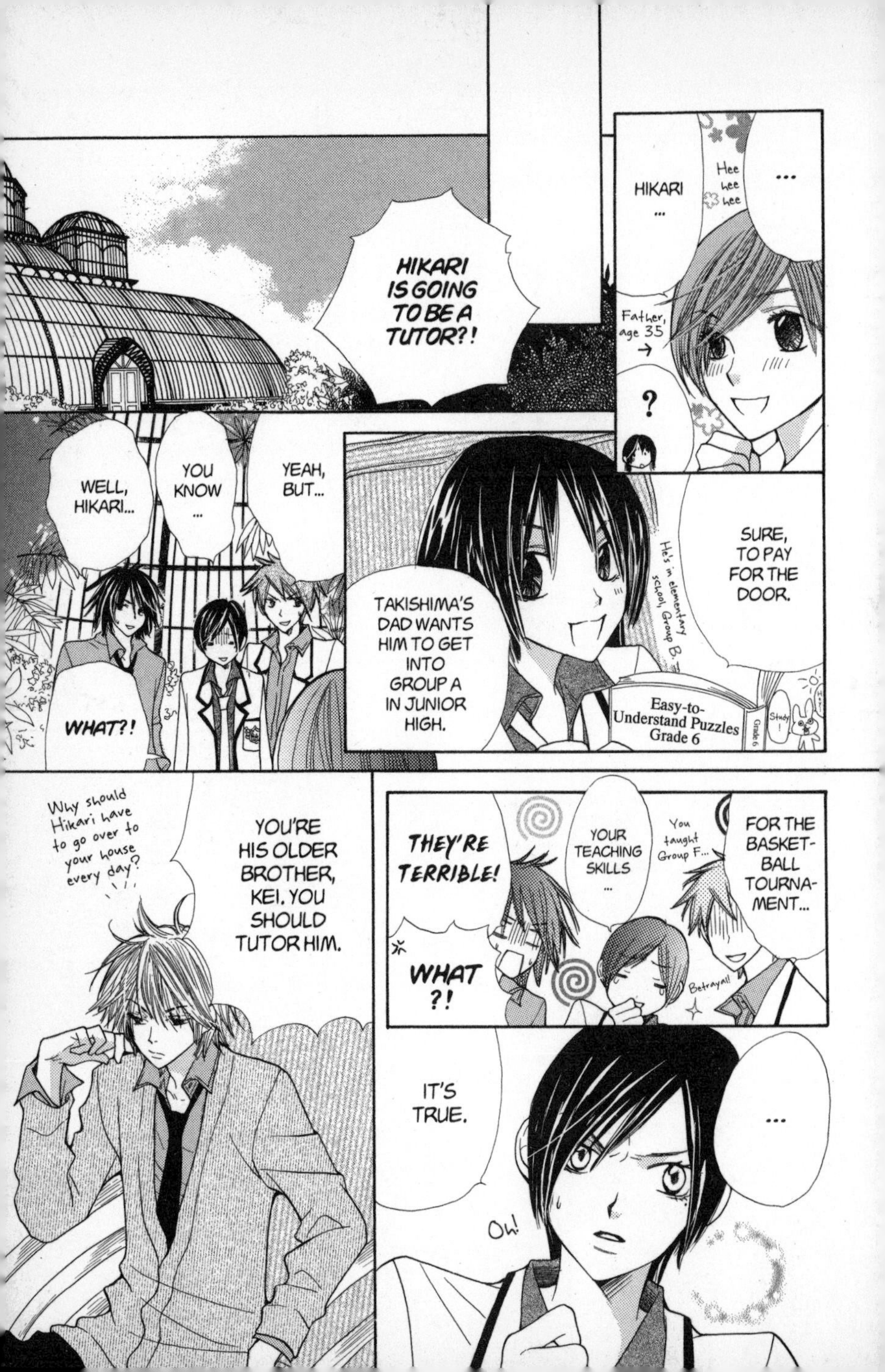
...
Hee hee hee
HIKARI ...
Father, age 35
?
HIKARI IS GOING TO BE A TUTOR?!
SURE, TO PAY FOR THE DOOR.
He's in elementary school, Group B.
TAKISHIMA'S DAD WANTS HIM TO GET INTO GROUP A IN JUNIOR HIGH.
Easy-to-Understand Puzzles Grade 6
Grade 6
Study!
YEAH, BUT...
YOU KNOW ...
WELL, HIKARI...
WHAT?!
FOR THE BASKET-BALL TOURNA-MENT...
Betrayal!
You taught Group F...
YOUR TEACHING SKILLS ...
THEY'RE TERRIBLE!
WHAT ?!
...
IT'S TRUE.
Oh!
YOU'RE HIS OLDER BROTHER, KEI. YOU SHOULD TUTOR HIM.
Why should Hikari have to go over to your house every day?

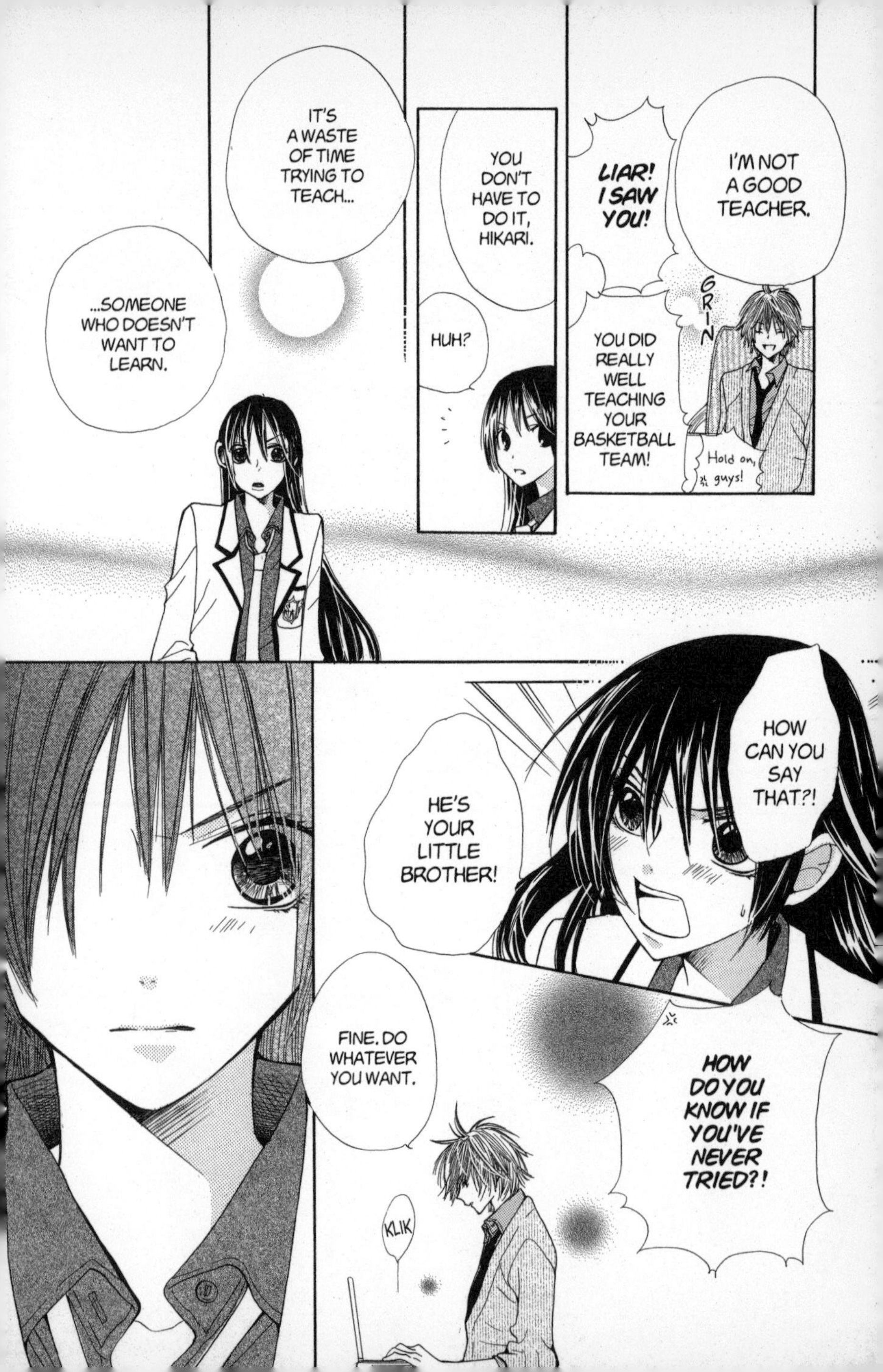
I'M NOT A GOOD TEACHER.
LIAR! I SAW YOU!
GRIN
YOU DID REALLY WELL TEACHING YOUR BASKETBALL TEAM!
Hold on, guys!
YOU DON'T HAVE TO DO IT, HIKARI.
HUH?
IT'S A WASTE OF TIME TRYING TO TEACH...
...SOMEONE WHO DOESN'T WANT TO LEARN.
HOW CAN YOU SAY THAT?!
HE'S YOUR LITTLE BROTHER!
HOW DO YOU KNOW IF YOU'VE NEVER TRIED?!
FINE. DO WHATEVER YOU WANT.
KLIK

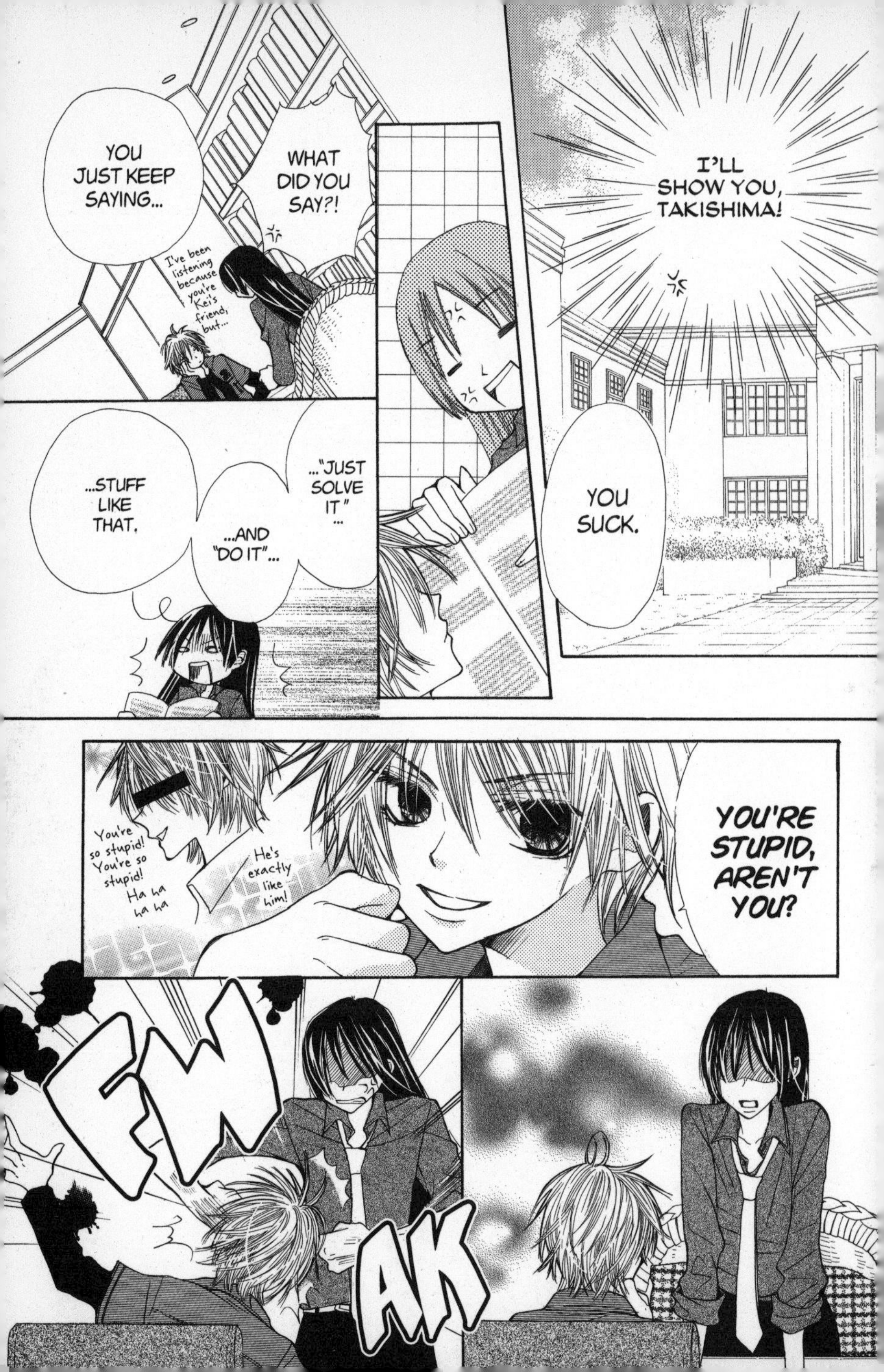
I'LL SHOW YOU, TAKISHIMA!
YOU SUCK.
WHAT DID YOU SAY?!
YOU JUST KEEP SAYING...
I've been listening because you're Kei's friend, but...
..."JUST SOLVE IT"...
...AND "DO IT"...
...STUFF LIKE THAT.
YOU'RE STUPID, AREN'T YOU?
He's exactly like him!
You're so stupid! You're so stupid!
Ha ha ha ha
FWAK

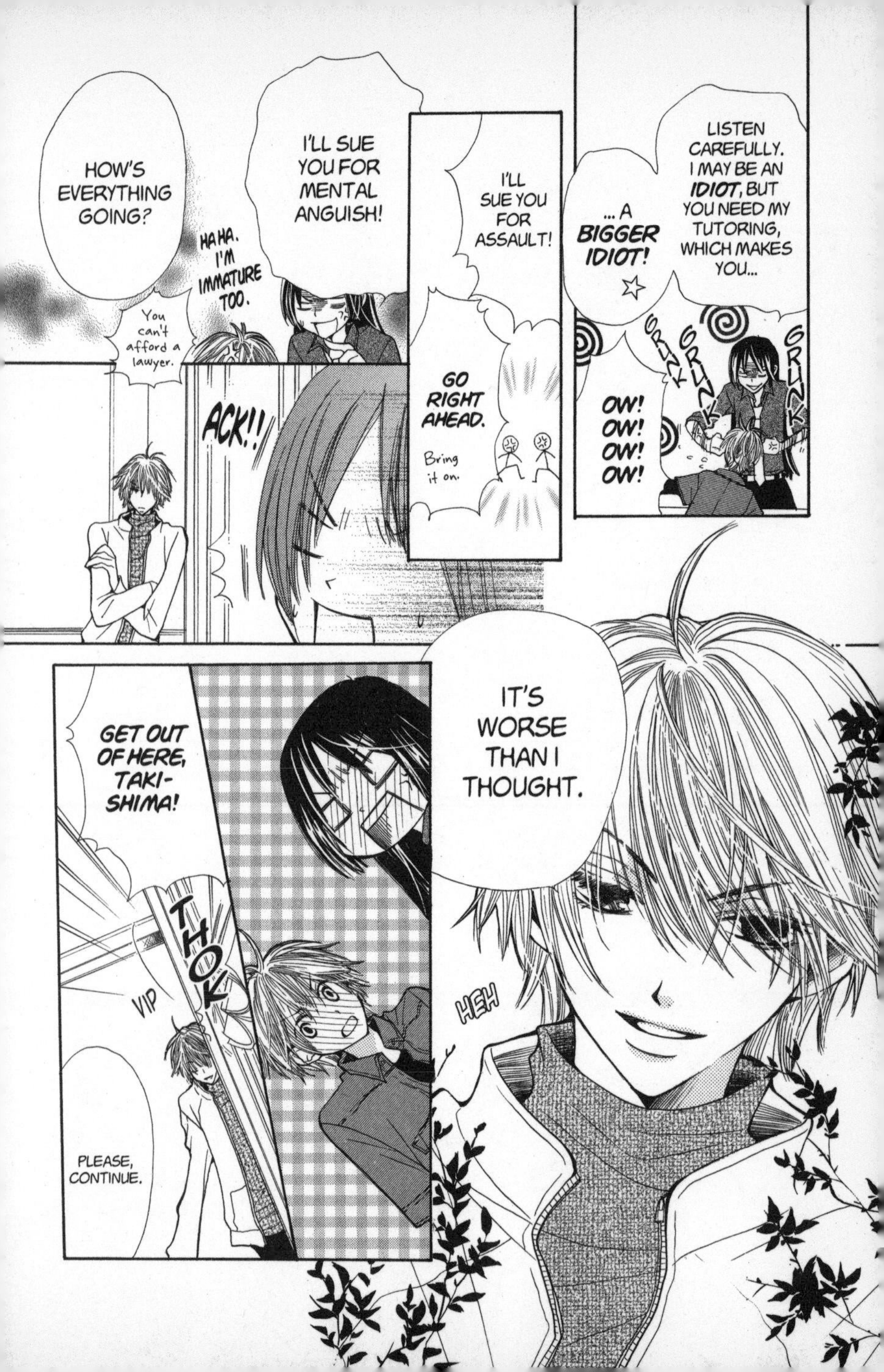
LISTEN CAREFULLY. I MAY BE AN IDIOT, BUT YOU NEED MY TUTORING, WHICH MAKES YOU...
... A BIGGER IDIOT! ☆
GRUNK
GRUNK
GRUNK
OW! OW! OW! OW!
I'LL SUE YOU FOR ASSAULT!
GO RIGHT AHEAD.
Bring it on.
I'LL SUE YOU FOR MENTAL ANGUISH!
HA HA. I'M IMMATURE TOO.
You can't afford a lawyer.
HOW'S EVERYTHING GOING?
ACK!!
IT'S WORSE THAN I THOUGHT.
HEH
GET OUT OF HERE, TAKI-SHIMA!
THOK
VIP
PLEASE, CONTINUE.

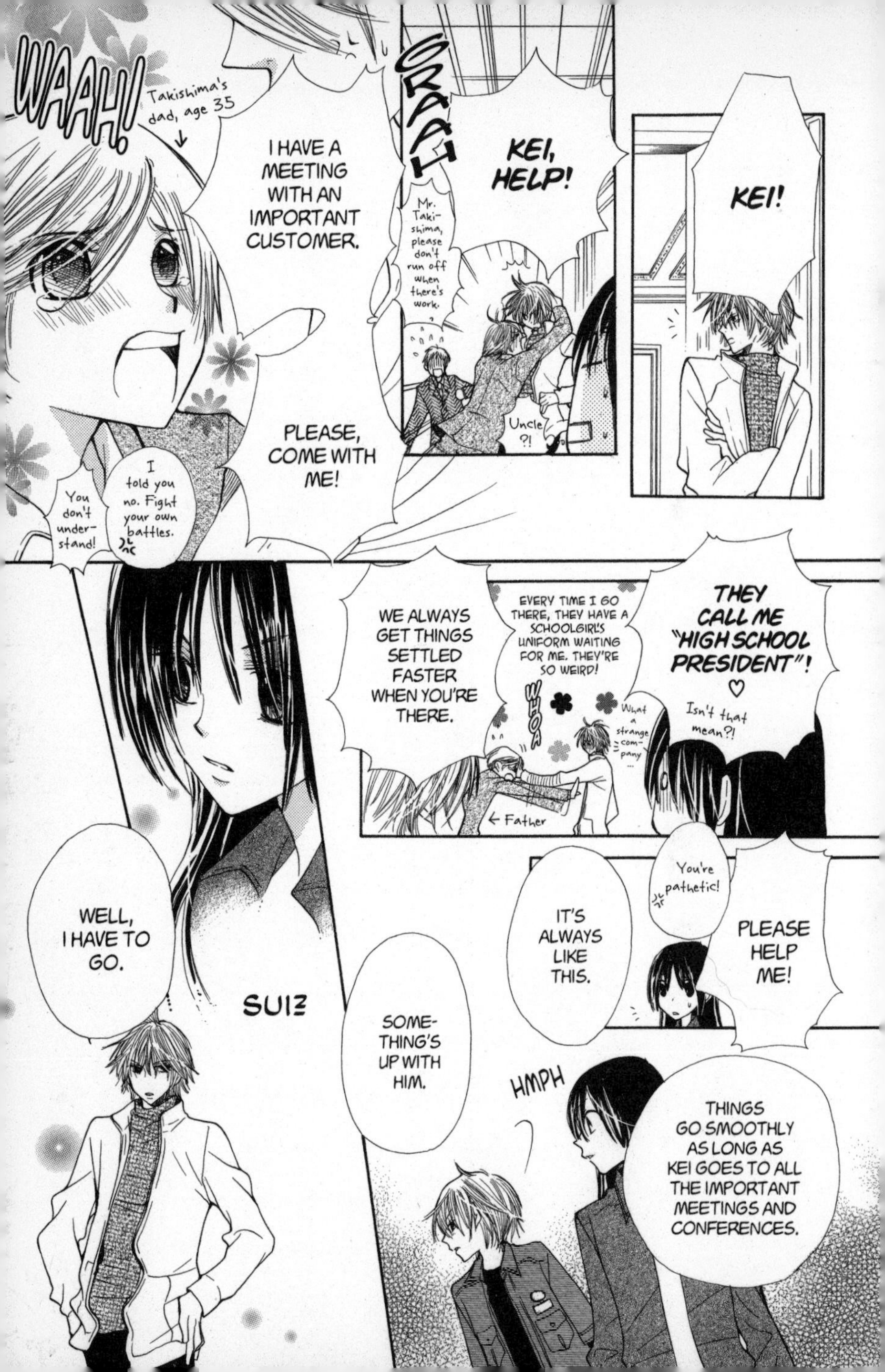
KEI!
ORAAAH
KEI, HELP!
Mr. Takishima, please don't run off when there's work.
Uncle?!
WAAH!
Takishima's dad, age 35
I HAVE A MEETING WITH AN IMPORTANT CUSTOMER.
PLEASE, COME WITH ME!
I told you no. Fight your own battles.
You don't understand!
THEY CALL ME "HIGH SCHOOL PRESIDENT"! ♡
Isn't that mean?!
EVERY TIME I GO THERE, THEY HAVE A SCHOOLGIRL'S UNIFORM WAITING FOR ME. THEY'RE SO WEIRD!
WHOA
What a strange company...
WE ALWAYS GET THINGS SETTLED FASTER WHEN YOU'RE THERE.
← Father
You're pathetic!
PLEASE HELP ME!
IT'S ALWAYS LIKE THIS.
SOMETHING'S UP WITH HIM.
HMPH
THINGS GO SMOOTHLY AS LONG AS KEI GOES TO ALL THE IMPORTANT MEETINGS AND CONFERENCES.
WELL, I HAVE TO GO.
SUI

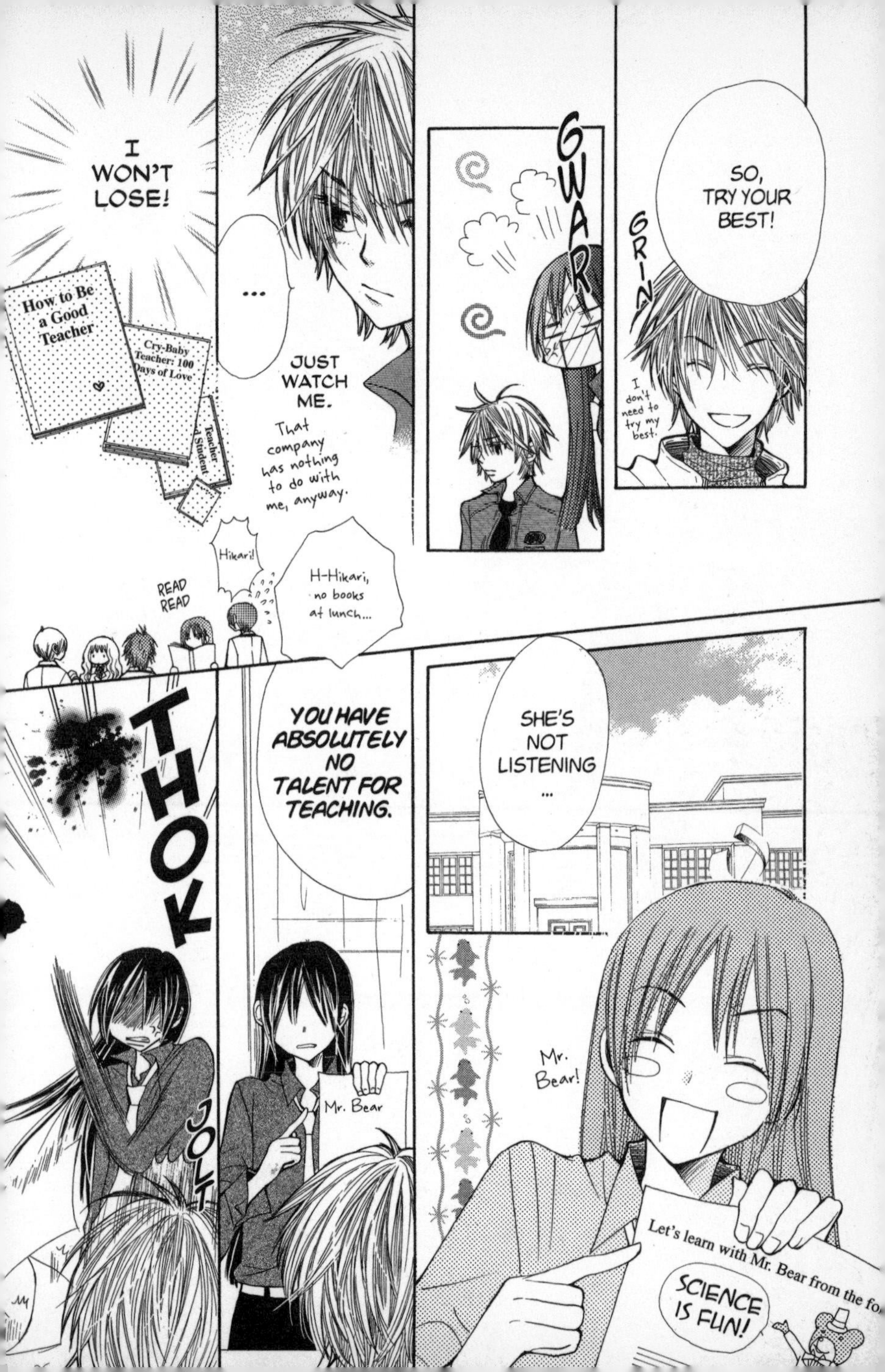
SO, TRY YOUR BEST!
GRIN
I don't need to try my best.
GWAR
...
JUST WATCH ME.
That company has nothing to do with me, anyway.
I WON'T LOSE!
How to Be a Good Teacher
Cry-Baby Teacher: 100 Days of Love
Hikari!
H-Hikari, no books at lunch...
READ READ
SHE'S NOT LISTENING ...
Mr. Bear!
Let's learn with Mr. Bear from the fo
SCIENCE IS FUN!
YOU HAVE ABSOLUTELY NO TALENT FOR TEACHING.
Mr. Bear
THOK
JOLT

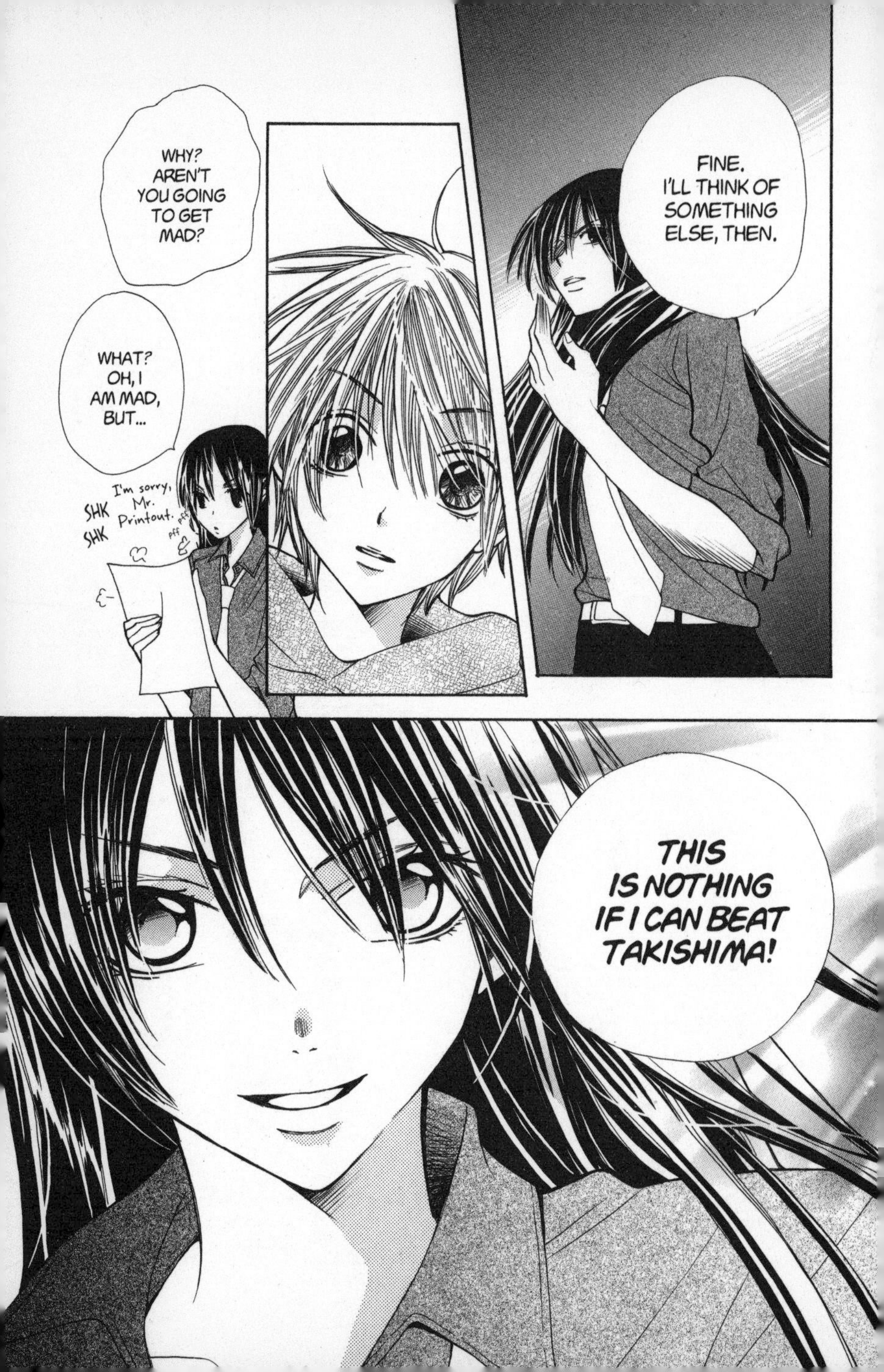
FINE. I'LL THINK OF SOMETHING ELSE, THEN.
WHY? AREN'T YOU GOING TO GET MAD?
WHAT? OH, I AM MAD, BUT...
I'm sorry, Mr. Printout.
SHK SHK
pff pff
THIS IS NOTHING IF I CAN BEAT TAKISHIMA!

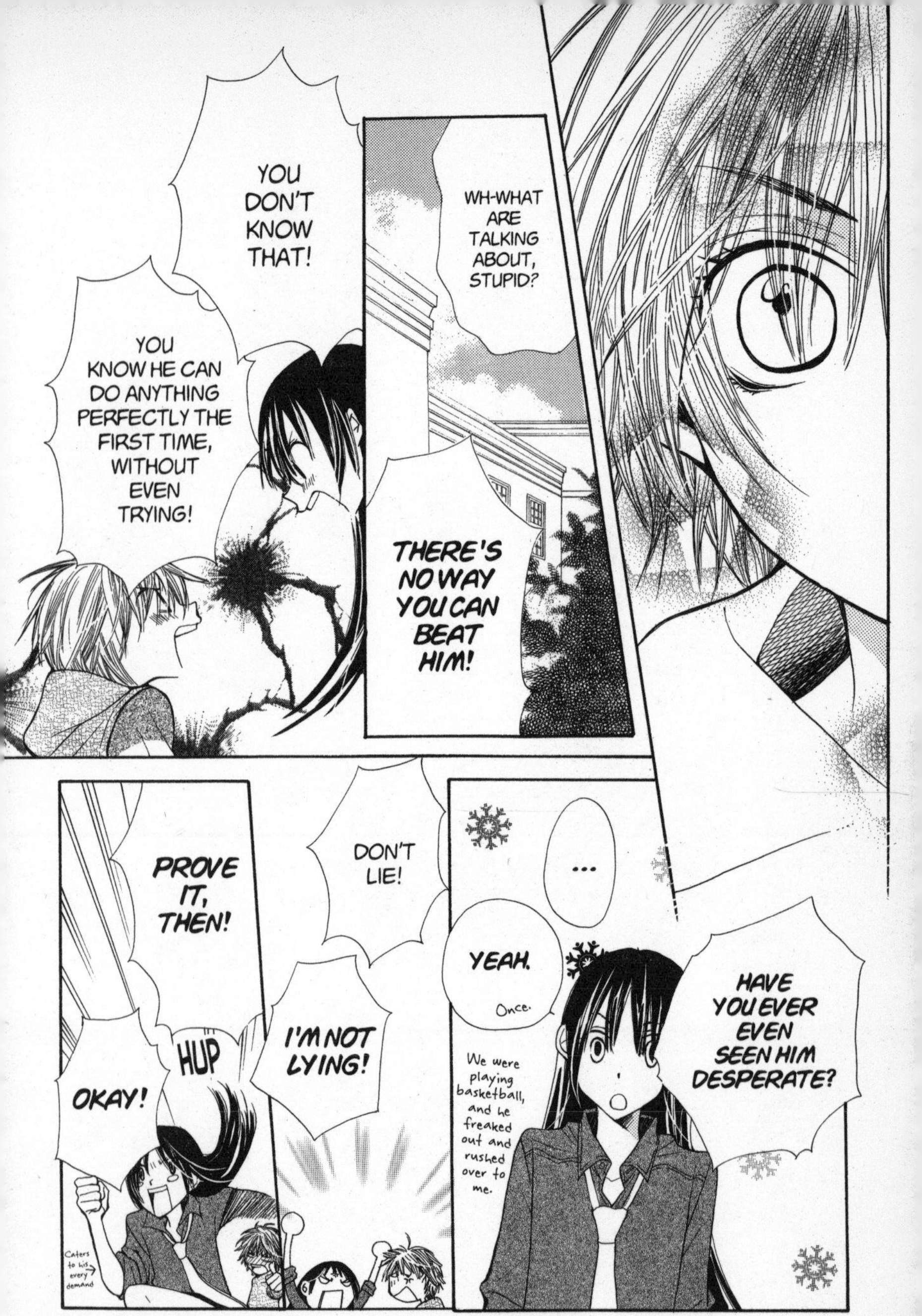

WH-WHAT ARE TALKING ABOUT, STUPID?
THERE'S NO WAY YOU CAN BEAT HIM!
YOU DON'T KNOW THAT!
YOU KNOW HE CAN DO ANYTHING PERFECTLY THE FIRST TIME, WITHOUT EVEN TRYING!
HAVE YOU EVER EVEN SEEN HIM DESPERATE?
...
YEAH.
Once.
We were playing basketball, and he freaked out and rushed over to me.
DON'T LIE!
I'M NOT LYING!
PROVE IT, THEN!
HUP
OKAY!
Caters to his every demand

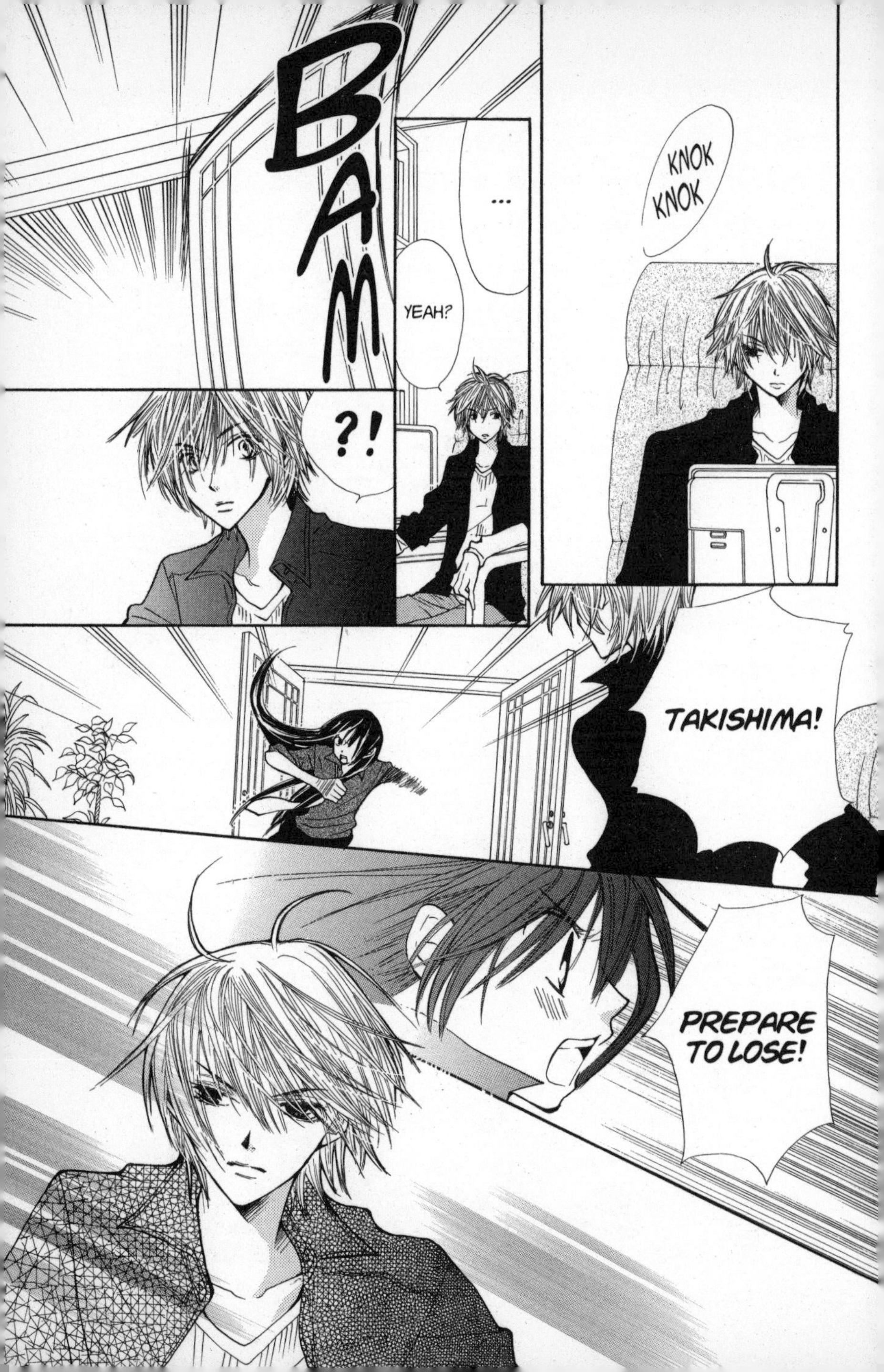
KNOK KNOK
...
YEAH?
BAM
?!
TAKISHIMA!
PREPARE TO LOSE!

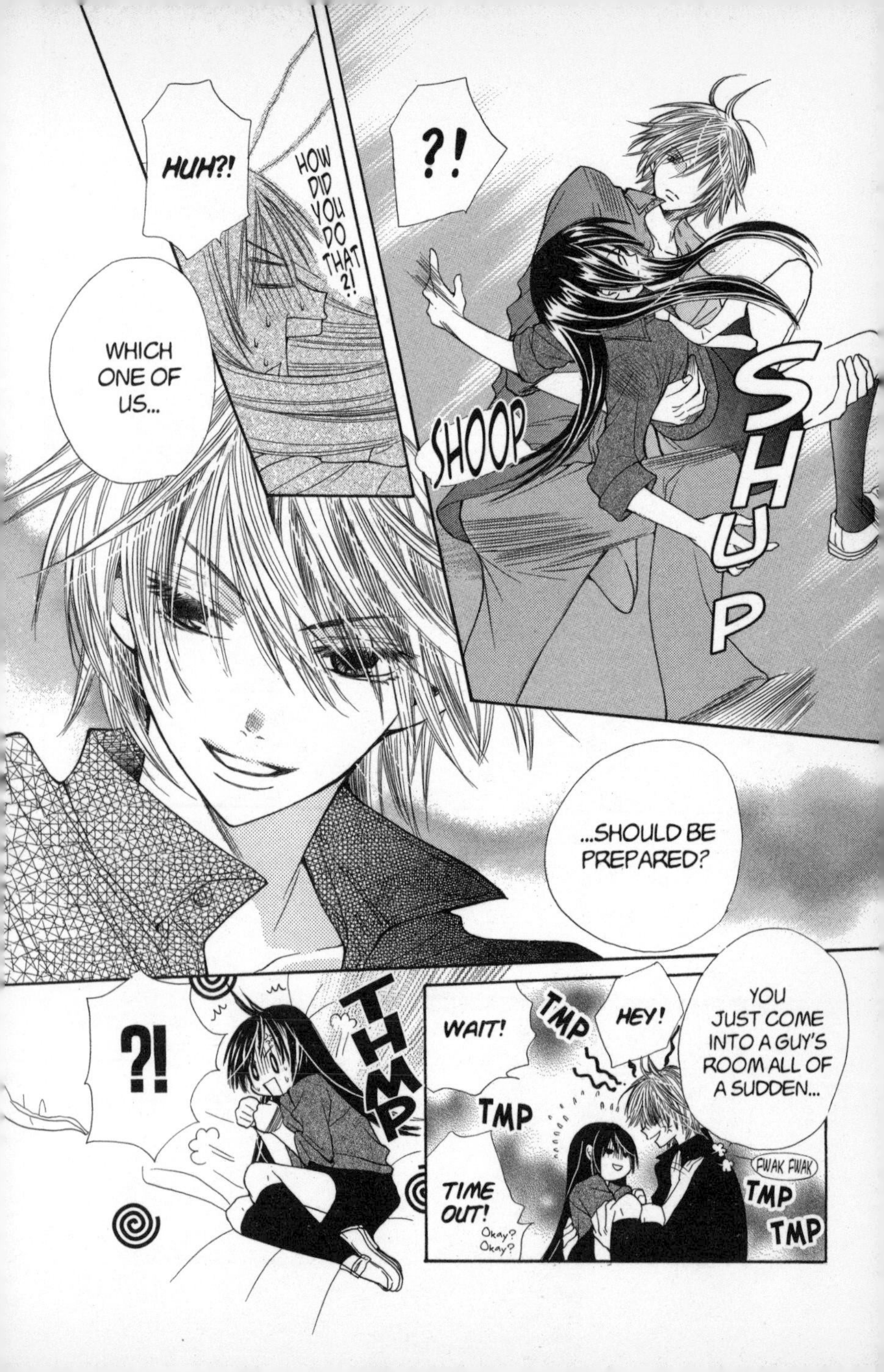
?!
SHUP
SHOOP
HOW DID YOU DO THAT?!
HUH?!
WHICH ONE OF US...
...SHOULD BE PREPARED?
YOU JUST COME INTO A GUY'S ROOM ALL OF A SUDDEN...
HEY!
TMP
WAIT!
TMP
TIME OUT!
Okay? Okay?
FWAK FWAK
TMP
TMP
THMP
?!

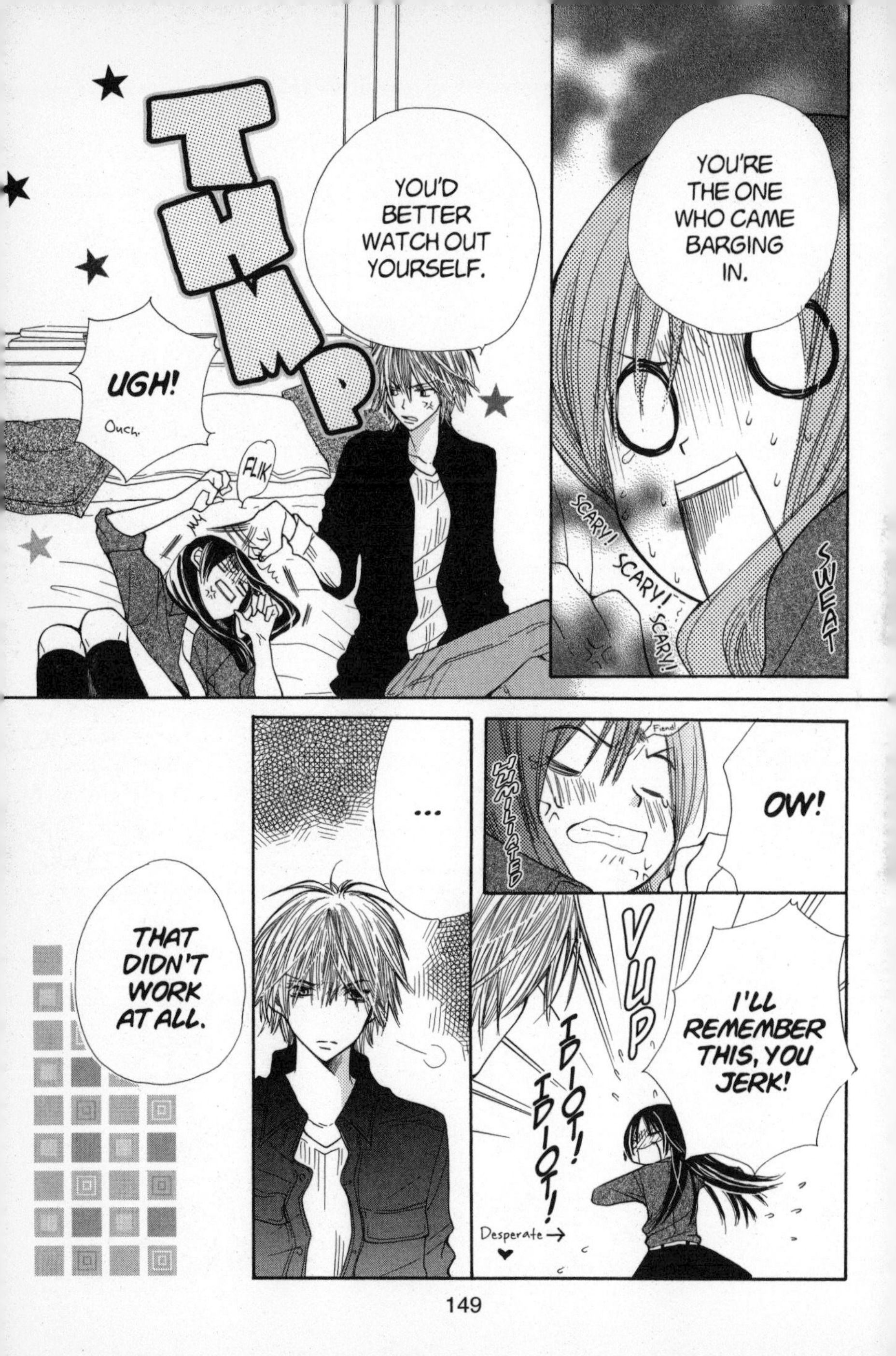
YOU'RE THE ONE WHO CAME BARGING IN.
SCARY! SCARY! SCARY!
SWEAT
YOU'D BETTER WATCH OUT YOURSELF.
THUMP
UGH!
Ouch.
FLIK
Fiend!
HUMILIATED
OW!
VUP
I'LL REMEMBER THIS, YOU JERK!
IDIOT! IDIOT!
Desperate →
...
THAT DIDN'T WORK AT ALL.

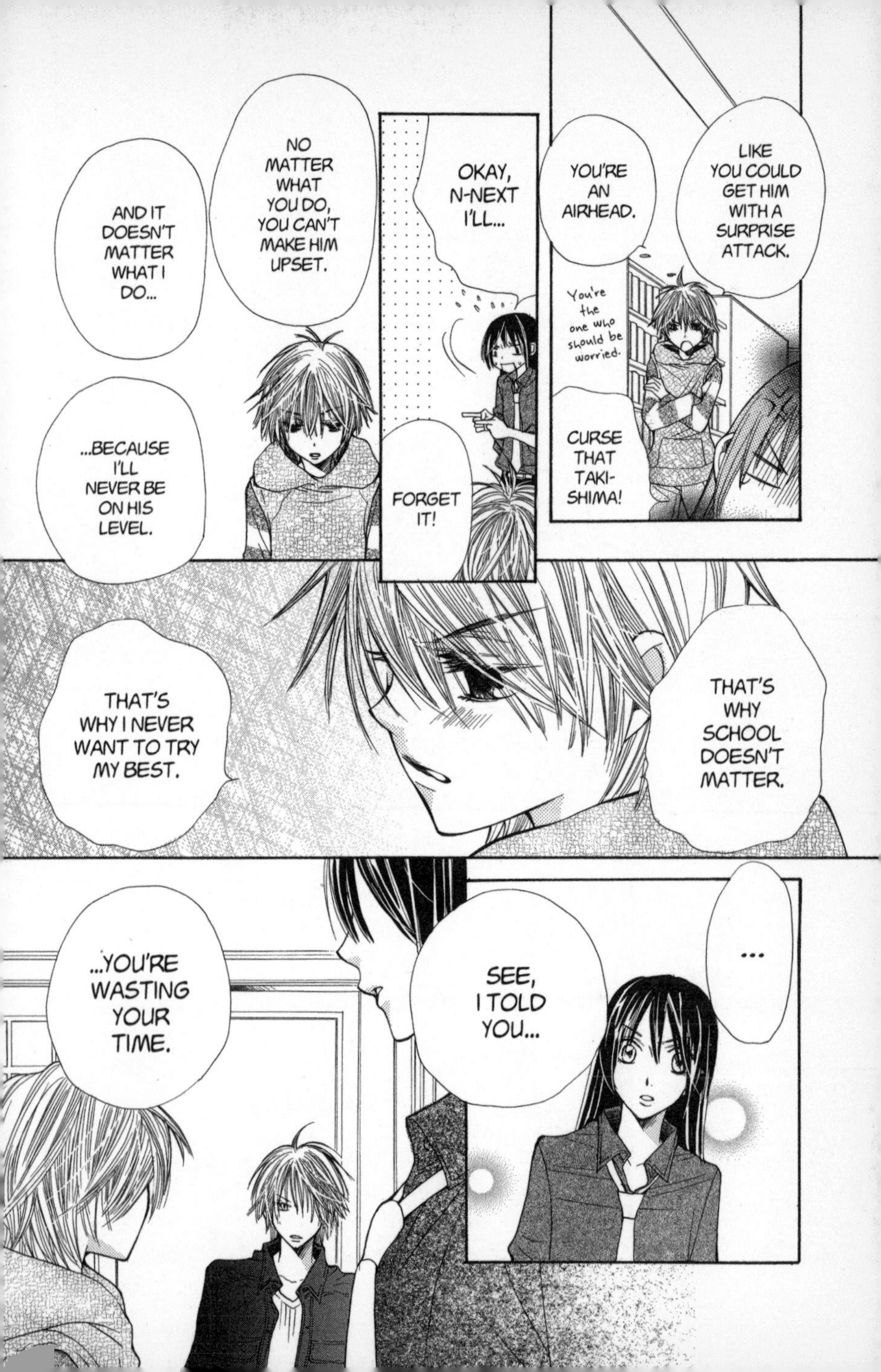
LIKE YOU COULD GET HIM WITH A SURPRISE ATTACK.
YOU'RE AN AIRHEAD.
You're the one who should be worried.
CURSE THAT TAKI-SHIMA!
OKAY, N-NEXT I'LL...
FORGET IT!
NO MATTER WHAT YOU DO, YOU CAN'T MAKE HIM UPSET.
AND IT DOESN'T MATTER WHAT I DO...
...BECAUSE I'LL NEVER BE ON HIS LEVEL.
THAT'S WHY SCHOOL DOESN'T MATTER.
THAT'S WHY I NEVER WANT TO TRY MY BEST.
...
SEE, I TOLD YOU...
...YOU'RE WASTING YOUR TIME.

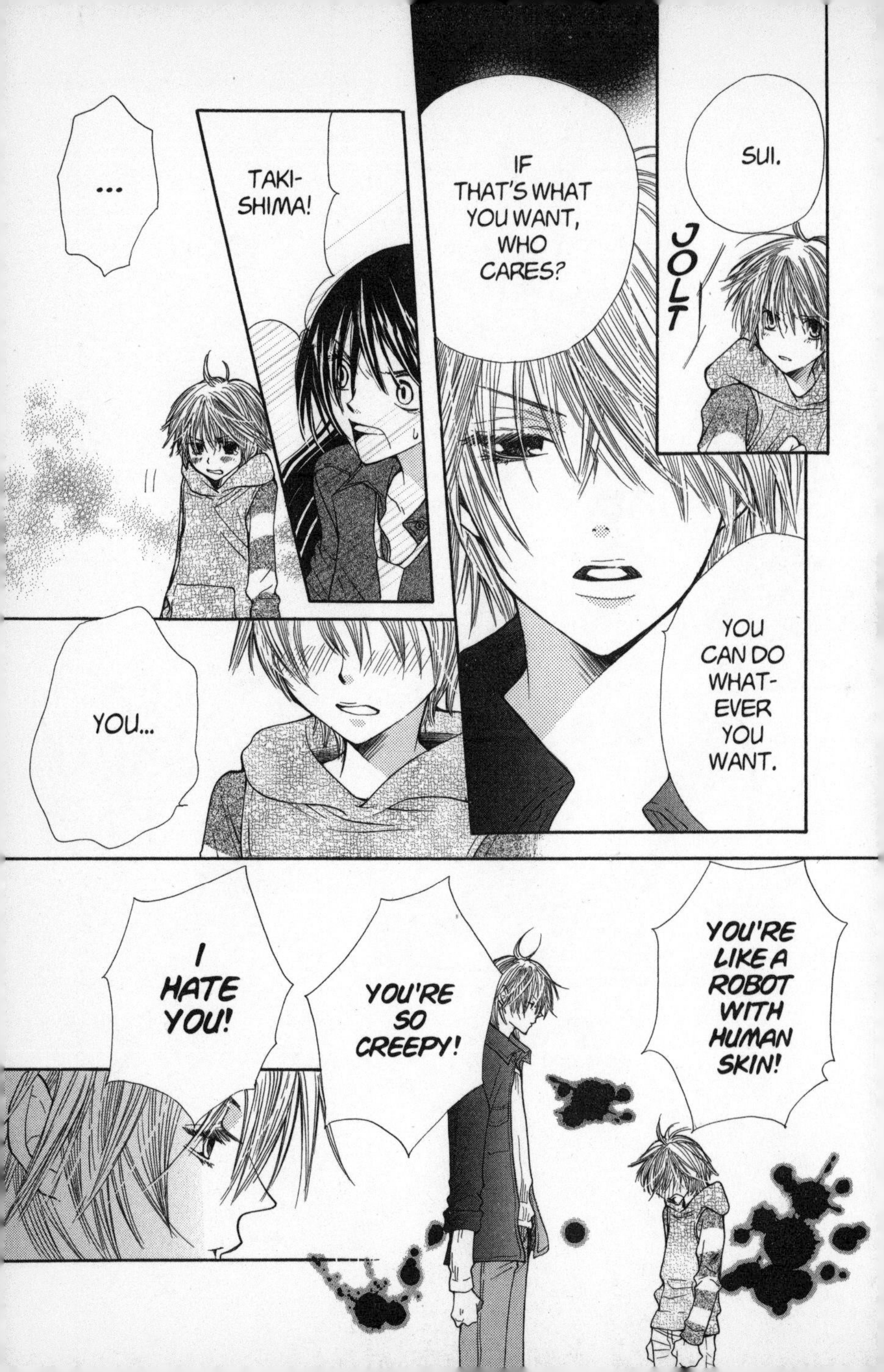
SUI.
JOLT
IF THAT'S WHAT YOU WANT, WHO CARES?
TAKI-SHIMA!
...
YOU CAN DO WHAT-EVER YOU WANT.
YOU...
YOU'RE LIKE A ROBOT WITH HUMAN SKIN!
YOU'RE SO CREEPY!
I HATE YOU!

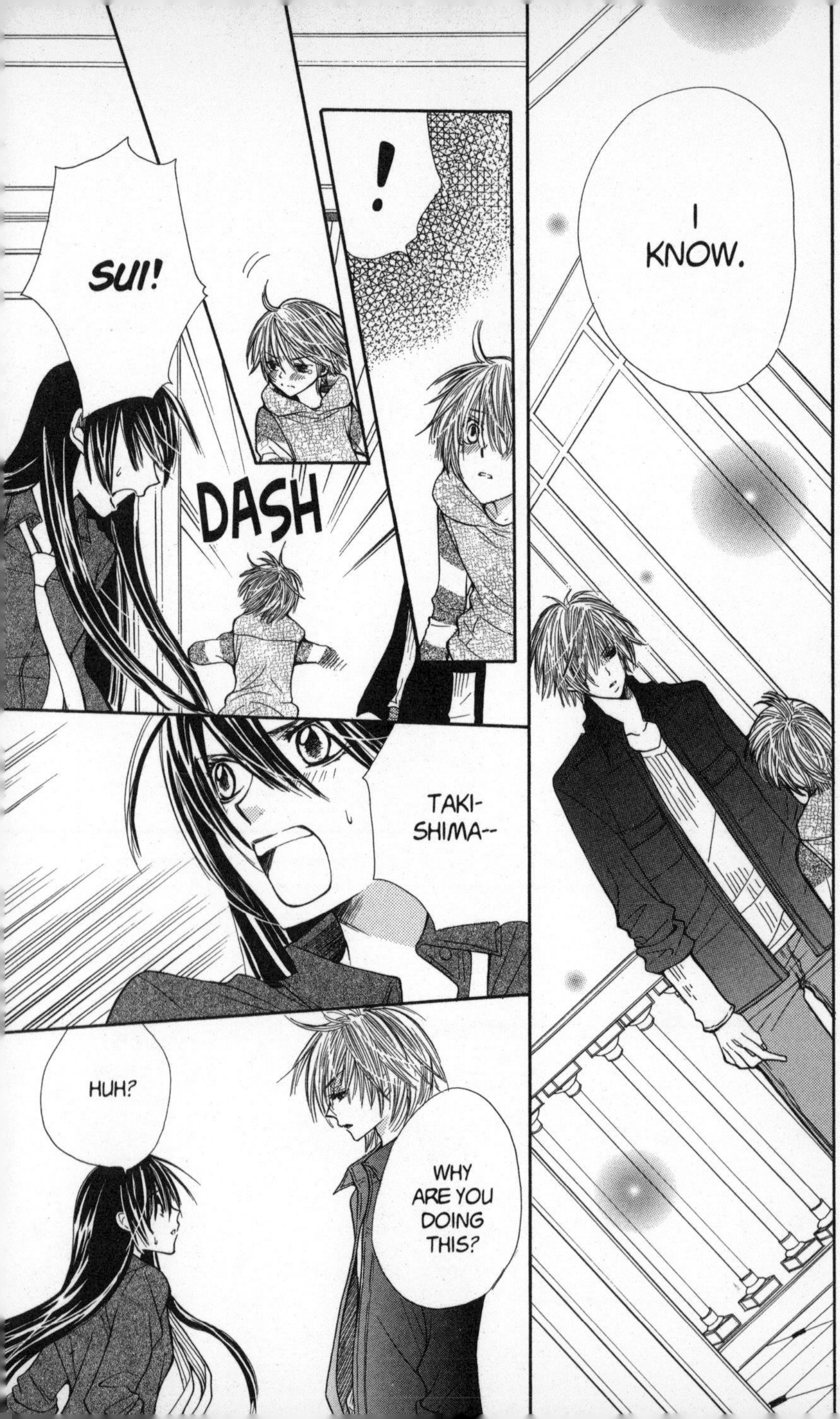
I KNOW.
!
SUI!
DASH
TAKI-SHIMA--
WHY ARE YOU DOING THIS?
HUH?

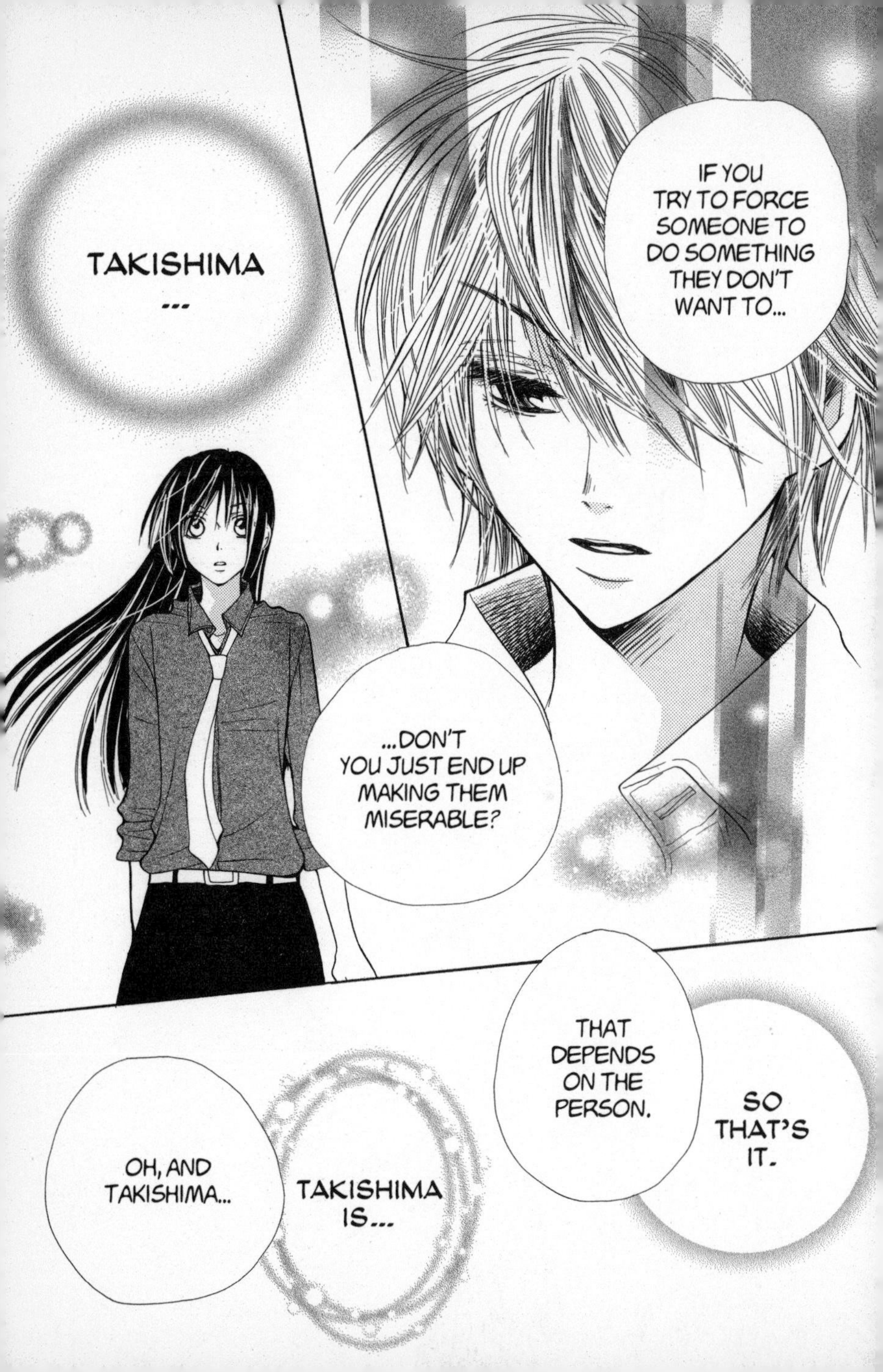
IF YOU TRY TO FORCE SOMEONE TO DO SOMETHING THEY DON'T WANT TO...
...DON'T YOU JUST END UP MAKING THEM MISERABLE?
TAKISHIMA ...
THAT DEPENDS ON THE PERSON.
SO THAT'S IT.
TAKISHIMA IS...
OH, AND TAKISHIMA...

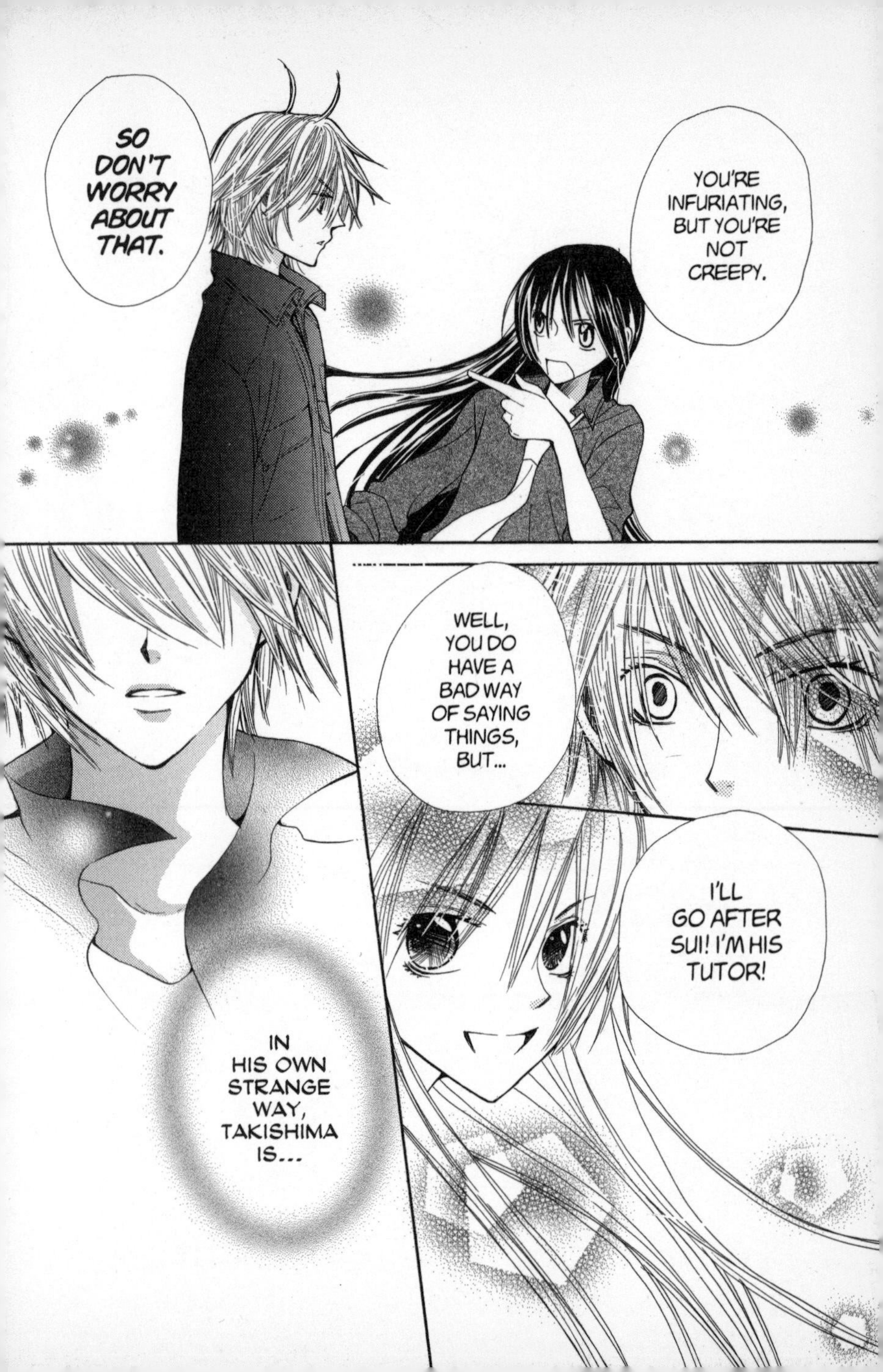
YOU'RE INFURIATING, BUT YOU'RE NOT CREEPY.
SO DON'T WORRY ABOUT THAT.
WELL, YOU DO HAVE A BAD WAY OF SAYING THINGS, BUT...
I'LL GO AFTER SUI! I'M HIS TUTOR!
IN HIS OWN STRANGE WAY, TAKISHIMA IS...

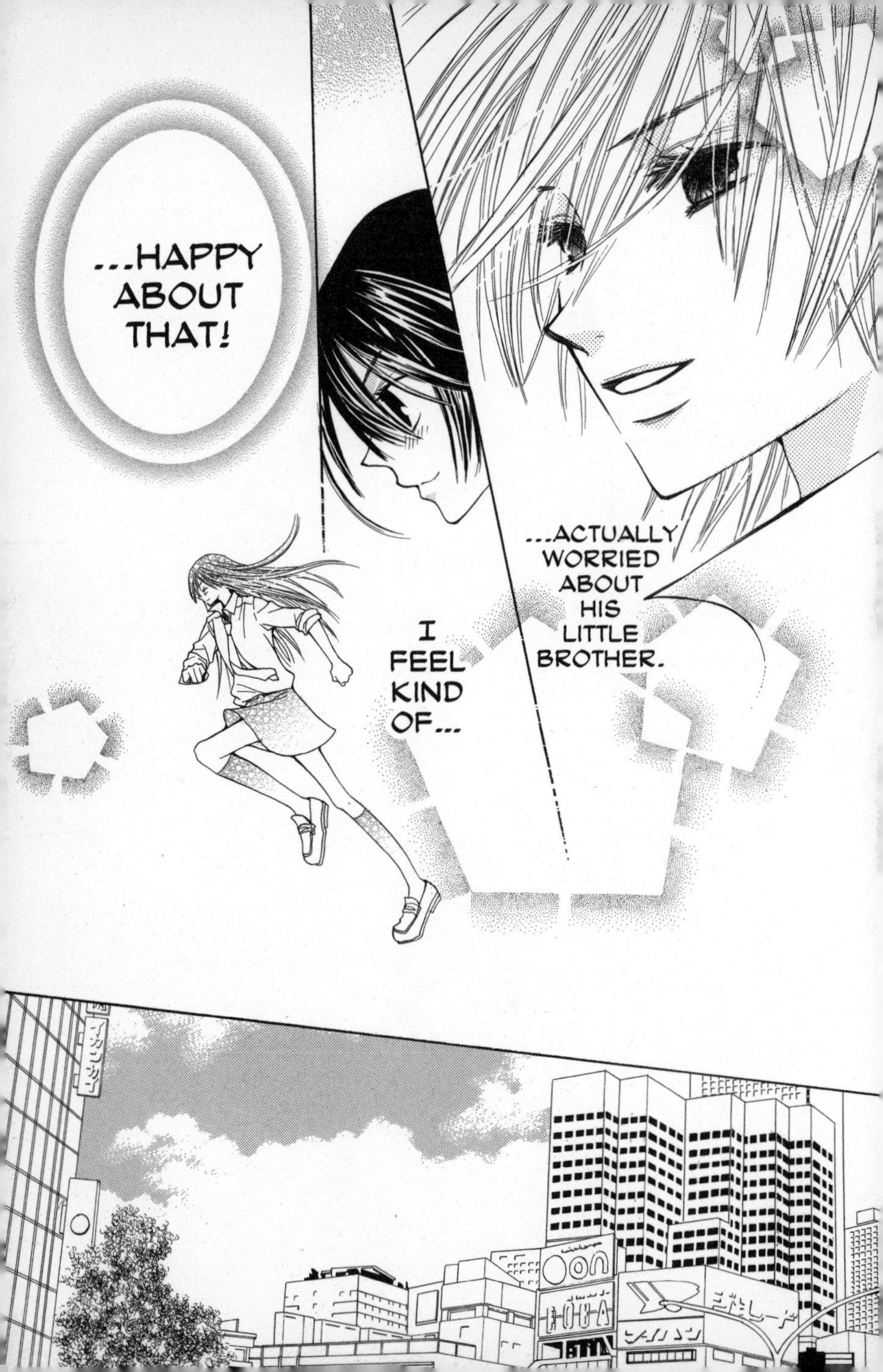
...ACTUALLY WORRIED ABOUT HIS LITTLE BROTHER.
I FEEL KIND OF...
...HAPPY ABOUT THAT!

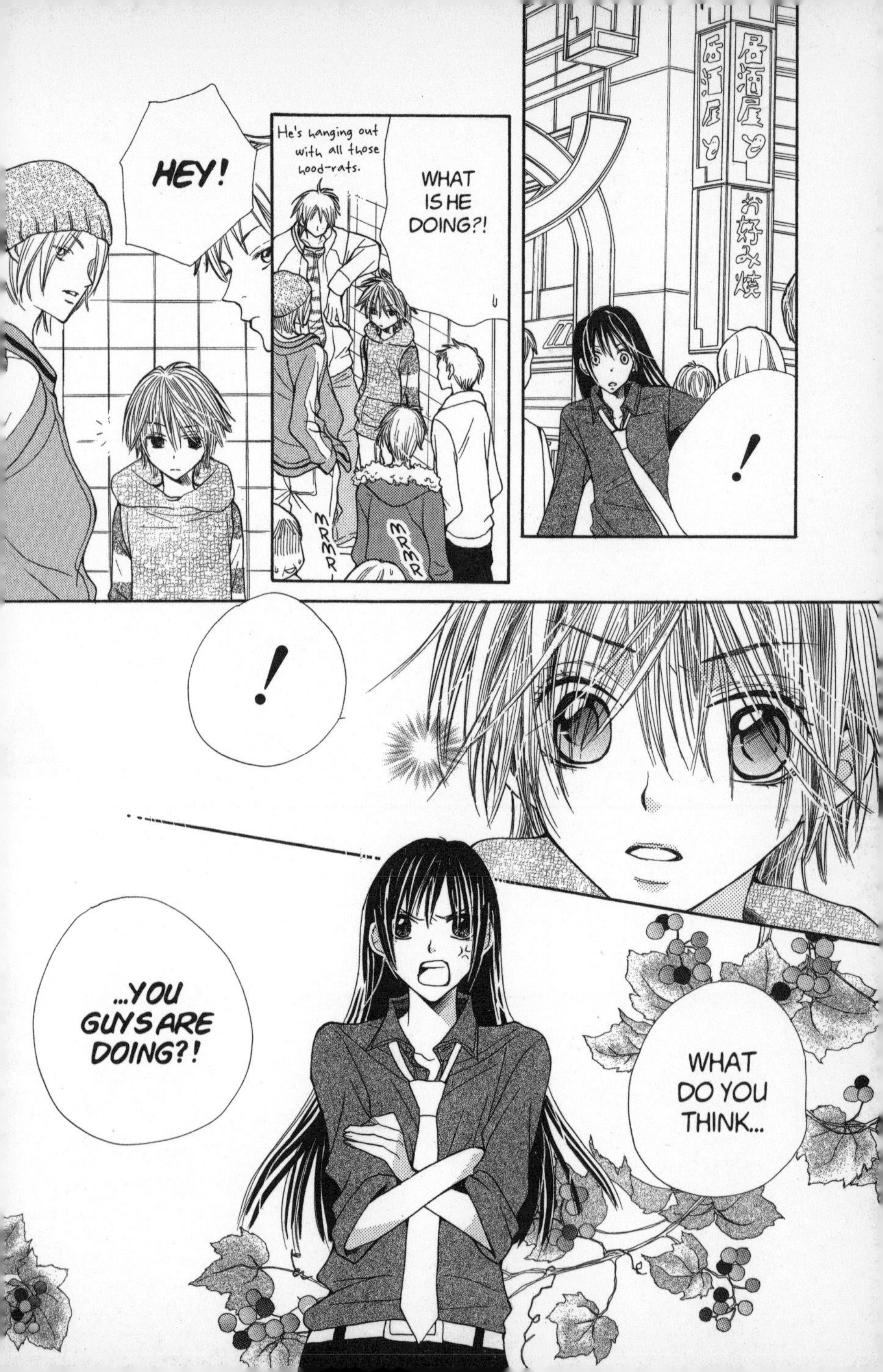
居酒屋と
お好み焼
!
WHAT IS HE DOING?!
He's hanging out with all those hood-rats.
MRMR
MRMR
HEY!
!
WHAT DO YOU THINK...
...YOU GUYS ARE DOING?!

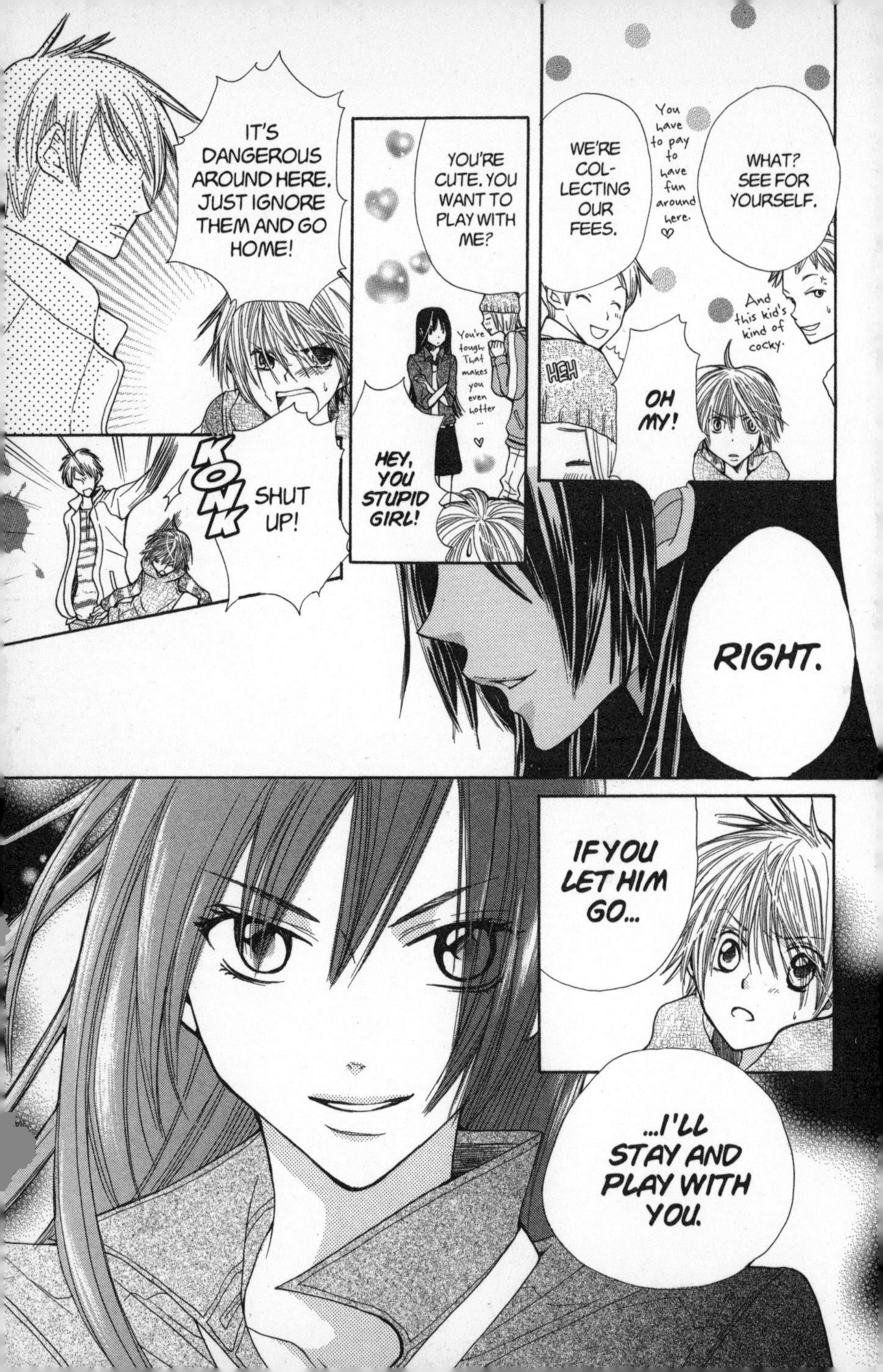
WHAT? SEE FOR YOURSELF.
You have to pay to have fun around here. ♡
WE'RE COL-LECTING OUR FEES.
And this kid's kind of cocky.
HEH
OH MY!
YOU'RE CUTE. YOU WANT TO PLAY WITH ME?
You're tough. That makes you even hotter... ♡
HEY, YOU STUPID GIRL!
IT'S DANGEROUS AROUND HERE. JUST IGNORE THEM AND GO HOME!
KONK
SHUT UP!
RIGHT.
IF YOU LET HIM GO...
...I'LL STAY AND PLAY WITH YOU.

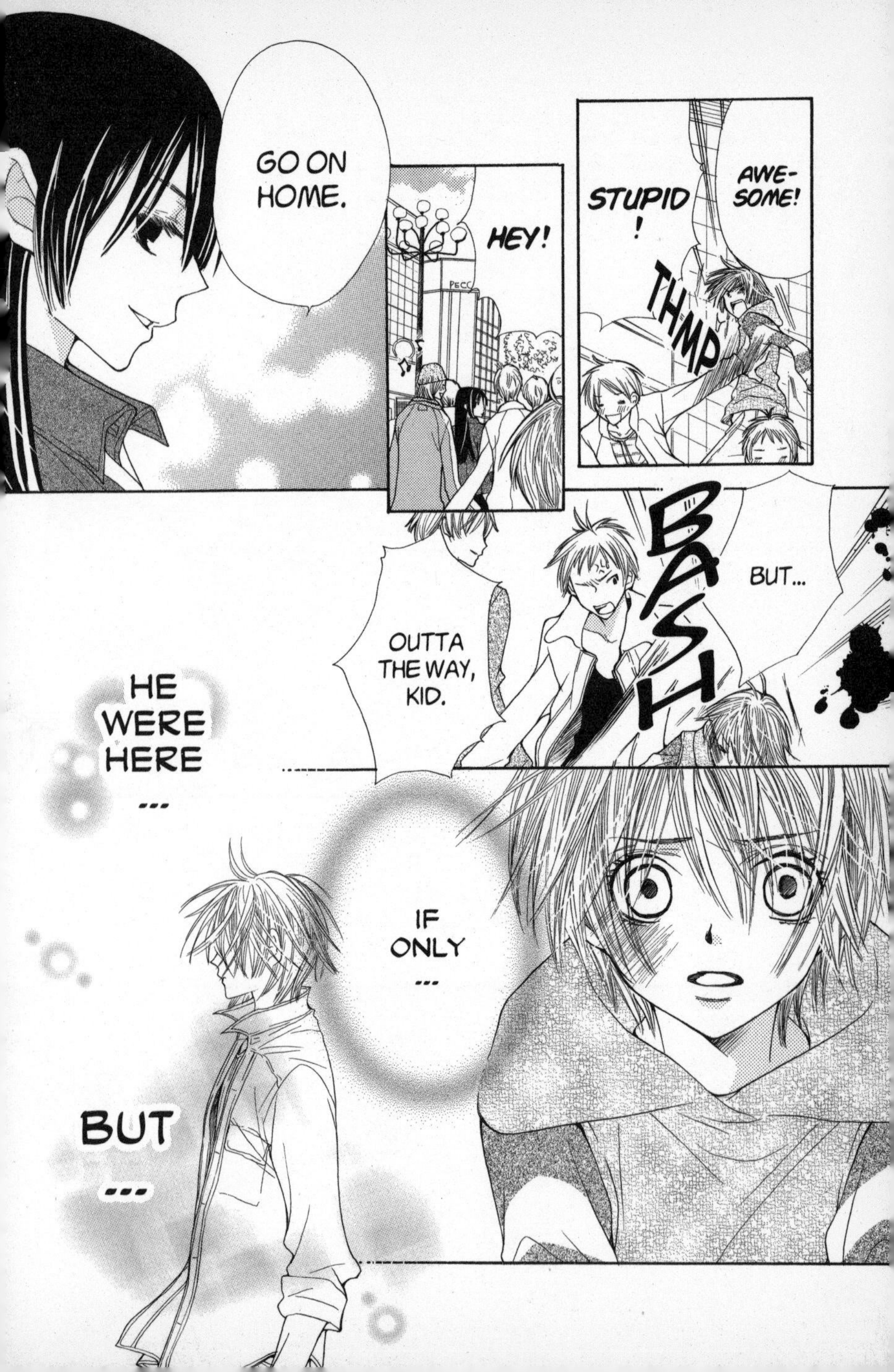
AWE-SOME!
STUPID!
THMP
HEY!
GO ON HOME.
BUT...
BASH
OUTTA THE WAY, KID.
IF ONLY ...
HE WERE HERE ...
BUT ...

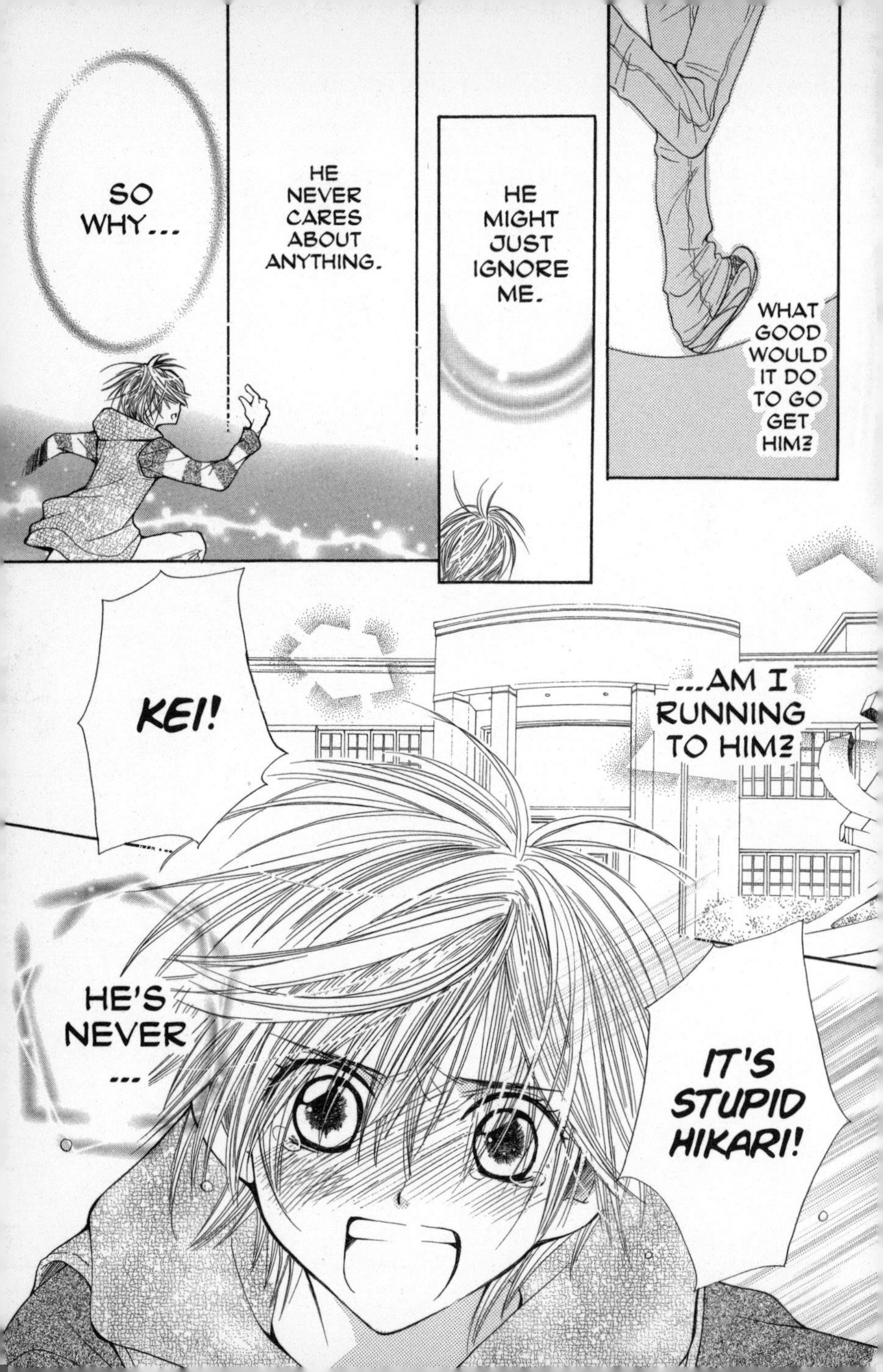
WHAT GOOD WOULD IT DO TO GO GET HIM?
HE MIGHT JUST IGNORE ME.
HE NEVER CARES ABOUT ANYTHING.
SO WHY...
...AM I RUNNING TO HIM?
KEI!
IT'S STUPID HIKARI!
HE'S NEVER ...

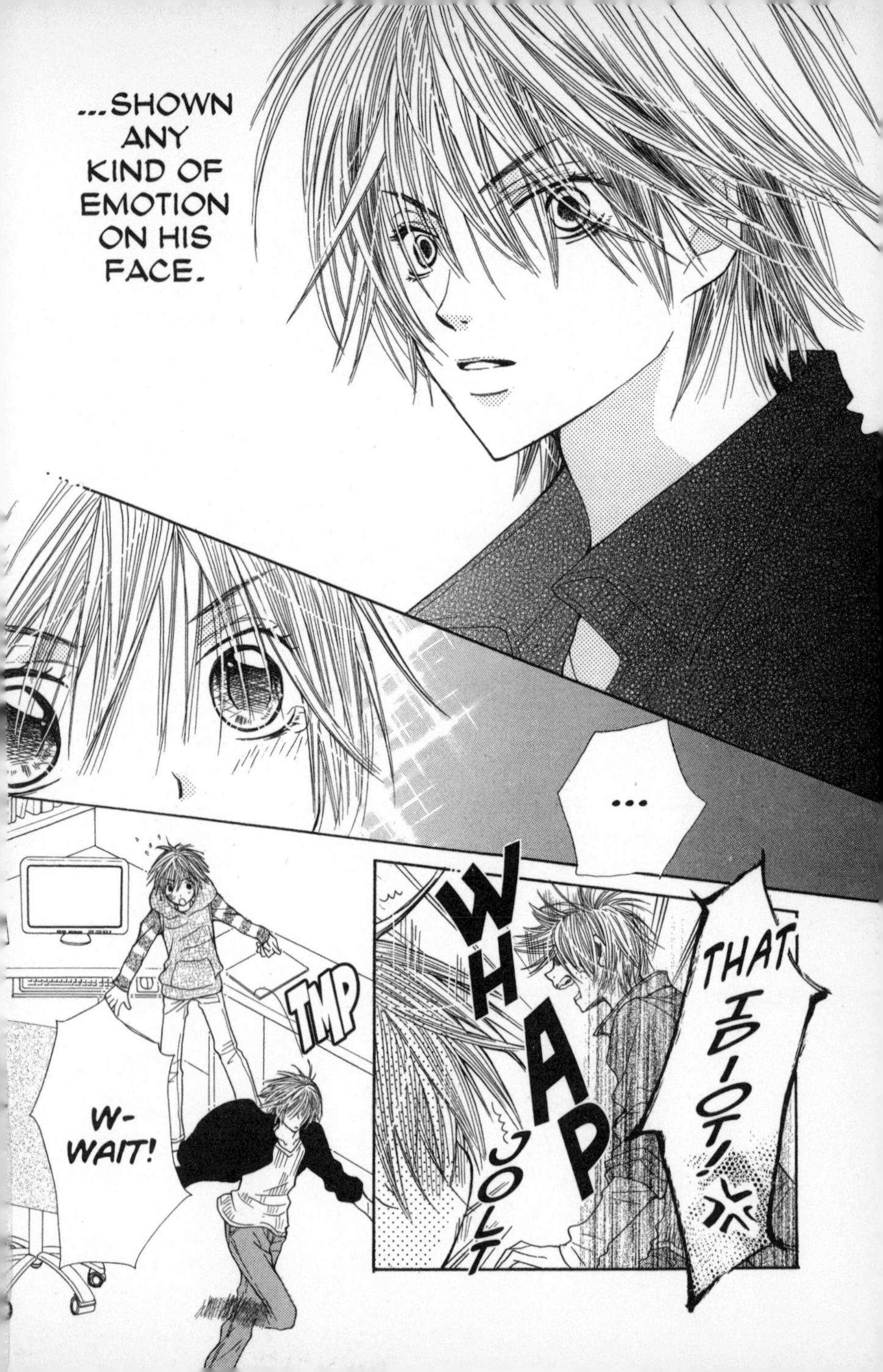
...SHOWN ANY KIND OF EMOTION ON HIS FACE.
...
THAT ID-IOT!!
WHAP
JOLT
TMP
W-WAIT!

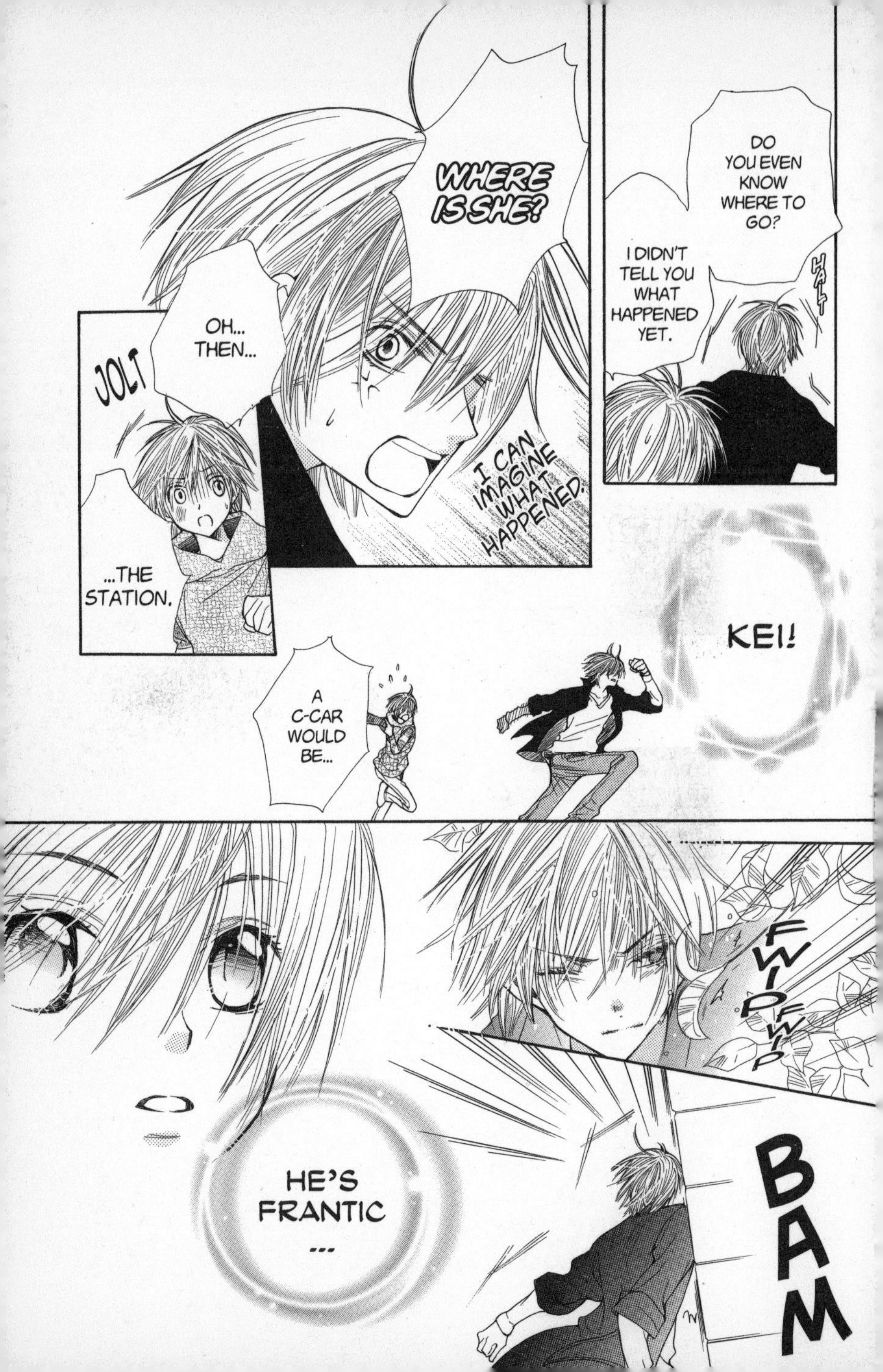
DO YOU EVEN KNOW WHERE TO GO?
I DIDN'T TELL YOU WHAT HAPPENED YET.
HALT
WHERE IS SHE?
I CAN IMAGINE WHAT HAPPENED.
OH... THEN...
JOLT
...THE STATION.
KEI!
A C-CAR WOULD BE...
FWIP FWIP
BAM
HE'S FRANTIC
...

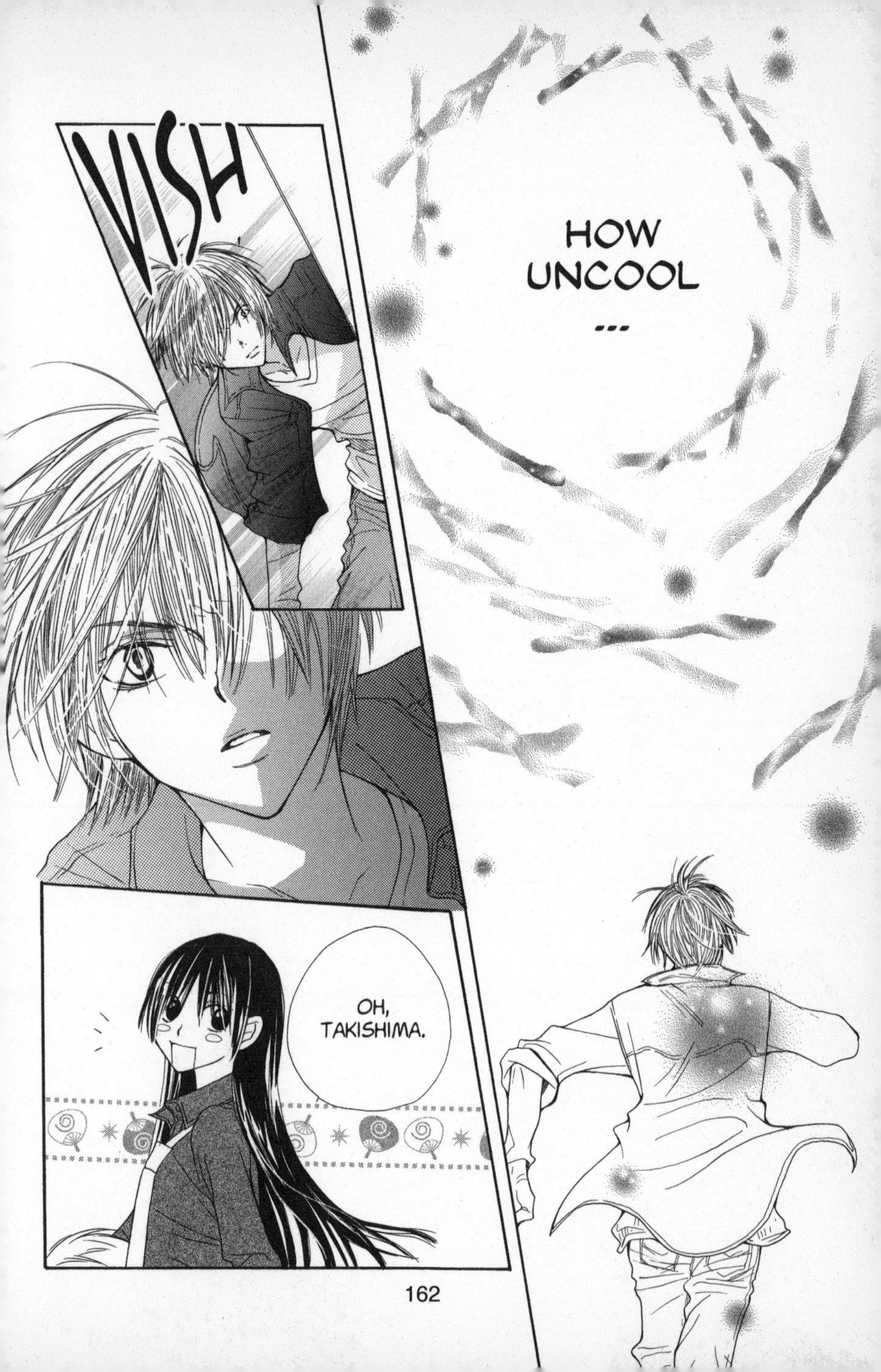
HOW UNCOOL ...
VISH
OH, TAKISHIMA.

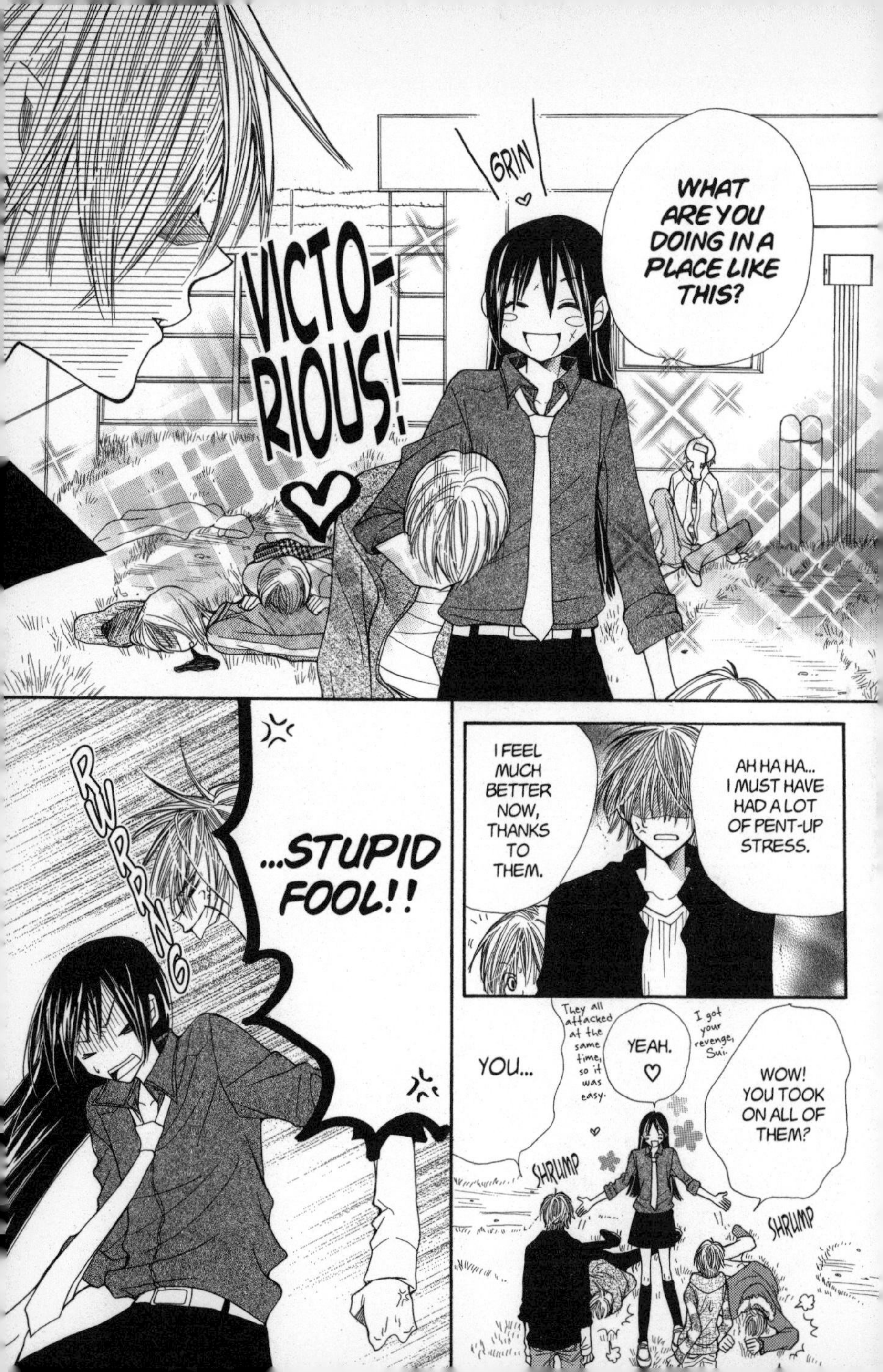
WHAT ARE YOU DOING IN A PLACE LIKE THIS?
GRIN ♥
VICTO-RIOUS! ♥
AH HA HA... I MUST HAVE HAD A LOT OF PENT-UP STRESS.
I FEEL MUCH BETTER NOW, THANKS TO THEM.
WOW! YOU TOOK ON ALL OF THEM?
I got your revenge, Sui.
YEAH. ♡
They all attacked at the same time, so it was easy.
YOU...
SHRUMP
SHRUMP
...STUPID FOOL!!
RWRRRNG

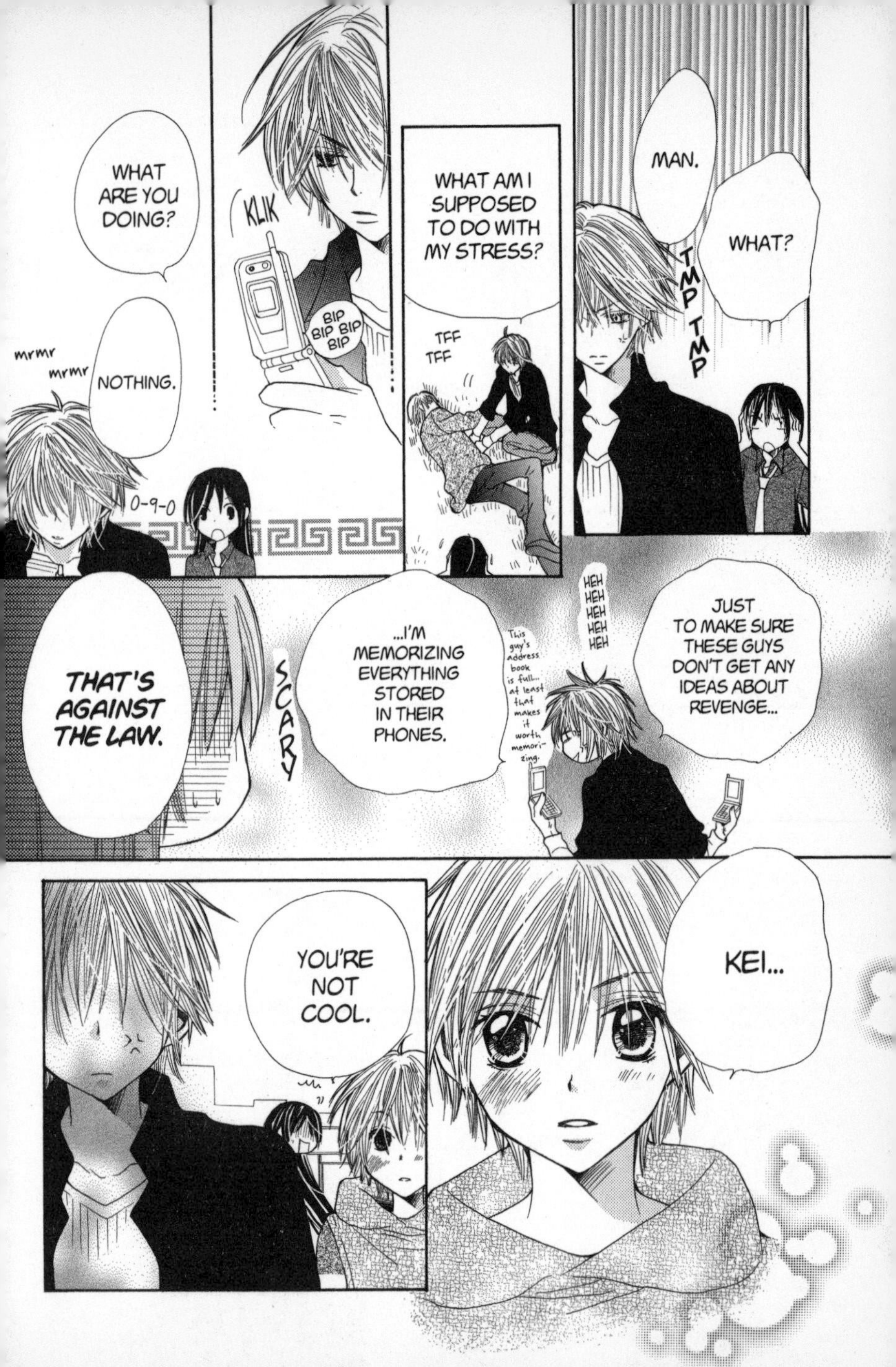
MAN.
WHAT?
TMP TMP
WHAT AM I SUPPOSED TO DO WITH MY STRESS?
TFF TFF
KLIK
BIP BIP BIP BIP
WHAT ARE YOU DOING?
NOTHING.
mrmr mrmr
0-9-0
JUST TO MAKE SURE THESE GUYS DON'T GET ANY IDEAS ABOUT REVENGE...
HEH HEH HEH HEH HEH
This guy's address book is full... at least that makes it worth memorizing.
...I'M MEMORIZING EVERYTHING STORED IN THEIR PHONES.
SCARY
THAT'S AGAINST THE LAW.
KEI...
YOU'RE NOT COOL.

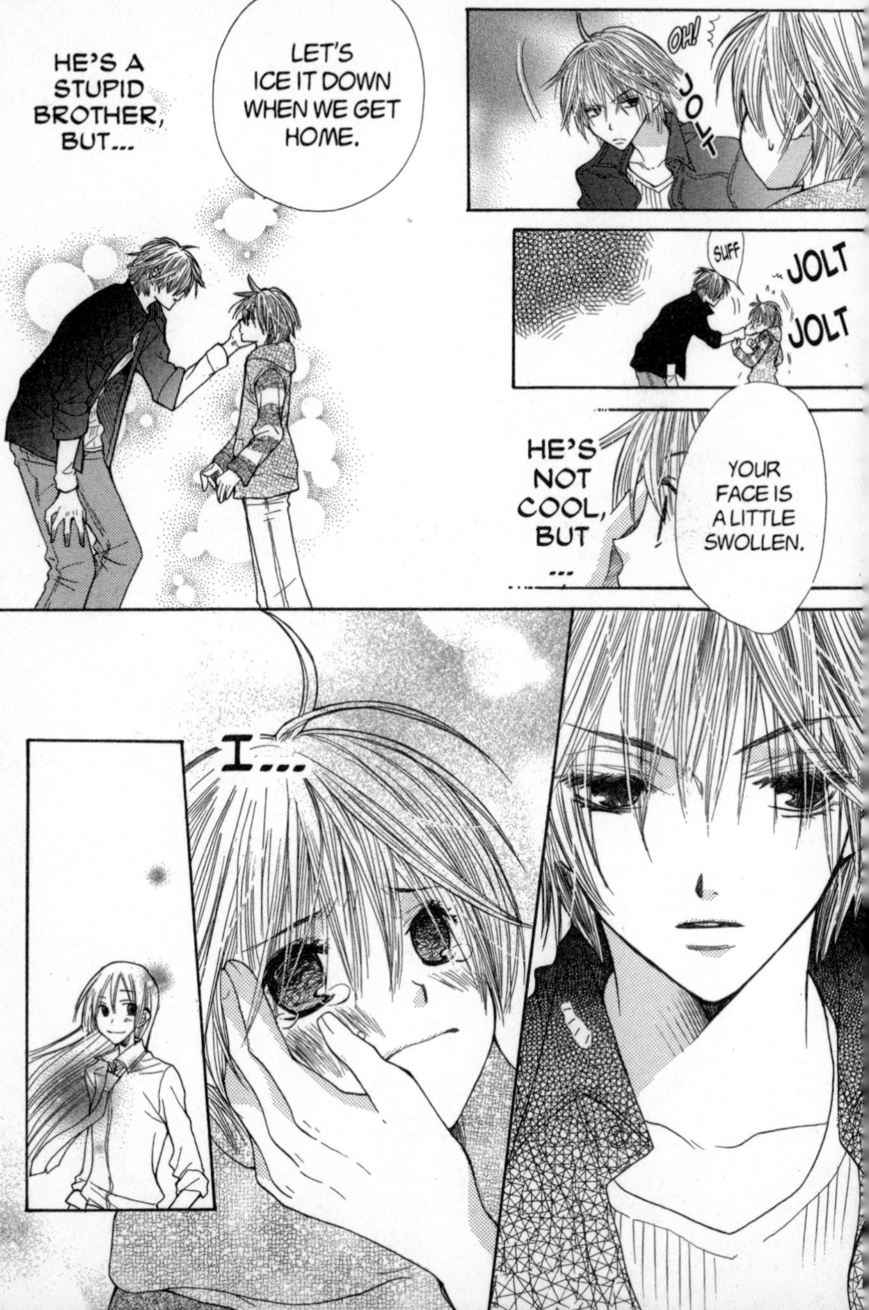
OH!
JOLT
SUFF
JOLT
JOLT
YOUR FACE IS A LITTLE SWOLLEN.
HE'S NOT COOL, BUT ...
LET'S ICE IT DOWN WHEN WE GET HOME.
HE'S A STUPID BROTHER, BUT...
I...

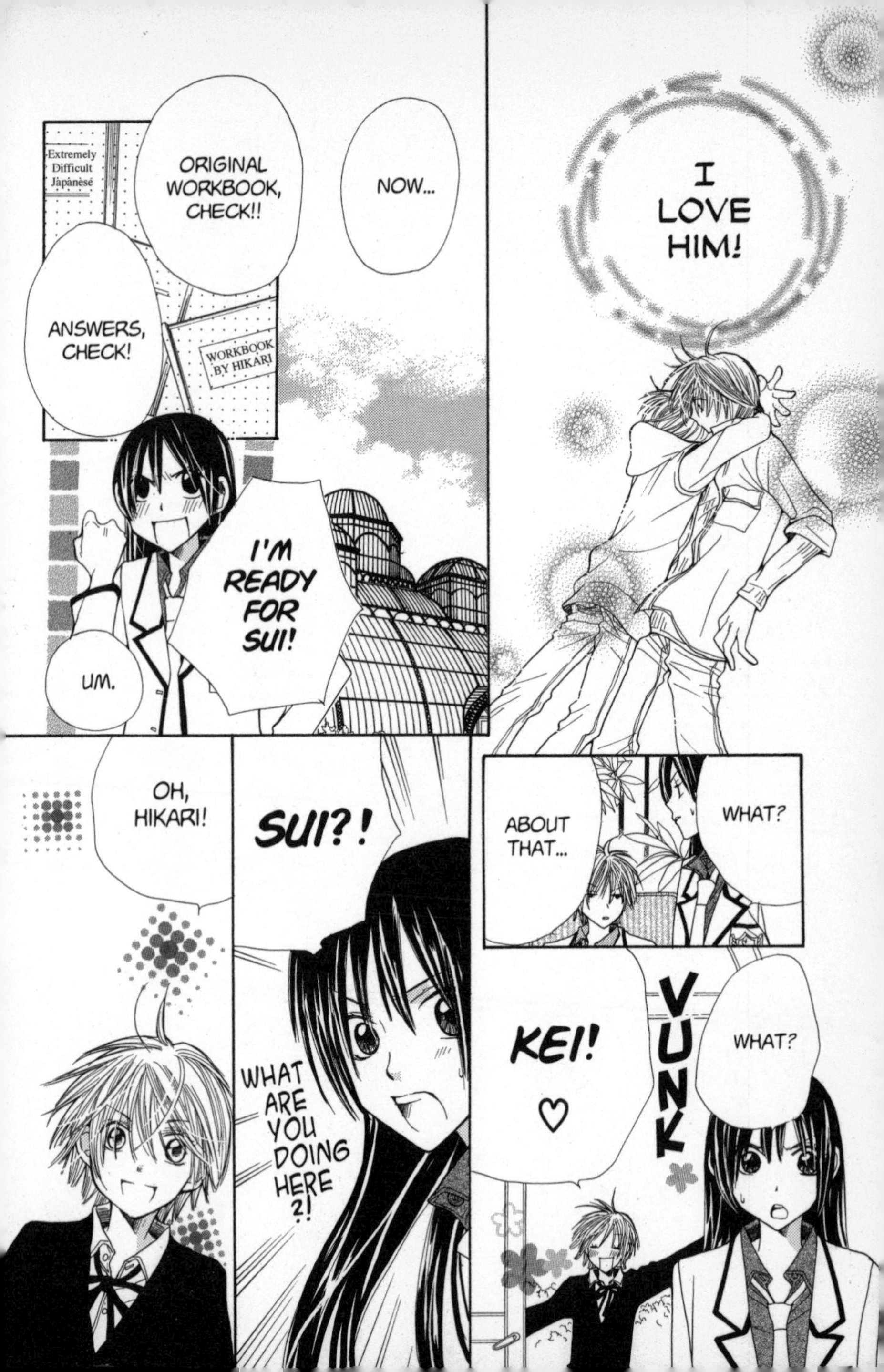
I LOVE HIM!
NOW...
ORIGINAL WORKBOOK, CHECK!!
Extremely Difficult Japanese
ANSWERS, CHECK!
WORKBOOK BY HIKARI
I'M READY FOR SUI!
UM.
WHAT?
ABOUT THAT...
WHAT?
VUNK
KEI! ♡
SUI?!
WHAT ARE YOU DOING HERE?!
OH, HIKARI!

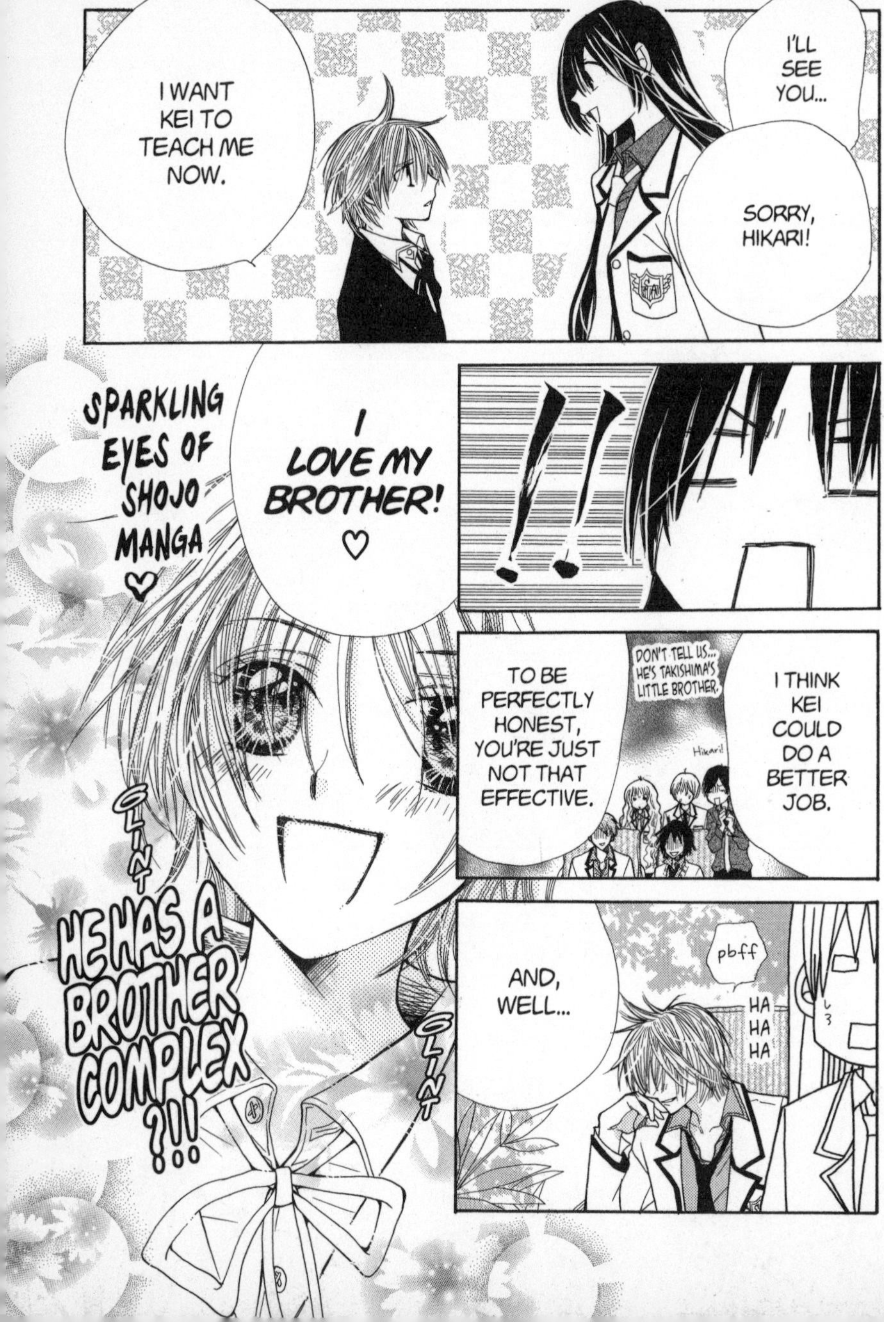
I'LL SEE YOU...
SORRY, HIKARI!
I WANT KEI TO TEACH ME NOW.
I THINK KEI COULD DO A BETTER JOB.
DON'T TELL US... HE'S TAKISHIMA'S LITTLE BROTHER.
Hikari!
TO BE PERFECTLY HONEST, YOU'RE JUST NOT THAT EFFECTIVE.
HA HA HA
pbff
AND, WELL...
I LOVE MY BROTHER! ♡
SPARKLING EYES OF SHOJO MANGA ♡
GLINT
GLINT
HE HAS A BROTHER COMPLEX ?!!

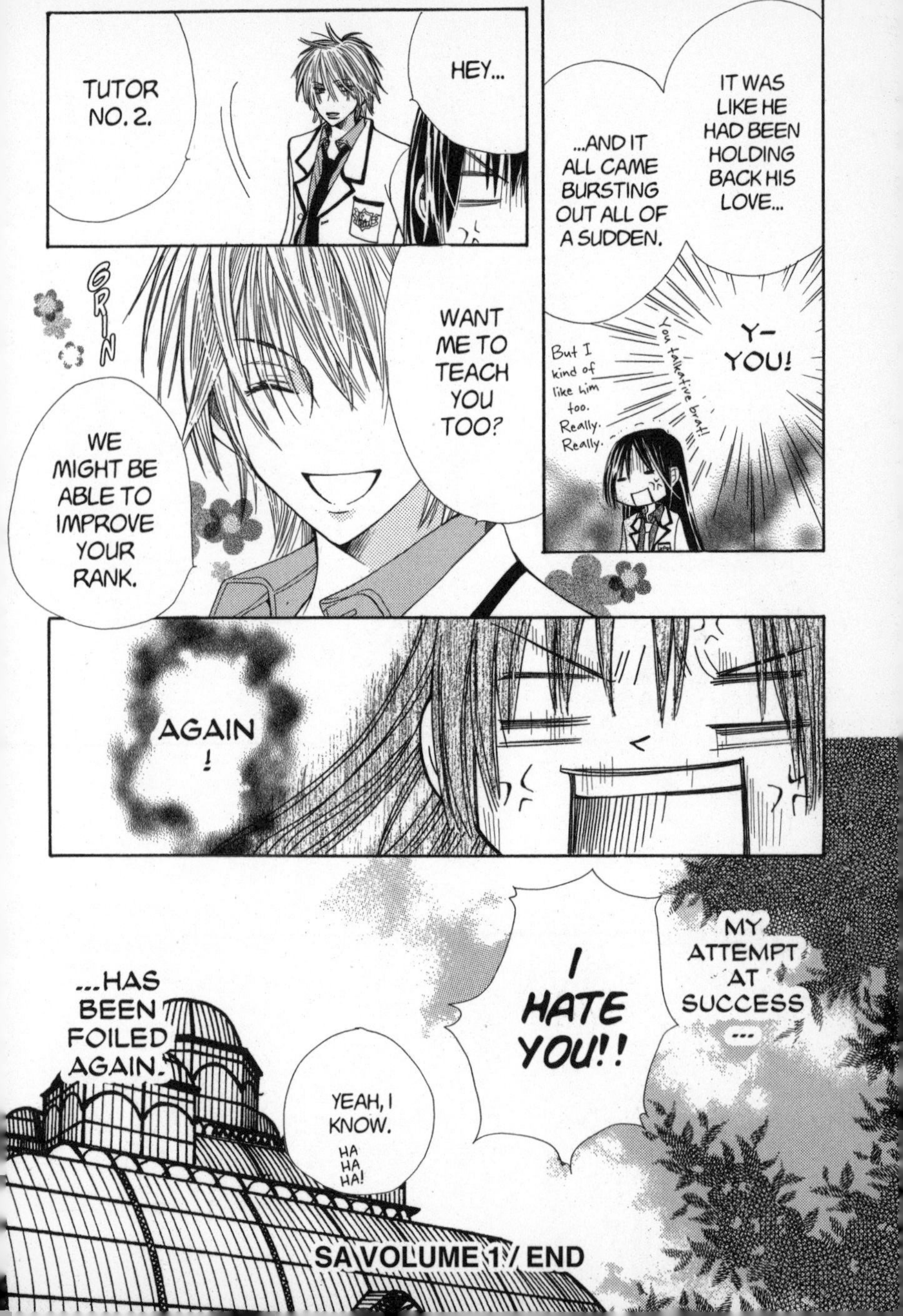
IT WAS LIKE HE HAD BEEN HOLDING BACK HIS LOVE...
...AND IT ALL CAME BURSTING OUT ALL OF A SUDDEN.
Y-YOU!
You talkative brat!!
But I kind of like him too. Really. Really.
HEY...
TUTOR NO. 2.
WANT ME TO TEACH YOU TOO?
GRIN
WE MIGHT BE ABLE TO IMPROVE YOUR RANK.
AGAIN!
MY ATTEMPT AT SUCCESS...
I HATE YOU!!
YEAH, I KNOW.
HA HA HA!
...HAS BEEN FOILED AGAIN.

SA VOLUME 1 / END

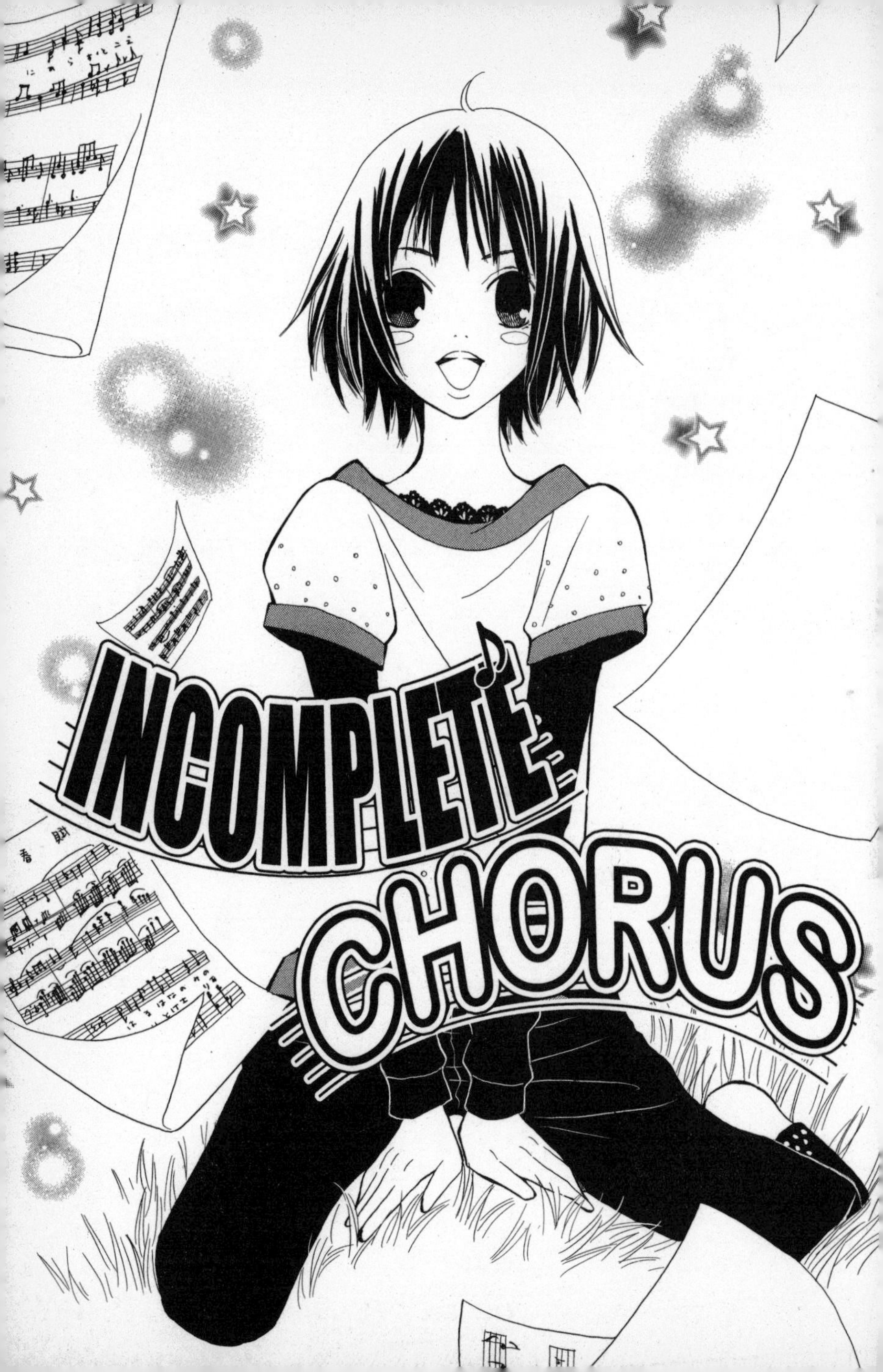
INCOMPLETE
CHORUS

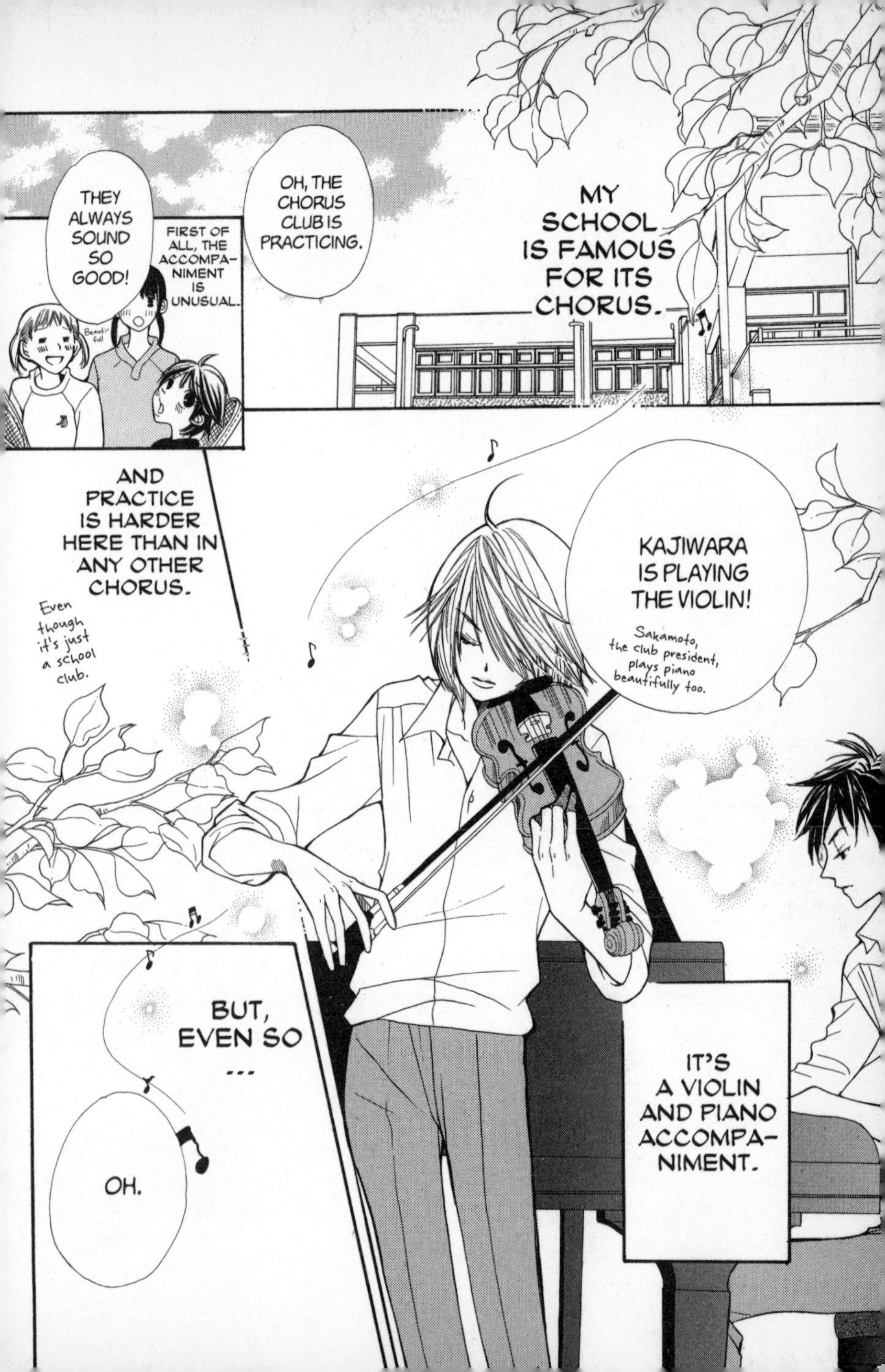
MY SCHOOL IS FAMOUS FOR ITS CHORUS.
OH, THE CHORUS CLUB IS PRACTICING.
THEY ALWAYS SOUND SO GOOD!
FIRST OF ALL, THE ACCOMPANIMENT IS UNUSUAL.
Beautiful!
KAJIWARA IS PLAYING THE VIOLIN!
Sakamoto, the club president, plays piano beautifully too.
AND PRACTICE IS HARDER HERE THAN IN ANY OTHER CHORUS.
Even though it's just a school club.
IT'S A VIOLIN AND PIANO ACCOMPANIMENT.
BUT, EVEN SO ...
OH.

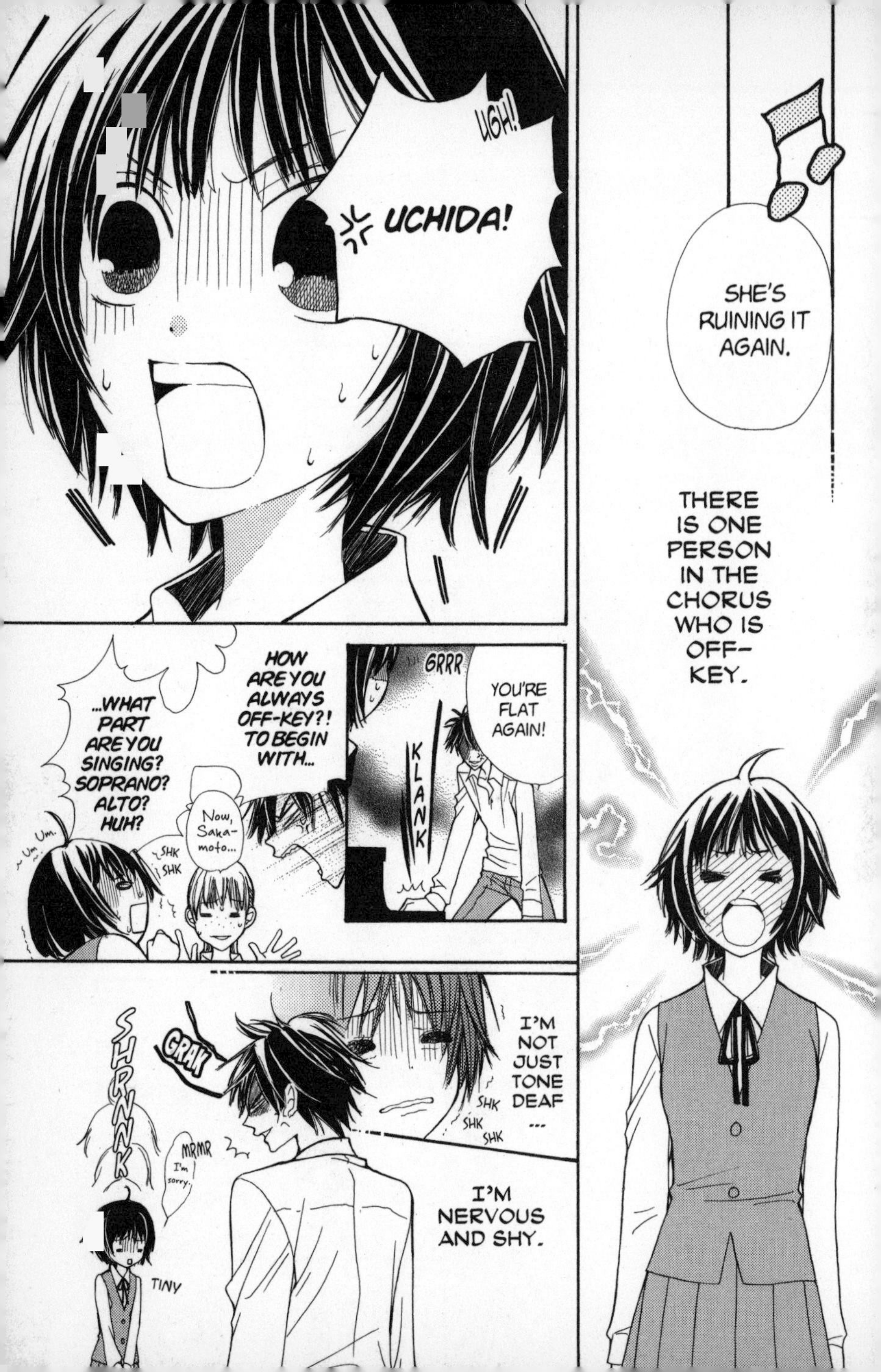
SHE'S RUINING IT AGAIN.
THERE IS ONE PERSON IN THE CHORUS WHO IS OFF-KEY.
UGH!
UCHIDA!
GRRR
YOU'RE FLAT AGAIN!
KLANK
HOW ARE YOU ALWAYS OFF-KEY?! TO BEGIN WITH...
...WHAT PART ARE YOU SINGING? SOPRANO? ALTO? HUH?
Now, Saka-moto...
SHK SHK
Um. Um.
I'M NOT JUST TONE DEAF...
SHK SHK SHK
GRAK
SHRNNNK
MRMR
I'm sorry.
I'M NERVOUS AND SHY.
TINY

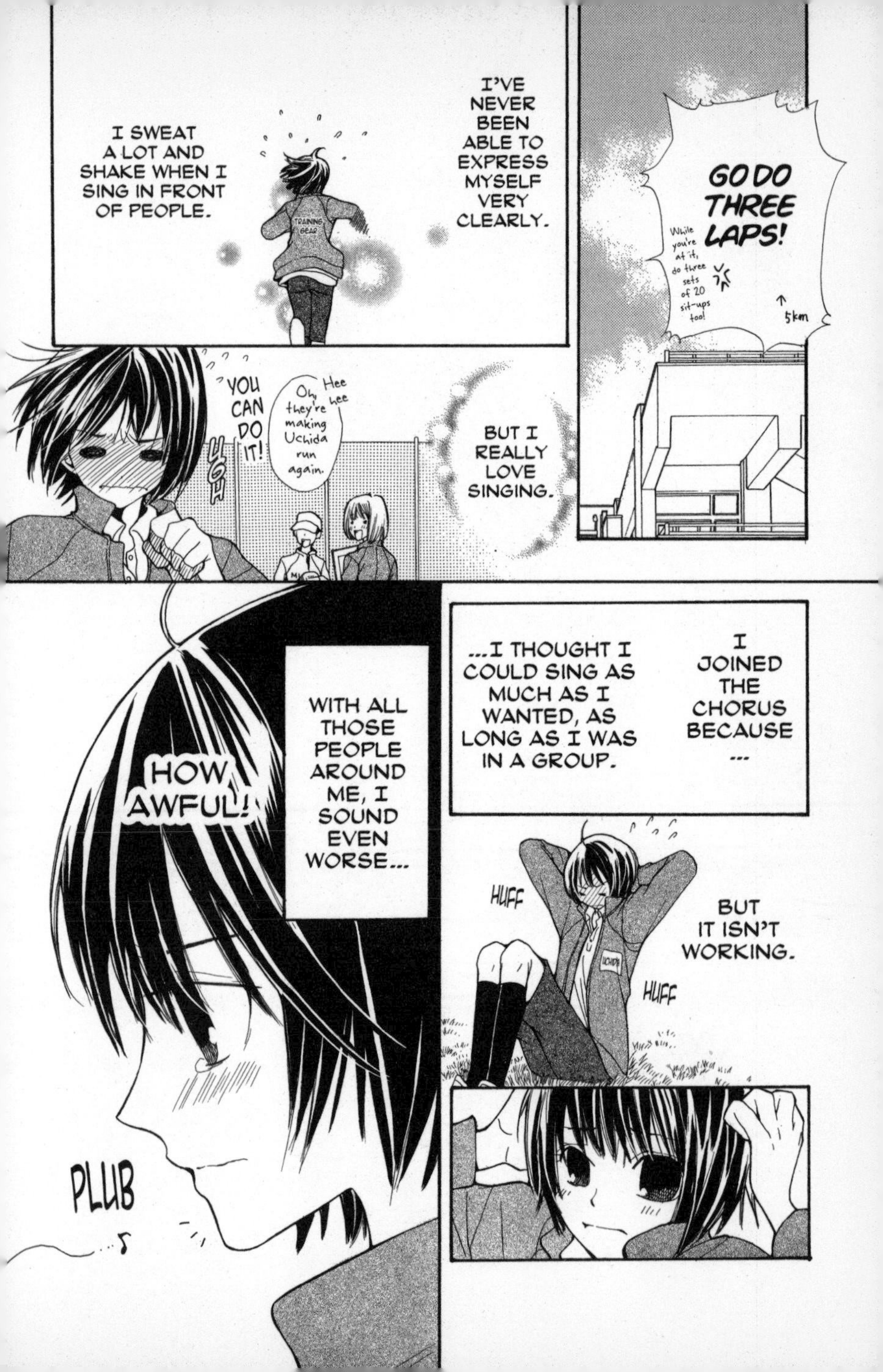
GO DO THREE LAPS!
While you're at it, do three sets of 20 sit-ups too!
5km
I'VE NEVER BEEN ABLE TO EXPRESS MYSELF VERY CLEARLY.
TRAINING GEAR
I SWEAT A LOT AND SHAKE WHEN I SING IN FRONT OF PEOPLE.
BUT I REALLY LOVE SINGING.
Hee hee
Oh, they're making Uchida run again.
YOU CAN DO IT!
UGH
I JOINED THE CHORUS BECAUSE...
...I THOUGHT I COULD SING AS MUCH AS I WANTED, AS LONG AS I WAS IN A GROUP.
BUT IT ISN'T WORKING.
HUFF
HUFF
WITH ALL THOSE PEOPLE AROUND ME, I SOUND EVEN WORSE...
HOW AWFUL!
PLUB
...♪

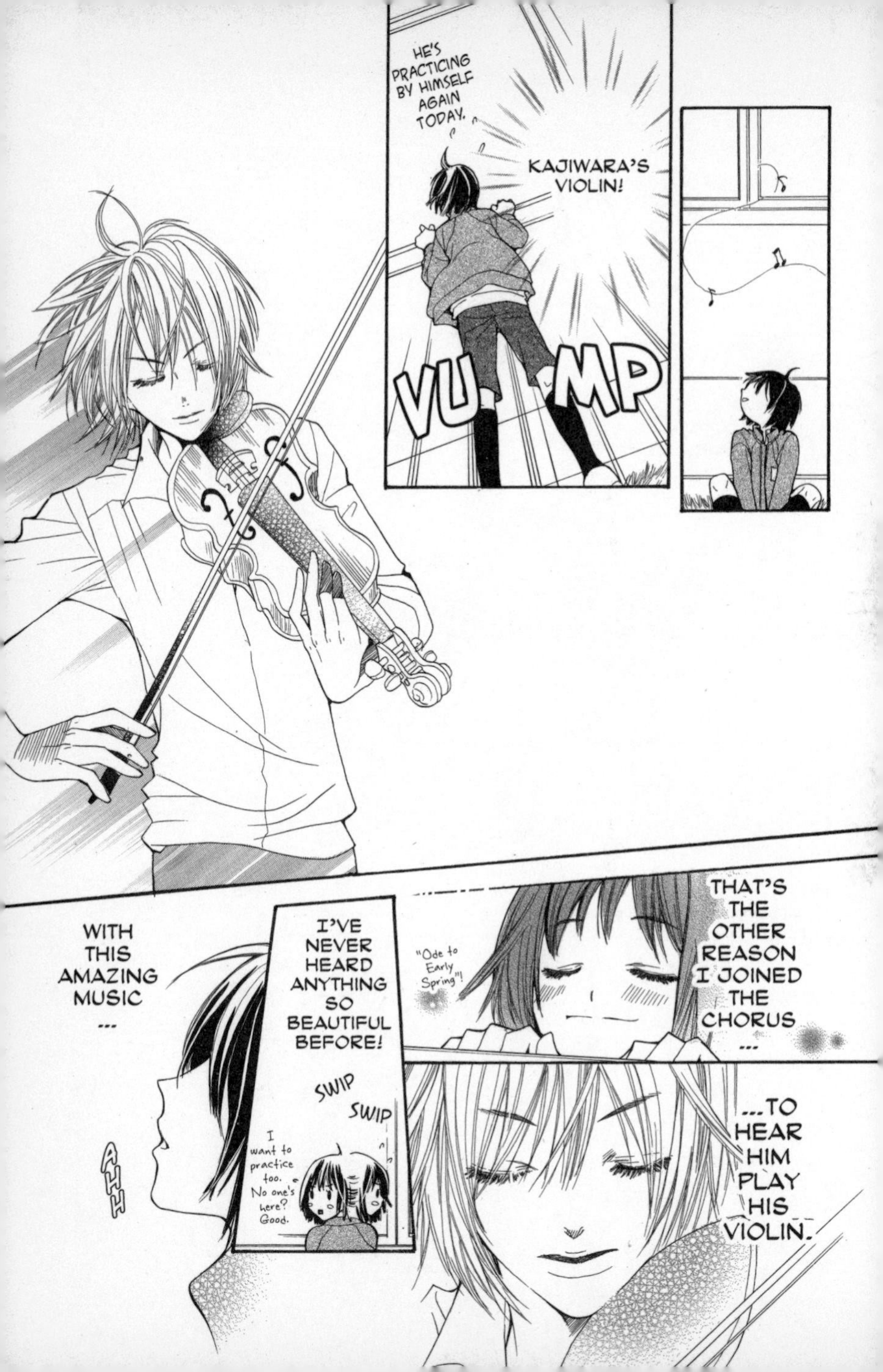
HE'S PRACTICING BY HIMSELF AGAIN TODAY.
KAJIWARA'S VIOLIN!
VUMP
THAT'S THE OTHER REASON I JOINED THE CHORUS...
"Ode to Early Spring"!
...TO HEAR HIM PLAY HIS VIOLIN.
I'VE NEVER HEARD ANYTHING SO BEAUTIFUL BEFORE!
SWIP
SWIP
I want to practice too. No one's here? Good.
WITH THIS AMAZING MUSIC...
AHHH

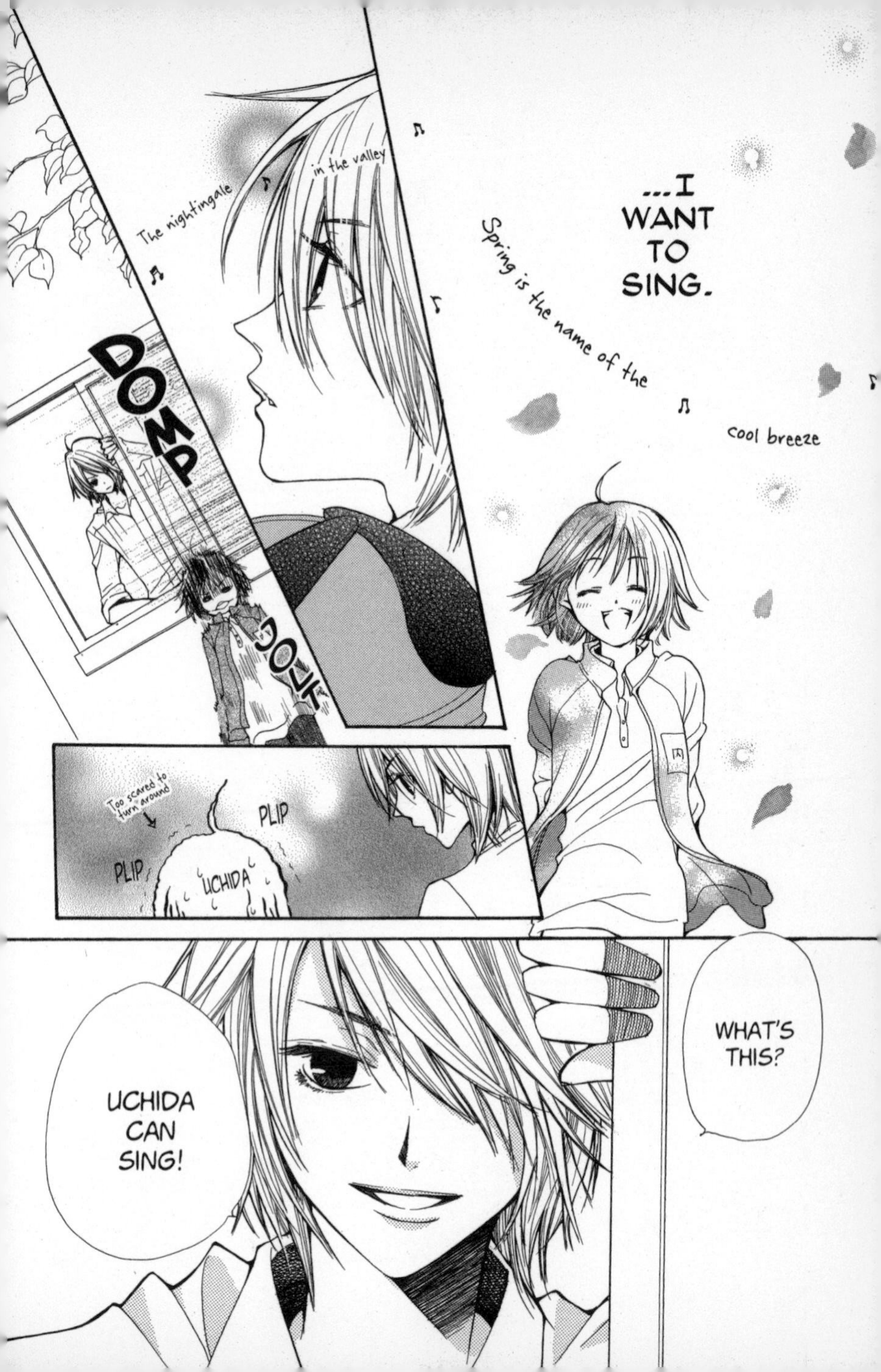
...I WANT TO SING.
Spring is the name of the
cool breeze
The nightingale
in the valley
DOMP
JOLT
Too scared to turn around
PLIP
PLIP
UCHIDA
WHAT'S THIS?
UCHIDA CAN SING!

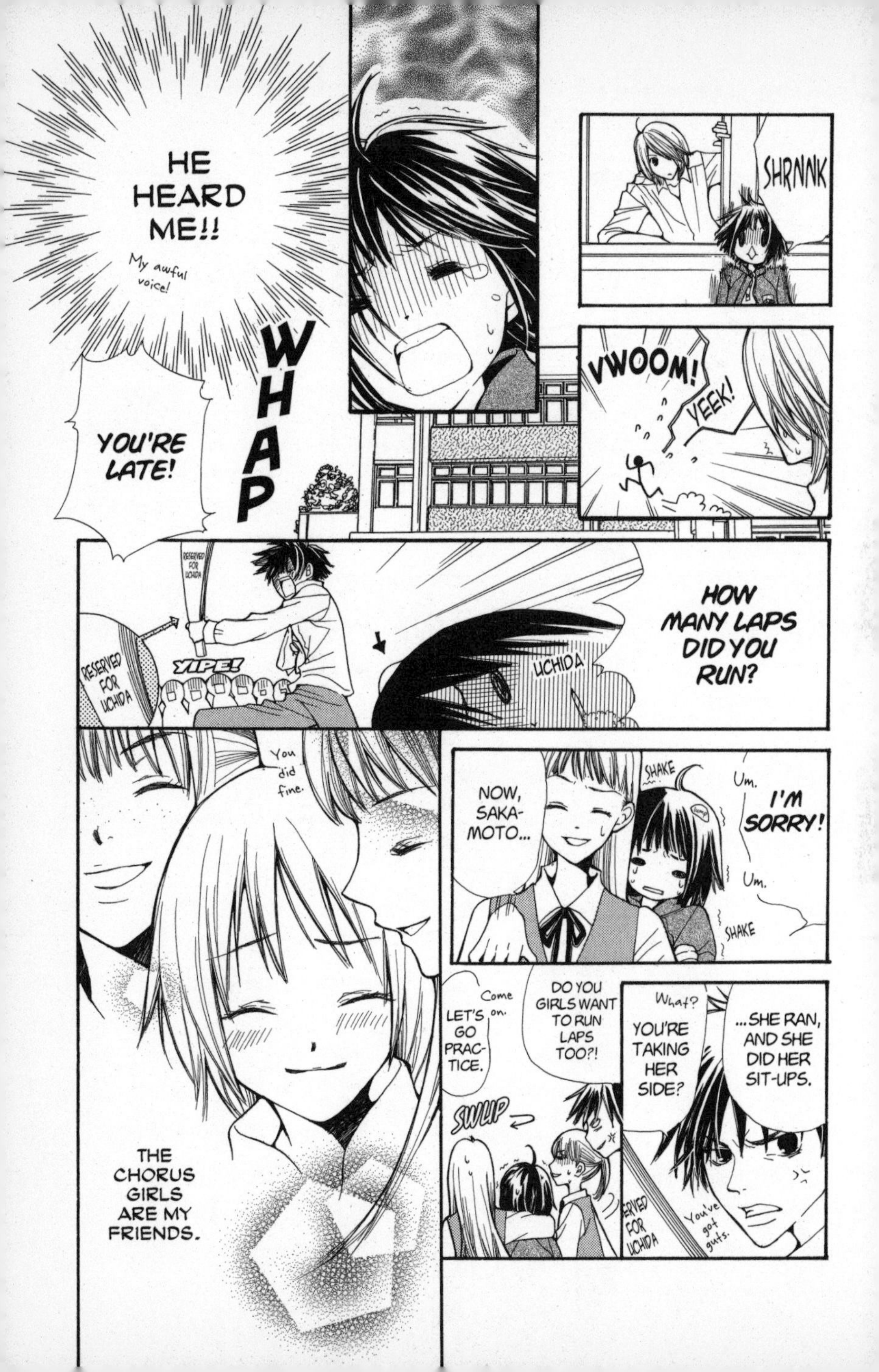
SHRNNK
VWOOM!
YEEK!
WHAP
HE HEARD ME!!
My awful voice!
YOU'RE LATE!
HOW MANY LAPS DID YOU RUN?
UCHIDA
YIPE!
RESERVED FOR UCHIDA
RESERVED FOR UCHIDA
SHAKE
Um.
I'M SORRY!
Um.
SHAKE
NOW, SAKAMOTO...
...SHE RAN, AND SHE DID HER SIT-UPS.
What?
YOU'RE TAKING HER SIDE?
You've got guts.
ERVED FOR UCHIDA
DO YOU GIRLS WANT TO RUN LAPS TOO?!
Come on.
LET'S GO PRACTICE.
SWLIP
You did fine.
THE CHORUS GIRLS ARE MY FRIENDS.

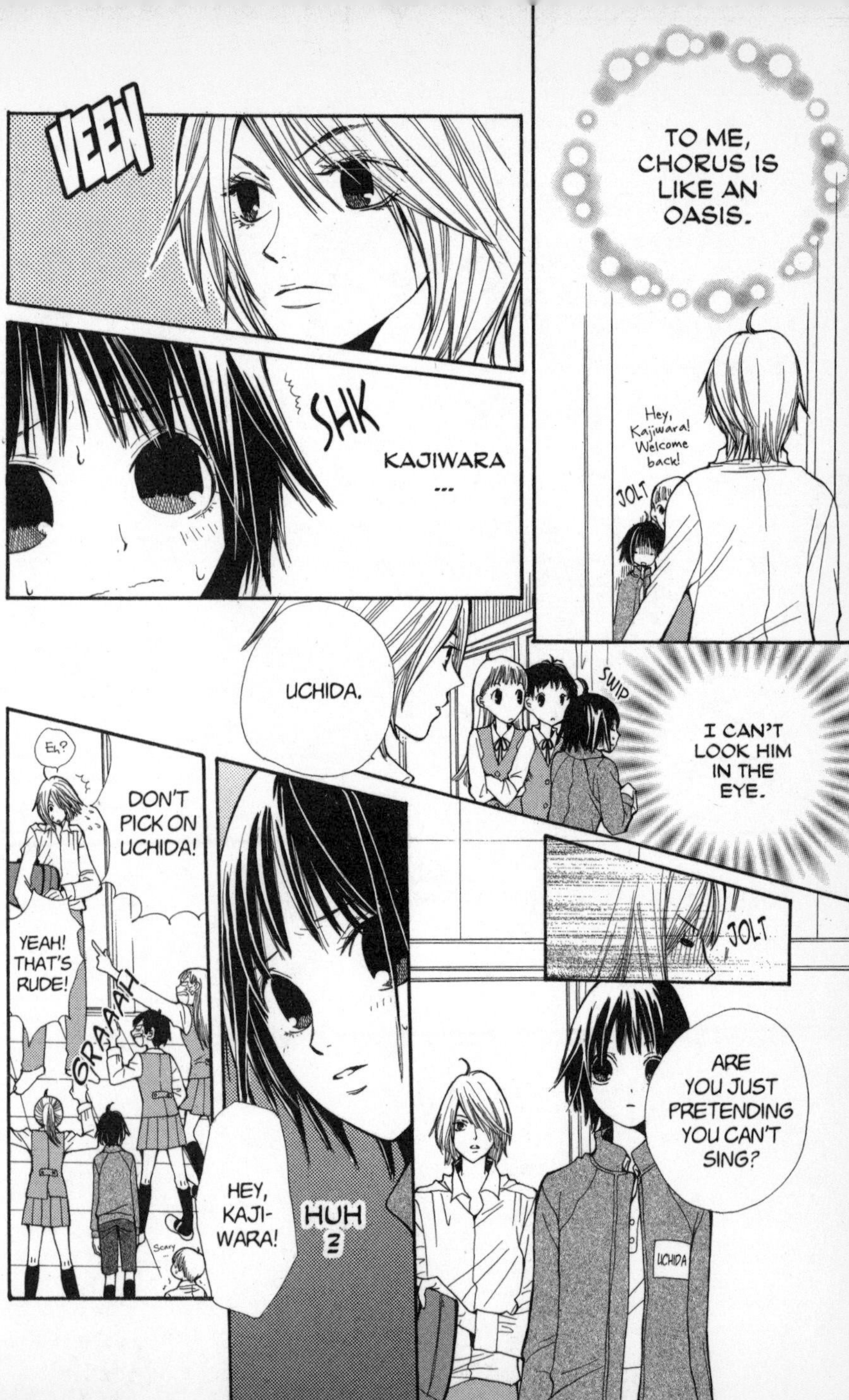
TO ME, CHORUS IS LIKE AN OASIS.
Hey, Kajiwara! Welcome back!
JOLT
VEEN
SHK
KAJIWARA...
SWIP
I CAN'T LOOK HIM IN THE EYE.
UCHIDA.
JOLT
ARE YOU JUST PRETENDING YOU CAN'T SING?
UCHIDA
HEY, KAJI-WARA!
HUH?
Eh?
DON'T PICK ON UCHIDA!
YEAH! THAT'S RUDE!
GRAAAH
Scary...

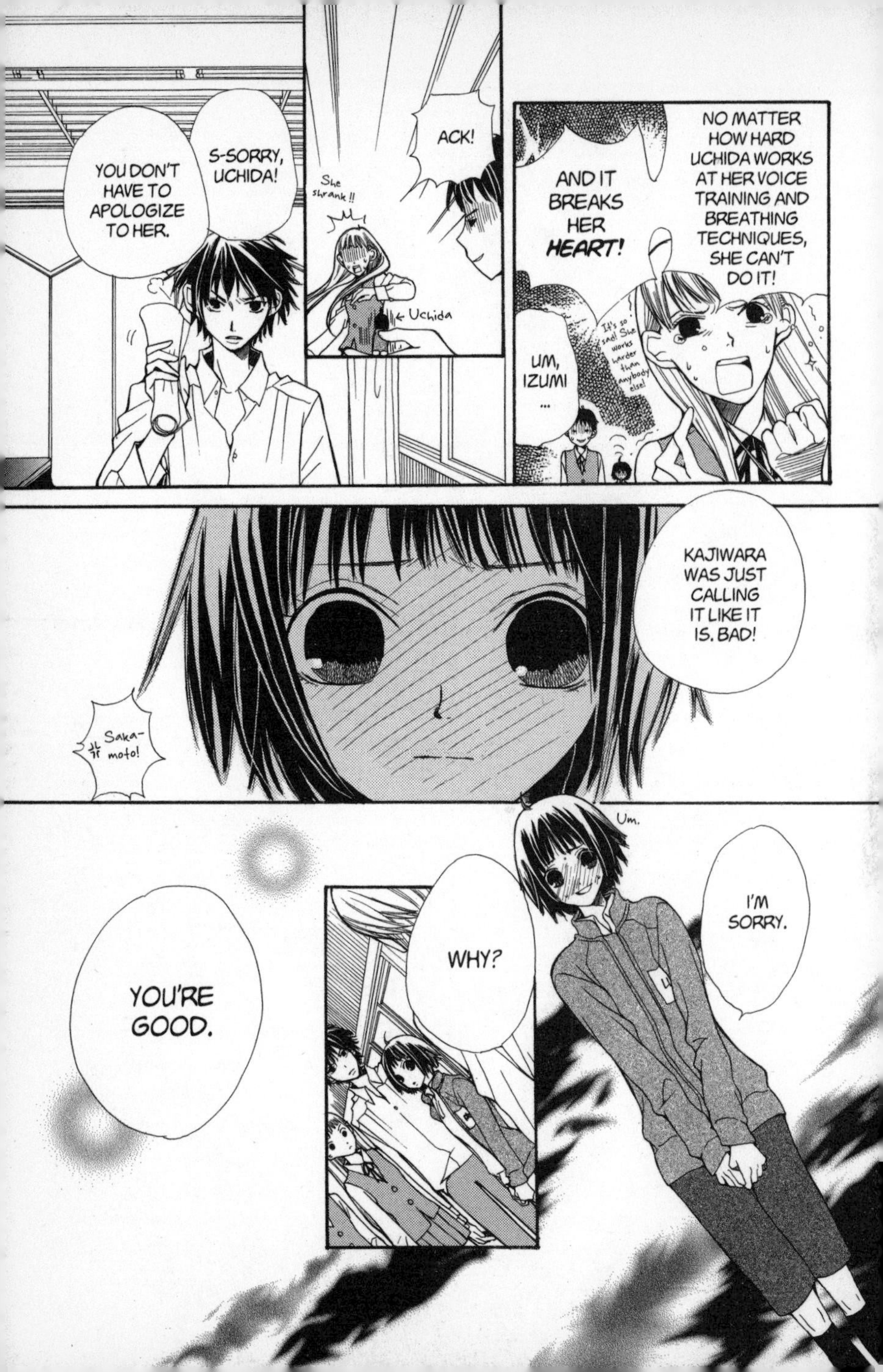
NO MATTER HOW HARD UCHIDA WORKS AT HER VOICE TRAINING AND BREATHING TECHNIQUES, SHE CAN'T DO IT!
AND IT BREAKS HER HEART!
It's so sad! She works harder than anybody else!
UM, IZUMI ...
ACK!
She shrank!!
← Uchida
S-SORRY, UCHIDA!
YOU DON'T HAVE TO APOLOGIZE TO HER.
KAJIWARA WAS JUST CALLING IT LIKE IT IS. BAD!
Saka-moto!
Um.
I'M SORRY.
WHY?
YOU'RE GOOD.

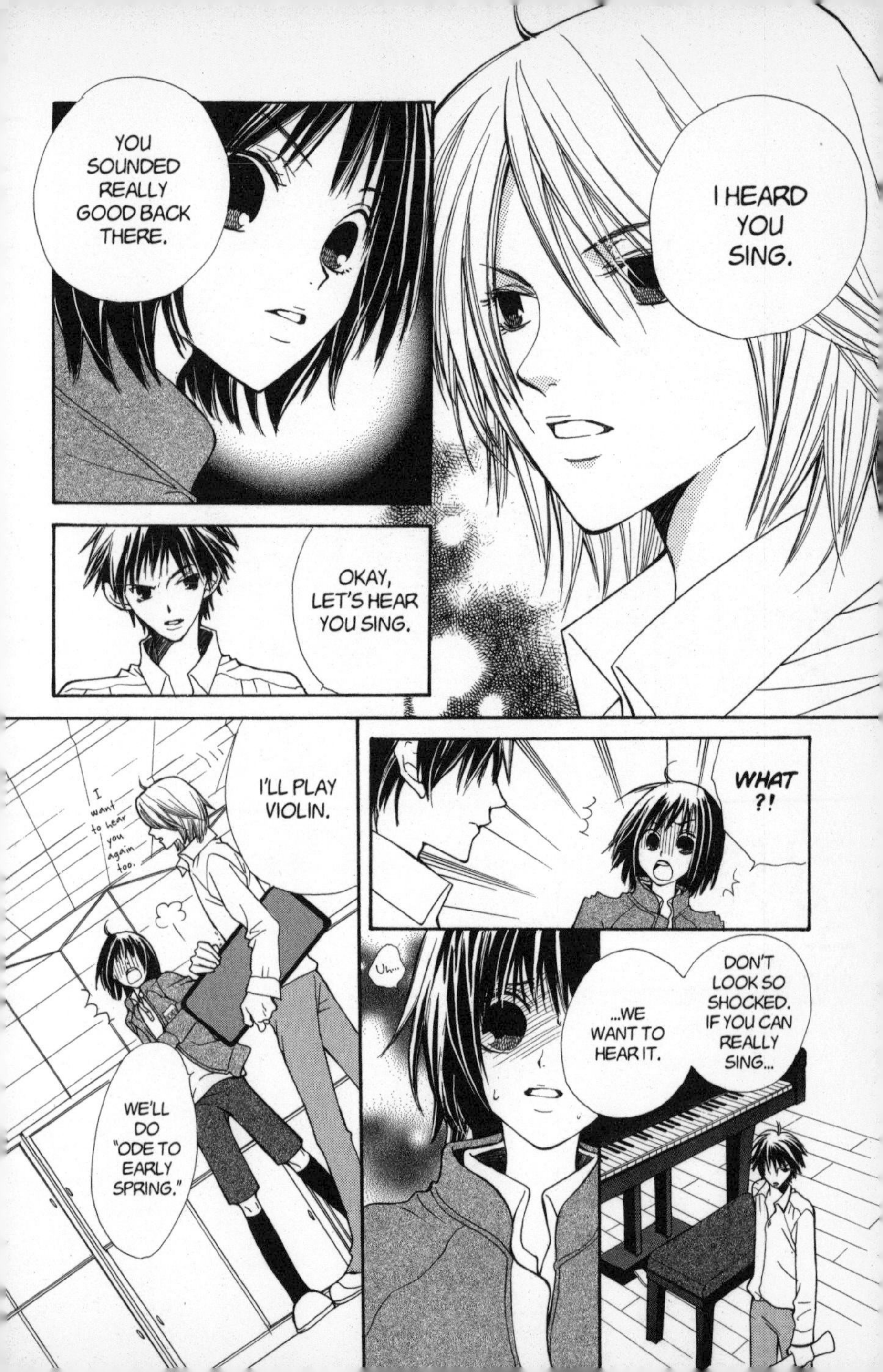
I HEARD YOU SING.
YOU SOUNDED REALLY GOOD BACK THERE.
OKAY, LET'S HEAR YOU SING.
WHAT?!
DON'T LOOK SO SHOCKED. IF YOU CAN REALLY SING...
...WE WANT TO HEAR IT.
Uh...
I'LL PLAY VIOLIN.
I want to hear you again too.
WE'LL DO "ODE TO EARLY SPRING."

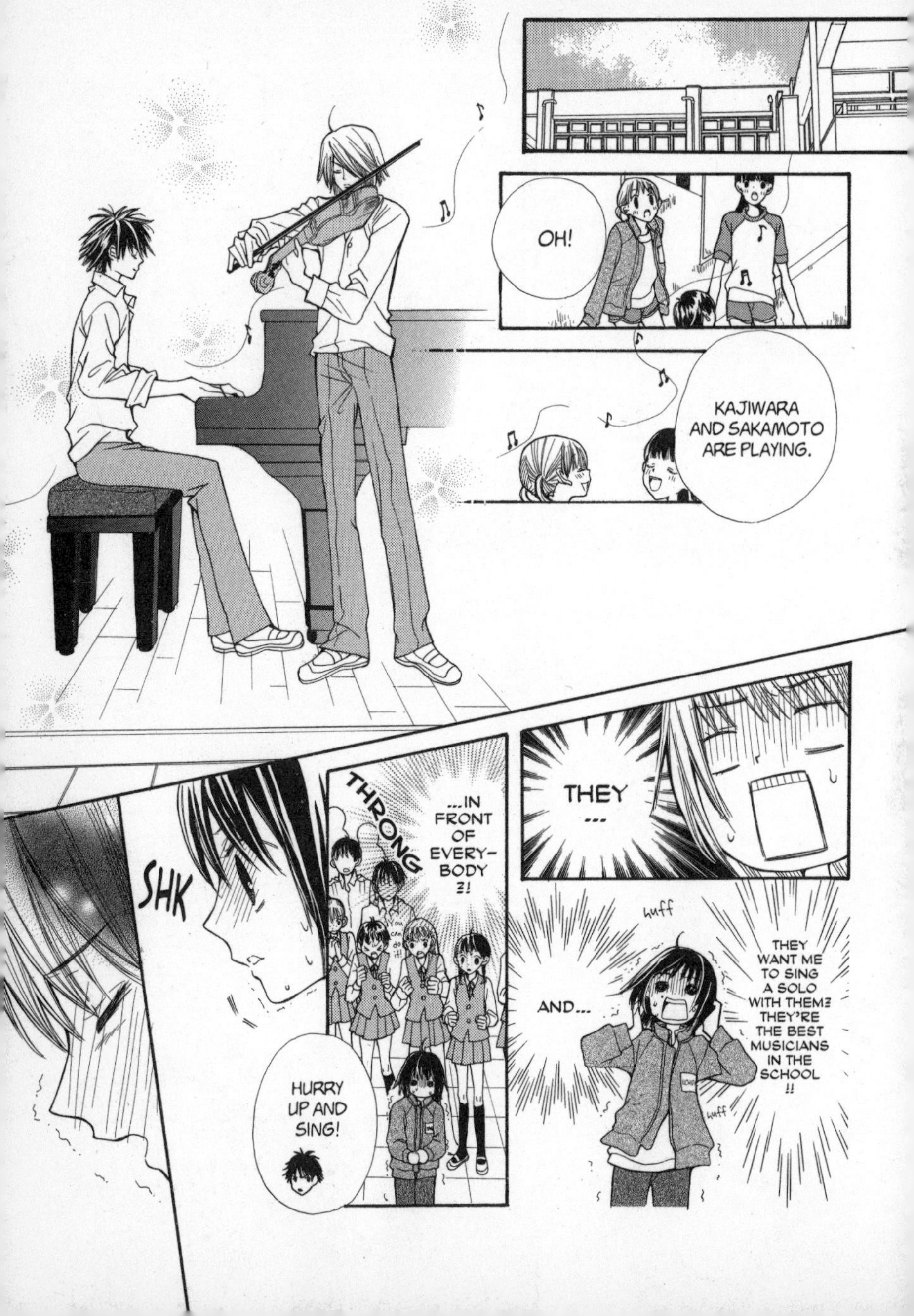
OH!
KAJIWARA AND SAKAMOTO ARE PLAYING.
THEY ...
huff
THEY WANT ME TO SING A SOLO WITH THEM? THEY'RE THE BEST MUSICIANS IN THE SCHOOL!!
AND...
huff
...IN FRONT OF EVERYBODY ?!
THRONG
You can do it!
HURRY UP AND SING!
SHK

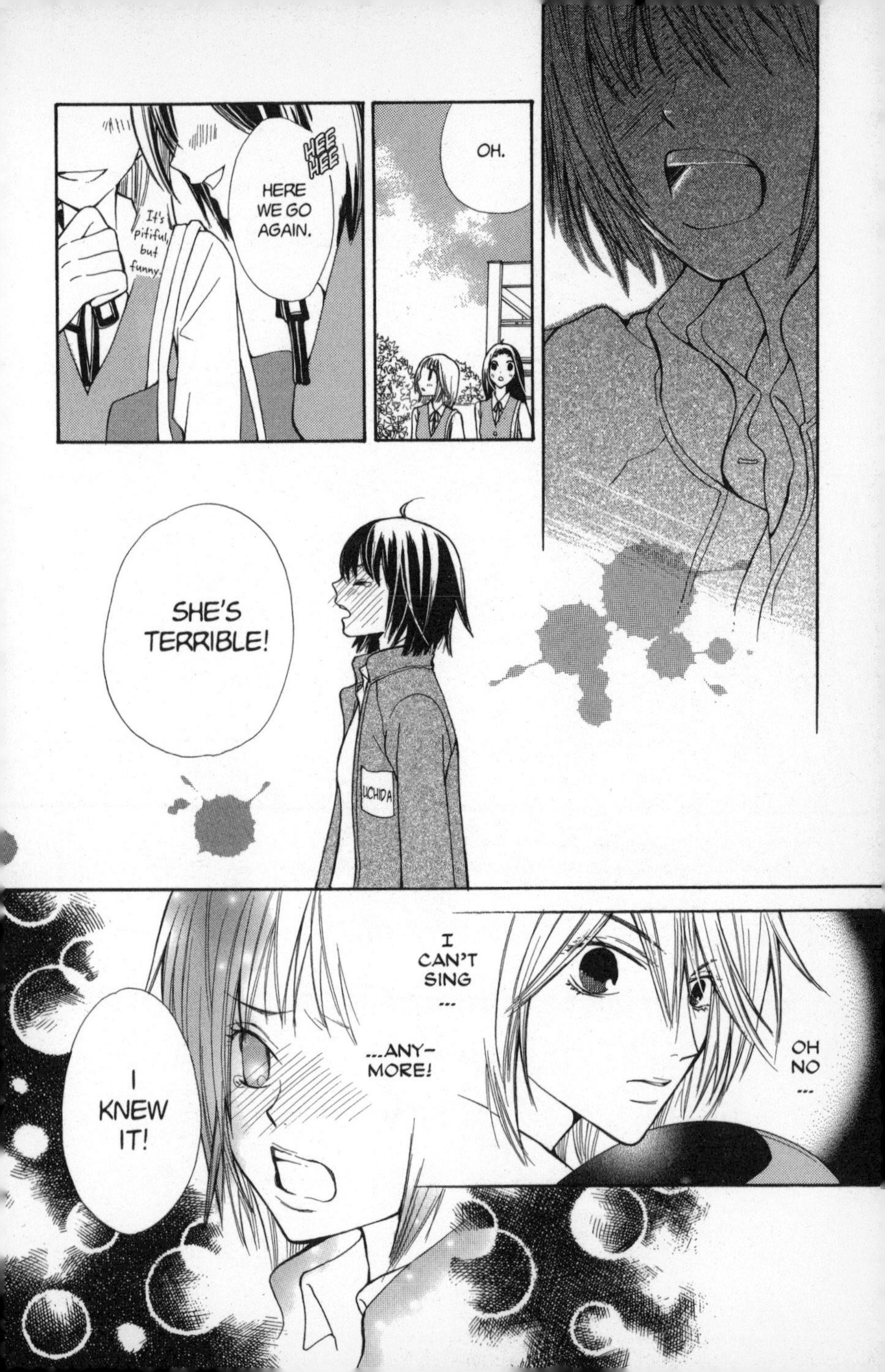
OH.
HEE HEE
HERE WE GO AGAIN.
It's pitiful, but funny.
SHE'S TERRIBLE!
UCHIDA
OH NO ...
I CAN'T SING ...
...ANY-MORE!
I KNEW IT!

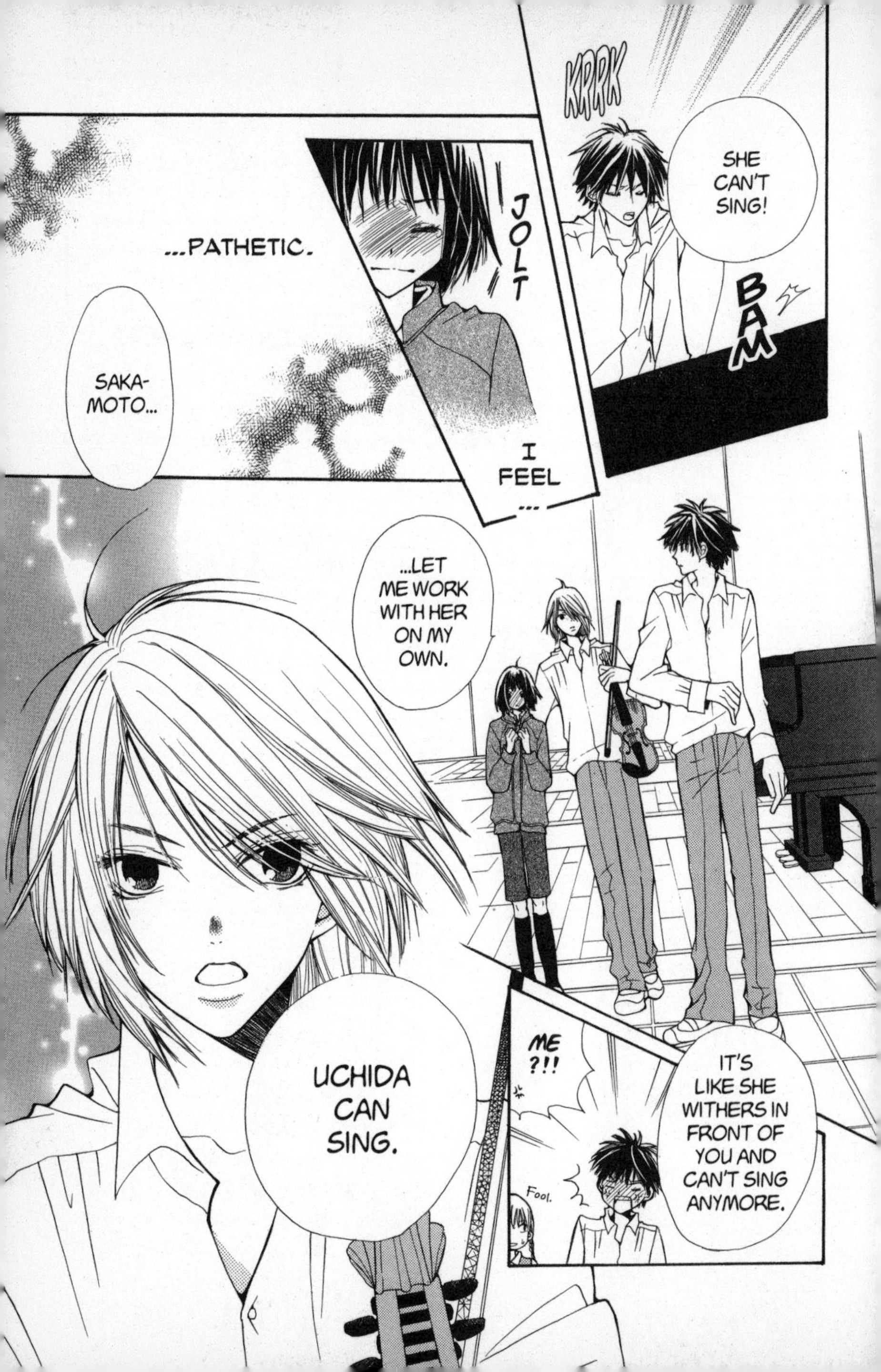
KRRK
SHE CAN'T SING!
BAM
JOLT
I FEEL ...
...PATHETIC.
SAKA-MOTO...
...LET ME WORK WITH HER ON MY OWN.
ME ?!!
IT'S LIKE SHE WITHERS IN FRONT OF YOU AND CAN'T SING ANYMORE.
Fool.
UCHIDA CAN SING.

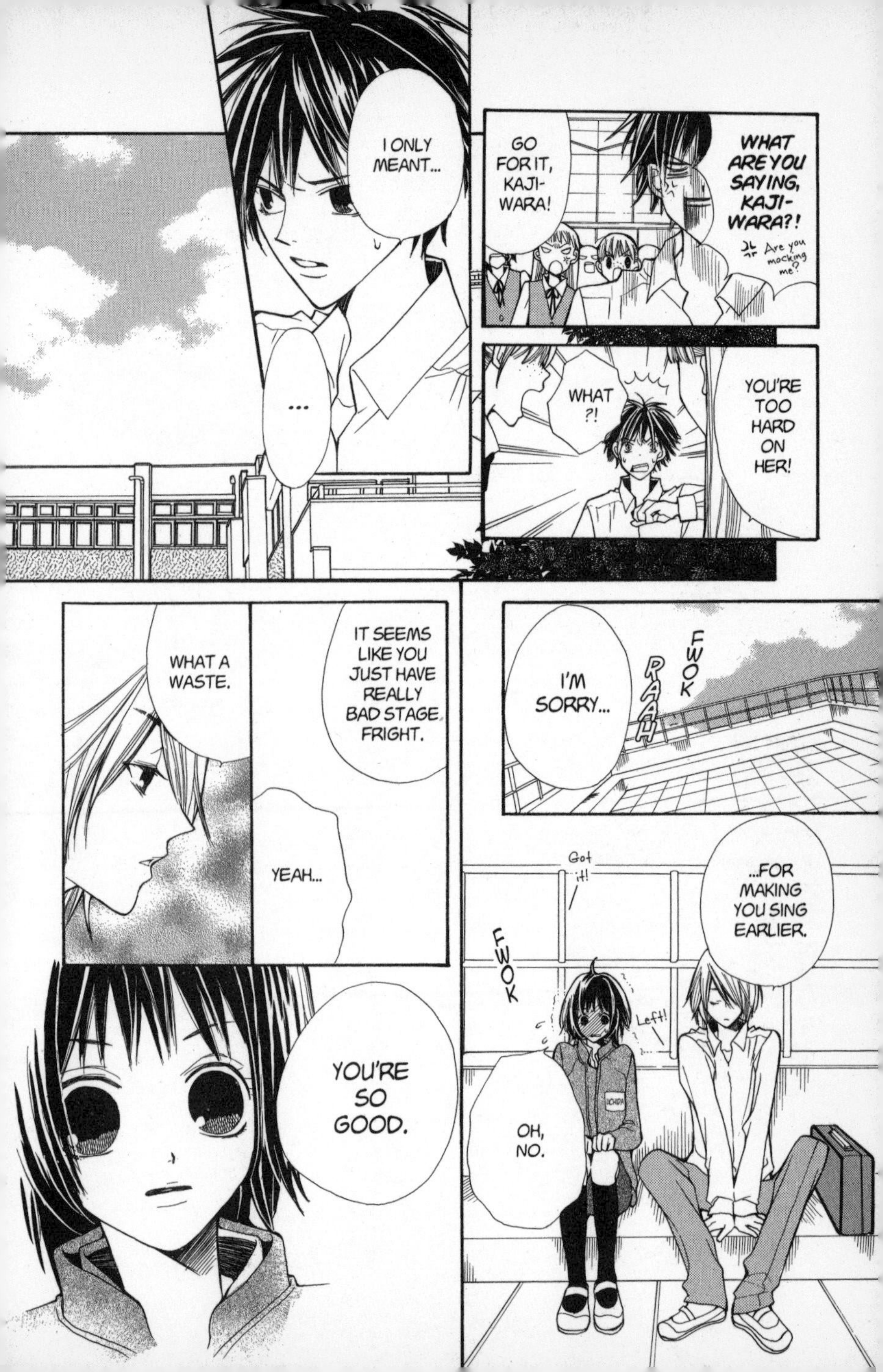
WHAT ARE YOU SAYING, KAJI-WARA?!
Are you mocking me?
GO FOR IT, KAJI-WARA!
YOU'RE TOO HARD ON HER!
WHAT ?!
I ONLY MEANT...
...
I'M SORRY...
FWOK
RAAAH
...FOR MAKING YOU SING EARLIER.
Got it!
Left!
FWOK
OH, NO.
IT SEEMS LIKE YOU JUST HAVE REALLY BAD STAGE FRIGHT.
WHAT A WASTE.
YEAH...
YOU'RE SO GOOD.

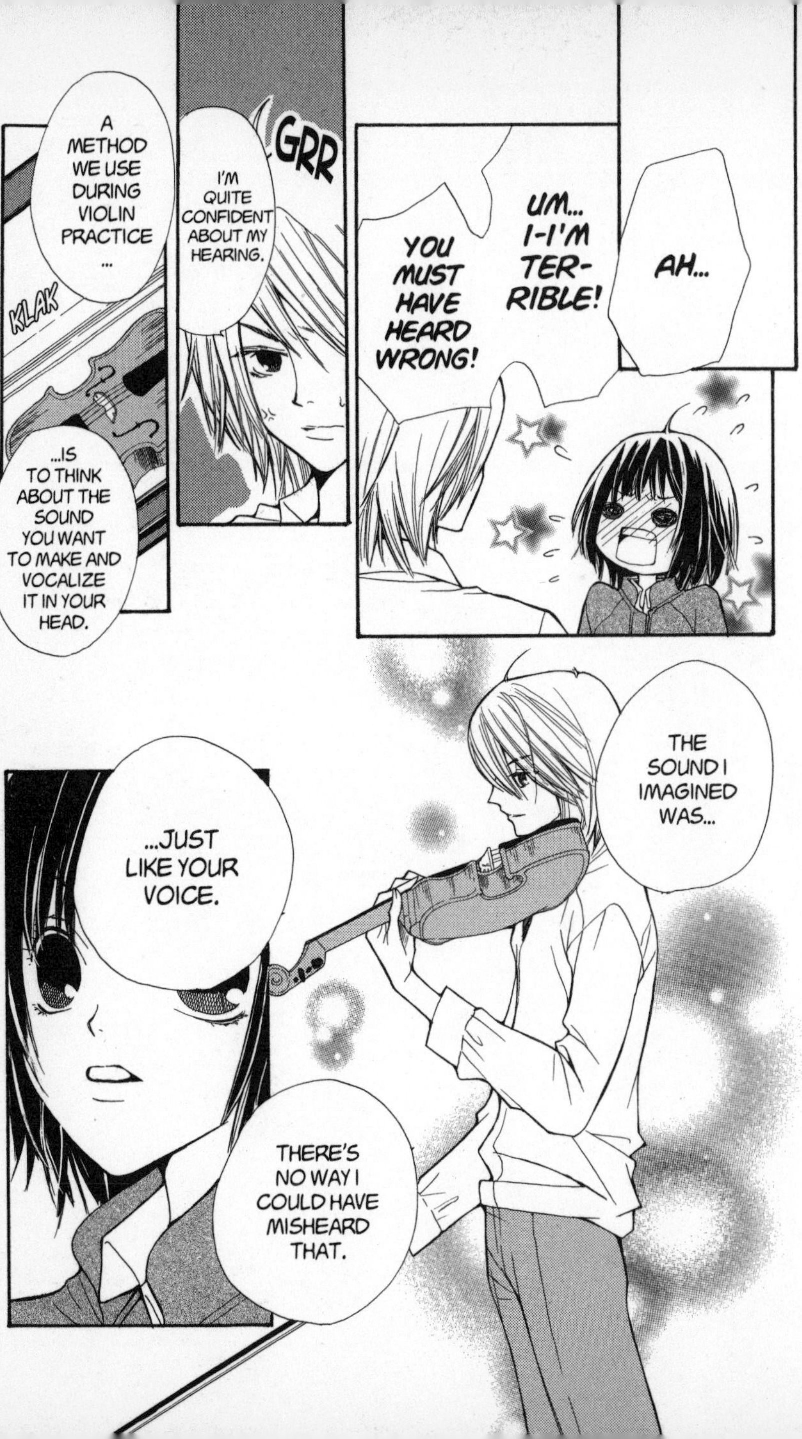
AH...
UM... I-I'M TER-RIBLE!
YOU MUST HAVE HEARD WRONG!
GRR
I'M QUITE CONFIDENT ABOUT MY HEARING.
A METHOD WE USE DURING VIOLIN PRACTICE ...
KLAK
...IS TO THINK ABOUT THE SOUND YOU WANT TO MAKE AND VOCALIZE IT IN YOUR HEAD.
THE SOUND I IMAGINED WAS...
...JUST LIKE YOUR VOICE.
THERE'S NO WAY I COULD HAVE MISHEARD THAT.

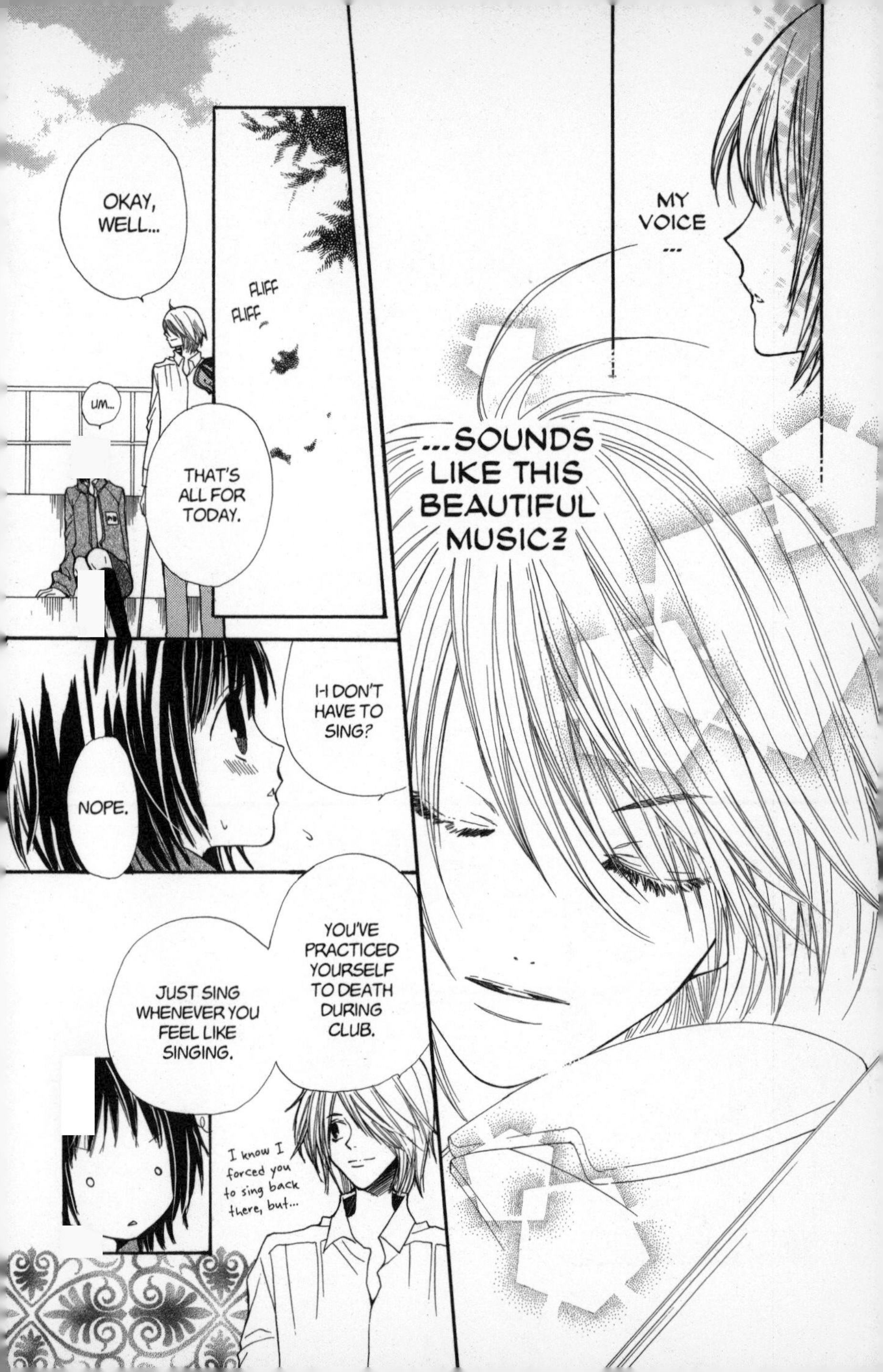
MY VOICE ...
...SOUNDS LIKE THIS BEAUTIFUL MUSIC?
FLIFF FLIFF
OKAY, WELL...
UM...
THAT'S ALL FOR TODAY.
I-I DON'T HAVE TO SING?
NOPE.
YOU'VE PRACTICED YOURSELF TO DEATH DURING CLUB.
JUST SING WHENEVER YOU FEEL LIKE SINGING.
I know I forced you to sing back there, but...

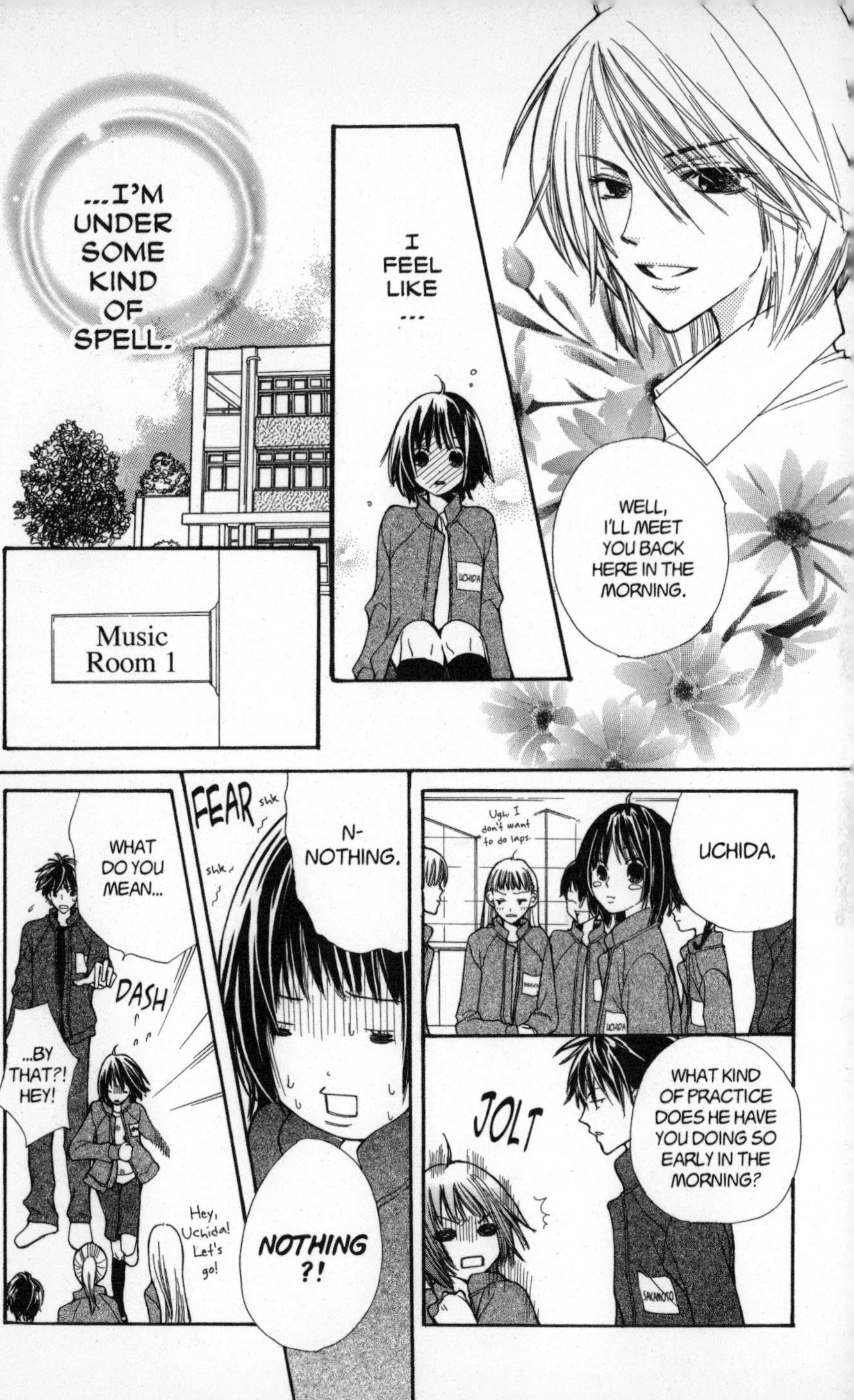
WELL, I'LL MEET YOU BACK HERE IN THE MORNING.
I FEEL LIKE ...
...I'M UNDER SOME KIND OF SPELL.
Music Room 1
UCHIDA.
Ugh, I don't want to do laps.
WHAT KIND OF PRACTICE DOES HE HAVE YOU DOING SO EARLY IN THE MORNING?
JOLT
N-NOTHING.
FEAR
shk
shk
NOTHING?!
WHAT DO YOU MEAN...
DASH
...BY THAT?! HEY!
Hey, Uchida! Let's go!

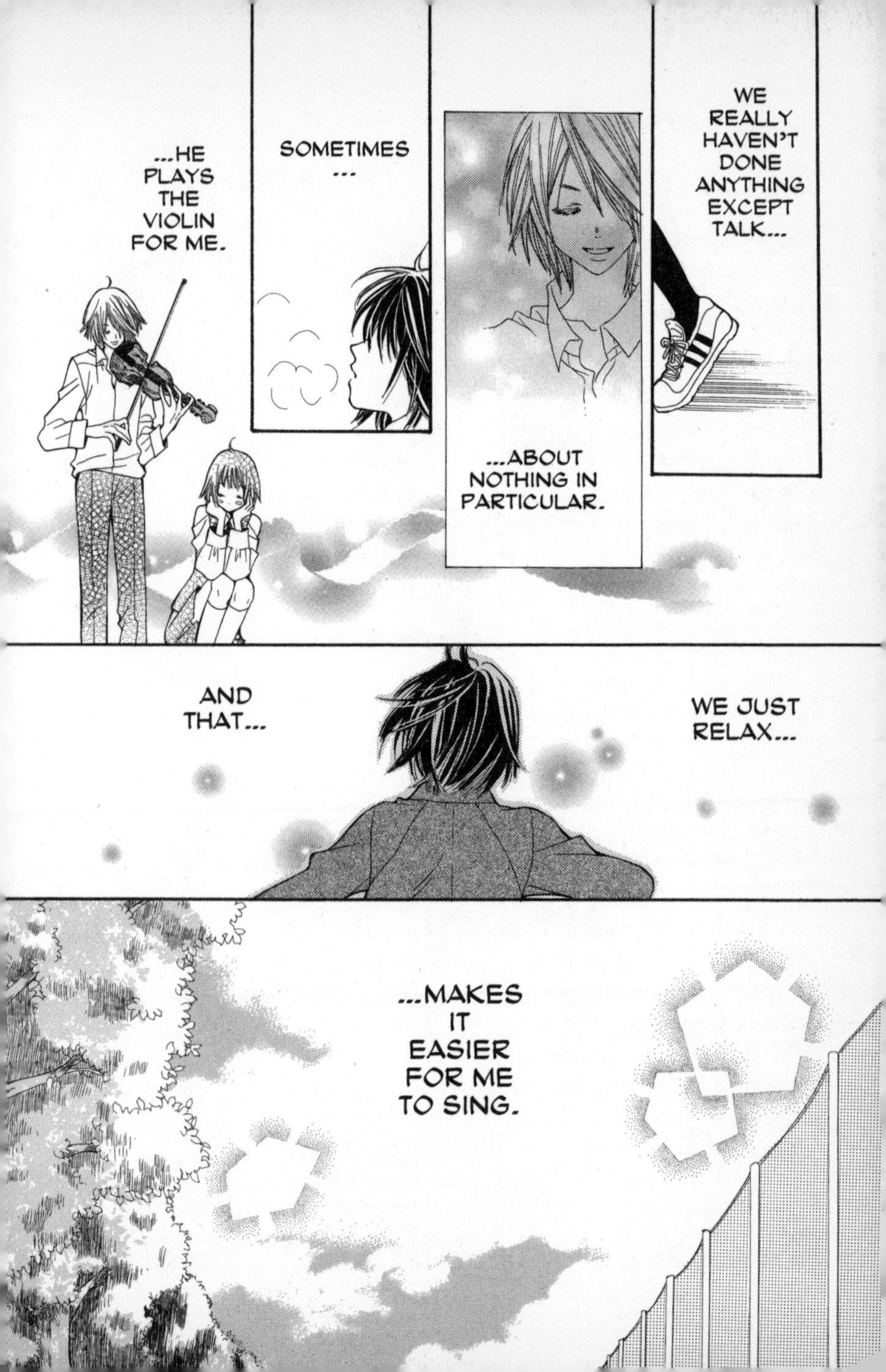
WE REALLY HAVEN'T DONE ANYTHING EXCEPT TALK...
...ABOUT NOTHING IN PARTICULAR.
SOMETIMES...
...HE PLAYS THE VIOLIN FOR ME.
WE JUST RELAX...
AND THAT...
...MAKES IT EASIER FOR ME TO SING.

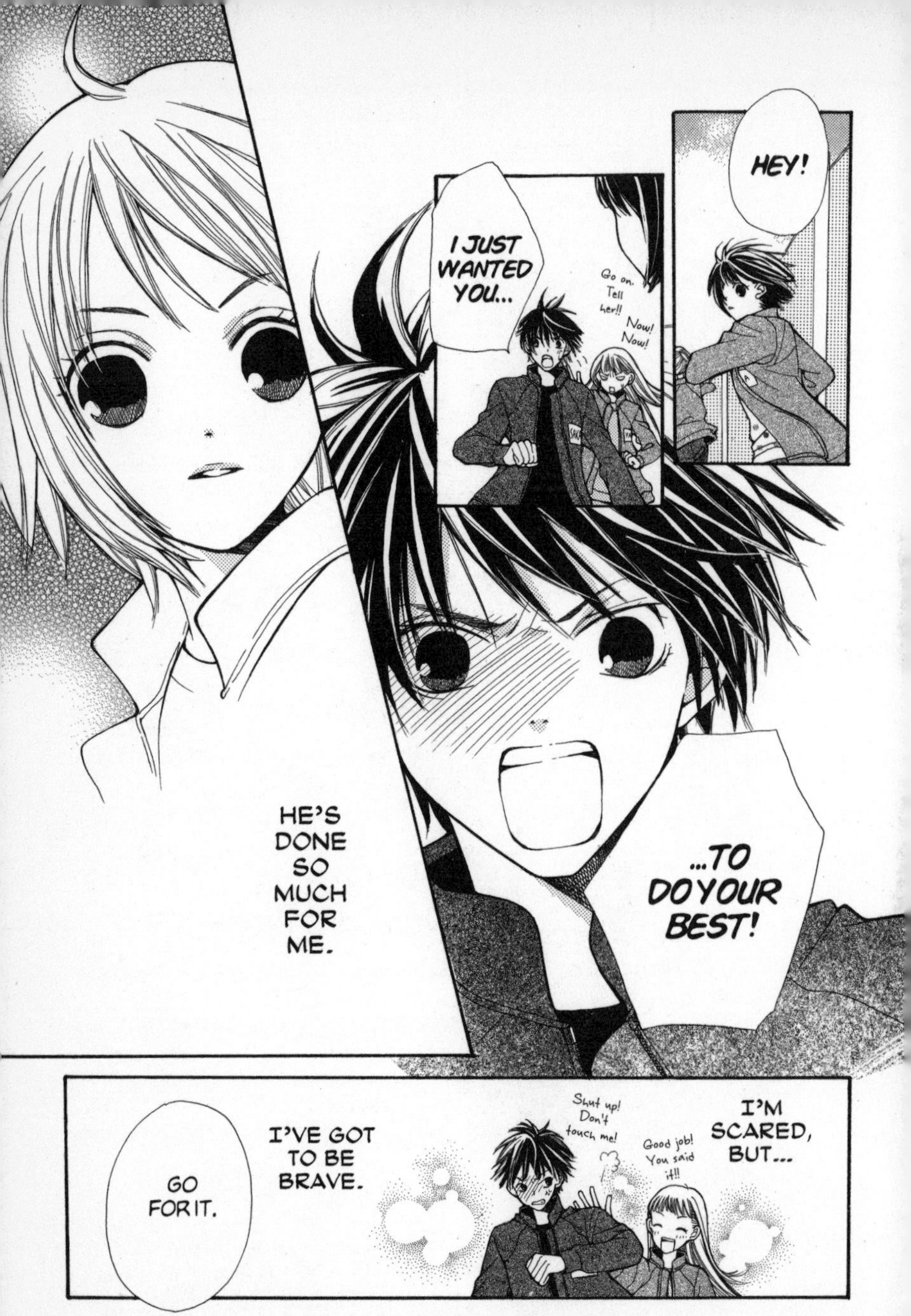
HEY!
I JUST WANTED YOU...
Go on. Tell her!!
Now! Now!
...TO DO YOUR BEST!
HE'S DONE SO MUCH FOR ME.
I'M SCARED, BUT...
Good job! You said it!!
Shut up! Don't touch me!
I'VE GOT TO BE BRAVE.
GO FOR IT.

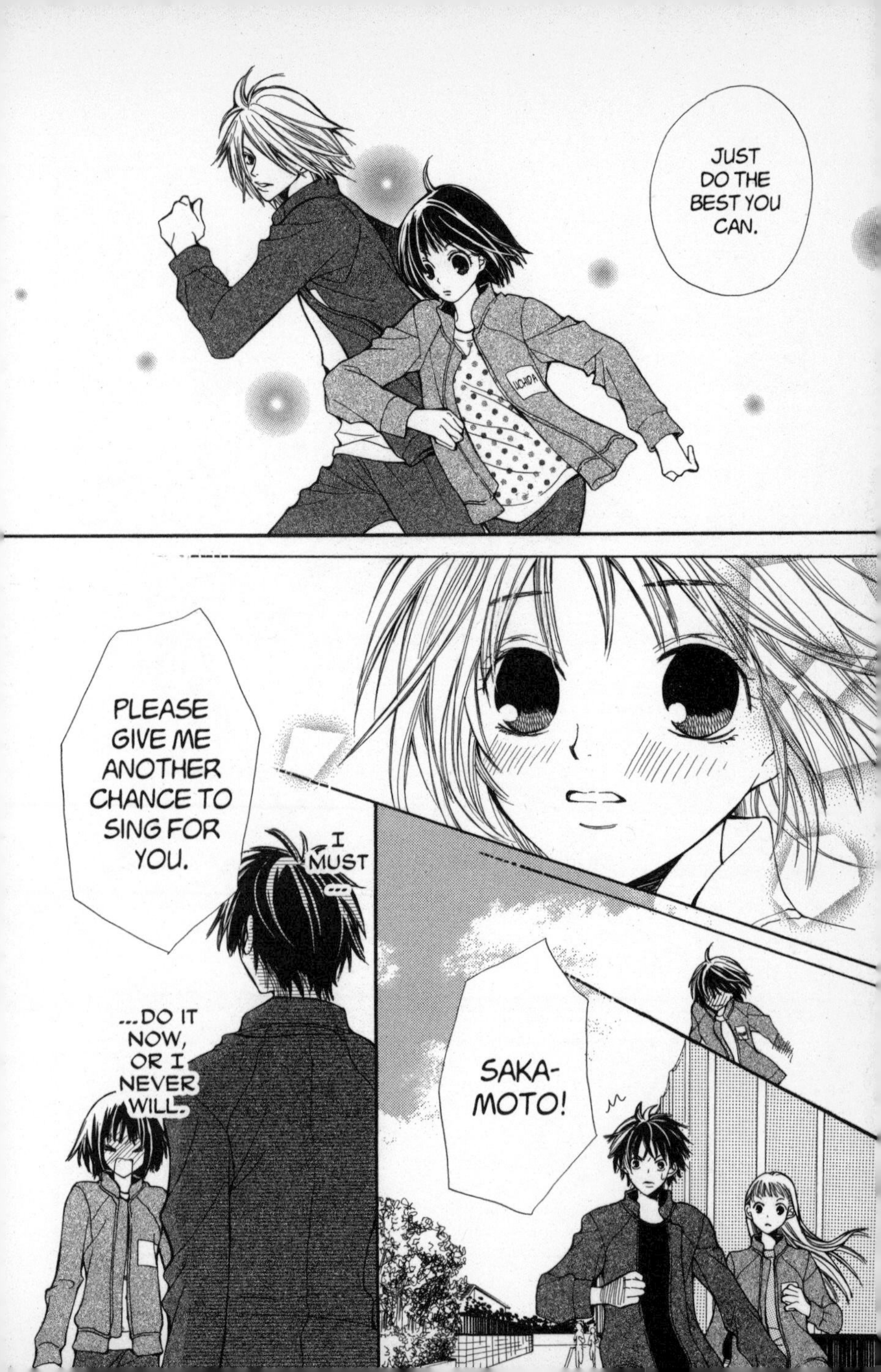
JUST DO THE BEST YOU CAN.
PLEASE GIVE ME ANOTHER CHANCE TO SING FOR YOU.
SAKA-MOTO!
I MUST...
...DO IT NOW, OR I NEVER WILL.

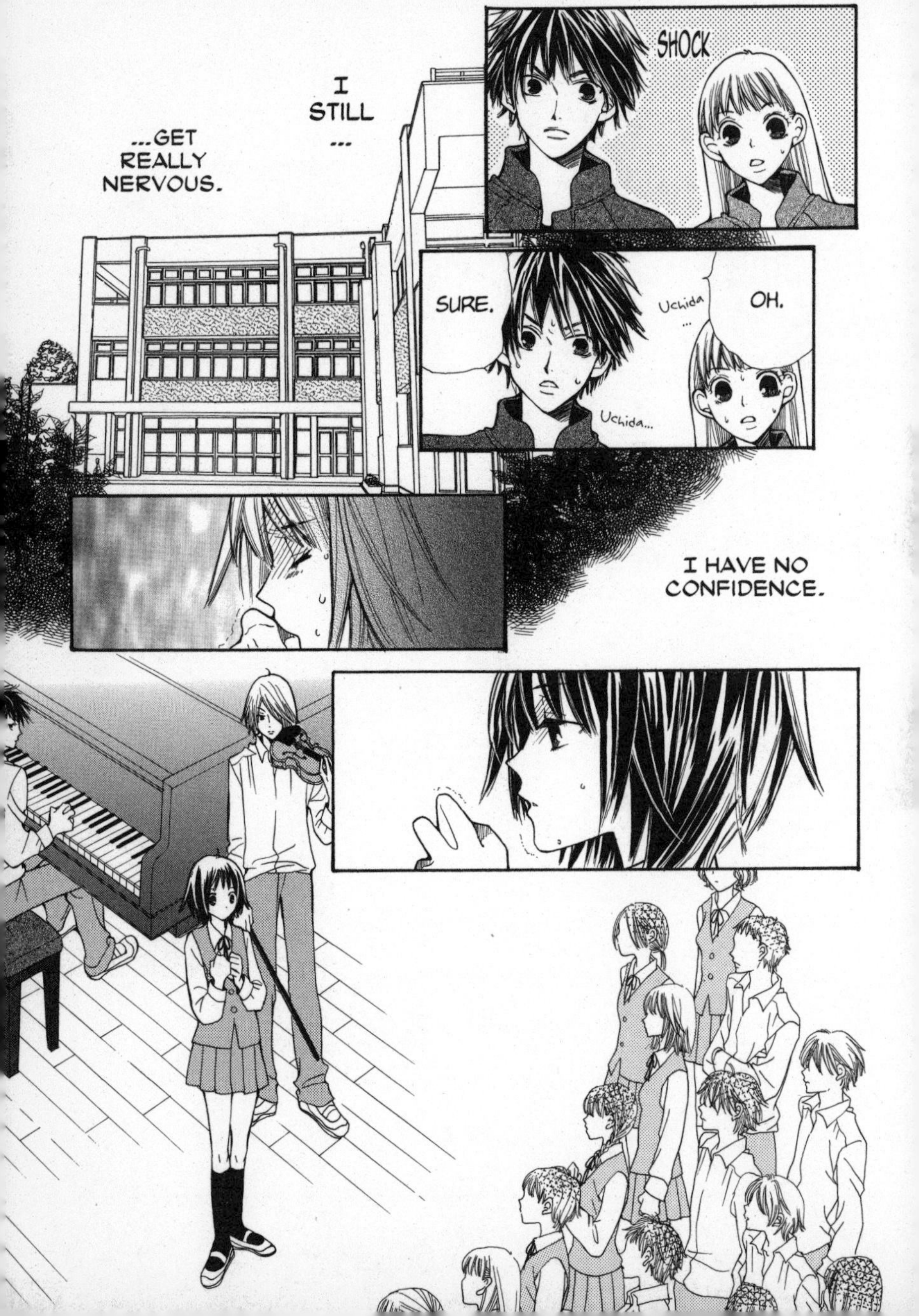
SHOCK
I STILL ...
...GET REALLY NERVOUS.
OH.
Uchida ...
Uchida...
SURE.
I HAVE NO CONFIDENCE.

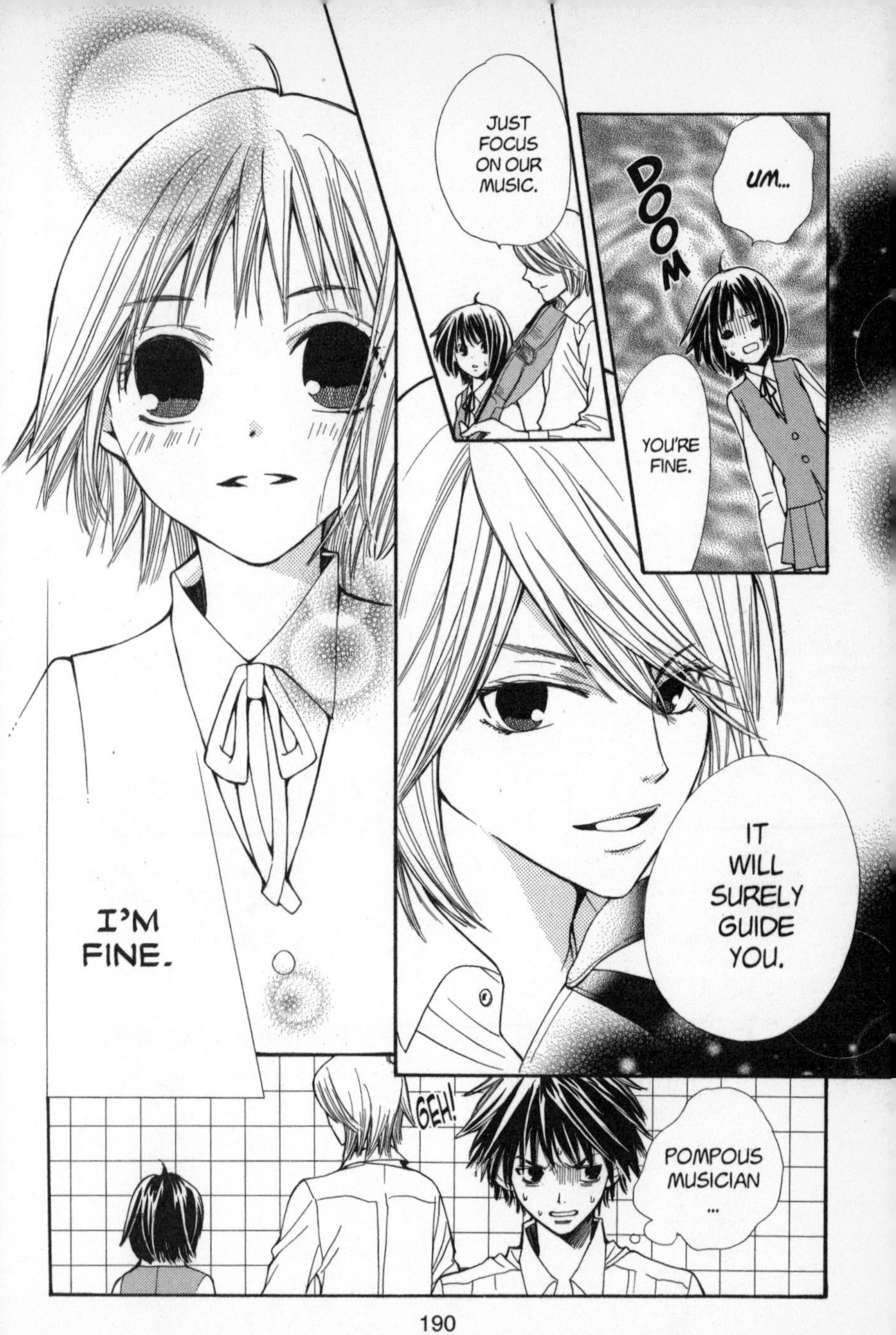
UM...
DOOM
YOU'RE FINE.
JUST FOCUS ON OUR MUSIC.
IT WILL SURELY GUIDE YOU.
I'M FINE.
GEH!
POMPOUS MUSICIAN ...

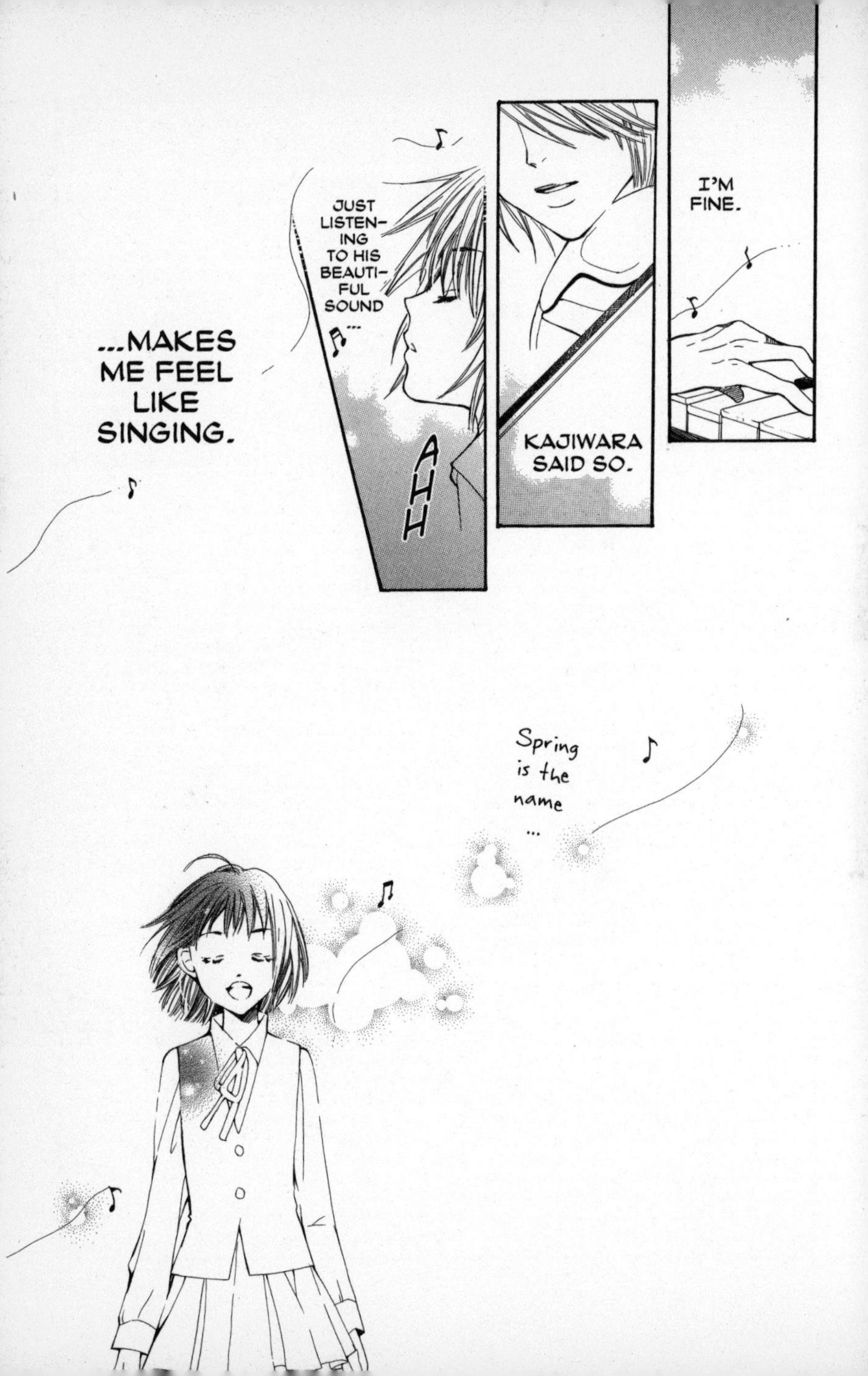
I'M FINE.
KAJIWARA SAID SO.
JUST LISTENING TO HIS BEAUTIFUL SOUND...
AHH
...MAKES ME FEEL LIKE SINGING.
Spring is the name ...

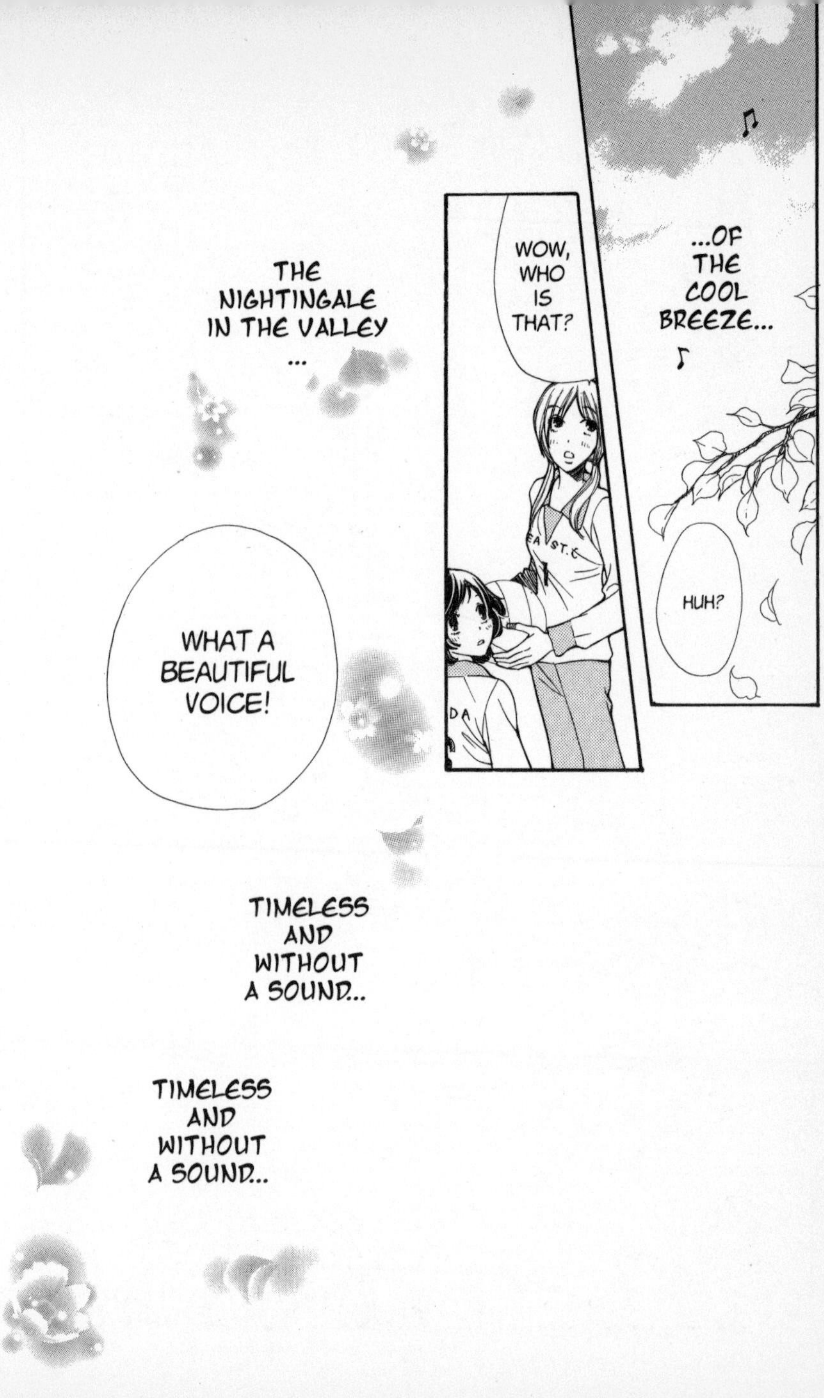
...OF THE COOL BREEZE...
HUH?
WOW, WHO IS THAT?
THE NIGHTINGALE IN THE VALLEY ...
WHAT A BEAUTIFUL VOICE!
TIMELESS AND WITHOUT A SOUND...
TIMELESS AND WITHOUT A SOUND...

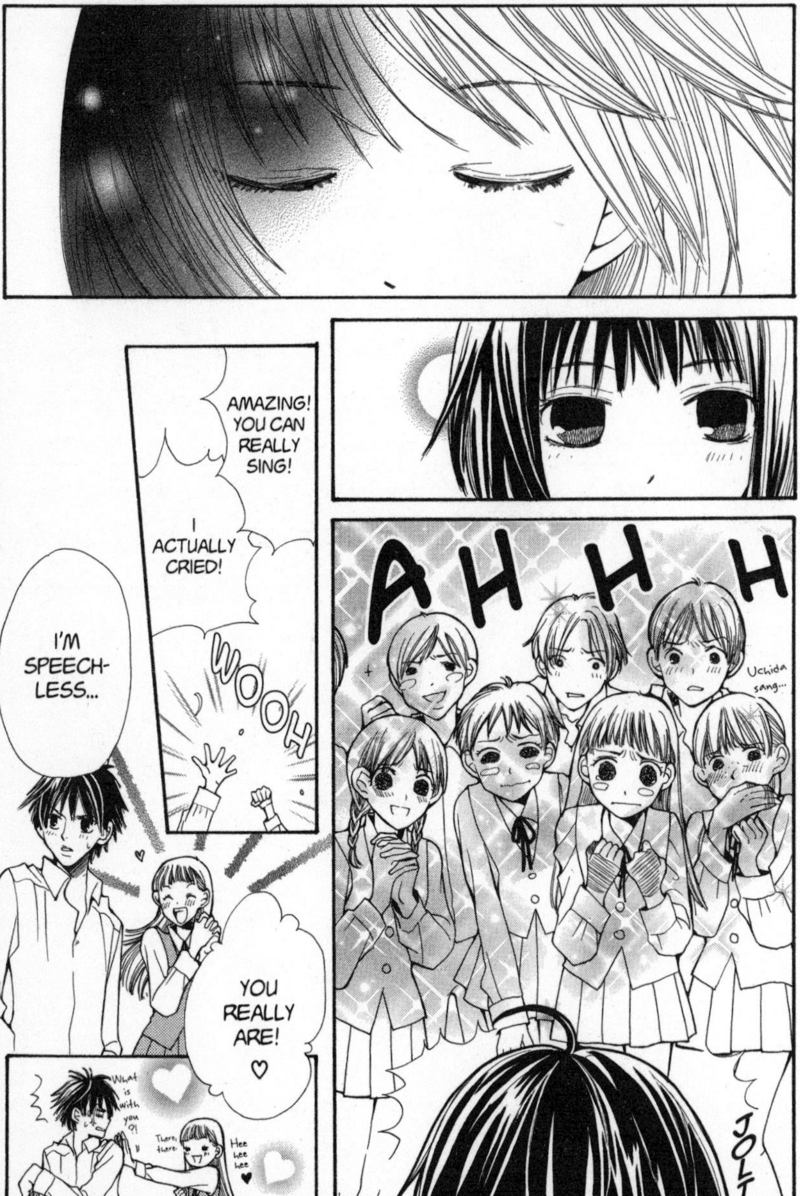

AMAZING! YOU CAN REALLY SING!
I ACTUALLY CRIED!
WOOH
AHHH
Uchida sang...
JOLT
I'M SPEECH-LESS...
YOU REALLY ARE! ♡
What is with you?!
There, there
Hee hee hee

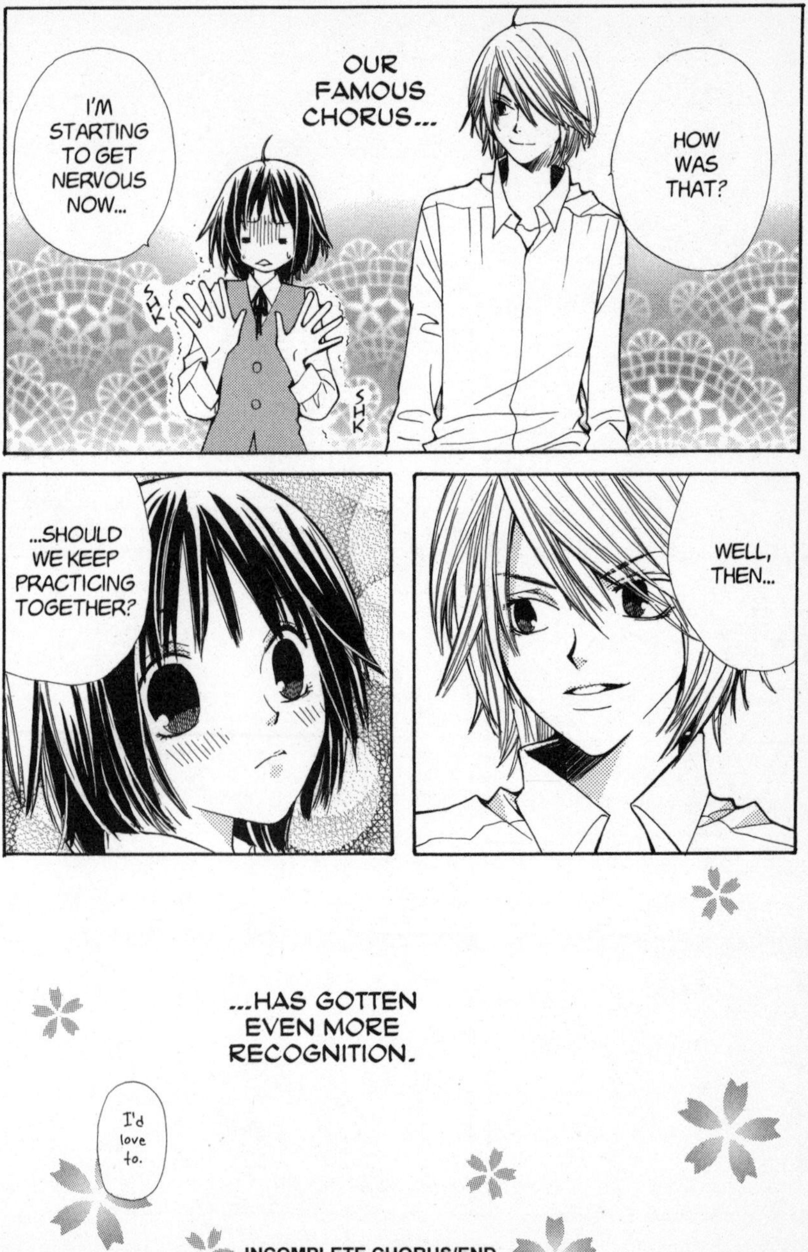
HOW WAS THAT?
OUR FAMOUS CHORUS...
I'M STARTING TO GET NERVOUS NOW...
SHK
SHK
WELL, THEN...
...SHOULD WE KEEP PRACTICING TOGETHER?
...HAS GOTTEN EVEN MORE RECOGNITION.
I'd love to.
INCOMPLETE CHORUS/END

Bonus Pages

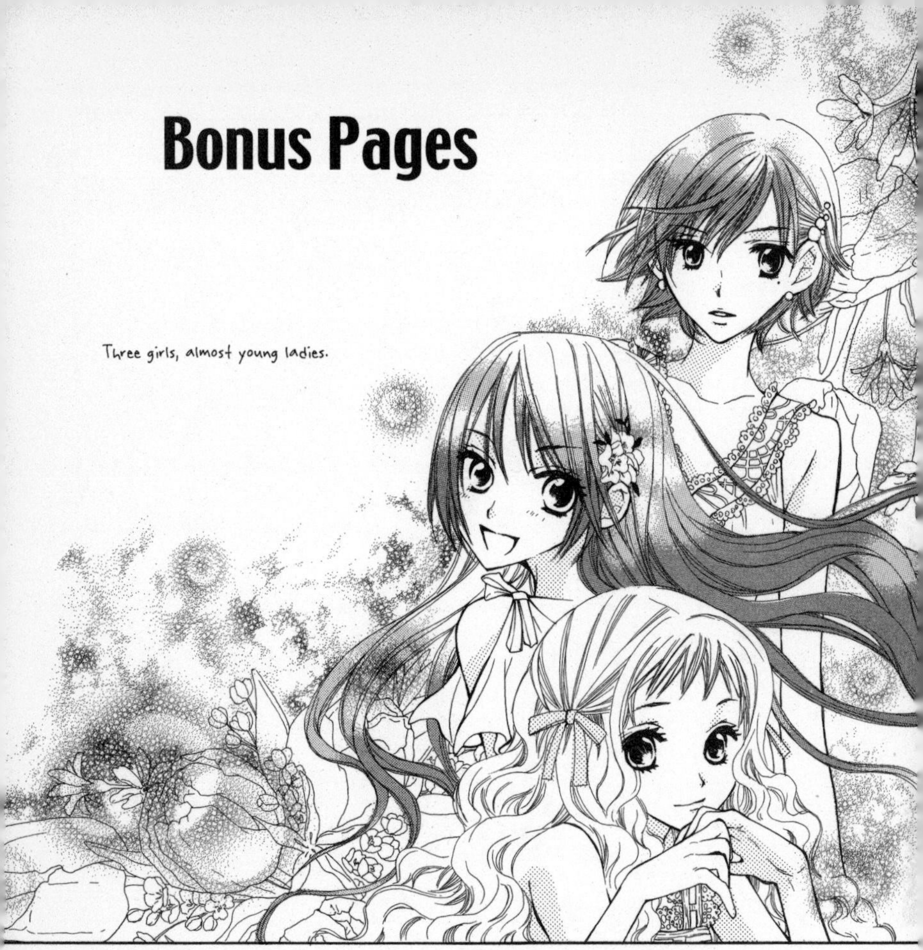
Three girls, almost young ladies.

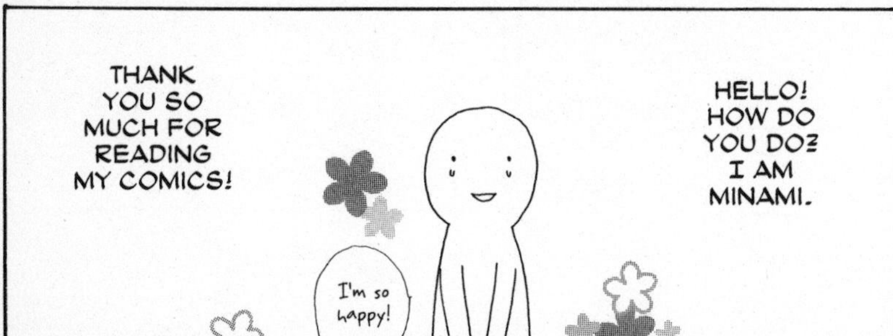
HELLO! HOW DO YOU DO? I AM MINAMI.
THANK YOU SO MUCH FOR READING MY COMICS!
I'm so happy!
Overjoyed!!

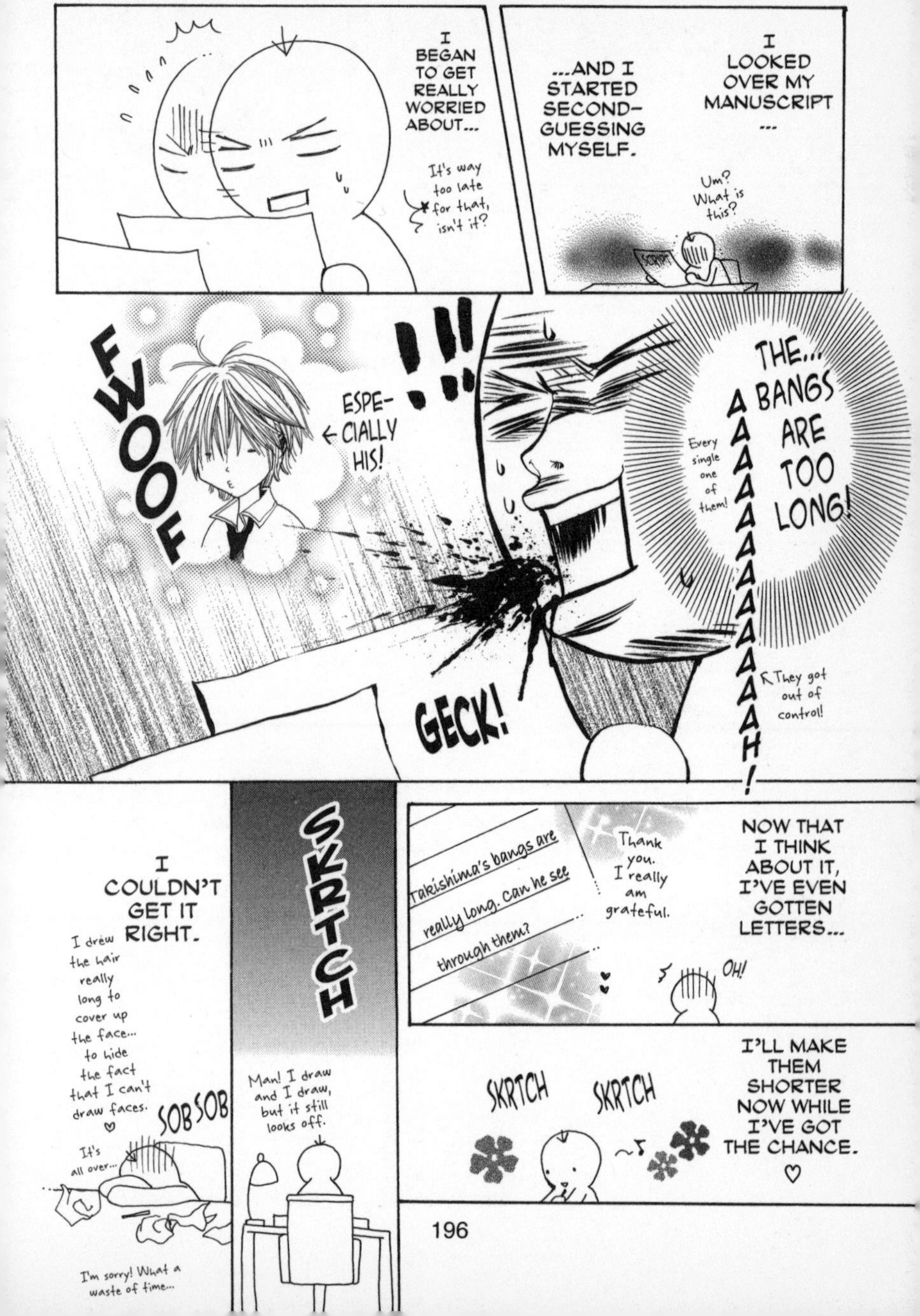

I LOOKED OVER MY MANUSCRIPT...
...AND I STARTED SECOND-GUESSING MYSELF.
Um? What is this?
SCRIPT
I BEGAN TO GET REALLY WORRIED ABOUT...
It's way too late for that, isn't it?
THE... BANGS ARE TOO LONG!
AAAAAAAAAAAAAAH!
Every single one of them!
They got out of control!
GECK!
!!!
ESPE-CIALLY HIS!
FWOOF
NOW THAT I THINK ABOUT IT, I'VE EVEN GOTTEN LETTERS...
Takishima's bangs are really long. Can he see through them?
Thank you. I really am grateful.
OH!
I'LL MAKE THEM SHORTER NOW WHILE I'VE GOT THE CHANCE. ♡
SKRTCH
SKRTCH
SKRTCH
Man! I draw and I draw, but it still looks off.
I COULDN'T GET IT RIGHT.
I drew the hair really long to cover up the face... to hide the fact that I can't draw faces. ♡
SOB SOB
It's all over...
I'm sorry! What a waste of time...

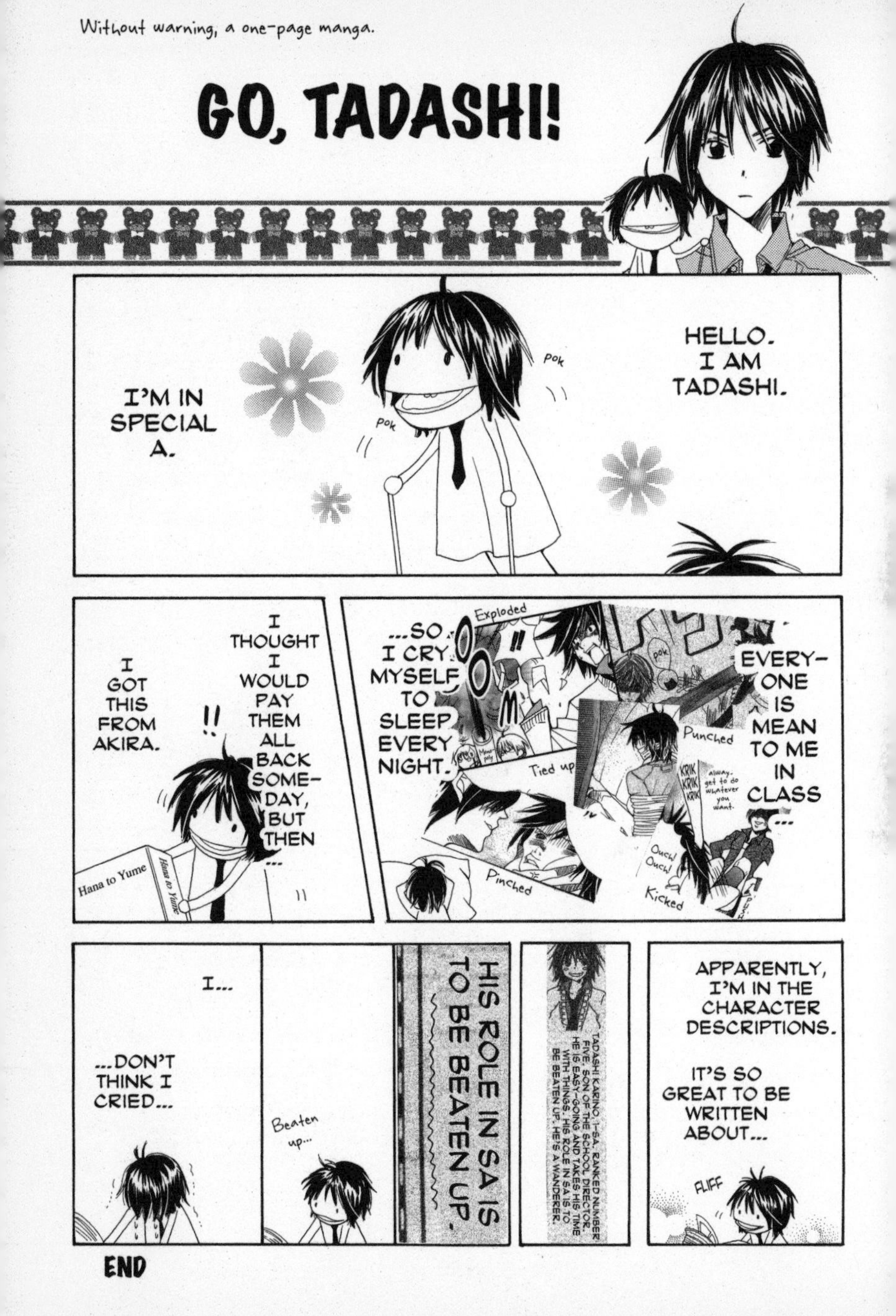
Without warning, a one-page manga.
GO, TADASHI!
HELLO. I AM TADASHI.
pok
pok
I'M IN SPECIAL A.
EVERY-ONE IS MEAN TO ME IN CLASS...
Exploded
pok
Punched
KRIK KRIK KRIK
Tied up
Ouch! Ouch!
Kicked
Pinched
...SO I CRY MYSELF TO SLEEP EVERY NIGHT.
I THOUGHT I WOULD PAY THEM ALL BACK SOME-DAY, BUT THEN...
!!
I GOT THIS FROM AKIRA.
Hana to Yume
Hana to Yume
APPARENTLY, I'M IN THE CHARACTER DESCRIPTIONS.
IT'S SO GREAT TO BE WRITTEN ABOUT...
FLIFF
TADASHI KARINO, 1-SA. RANKED NUMBER FIVE. SON OF THE SCHOOL DIRECTOR. HE IS EASY-GOING AND TAKES HIS TIME WITH THINGS. HIS ROLE IN SA IS TO BE BEATEN UP. HE'S A WANDERER.
HIS ROLE IN SA IS TO BE BEATEN UP.
Beaten up...
I...
...DON'T THINK I CRIED...
END

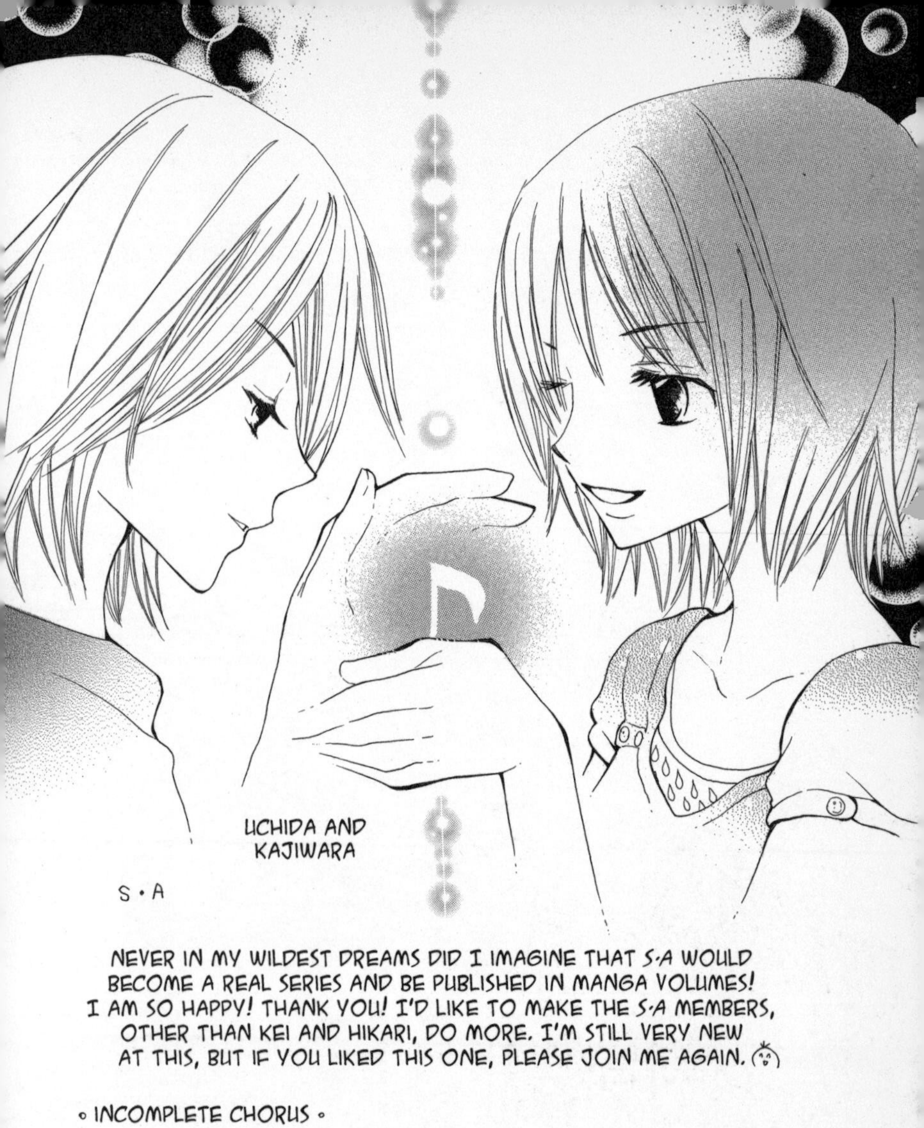
UCHIDA AND KAJIWARA

S • A

NEVER IN MY WILDEST DREAMS DID I IMAGINE THAT S·A WOULD BECOME A REAL SERIES AND BE PUBLISHED IN MANGA VOLUMES! I AM SO HAPPY! THANK YOU! I'D LIKE TO MAKE THE S·A MEMBERS, OTHER THAN KEI AND HIKARI, DO MORE. I'M STILL VERY NEW AT THIS, BUT IF YOU LIKED THIS ONE, PLEASE JOIN ME AGAIN.

◦ INCOMPLETE CHORUS ◦

VOICE AND VIOLIN AND PIANO? I LOVE MUSIC, SO I'M GLAD I GOT A CHANCE TO DRAW THE PARTS WHERE SHE'S SINGING. THIS PART DEFINITELY SHOWS THE EXTENT OF MY INEXPERIENCE, BUT IF YOU LIKED IT, EVEN JUST A LITTLE BIT, I'M HAPPY.

• FINALLY •

THANKS FOR READING ALL THE WAY TO THE END! ◦

MY THANKS ALSO GOES TO EVERYONE WHO SUPPORTED ME--MY LOVING FAMILY, THE LP PEOPLE, MY FRIENDS--BEFORE THIS MANUSCRIPT WAS DONE, BUT ALSO TO THOSE WHO HAVE HELPED ME AFTER THE SERIALIZATION: MY PREVIOUS EDITOR, AND MY CURRENT EDITOR.

ALSO, THANKS TO ALL THOSE WHO READ THIS VOLUME, AND TO THOSE WHO ENCOURAGED ME WITH THEIR LETTERS. I COULD NEVER EXPRESS THE GRATITUDE I FEEL!!! I'M STILL VERY NEW AT THIS, BUT I HOPE TO WRITE MANY MORE BOOKS FOR THE READERS TO ENJOY. UNTIL NEXT TIME!

maki minami

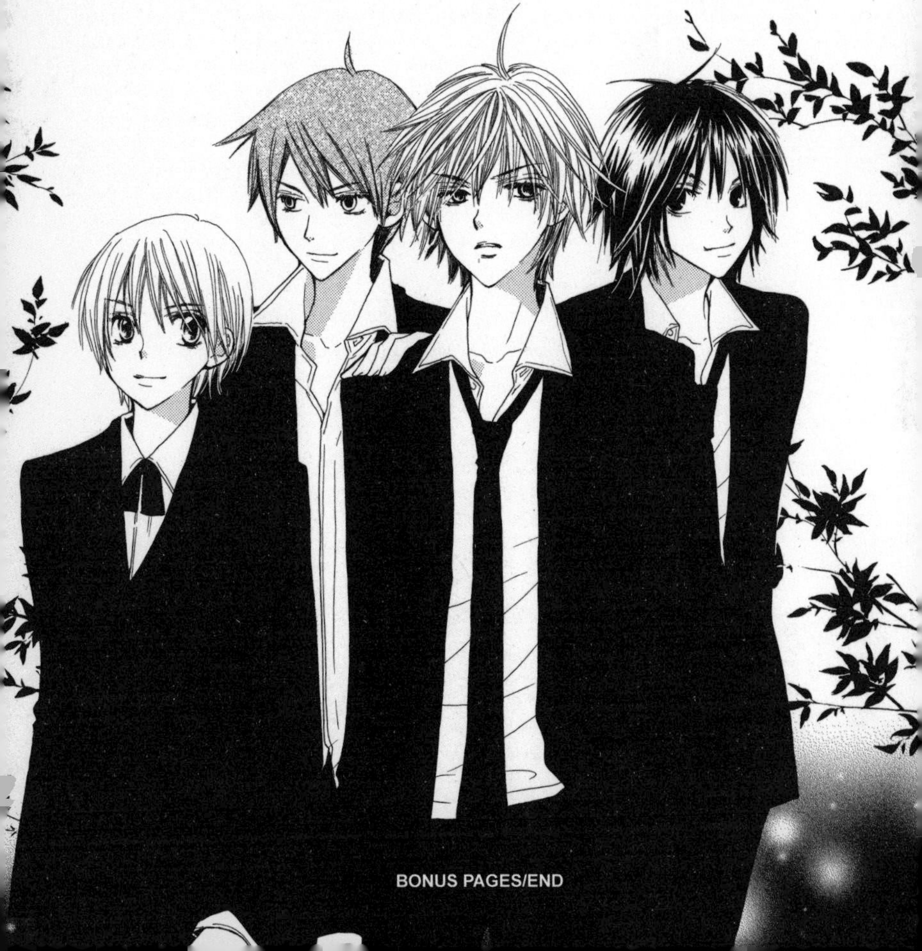

BONUS PAGES/END

Maki Minami is from Saitama
prefecture in Japan. She debuted
in 2001 with *Kanata no Ao*
(Faraway Blue). Her other works
include *Kimi wa Girlfriend*
(You're My Girlfriend), *Mainichi
ga Takaramono* (Every Day Is a
Treasure) and *Yuki Atataka*
(Warm Winter). *S•A* is her current
series in Japan's *Hana to Yume*
magazine.

S•A

Vol. 1
The Shojo Beat Manga Edition

STORY & ART BY
MAKI MINAMI

English Adaptation/Amanda Hubbard
Translation/JN Productions
Touch-up Art & Lettering/Rina Mapa
Design/Izumi Hirayama
Editor/Nancy Thistlethwaite

Editor in Chief, Books/Alvin Lu
Editor in Chief, Magazines/Marc Weidenbaum
VP of Publishing Licensing/Rika Inouye
VP of Sales/Gonzalo Ferreyra
Sr. VP of Marketing/Liza Coppola
Publisher/Hyoe Narita

Printed in Canada

Published by VIZ Media, LLC
P.O. Box 77010
San Francisco, CA 94107

Shojo Beat Manga Edition
10 9 8 7 6 5 4 3 2
First printing, November 2007
Second printing, February 2008

www.viz.com   store.viz.com

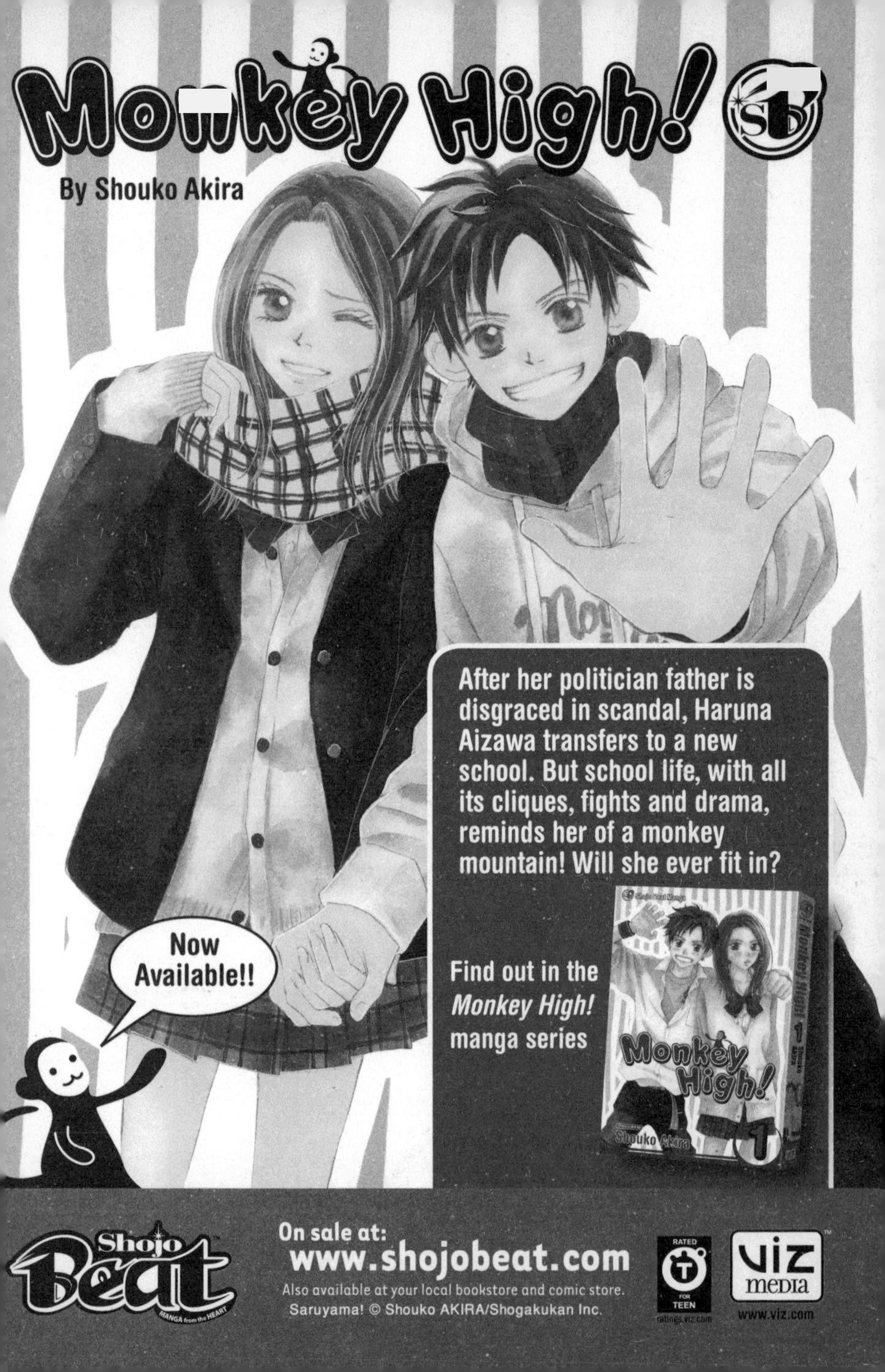
Monkey High!
By Shouko Akira
After her politician father is disgraced in scandal, Haruna Aizawa transfers to a new school. But school life, with all its cliques, fights and drama, reminds her of a monkey mountain! Will she ever fit in?
Find out in the *Monkey High!* manga series
Now Available!!
Monkey High!
Shouko Akira
1
Shojo Beat
MANGA from the HEART
On sale at:
www.shojobeat.com
Also available at your local bookstore and comic store.
Saruyama! © Shouko AKIRA/Shogakukan Inc.
RATED T FOR TEEN
ratings.viz.com
VIZ MEDIA
www.viz.com

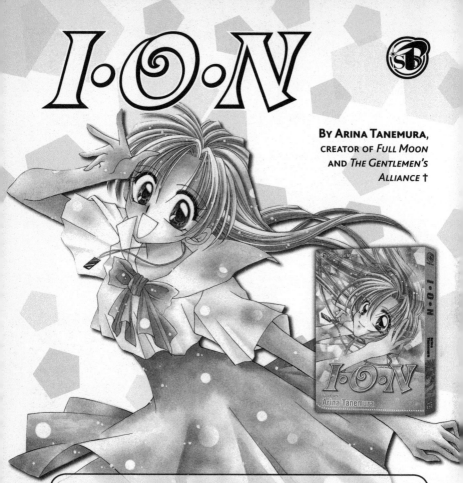

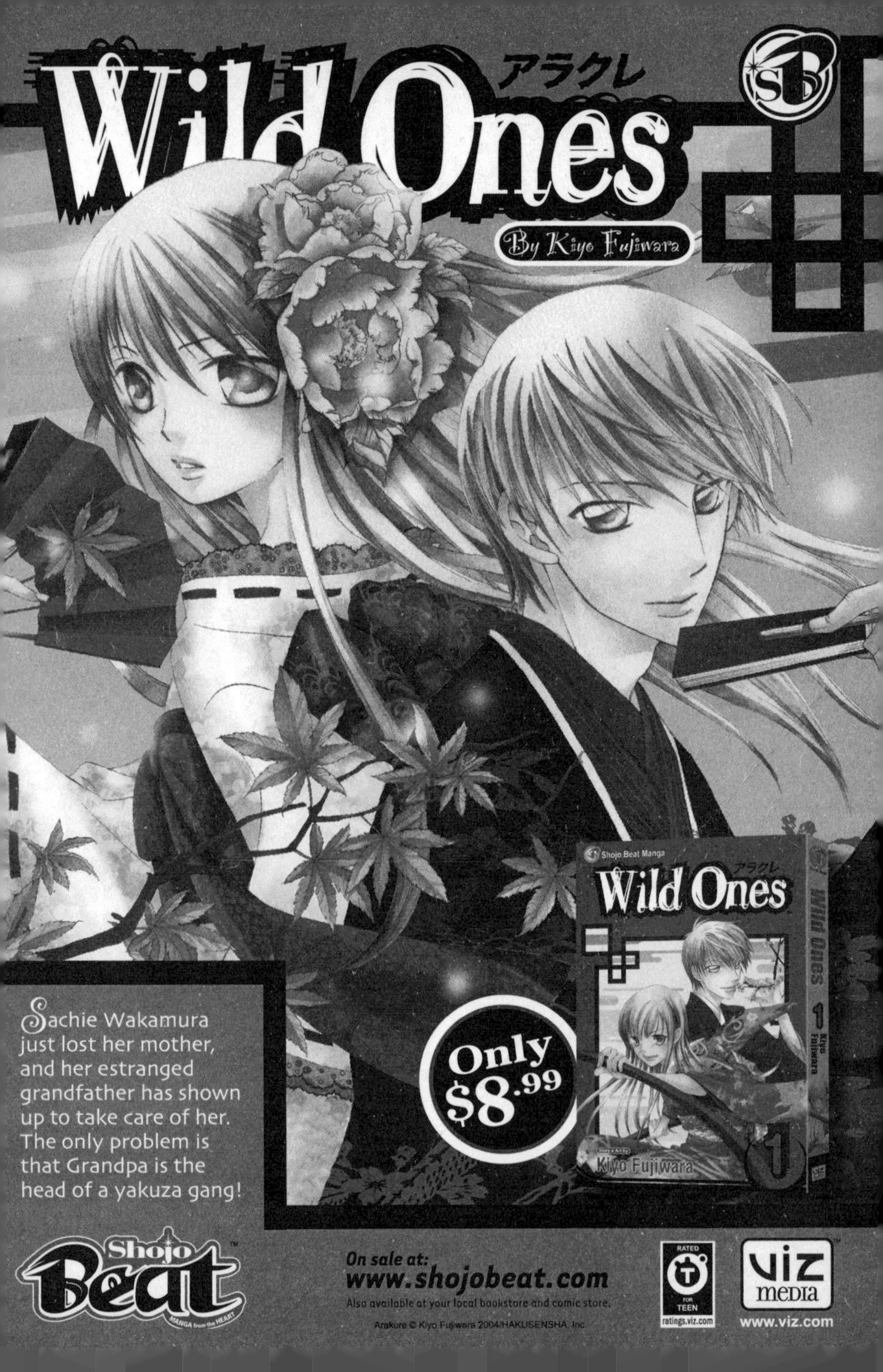
Wild Ones
アラクレ
By Kiyo Fujiwara
Shojo Beat Manga
Wild Ones
Kiyo Fujiwara
Sachie Wakamura just lost her mother, and her estranged grandfather has shown up to take care of her. The only problem is that Grandpa is the head of a yakuza gang!
Only $8.99
Shojo Beat
MANGA from the HEART
On sale at:
www.shojobeat.com
Also available at your local bookstore and comic store.
Arakure © Kiyo Fujiwara 2004/HAKUSENSHA, Inc.
RATED T FOR TEEN
ratings.viz.com
VIZ media
www.viz.com

Tell us what you think about Shojo Beat Manga!

Our survey is now available online. Go to:

shojobeat.com/mangasurvey

Help us make our product offerings better!